Relocating World Christianity

Theology and Mission in World Christianity

The titles published in this series are listed at *brill.com/tmwc*

Relocating World Christianity

*Interdisciplinary Studies in Universal and Local
Expressions of the Christian Faith*

Edited by

Joel Cabrita
David Maxwell
Emma Wild-Wood

BRILL

LEIDEN | BOSTON

Cover illustration: 'Zion Prayer Reminder' from *Leaves of Healing*, Vol. X, No. 11, 4 January 1902, p. 478. Source: Flower Pentecostal Heritage Centre.

The Library of Congress Cataloging-in-Publication Data

Names: Cabrita, Joel, 1980- editor.
Title: Relocating world Christianity : interdisciplinary studies in universal and local
    expressions of the Christian faith / edited by Joel Cabrita, David Maxwell,
    Emma Wild-Wood.
Description: Boston : Brill, 2017. | Series: Theology and mission in world
    Christianity, ISSN 2452-2953 ; VOLUME 7 | Includes index.
Identifiers: LCCN 2017033076 (print) | LCCN 2017037109 (ebook) | ISBN
    9789004355026 (e-book) | ISBN 9789004342620 (hardback) : alk. paper)
Subjects: LCSH: Christianity.
Classification: LCC BR50 (ebook) | LCC BR50 .R425 2017 (print) |
    DDC 270.8–dc23
LC record available at https://lccn.loc.gov/2017033076

Typeface for the Latin, Greek, and Cyrillic scripts: "Brill". See and download: brill.com/brill-typeface.

ISSN 2452-2953
ISBN 978-90-04-34262-0 (hardback)
ISBN 978-90-04-35502-6 (e-book)

Contents

Acknowledgements

This edited collection emerged out of two related series of scholarly events. The first was a research network, 'Locating Religion', from 2013 to 2015, convened by Joel Cabrita and David Maxwell. Funded by the University of Cambridge's Centre for Research in the Arts, Social Sciences and Humanities (CRASSH), the network enabled us to draw together a diverse group of scholars in history, divinity, anthropology, sociology and music from the University of Cambridge and beyond to debate issues relating to the locus and scale of Christian activity across the globe. We are grateful to Esther Lamb's extensive assistance in organising the network. The second event was the Biennial Henry Martyn Lectures, from 3 to 5 February 2015, on the subject of World Christianity across the disciplines. The lectures were organised by the Cambridge Centre for Christianity Worldwide (CCCW) under the directorship of Emma Wild-Wood and were supplemented by a workshop convened by all three editors of the present volume – Cabrita, Maxwell and Wild-Wood. The conference and workshop were generously hosted by CCCW at Westminster College, Cambridge, and we wish to express our thanks to Polly Keen for her efficient administration of these events. Our extended discussions would not have been possible without generous grants from the George Macaulay Trevelyan Fund in the Faculty of History, trust funds in the Faculty of Divinity and financial support from the CCCW, in addition to funding from CRASSH.

Ankur Barua, Tom Boylston, Fenella Cannell, Shinjini Das, Matthew Engelke, Charlie Farhadian, Martha Frederiks, James Gardom, Andrea Grant, Jörg Haustein, Marloes Jansen, Timothy Jenkins, Jamie Klair, Miriam Levin, Ruth Prince, Gabriela Ramos, Aparecida Vilaca, Richard Werbner, Chris Wingfield, Johannes Zeiler and Jesse Zink all participated in the debates that shaped this volume and we gratefully acknowledge their contribution.

We are obliged to the two anonymous reviewers of the first draft for their thoughtful and detailed responses. At Brill, Mirjam Elbers was encouraging from the outset and Ingrid Heijckers-Velt put up with many questions and provided efficient support. We thank them both. We are indebted to the Flower Pentecostal Heritage Center for permission to reproduce the image used for the front cover illustration (*Leaves of Healing*, Vol. X, No. 11, 4 January 1902). Finally, we are grateful to Judith Forshaw for her sterling work in copyediting the manuscript.

Abbreviations

ACF	Action Catholique Familiale
ACI	Action Chapel International
AIADMK	All India Anna Dravida Munnetra Kazhagam
AIC	African Independent/Initiated Church
AMECEA	Association of Bishops of Eastern Africa
ASEAN	Association of Southeast Asian Nations
BFB-IEF	Biblioteca Fernandes Braga – Igreja Evangélica Fluminense
BFBS	British and Foreign Bible Society
BGEA	Billy Graham Evangelistic Association
BJP	Bharatiya Janata Party
BSA	Bible Society Archives
CARTS	Centre for Advanced Religious and Theological Studies, Faculty of Divinity, University of Cambridge
CATC	Confédération Africaine des Travailleurs Croyants
CCC	Campus Crusade for Christ
CCCW	Cambridge Centre for Christianity Worldwide
CCPA	Chinese Catholic Patriotic Association
CFTC	Confédération Française des Travailleurs Chrétiens
CGT	Confédération Générale du Travail
CIA	Central Intelligence Agency
CLADE	Congresso Latinamericano de Evangelización (Latin American Congress for Evangelisation)
CT	*Christianity Today*
CWC	Currents in World Christianity
DMK	Dravida Munnetra Kazhagam
EATWOT	Ecumenical Association of Third World Theologians
ESITIS	*European Society for Intercultural Theology and Interreligious Studies*
ETS	Evangelical Theological Society
EU	European Union
FBO	faith-based organisation
FIDES	Fonds pour l'Investissement en Développement Économique et Social
FTL	Fraternidad Teológica Latinoamericana (Latin American Theological Fraternity)
GAFCON	Global Anglican Future Conferences
ICGC	International Central Gospel Church
IFES	International Fellowship of Evangelical Students
IRFA	International Religious Freedom Act

IS	Islamic State
ISIS	Islamic State
IVCF	InterVarsity Christian Fellowship
IVF	Inter-Varsity Fellowship
JOC	Jeunesse Ouvrière Chrétienne
KICC	Kingsway International Christian Centre
LMEF	Ligue Missionnaire des Étudiants de France
LUCEM	Ligue Universitaire Catholique et Missionnaire
MRP	Mouvement Républicain Populaire
NAMP	North American Missiology Project
NGO	non-governmental organisation
OMF	Overseas Missionary Fellowship
PNG	Papua New Guinea
PRC	People's Republic of China
RCCG	Redeemed Christian Church of God
RTS	Religious Tract Society
SC	scheduled caste
SMEP	Société des Missions Évangéliques de Paris
TSPM	Three-Self Patriotic Movement
UCCF	Universities and Colleges Christian Fellowship
UCJG	Union Chrétienne des Jeunes Gens
UFER	Union Fraternelle des Races
UPA	United Progressive Alliance
UPC	Union des Populations du Cameroun
VHP	Vishwa Hindu Parishad (World Hindu Federation)
WCC	World Council of Churches
YPG	Yekîneyên Parastina Gel (People's Protection Units)
ZAOGA	Zimbabwe Assemblies of God Africa

Contributors

J. Kwabena Asamoah-Gyadu

FGA, PhD (Birmingham, UK, 2000) is currently the Baëta-Grau Professor of Contemporary African Christianity and Pentecostal/Charismatic Theology and Vice President of the Trinity Theological Seminary, Legon, Ghana. He has researched and written extensively on contemporary Christianity in Africa and Pentecostalism, including on African immigrant churches in both Europe and North America.

Naures Atto

is research associate at the Faculty of Asian and Middle Eastern Studies, University of Cambridge, and research associate at Wolfson College. Atto received her PhD from Leiden University in 2011. She is the author of *Hostages in the Homeland, Orphans in the Diaspora: Identity Discourses among the Assyrian/ Syriac Elites in the European Diaspora* (Leiden University Press, 2011). Atto is Director of the Inanna Foundation.

Joel Cabrita

is a historian of Christianity in Southern Africa, and teaches in the Faculty of Divinity and the Centre for African Studies at the University of Cambridge. Her first book was a history of the production, use and reception of sacred texts, *Text and Authority in the South African Nazaretha Church* (Cambridge University Press, 2014). Her latest book (Harvard University Press, 2018) tells the transatlantic story of Zionist Christianity. Cabrita's articles have been published in *Africa, Comparative Studies in Society and History*, and *Journal of African History*.

Pedro Feitoza

is a PhD candidate reading history at Emmanuel College, University of Cambridge. His doctoral research is entitled 'Protestants and the Public Sphere in Brazil, 1874–1962' and investigates how mainline Protestants engaged in wider social and political debates in Brazil and how religious literature circulated in Evangelical arenas. Previously, he taught at the Instituto Federal de Educação, Ciência e Tecnologia de Brasília.

David C. Kirkpatrick

gained his PhD in World Christianity from the University of Edinburgh. He was a teaching fellow in the Centre for the Study of World Christianity at the

University of Edinburgh. He is presently the T. Gannon Postdoctoral Associate in Religion at Florida State University. As a historian, he focuses especially on the intersection of Latin America and the global North.

Chandra Mallampalli

is Professor of History at Westmont College. His work addresses the intersection of religion, law and society in colonial South Asia. His publications include *Christians and Public Life in Colonial South India* (RoutledgeCurzon, 2004) and *Race, Religion and Law in Colonial India* (Cambridge University Press, 2011). His most recent book is entitled *A Muslim 'Conspiracy' in British India* (Cambridge University Press, 2017).

David Maxwell

is Dixie Professor of Ecclesiastical History at the University of Cambridge and a fellow of Emmanuel College. He is author of *Christians and Chiefs in Zimbabwe: A Social History of the Hwesa People c.1870s–1990s* (International African Library/Edinburgh University Press, 1999) and *African Gifts of the Spirit: Pentecostalism and the Rise of a Zimbabwean Transnational Religious Movement* (James Currey, 2006). With Patrick Harries he co-edited *The Spiritual in the Secular: Missionaries and Knowledge about Africa* (Eerdmans, 2012). He was long-time editor of *The Journal of Religion in Africa*. Currently, he is writing a book about missionaries and African agents in the creation of colonial knowledge in Belgian Congo.

Dorottya Nagy

is Professor of Missiology at the Protestant Theological University in Amsterdam, the Netherlands, with a research interest in migration, mission studies, ecclesiology, Christianity in post-communist Europe, and innovative ways of theologising. Her publications include *Migration and Theology: The Case of Chinese Christian Communities in the Globalisation Context* (Boekencentrum, 2009) and 'Minding Methodology: Theology-Missiology and Migration Studies' (*Mission Studies* 32 (2), 2015). Nagy is President of the Central and Eastern European Association for Mission Studies (CEEAMS) and a member of the editorial board of its journal.

Peter C. Phan

holds the Ignacio Ellacuría Chair of Catholic Social Thought at Georgetown University and is Director of the PhD programme in theology and religious studies. He earned three doctorates: an STD from the Università Pontificia Salesiana, Rome, and a PhD and DD from the University of London. He has received two honorary doctoral degrees: from the Catholic Theological Union and from Elms College. He has published widely on the theology of icons in Orthodox theology, patristic theology, eschatology, the history of Christian missions in Asia, and liberation, inculturation and interreligious dialogue.

Andrew Preston

is Professor of American History and a fellow of Clare College, Cambridge University. He is the author of *The War Council: McGeorge Bundy, the NSC, and Vietnam* (Harvard University Press, 2006) and *Sword of the Spirit, Shield of Faith: Religion in American War and Diplomacy* (Knopf, 2012), and editor of four other books. He is currently writing a book on the idea of national security in American history as well as editing Volume 2 of *The Cambridge History of the Vietnam War*.

Joel Robbins

is Sigrid Rausing Professor of Social Anthropology at the University of Cambridge. He has long been active in the anthropological study of Christianity as well as in the study of global Pentecostalism, ethics and ritual. He is the author of *Becoming Sinners: Christianity and Moral Torment in a Papua New Guinea Society* (University of California Press, 2004).

Chloë Starr

is Associate Professor of Asian Christianity and Theology at Yale Divinity School. Her research focuses on Chinese theological texts and the interaction between literature and theology in China, and her most recent volume is *Chinese Theology: Text and Context* (Yale University Press, 2016). She is currently translating an anthology of Chinese theology into English and preparing a volume on contemporary Chinese Christian fiction.

Charlotte Walker-Said

is Assistant Professor of Africana Studies at John Jay College of Criminal Justice, City University of New York (CUNY). Her research examines the transnational character of Christianity and its influence on gender politics, family law and human rights in Africa in the colonial and postcolonial periods. Her most recent book is entitled *Faith, Power, and Family: Law and Christianity in Interwar Cameroon* (James Currey, 2018). With John D. Kelly she edited *Corporate Social Responsibility? Human Rights in the New Global Economy* (University of Chicago Press, 2015).

Emma Wild-Wood

lectures in World Christianities at the University of Cambridge. She was Director of the Cambridge Centre for Christianity Worldwide and taught in DR Congo and Uganda. She has published widely on African Christianity, including *Migration and Christian Identity in Congo* (Brill, 2008). She co-edited with Kevin Ward *The East African Revival: History and Legacies* (Ashgate, 2012), and with Peniel Rajkumar *Foundations for Mission* (Regnum, 2014). She is currently writing on religious change in the Great Lakes region through the life of Apolo Kivebulaya. From January 2018 she will be Senior Lecturer in African Christianity and African Indigenous Religions in the School of Divinity, University of Edinburgh.

Relocating World Christianity

Joel Cabrita and David Maxwell

In recent years, World Christianity has become a new catchphrase in theological and missiological circles. It denotes the growing interest in studying regional Christianities in multiple geographical locations in the non-Western world, often deliberately excluding Christianity in the West – considered to have long attracted a disproportionate share of scholarly attention – from its purview. Western-based theologians and missiologists have sought to engage with non-Western theologies and local expressions of Christianity in order to critique their own ethnocentric constructions of the faith. The term thus represents a shift away from viewing Christianity in Western Europe and North America as in any sense normative of Christianity, and it also reflects the remarkable demographic movement in the axis of Christianity from the West to the global South that occurred in the twentieth century. The chapters in the present volume, a combination of regionally focused case studies and thematic essays, seek to both conceptualise and map out the broad dimensions of this transformative shift within the scholarship. This introduction, in particular, aims to explain some of the factors prompting the emergence of World Christianity as an oft-cited term in certain academic circles. Our goal is to focus on the rise of the phenomenon in scholarship; here, we account for and explain a historiographical shift, rather than comment on the demographic shift of Christianity to the non-Western world described by the term.

We begin, then, by noting the increasingly ubiquitous nature of the term in academic circles in the West. For example, numerous research centres for the study of World Christianity have sprung up in recent years, mainly in the United Kingdom and the United States: the University of Edinburgh's School of Divinity has a Centre for the Study of World Christianity; Boston University's School of Theology has a Center for Global Christianity and Mission; Yale University's Divinity School boasts a World Christianity Initiative; and the University of Cambridge works in association with the self-professedly Christian Henry Martyn Centre, an institute for 'understanding Mission and World Christianity', recently and significantly renamed the Cambridge Centre for Christianity Worldwide (CCCW), hence substituting the new term for the older, more traditional 'missionary luminary' nomenclature. Beyond the UK and USA, the so-called 'Munich School' of World Christianity, based at Ludwig Maximilian

© KONINKLIJKE BRILL NV, LEIDEN, 2017 | DOI: 10.1163/9789004355026_002

University, Germany, under the leadership of Klaus Koschorke, has been rising in prominence. And the University of Basel, renowned for its long tradition of scholarship on the history of missions, particularly its own Basel Mission, has recently created a chair in *Aussereuropäisches Christentum* ('non-Western Christianity'). Book series and journals devoted to the study of World Christianity have appeared on both sides of the Atlantic, including Baylor University Press's *Studies in World Christianity* and Wiley's *Blackwell Guides to Global Christianity*, as well as the Edinburgh University-published journal *Studies in World Christianity* and the North American *Journal of World Christianity*. Academic posts in the area, too, abound (Phan 2012: 171–5). A recent trawl of the internet revealed that posts in 'World Christianity' or 'Global Christianity' are fast becoming a standard feature of international job postings in theology and religious studies. More faculty positions in seminaries, divinity schools and the religion and theology departments of colleges and universities include World Christianity in their titles. Indeed, Joel Cabrita's own position at Cambridge confirms this trend, with the Faculty of Divinity approving the creation of a new post – 'Lecturer in World Christianities' – in 2012, while David Maxwell, as an Africanist, is the first specialist on Christianity in the global South appointed as the Dixie Professor of Ecclesiastical History in Cambridge (2010) since the foundation of the Chair in the Faculty of History in 1884. Finally, mission societies themselves have consciously adopted the term to reflect upon the way in which increased connectedness creates new opportunities for cross-cultural partnerships and new dangers in the form of cultural homogenisation (Beattie 2005: 6–8).

Responding to the new attention to Christianity's demographic strength outside the Western world, as well as a failure of confidence in old assumptions about the value of mission work and conventional missionary studies, many scholars within theology and missiology stables have come to invoke the term in a revisionist manner. It has become their shorthand for advocating that Western researchers discard older Eurocentric categories of normative Christian faith, and instead invest in the study of culturally and linguistically particular expressions of the faith outside the West. Admittedly, this recent theological turn to Christian specificity stands in a much longer tradition of area studies of religious communities conducted by historians and anthropologists. For a long time the field was dominated by Africanists, who, following in the footsteps of Bengt Sundkler, examined the dynamics of missionary encounters with local societies and the subsequent emergence of African Christian movements (Sundkler 1948).[1] But scholars studying the Pacific, India and Latin America

---

have shared these interests.[2] Yet while historically minded scholars in the social sciences were fascinated by processes of reception and adaptation that made Christianity indigenous, such analyses were largely ignored by mid-twentieth-century theologians and missiologists, who largely remained convinced that the Christian faith was an alien import awaiting absorption into an essentialised traditional culture.[3]

What is now distinctive is the far more widespread interest of theologians and missiologists in mapping out specific case studies of local, non-Western Christianities (see, for example, Farhadian 2012; Sanneh 2003). Global Pentecostal and Charismatic Christian communities have been considered particularly well suited to this trend of emphasising decentralised local expressions of the faith autonomous of Western control; a recent example of this scholarship is Allan Anderson's *To the Ends of the Earth: Pentecostalism and the Transformation of World Christianity* (Anderson 2013). The analytical shift prompted in part by populist commentary on data proclaiming the southwards migration of Christianity (Barrett 2001), and a growing sociological awareness of globalisation, has had considerable benefits for those interested in charting the manifold expressions – both historical and present-day – of Christianity around the world. Non-Western forms of Christianity are no longer viewed as derivative of, or dependent on, prior – both chronologically and conceptually – expressions of Western Christianity. Instead of being seen as peripheral to the main narrative of the Christian faith, the shift to World Christianity has allowed scholars to view Christianity in Africa, Asia, the Pacific and Latin America as stories with their own integrity and their own centres of gravity; constitutive of unique trajectories of the Christian faith, often developed with little or no recourse to Western missionary influence. In this way, the adoption of World Christianity as an analytical framework has facilitated a valuable move away from viewing non-Western Christians as merely an extension of 'missionary history', seeing them instead as an important expression of the Christian faith in its own right.

However, this introduction argues that the term, and the scholarly field it has generated around it, are now due a critical reappraisal. We suggest here that the label 'World Christianity' in fact accomplishes significant – largely implicit – intellectual work. Rather than being a purely descriptive term, scholars' focus on World Christianity actively shapes their material in mainly unacknowledged

---

Peel (1968; 2000); Ranger and Kimambo (1972); Ranger and Weller (1975); Comaroff and Comaroff (1991; 1997); Maxwell (1999; 2006a).

2 For example: Gunson (1978); Barker (1990); Austin-Broos (1997); Robbins (2004); Grimshaw and May (2010); Frykenberg (2008); Annis (1987).

3 This point was made by Hastings (1989: 31) and Etherington (1996).

ways. We argue that, far from describing an objective state of things 'out there in the world', the intellectual genealogy of the phrase highlights that 'World Christianity' is best understood as a normative term rather than a purely descriptive one. In other words, it does not merely give an account of a shift that has taken place, traceable in empirical reality; rather, it offers a moral commentary on the shape and future of contemporary Christendom. In particular, we aim to show in this introduction that the ideological thrust of the term as used in current theological-missiological discourse above all privileges attention to the local, the particular and the regional, and thus simultaneously obscures larger-scale connections and networks as well as cross-cultural continuities. Another way of putting this – as we shall shortly explain – is that the turn to World Christianity, best understood in the context of postcolonial unease about the missionary endeavour, leans heavily on a relatively recent, theologically inflected grammar of cultural specificity and essentialism, rather than on older missionary discourses around notions of Christian universality and human cosmopolitanism.

In what follows of this introduction, we unpack some of the theoretical assumptions underlying the term, as well as draw out some constraining implications that result from its uncritical use. First, we situate the emergence of the term 'World Christianity' in a particular theological and political milieu of postcolonial anxiety. Missiologists pioneered the use of the term in a period when they were grappling with the legacy of missions' ties to a colonial past as well as forging a new vocabulary with which to positively articulate a theology of culture – the latter development linked to the rise of Africanist scholarship on Christianity in the second half of the twentieth century. Second, we locate the increasing popularity of the label within a broader turn across the humanities to wider studies of the 'World'. We explain some of the implications arising from this, paying particular attention to the danger of an over-simplistic bifurcation of the globe into the 'West' and the 'World', and instead argue for a research agenda that is attentive to connections – as well as ruptures – between different parts of the globe. While remaining cognisant of the inherent limitations of the term, we are nonetheless hopeful about the possibility of subjecting the concept of World Christianity to rigorous critical interrogation, where, with some notable exceptions (Koschorke 2014; Sanneh 2003), it has hitherto been taken for granted.

Finally, this volume also seeks to bring a fresh perspective to the field by incorporating contributions from a range of humanities disciplines, while also seeking to add to and enhance those disciplines' insights and conceptual frameworks. While several scholars have already called for an interdisciplinary approach (Burroughs 1995: 172; Walls 1991: 154), much World Christianity scholarship tends to be carried out by theologians and missiologists. This volume engages theologians and missiologists in explicit dialogue with historians, anthropologists and political scientists who are well versed in thinking in terms of units beyond the nation-state and alert to the dangers of cultural essentialism. It is true that many of the historians, anthropologists and political scientists represented in this volume would not ordinarily think of their research in terms of 'World Christianity'. Yet here we argue that by building on these disciplines' by now well-established methods of conceptualising phenomena in ways that transgress local or national or culturalist boundaries, a valuable complement is added to missiologists' and theologians' competency in attending to local, contextualised religious practice. The volume thus approaches World Christianity from a variety of perspectives. Although its geographical scope is by no means exhaustive, one or more chapters address each of the globe's major inhabited regions. We have also been at pains to include Europe and North America in our discussions of World Christianity and to ensure that the four broad Christian traditions are represented: Catholicism, Orthodoxy, Pentecostalism and Protestantism. The inclusion of Catholicism and Orthodoxy is intended as an antidote to the strong focus on Protestantism in scholarship on World Christianity. The chapters by historians take a long view of the history of connectivity and consciousness while those by theologians and social scientists tend to focus on recent or current developments. Where relevant, the contributors examine the interaction of Christian traditions with each other and with other religions, whether Confucianism, Hinduism, Islam or ancestral religion. Our twelve contributors investigate how the flourishing of diverse religious communities coexists alongside more universal theologies and adherents' lived practices of Christianity as a single, worldwide faith. Rather than merely drawing on an unproductive dichotomy between Western and non-Western Christianity, our diverse contributors examine large-scale networks within the global South as well as within diasporic global South communities in the northern hemisphere. Before discussing some of these contributions in more depth, however, we now discuss the intellectual precursors that paved the way for the current World Christianity turn.

From Mission Studies to World Christianity

By the 1980s, missiologists shared a widespread perception that their academic field was increasingly under threat. First and foremost was the changed political context of the second half of the twentieth century. For many Christians in

Africa, Asia and Latin America, the success of anti-imperialist independence movements across much of the world served to underscore the ambiguous relationship between Western mission agencies and European imperialism. From the 1950s onwards, churches around the world increasingly accused Western missionaries of paternalism, racism and cultural imperialism, seeing their continued presence as inappropriate in a postcolonial landscape. In 1971, Christian leaders in the Philippines, Kenya and Argentina called for a moratorium on missionaries to end the dependence of younger churches on older ones. In 1974, the All Africa Conference of Churches, meeting in Lusaka, issued a block on Western missionaries and money sent to Africa, reflecting the period's widespread conviction that foreign assistance created undesirable dependency and stifled African leadership (Robert 2000: 52). Furthermore, there were also outright rejections of Christianity within many independence-era revolutionary movements (many Marxist in orientation), as in Mobutu's newly independent Zaire, which abolished the celebration of Christmas as a vestige of colonialism (Maxwell 2006b).

Moreover, further eroding the moral defensibility of missions in the eyes of many – including missiologists themselves – was the social sciences' simultaneous discovery of the missionary as an agent of imperialism. The 1980s witnessed an explosion of new scholarly interest in the history of European and American missions. Mission history written in the first half of the twentieth century had been largely institutionally focused, told from the perspective of individual denominations attempting to spread their form of Christianity across the globe (Latourette 1937–45). Moreover, mirroring Eurocentric imperial history, missionaries were cast in these narratives as the sole agents of change. By the 1970s, however, a new interest in the dynamics of the colonial encounter portrayed missionaries in a very different light: rather than heroes, they were handmaids of colonialism who mediated Western values and ideas, as well as formal structures of empire, to local converts. The idea that Protestant and Catholic foreign missions were a tool of nationalism at home, and imperialism abroad, proved 'an irresistible thesis', generating numerous monographs from the late 1950s to the present (Robert 1994: 148). Entanglement with empire has long been deemed true of British missions; a more recent body of literature focused on American expansion in the Pacific world, and the role of American missionaries in these processes (Grabill 1971; Comaroff and Comaroff 1991; 1997). The argument was nuanced by the recognition that missionaries and their apologists were not always active agents of American or European colonialism, but rather ideologues of it, providing a 'moral equivalent for imperialism' (Hutchinson 1982: 174). Subsequently, many studies showed that missionaries' role in colonialism was highly ambivalent; they critiqued the imperial enterprise as much as they supported it (Etherington 2005). And some of the most interesting scholarship has insisted that local colonial subjects were creative agents engaged in a 'long conversation' with Western missionaries, often taking on, and simultaneously transforming, the ideologies and cultural and material artefacts of their European and North American interlocutors (Cooper 2010; Dirks 1992; Peel 2000; Landau 1995).

Added to these historiographical and political shifts was also a much-commented upon demographic transformation in the worldwide distribution of Christianity. The 2002 publication of Philip Jenkins' populist *The Next Christendom: The Coming of Global Christianity* drew widespread attention to this. Jenkins' argument was simple: over the course of the twentieth century, he maintained, there had been a great southwards migration of the Christian faith, a vast demographic movement of Christians to Africa, Latin America, Asia and the Pacific. The corollary to this was that Christianity in the region known as the 'global North' – primarily Europe and North America – was now in terminal decline, its Northern congregations dwindling and church buildings emptying (Jenkins 2007: 115–20). Jenkins argued that Christianity was poised on, or indeed already passing over, the threshold of another great Reformation, with vast and unprecedented growth occurring in the 'global South', coming to constitute a theologically conservative, supernaturally oriented and enspirited version of the faith that challenged the supposed relativism of liberal Northern Christians. A major survey of global Christianity published in 2011 by the Pew Research Forum affirmed Jenkins' findings, revealing that, between 1910 and 2010, although the total number of global Christians remained relatively stable at about 32–25 per cent, there had nonetheless been a significant shift in where these Christians were found. While in 1910 Europe and the Americas had contributed 93 per cent of the world's Christians, in 2010 this figure had dropped to 63 per cent. At the same time, the survey's results showed that Christianity had grown enormously in other regions – particularly in sub-Saharan Africa, where the continent's share of the world's Christian population had grown from 1.4 per cent in 1910 to a whopping 23.6 per cent in 2010 (62.7 per cent of all Africans). Another area of major growth has been in what the survey dubs the 'Asia-Pacific' region; this contributed 4.5 per cent of the world's Christian population in 1910, but that figure had grown threefold to 13.1 per cent by 2010.[4] These

---

4   In December 2012, the Pew Forum on Religion and Public Life released *The Global Religious Landscape: A Report on the Size and Distribution of the World's Major Religious Groups as of 2010*. Notable data included: Europe has more Christians than any other continent (558 million), with South America and Africa gaining ground; Asia remains far behind; the Christian

dramatic changes – and the debate they precipitated – further undermined traditional conceptions of the necessity and value of missionary work. It was clearly seen by many that there needed to be a scholarly model that recognised Christian activity beyond the West in its own right, rather than as a derivative of missionary activity originating in Western Europe or North America. Given the vitality of church growth in Asia and Africa, a figure such as prominent World Christianity proponent Lamin Sanneh could recently acknowledge that 'the fact that disadvantaged peoples and their cultures are buoyed by new waves of conversion has created alignments of global scope at the margins of power and privilege' (Sanneh 2008: 287).

Responding to this dramatic shift in mood – comprising political, historiographic and demographic elements – many Western missionaries became highly self-critical of their own role in structures of colonial domination and Eurocentric assumptions about where Christianity found its 'normative' home. Indeed, anxiety about the missionary enterprise had been alive in missionary circles at least since the turbulent 1970s, the era when independence movements swept across the African continent. The Lausanne Movement (founded in 1974) and the Commission on World Mission and Evangelism (inaugurated in 1961) were key voices in this regard. Both addressed themselves to the task of reconceptualising mission in a postcolonial age. Inspired by Billy Graham, the Lausanne Movement brought together Protestant leaders from across the world to pray and reflect upon world evangelisation, infused with a sense of 'penitence by our failures' (Clarke 2014: 196) and critically reflecting on how the theology and practice of Christian mission were tainted by an 'imperial' past. There was intense self-scrutiny of the ways in which Christian mission had historically allied itself with imperial and colonial regimes: 'a turning toward past colonial alliances to prophetically indict such systems of power and a turning away from the lure of such hegemonic practice' (Clarke 2014: 201).

By the 1980s, building on insights garnered at these international meetings, a number of missiologists had begun to independently voice the need for dramatic transformation in the academic practice of missiology. The leading British historian of Christian missions, Andrew Walls, was a vocal proponent of such acts of self-examination, as well as an advocate for charting a new, more

---

median age worldwide is thirty (compared with twenty-three for Muslims), with large geographic disparities – for example, European and North American Christians are far older than those in Africa, Latin America and Asia; Christians are by far the most evenly distributed religious group; Asia houses the majority of Muslims, Hindus, Buddhists, members of 'folk religions' and the religiously unaffiliated. See http://www.pewforum.org/2011/12/19/global-christianity-exec/, accessed November 2016.

dialogical agenda for mission in a postcolonial world. Walls asserted the need
for a radical rupture with old 'modes' of mission:

> the [imperial] crusading mode and the [postcolonial] missionary mode
> are sharply differentiated means of extending the Christian faith ... The
> [imperial] crusader may first issue his invitation to the Gospel but, in
> the end, he is prepared to compel. The [postcolonial] missionary, even
> if his natural instinct is to desire compulsion, cannot compel, but only
> demonstrate, invite, explain, entreat and leave the results to God.
>
> WALLS and ROSS 2008: 196–7; BURROUGHS et al. 2011

While Walls urged a new practice of mission itself, he also called for an academic 'renaissance' of the discipline of mission studies in response to these
crippling 'structural problems' (Walls 1991: 150) and for mission history to now
be written in engagement with histories of Christianity in the South. Another
milestone in the journey to a new and more self-reflexive missiology was a
publication from the renowned South African missiologist David J. Bosch, who
in 1991 completed *Transforming Mission: Paradigm Shifts in the Theology of
Mission* (Bosch 1991). This was a magisterial study of 'mission in the wake of
Enlightenment', arguing that mainstream understandings of mission still portrayed it as an essentially Western initiative. Echoing Walls, Bosch's influential
argument was also for a renewed understanding of mission that strove to be
less culturally blinkered and more sensitive to the diversity of Christian practice and belief in different parts of the globe.

In an era, then, when older models of mission studies seemed increasingly
untenable – Walls noted that 'studies of the activities of Western missionaries
nowadays often need an explanation or apology' (Walls 1991: 146) – the emergence of World Christianity as a new analytical framework within missiological circles happily promised to rehabilitate the older discipline. The notion
seemed to work best in exactly those areas where older conceptions of mission no longer did: it was sensitive to local cultural difference, intensely self-
conscious about postcolonial political dynamics, and made a distinct effort
to overcome Western cultural preconceptions. Moreover, this was a term that
already had credibility in the sense that it had circulated in missiological circles
since the early twentieth century. Then, as now, the notion carried theological weight. Missionary publications before the First World War referred to
'world evangelisation' but largely stopped short of invoking World Christianity (understandable, after all, because the vast majority of all Christians was
still concentrated in Western Europe and North America). It was only after
the First World War that the term emerged in more frequent usage, not only

a recognition of the increasing numerical strength of worldwide Christianity, but also a reflection of the profound loss of confidence in Western culture after the horrors of the trenches, and the resultant willingness on the part of many intellectuals to question the hitherto unquestioned superiority of Western values and religion.[5] Along these lines, the missiologist Michael Poon has shown how the notion of World Christianity emerged out of ecumenical thinking in the first half of the twentieth century, shaped by a focus on international friendship and interdenominational fellowship as the answer to the world's bloody woes (Johnson and Kim 2005: 81). Works such as Francis McConnell's *Human Needs and World Christianity* (1929) and Henry Leiper's *World Chaos or World Christianity* (1937) argued that only a unified church could effectively deal with the turmoil of war, economic crises and totalitarianism. Henry Van Dusen's *World Christianity: Yesterday, Today and Tomorrow* (1947), published just after the global catastrophe of the Second World War, made a similar argument for 'World Christianity' – here deployed as a shorthand for Christian unity and ecumenical collaboration – in the face of a hostile world:

> To an age destined to survive, or to expire, as 'one world', we bring a world Church. We have seen that in the past century Christianity has become, for the first time, a world reality. For the first time – and in the nick of time.
>
> VAN DUSEN 1947: 251

By the late twentieth century, in the hands of missiologists such as Walls and others, the term was given new theological mileage in a context of increasing anxiety about the missionary enterprise's relevance, and a guilty conscience about colonialism. Andrew Walls wrote in 1996 of the need 'to come to terms with Christianity as a non-Western religion' (Walls 1996: xix). But he had founded his Centre for the Study of Christianity in the non-Western World at the

---

5   The term 'World Christian' was also coined in this post-war era and probably first used by Daniel Fleming in a 1920 YMCA book entitled *Marks of a World Christian*. More recently it has appeared in publications by Evangelical groups such as the World Team missions, Conservation Baptist Foreign Missionary Society, United Presbyterian Center for Mission Studies and, in particular, student bodies such as Campus Crusade for Christ and InterVarsity Christian Fellowship. One such student movement, the Travelling Team, which traces its ancestry through John Mott to the Student Volunteer Movement (1886) and mobilises on campuses for mission work, defines a World Christian as someone who determines 'to make Christ's global cause the unifying focus – the context – for all they are and do'. See http://www.thetravelingteam.org/articles/to-be-a-world-christian, accessed 26 April 2016.

University of Aberdeen as early as 1983, moving it to the School of Divinity at the University of Edinburgh in 1987, where it was subsequently renamed the Centre for the Study of World Christianity.[6] With Lamin Sanneh (discussed below), Walls stands out as one of the two principal architects of World Christianity, a figure upon whose shoulders Philip Jenkins' intervention clearly stands. In a remarkable and multifaceted career that commenced in the 1950s, Walls has perhaps done more than any other scholar to formulate the notion of a 'World Christianity'. In his collection of source materials on contemporary Christian expressions around the globe, his supervision of missionaries and local church leaders, and a breadth of teaching that has taken him to Freetown, Nsukka, Aberdeen, Edinburgh, Princeton, New Haven, Akropong, Singapore, Hong Kong, Seoul and Liverpool, Walls' career embodies the diversity of the Christian church.

Yet it was the complex interplay between diversity of Christian expression and ecclesial unity that was perhaps Walls' most enduring interest. Walls' early career in West Africa (1957–66) grounded him in the area studies approach to African Christianity referred to above. On his move to Aberdeen in 1967 he founded the *Journal of Religion in Africa*, a periodical committed to examining Christianity in specific regions of the continent and its encounter with Islam and traditional religion in context.[7] But his interests extended well beyond Africa, incorporating a robust sense of the church as a worldwide communion. As early as 1987 he argued for 'the end of Christendom': 'In the continuing Christian histories of Africa, Asia and the Pacific, the missionary period is already an episode.' He also noted how the 'Great Reverse Migration' of peoples from the global South into Europe and North America enriched the nature of Christianity within the West. Moreover, while celebrating the worldwide church in all its diversity, he also shared Van Dusen's much older vision of an operational unity: 'The Ephesian question at the Ephesian moment is whether or not the church in all its diversity will demonstrate its unity by the interactive participation of all its culture-specific segments, the interactive participation that is to be expected in a functioning body' (Walls 1987: 85; Walls 2002: 81). In this sense, Walls was a bridging figure between the older ecumenical sense of a global communion – 'World Christianity' – and the newer, emerging concept of

---

6 Michael Poon, 'Reimagining World Christianity: Andrew Walls and His Legacy', https://www.fulcrum-anglican.org.uk/articles/re-imagining-world-christianity-andrew-walls-and-his-legacy/, accessed 19 February 2016.

7 Walls was also co-founder of the journal *Studies in World Christianity* (1995) and a joint convener of the Yale–Edinburgh Group on the History of the Missionary Movement and World Christianity.

World Christianity as scholarship focused on culturally specific, non-Western Christian practice in a postcolonial context.

Many soon followed in Walls' pioneering footsteps. An important moment in the making of World Christianity as new sub-discipline, both in terms of resourcing and intellectual ambition, was the formation of the Currents in World Christianity (CWC) project in 1999. Located in the Centre for Advanced Religious and Theological Studies (CARTS) in the Faculty of Divinity, University of Cambridge, and lavishly funded by the Pew Charitable Trust, the project represented the marriage of two research groups.[8] The first was the CARTS-based North American Missiology Project (NAMP) directed by Brian Stanley (currently director of the Centre for the Study of World Christianity at the University of Edinburgh), which had sought to examine the inter-relationships between theology, theory, policy and experience in Protestant missions in Britain and North America in the period 1740–1910. The second project was co-ordinated by Mark Hutchinson, a historian of Evangelical Christianity currently at Western Sydney University as well as loosely based at the Institute for the Study of American Evangelicals at Wheaton, Illinois. Hutchinson's project comprised a group of scholars – including historians of American Christianity Edith Blumhofer and Mark Noll – all working on evangelicalism and globalisation. The fusion of these two research agendas into the CWC under the joint directorship of Stanley and Hutchinson brought sociological perspectives on globalisation to the NAMP history of missions, expanding its focus into the twentieth century as well as from the North Atlantic world into the global South. In particular, the CWC project examined whether the spread of evangelicalism into the so-called Two-thirds World was the result of the globalisation of capital, institutions and concepts, or the contrary: a phenomenon that subverted these homogenising processes. Further, it asked whether the term 'evangelicalism' could be used as a uniform category to describe non-Western Christian traditions descended from Evangelical missions but which, over time, had localised considerably. The project's expanded geographical vision came in part via the prior participation in the American project of historian of Christianity in Africa Ogbu Kalu as well as the Latin Americanist Paul Freston, and its global purview was also symbolised by setting the project's third conference in Pretoria, South Africa in 2001.

---

8 The Pew Charitable Trusts funded other research that raised the profile of scholars of World Christianity. From 1991 to 1999, the Overseas Ministries Studies Center in New Haven administered Pew's Research Enablement Program, awarding about twenty grants a year to early career and established scholars in 'mission and Third World Christianity'. In the same decade, Pew also sponsored separate large-scale research on Africa and China.

The significance of the CWC project for our current mapping of the scholarly turn to World Christianity was threefold: first, by means of its extensive seminars, international conferences and plentiful publications, it placed World Christianity on the scholarly agenda, if only loosely defined, as a description of the global expansion of the Christian church and as a category of analysis. Second, it created a strong association between World Christianity and evangelicalism by viewing Evangelical religion as the pre-eminent global religion due to its 'sense of shared vision and theological inheritance which transcends denominational and national allegiances'.[9] Scholars who had an expertise in the study of evangelicalism and who were often also Evangelical by confession also dominated CWC's membership, highlighting once again that the World Christianity turn has largely been pioneered by individuals who self-identify as insiders in the Christian tradition. Lastly, the project helped establish and shape the careers of the second generation of World Christianity scholars. It prompted Stanley to embark on a study of the World Missionary Conference in 1910 and a subsequent study of global evangelicalism, and Hutchinson followed a very similar trajectory (Stanley 2009: xiii; 2013; Hutchinson and Wolffe 2012). Other prominent academics involved in CWC's US-based seminars, such Mark Noll (2009) and Dana Robert (2009), also went on to make significant interventions in the scholarship.

From the 1990s and up to the present day, institutions, organisations and publications previously defined as 'missiological' now increasingly began to redefine themselves as addressing Christianity in its 'non-Western' or 'world' incarnations, attempting to free mission studies from its imperial associations by allowing Southern and Eastern voices and texts into the canon. In 2007, Uppsala University's Mission Studies section within the Faculty of Theology was renamed 'World Christianity and Interreligious Studies', maintaining on its website that the new name 'better describes' the international and multidisciplinary content of the course (Uppsala was, in turn, inspired by the Netherlands' Radboud University Nijmegen Institute for Mission Studies' own shift in this direction).[10] Cambridge University's Theological Federation was slower to change: while its Henry Martyn Centre for the Study of Mission had been set

---

9   David Thompson, 'Grant Proposal to the Pew Charitable Trusts' Centre for Advanced Religious and Theological Studies, Faculty of Divinity, University of Cambridge, July 1998' (archived in the Cambridge Centre for Christianity Worldwide). See also Stanley (1999) and Hutchinson (1999).

10   See http://www.teol.uu.se/Research/Research_Disciplines/world-christianity-and -interreligious-studies+/, accessed 21 February 2016; personal communication, Johannes Zeiler, 2 July 2016.

up in 1998, it was only in 2014 that it was renamed the Cambridge Centre for Christianity Worldwide; it was noted that the new name 'encourages a deeper understanding of the worldwide and missionary nature of the church'.[11] Publications as well as institutions joined the trend towards replacing mission nomenclature with the rhetoric of World Christianity. Even cautious renaming provides evidence of the overall trend. In 2016, the *International Bulletin of Missionary Research* – the flagship journal of mission studies – became the *International Bulletin of Mission Research*, admitting that 'for some readers, "missionary" can too easily bring to mind previous centuries of cross-cultural ministries in the context of colonialism'. The journal's editors found 'mission' to be a less historically loaded term: 'both ancient and contemporary' (Whiteman 2016: 4).

What is noteworthy from the survey above is that the notion of 'World Christianity' tends to be a largely Protestant preoccupation. With one or two notable exceptions, such as Peter Phan or Lamin Sanneh, there is an absence of an explicit World Christianity turn in Catholic literature. And while Sanneh does deploy the term, as we will see below he is at pains to stress its disaggregated vernacular forms.[12] If, as we suggest, World Christianity is partly the product of missionaries and missiologists' postcolonial guilt, then the Roman Catholic Church had a clearer conscience, having begun to indigenise its clergy either several decades before or on the cusp of decolonisation.[13] But the explanation for a lack of engagement with World Christianity also lies in the particularities of Catholic missiology and ecclesiology. The incarnationalist aspects of Catholic teaching have stimulated nationalism, particularly in early twentieth-century Europe, while Catholic clericalism has made it less responsive to local pressures than is the case for many other churches. But these particularities are countered by an equally strong universalist tradition, which has asserted a global communion and is embodied in *Propaganda Fide*, the congregation of the Roman Curia responsible for missionary work, which has a global vision and reach that is 'catholic' in the true sense of the word. One can see these tensions at work in the fascinating autobiography of the Malawian Catholic bishop Patrick Kalilombe, *Doing Theology at the Grassroots* (1999). Convinced of the historical and cultural relativity of Catholic traditions and of the need for local expressions of the faith, he is nevertheless proud of his cosmopol-

---

11   Personal communication, Emma Wild-Wood, 19 February 2016; see also http://www.cccw .cam.ac.uk/, accessed 21 February 2016.

12   Sanneh is, of course, the product of a strong Methodist formation before his conversion to Catholicism in the early 2000s.

13   Pentecostals and Methodists also ordained indigenous clergy prior to decolonisation and were often criticised for doing so by fellow Protestants.

itan formation in the 'Eternal City' of Rome, where he came to appreciate the divine aspects of church government and to see himself as a missionary to other nations (Kalilombe 1999: 26–8).

Throughout the last century, the Catholic Church struggled with the same issues that animated Protestant theologians: namely imperialism, nationalism, war, decolonisation and the emergence of the global South with distinct political and economic agendas. The Vatican's response was manifested in moments of reform in the face of resistance from national churches and reluctant clerical hierarchies; in these, it attempted to decentralise power and authority in order that the church might better realise its vision of world mission. The first manifestation of these tensions came with the election of Benedict XV as Pope in 1914 just as the Great War was breaking out. Much challenged by the destructive force of nationalism, in 1919 he issued one of the most significant mission encyclicals, *Maximum Illud*. Foreshadowing Van Dusen's later insistence on an ecumenical, supra-nationalist 'World Christianity' in the aftermath of the Second World War, the Pope used the encyclical to warn missionaries to avoid furthering the interests of their own countries because it created the impression that 'the Christian religion is the exclusive property of some foreign nation', whereby acceptance appeared to entail 'submission to a foreign country' and 'the loss of one's national dignity'. Benedict placed great emphasis on the development of local clergy who were to be responsible for their own churches rather than serve as auxiliaries to missionary priests:

> In this policy lies the greatest hope of the new churches. For the local priest, one with his people by birth, by nature, by his sympathies and his aspirations, is remarkably effective in appealing to their mentality and thus attracting them to the Faith.

Citing the 'one billion souls' yet to be reached by the church, the encyclical signalled the renewal of Catholic mission after its loss of momentum to Protestantism during the nineteenth century.[14] Benedict's appointment of Cardinal van Rossum as head of *Propaganda Fide* was critical for the implementation of his policies. So too was the subsequent papacy of Pius XI (1922–39), whose *Rerum Ecclesiae* of 1926 consolidated Benedict's vision. By the time of Pius's death in 1939, forty-eight mission church territories were under native bishops,

---

14   Benedict XV, '*Maximum Illud*: Apostolic Letter on the Propagation of the Faith Throughout the World', 30 November 1919. Translated by Thomas J. M. Burke, SJ. Washington DC: National Catholic Welfare Office, http://www.svdcuria.org/public/mission/docs/encycl/mi-en.htm, accessed 7 February 2017.

including twenty-six in China and thirteen in India, three in Japan and three in Vietnam (Ward 2006: 75–6; Hastings 2001: 748–9).

The Second Vatican Council (1962–65), inaugurated by Pope John XXIII, gave a huge impetus to Catholic programmes of mission and decentralisation, paralleling similar developments that were occurring in Protestant circles in this period. *Ad Gentes* ('To the Nations') – the Council's decree on mission-ary activity – stressed the priorities of proclamation and preaching, reminding the faithful that these were 'the greatest and holiest duty of the church', while highlighting the needs of the now two billion unreached.[15] Equally significant was *Lumen Gentium* (the Dogmatic Constitution on the Church), which shifted emphasis from the church as a monarchy, preoccupied with its authority, to a communion in which other Christians were recognised, and where missionar-ies were encouraged to adopt what was good in other religions so that the faith might be ennobled to the glory of God. This new model of church enabled novel expressions of the gospel such as base communities in Latin America and Cent-ral Africa, the former more overtly political, the latter more pastoral (Yates 1994: 168–71).

As was the case with the Protestant turn to World Christianity, the con-tinent of Africa was central to the articulation of similar ideas within Cath-olic circles.[16] The renowned scholar of African Christianity Adrian Hastings was ordained as a secular Catholic priest in Uganda just four years prior to Vatican II, and, with his considerable skills, he was soon redeployed to work with the Association of Bishops of Eastern Africa (AMECEA) with the task of post-conciliar reorientation. Reflecting on the happy convergence between the church's new openness to cultural difference on the one hand, and a self-conscious celebration of African agency in recently independent East Africa on the other, Hastings observed that 'probably in no other continent did the Vat-ican Council coincide quite so neatly with and sympathetically with a major process of secular change in Africa' (Hastings 1986: 315). He recalled the dec-ade of optimism and openness in the region that followed the Council, with the increased pace of the Africanisation of the clergy, particularly female religious orders, innovation in music, liturgy and song, and a new ecumenism. Eventu-

---

15 'Decree *Ad Gentes* on the Mission Activity of the Church' (1965), http://www.vatican.va/ archive/hist_councils/ii_vatican_council/documents/vat-ii_decree_19651207_ad-gentes_ en.html, accessed 7 February 2017.

16 Although Latin American bishops adopted Vatican II's recommendations with alacrity, Catholic thought in Latin America has been less central to the emergence of the World Christianity paradigm – perhaps, in part, another effect of the dominance of Protestant Anglophone scholarship in articulating the study of Christianity worldwide.

ally, the movement was stemmed by the barriers of canon law, curia control, clerical privilege and sheer lack of resources, but not before it had profoundly shaped Hastings' intellectual agenda, spurring him to produce a remarkable body of work on inculturated or indigenous forms of African Christianity, and eventually to take on the editorship of the *Journal of Religion in Africa* from Andrew Walls (Hastings 1989: 122–37). This broader context of intellectual ferment in newly independent Africa also shaped the work of Hastings' collaborators and colleagues, such as Terence Ranger, Richard Gray and John Peel, who worked in Africa in this period as researchers or lecturers in new universities and sought to historicise African seizures of Christianity (Maxwell 2001: 1–24).

It was in the decades following the Second Vatican Council that the shift in the centre of gravity of the church gathered pace. If Western scholars and media were slow to grasp the significance of what was happening, Pope John Paul II (1978–2005) was not. Devoting the bulk of his papal visitations to the global South, he sought to affirm and give equal significance to the Catholicism of those who were previously deemed to live on the margins of Christendom. The election in March 2013 of Cardinal Archbishop of Buenos Aires Jorge Mario Bergoglio as Pope appears a logical if overdue recognition of that geographical shift. He is the first to choose the name Francis, the Poverello or little poor man, the first Jesuit, and, most significantly, the first modern Pope from the southern hemisphere. Although it is too early to assess his papacy, Pope Francis has already changed the way the institution is perceived. Determined to continue the simple life he had lived as Archbishop of Buenos Aires, where he had taken the bus to work, cooked his own meals and resided in a simple apartment, he shocked the Vatican by announcing that he would not take up rooms in the papal apartments but instead live in the Vatican guesthouse, the home of some priests and bishops who work in Rome. Having criticised clericalism and ecclesiastical careerism, he quickly convened a committee of eight cardinals from around the world to aid him in the reform of the Roman Curia. His first apostolic letter, *Evangelii Gaudium* (2013) ('The Joy of the Gospel'), called for recognition of the authority and juridical status of episcopal conferences, citing the concerns of conferences from Africa, Asia and Latin America. He preferred the church 'bruised, hurting and dirty' at the service of the poor, one preaching not a multitude of doctrines but the saving love of God manifest in Jesus. And drawing from the perspective of the southern hemisphere, he argued that neoliberal trickle-down theories of economic growth fail to bring about greater justice or inclusiveness in the world (Raucsch 2016: 615–16).[17]

---

17   Pope Francis (2013) *Apostolic Exhortation* Evangelli Gaudium *of the Holy Father Fran-*

Evident within both Catholic and Protestant thought, one of the most important features of the current 'world' turn within missiology has been a renewed and sympathetic attention to culture. An earlier generation of missiologists and missionary practitioners had famously wrestled with the 'problem' of syncretism, how local Christians across the world were perceived by missionaries to have corrupted the gospel with inappropriate residues of their heathen and pagan pasts. The self-perceived role of the missionary was to encourage a wholesale conversion to Christianity and rejection of the past – both in a spiritual and a cultural sense. In the 1930s, eminent missionary and Africanist Dietrich Westermann argued that 'the aim of missionary work is to give the African a life-power which remakes not only individuals but tribes and people as a whole … giving the new means taking away the old. In trying to build up a new society, the missionary cannot help destroying age-old institutions and ideals' (Westermann 1937: 57). Even Lutheran missionary Bengt Sundkler's sympathetic study of local forms of South African Christianity in the 1940s lamented that these practices were ultimately a means for mid-twentieth-century Africans to give 'a more honored place … to the religious and cultural heritage of the Zulus' than to Christian belief (1948: 17). For Sundkler, Zionist healing rituals were evidence not of the strength of popular Christianity but rather more unfortunately of 'the pull from the heathen heritage' (1948: 240).

But in the postcolonial period, the new school of missiologists avowed – in the words of North American missiologist William R. Shenk – that rather than treating culture as a 'problem to be solved', they would espouse a 'Christological openness to culture, not its rejection' (Shenk 2001: 100–1). In recent years, cultural difference has come to be seen as constitutive of and fundamental to an authentic worldwide or non-Western Christianity. As alluded to above, it was a rich swathe of Africanist scholarship on Christianity in the second half of the twentieth century that led the way for later missiological developments, especially by focusing on popular Christian movements known as the independent churches as pre-eminent examples of the rich mingling of local culture with the Christian gospel (Peel 1968; Welbourn 1961; Turner 1967). African authors, many working in Nigerian higher education institutions, began to make their own contributions, with an important article 'Writing African Church History' by J. F. Ade Ajayi and E. A. Ayandele arguing that Africans in Africa must interpret Christianity through their own cultural terms: 'an African Church

---

cis. Vatican City: Libreria Editrice Vaticana, https://w2.vatican.va/content/francesco/en/ apost_exhortations/documents/papa-francesco_esortazione-ap_20131124_evangelii -gaudium.html, accessed 7 February 2017.

must necessarily be the product of an organic growth on the African soil, an institution in which Christianity is incarnate within the African milieu' (Ade Ajayi and Ayandele 1969: 90–1). It is no coincidence, then, that many of the first-generation scholars of World Christianity – Andrew Walls, Lamin Sanneh, Kwame Bediako – have all been Africanists, primed by this rich tradition of twentieth-century scholarship to emphasise indigenous agency and local cultural appropriations of Christianity. In this way, then, we see that – despite important differences – both Protestant and Catholic intellectuals were indebted to formative experiences on the independence-era African continent in articulating their turn to the local and to the particular in their understanding of World Christianity.

Perhaps no figure has emphasised the culturalist dimensions of World Christianity as much as Lamin Sanneh, Walls' former colleague at Aberdeen University and currently D. Willis James Professor of Missions and World Christianity at Yale Divinity School, as well as a practising Roman Catholic. Sanneh's scholarship was less formally concerned with ecumenism and unity than Walls' was, but it fully embodied the more recent emphasis on cultural difference being *the* legitimating feature of World Christianity.[18] Of his many significant publications, *Translating the Message* (2009 [1989]) stands out as the most influential, because, as Dana Robert observes, it 'completely reframed the colonial discourse in which mission studies had functioned'. Moreover, as a West African Muslim convert to Christianity, he could not easily be dismissed as a Western apologist (Robert 2014: 5). In *Translating the Message*, Sanneh described how, as Christianity expanded and spread into new environments beyond its original Middle Eastern milieu, it faced new challenges as a minority religion within non-Christian societies (Sanneh 2009 [1989]). The key to Christianity's great subsequent success lay in its 'translatability'. According to Sanneh, this was its capacity not to be encapsulated within any single language or cultural system. Rather, Sanneh argued that God's spirit showed a remarkable willingness to move into any language and assume the garb of various cultures, most importantly seen in the Christian belief in the doctrine of the incarnation – or God's being made person in the form of Jesus Christ. This foundational act of the religion subsequently lent great weight to the particular, the local and the material – all these could manifest the universal, transcendent and invisible truth of God. An important scriptural instance of this dynamic, according to Sanneh, was the descent of the Holy Spirit at the Feast

---

18   However, Sanneh's recent autobiography (2012) shows a deep personal commitment to issues of ecumenism and unity.

of Pentecost, when human linguistic difference was mediated into divine and harmonious interchange and mutual understanding (see also Walls 1996). Here, we need also to acknowledge Kwame Bediako, another figure within World Christianity who developed a theology of culture based on Christological openness. Bediako held up the Apostle Paul as an important model for sympathetic attentiveness to culture in the transmission of Christianity, pointing out that 'Paul understood that whoever encounters Jesus Christ does so as a whole person – a person in a web of relationships, with a history, living in a particular culture, speaking the vernacular ... the work of redemption takes place in the individual's indigenous environment' (Bediako 1990: 5–6).

This theological move ('baptising' culture by invoking the principle of the incarnation) has had profound consequences for the ethnographic and historical study of Christianity worldwide. Above all, it has led scholars to adopt an almost entirely positive estimation of the regional features of Christian belief and practice. Accordingly, Sanneh has expressed his dislike of the phrase 'Global Christianity', arguing that the homogeneity it implies erases worldwide Christian particularity and difference (Sanneh 2003) and instead privileges the extension of European forms of Christianity – while assuming the garb of 'diversity'. For Sanneh, Global Christianity is nothing more than the 'expansion of western Christendom' inaugurated by European and North American missionaries (ibid.: 35). Sanneh pits the homogenising, Eurocentric forces of globalisation against the divergent, grassroots expressions of Christianity; globalisation and the worldwide spread of Christianity can move in tandem but also diverge: '[W]orld Christianity is not merely an echo of globalization, though there is overlap in certain important sectors. On the contrary, in some instances new Christian movements are a reaction to the ravages and threats of globalization with concerted attention to the value of local cultures and economies' (ibid.: 75). It is the diverse heterogeneity of World Christianity that allows the voices of global South Christians to speak freely and for themselves over and against globalisation's often deleterious effects: 'World Christianity is not one thing, but a variety of indigenous responses through more or less effective local idioms, but without necessarily the European Enlightenment frame' (ibid.: 22).

In this context, then, World Christianity has become shorthand for the study of Christianity in very particular territories and locations around the globe, rather than the more unitary phenomenon that is usually suggested by the use of the word 'world', and indeed by older invocations of World Christianity in the interwar period as an ecumenical international fellowship. Current scholarship is largely invested in studying how Christians imprint local concerns upon a universal faith, rather than in how a universal faith provides a basis for imagined and actual solidarities between highly divergent believers across the world. A brief glance through a single issue of the Andrew Walls-founded flagship journal in the area, Edinburgh University Press's *Studies in World Christianity*, underscores this interest in disconnected local appropriations of Christianity. A 2003 issue featured research articles on Christianity and ancestral worship in Botswana; Mongolian identity and Christianity; and tropes of popular culture in Argentina and Christianity.[19] A recent commentary on World Christianity as an emerging discipline aptly captures its particularist thrust:

> [It is] a field that seeks to understand Christian communities, faith, and practice as they are found on six continents, expressed in diverse ecclesial traditions, and informed by the multitude of historical and cultural experiences ... It is concerned with the diversity of local or indigenous expressions of Christian life and faith throughout the world.
>
> IRVIN 2008: 1–2

However, in emphasising the autonomy and cultural specificity of local Christianities, this scholarship largely neglects the older interwar sense of World Christianity as an international community of Christians. This includes the way in which local Christians across the world have valued exchange and communication with Christians in the so-called global North as well as with fraternities in other parts of the southern hemisphere. In these situations, many Christians take great pride in situating themselves as part of a worldwide ecclesia (see Maxwell, Chapter 1 in this volume). The current focus on culture in World Christianities runs the risk of becoming an exoticising reification of the local, a fetishistic commitment to regional particularity, regardless of whether this is in fact how Christians choose to define themselves and their activities. For one, an important strand of Africanist scholarship has called attention to the provisional, invented nature of much that is labelled 'traditional' or 'cultural' on the continent (Vail 1989). Rather than residues of a timeless past, many ethnic traditions in present-day Africa – and by extension elsewhere – were self-consciously crafted for strategic ends in the colonial period via complex and long-lived collaborations between traditional authorities and European administrators. Many World Christianity scholars delight in demonstrating the imprint of so-called 'traditional' religion on Christian practice around the globe (further proof of Christianity's 'translatability'), and yet 'traditional religion' was just as much a product of modernity as ethnicity has been shown to be,

---

19   *Studies in World Christianity* 9 (1) (2003).

as Valentine Mudimbe powerfully reminds us (Mudimbe 1997). Furthermore, for many on the African continent, traditionalism today is not always a trope to be profitably invoked in fashioning identities. As Ruth Marshall observes in the contemporary Nigerian context: 'Where did all this fear, confusion, need for fixed identities appear from? ... Today in Africa, a great majority of the population is only too eager and willing to hasten the erosion of established lifeways, and such a politics of nostalgia is a peculiarly Western obsession' (Marshall 2009: 28–9).

Moreover, it is one of the staples of current World Christianity scholarship – Pentecostal and Charismatic Christianity – that itself challenges many of the field's assumptions. Recent studies of Pentecostalism provide empirical evidence demonstrating that believers across the globe have chosen, both historically and in the present day, to stress that fidelity to Christ does not 'baptise' their existing culture but rather enacts a radical break with pasts frequently characterised by them as degenerate, corrupt and sinful (Meyer 1998; Maxwell 2006a). That worldwide Pentecostals frequently denounce their own cultural baggage as sinful or even demonic should give some pause to the current World Christianity approbation of localism and tradition. This Pentecostal tendency towards iconoclasm and the de-sacralisation of pre-conversion beliefs and practices is powerfully demonstrated in Joel Robbins' description of the effects of revival on the Urapmin of Papua New Guinea in this volume (Chapter 9). Indeed, in an earlier influential essay, Robbins deploys the notion of rupture to argue that, until now, anthropologists have tended to diminish the significance of cultural and religious change through a long-seated tendency towards 'continuity thinking' in conceptualising the effects of conversion (Robbins 2007). Moreover, as Kwabena Asamoah-Gyadu's chapter in this volume (Chapter 12) also shows us, in place of investing in idioms of culture and tradition, West African Pentecostals more usually emphasise their triumphant march into a future confidently anticipated to be marked by financial prosperity, good health and overall 'dominion' over life's manifold problems and obstacles. Asamoah-Gyadu reminds us that Pentecostals steadfastly look forward; rarely do they cast backward glances.

Furthermore, given that the culturalist model of World Christianity is profoundly rooted in case studies drawn from the African continent (and, paradoxically, also critiqued by newer Africanist scholarship on ethnic identities), the question of whether this is an analytical framework applicable to studies of Christianity in other parts of the globe is well worth asking. What would the study of World Christianity look like if its key proponents had drawn their case studies from the continent of Asia, engaging not with the very many indigenous religions of Africa (highly amenable, as we have seen, to culturalist analyses, and particularly in the politically charged independence-era decades) but with the vast world religions of Hinduism or Buddhism that cut across cultures, language groups and huge geographical areas? Moreover, World Christianity scholars' determination to move beyond traditional missionary history and its preoccupation with replacing Eurocentric accounts of Christianity's transmission has resulted in potentially deleterious consequences for our understanding of Christianity's complex history in the world, and of the nuanced interactions between different regions. Philip Jenkins claimed that 'while missionaries began the process of Christianization, they had little control over how or where that path might go' (Jenkins 2006: 20). In fact, much careful historical work reveals the important role of missionaries and mission societies in shaping Christian practice in worldwide contexts. Missionaries may have lost control of Christian movements in the pioneering phase of their work, but the second generation of overseas workers did their best to catch them up and assert orthodoxy. And it was this heavy-handedness that was often the precursor of the schisms that created breakaway movements of Christian independency, indicating once again missionaries' centrality – even if only indirectly, as in these cases – to the development of Christianity outside of the West.

And despite many World Christianity scholars' wistful aspiration for a 'post-imperial' Christian landscape, it would also be hard to underestimate the power of North American Christianity in shaping Christian practice across the globe. Robert Wuthnow has argued that American faith-based non-governmental organisations (NGOs), overseas missionary efforts, congregational activities and faith-influenced foreign policy initiatives continue to significantly affect Christian communities around the world (Wuthnow 2009). Neither Wuthnow nor others making related arguments (Noll 2009) are claiming a hegemonic role for the United States in World Christianity; instead, they argue for local autonomy and independent initiatives. Nevertheless, they marshal data that shows how deeply involved North American religious actors are in the worldwide Christian landscape. The ideological push towards a non-imperial church history therefore risks obscuring the historical and ongoing contribution of 'imperial' powers – formerly in Western Europe, now, perhaps, in the United States – to shaping Christian practice worldwide. And it is precisely the influence of the United States on worldwide Christianity that Andrew Preston's chapter in this volume (Chapter 10) highlights. Nuancing usual portrayals of the United States as a melting pot of religious traditions, and as a country where church and state exist independently of each other, Preston shows that a Judeo-Christian tradition still lies at the very heart of the country's identity and still shapes many aspects of that identity, ranging from domestic matters to foreign policy. In the realm of the latter, it is the United States' conception of itself as a 'defender of the faith' that causes it to insist on protecting the rights of minority religions (usually Christianity) in areas such as Vietnam and the Middle East. Providing an instructive parallel with Naures Atto's chapter in this volume on persecuted Assyrian Christians in the Middle East (Chapter 11), Preston shows that the current administration's advocacy for Arab Christians forms a key component of ongoing debates about the desirability of Muslim immigration to the United States and the growth of Islamophobia within the Republican party. In recent months, this long-standing dynamic within American foreign policy has dramatically come into focus in the form of President Donald Trump's controversial statement of preferential treatment for Christian refugees from Middle Eastern and African countries seeking to enter the United States. Preston's and Atto's chapters thus remind us that to exclude entirely the West – and its constitutive role in shaping power relations – from our analytical framework of worldwide Christianity would be a grave mistake.

In the remainder of this introduction, we show how the chapters in this volume collectively make a case for a future research agenda for World Christianity that takes into account the shortcomings we have pointed out. We have already begun to highlight what we consider to be some of our authors' varied contributions to the existing scholarship on this topic. Despite World Christianity's early origins in an impetus towards global unity and ecumenism, it is precisely this attention to transnational networks and cross-cultural linkages that has been lost in recent scholarship's focus on cultural particularity. In this sense, we are building upon Wuthnow's and Preston's arguments that the West – particularly North America – needs to be taken into account. But we are also going beyond this to argue that what is needed is a robust sense of global connections and networks more broadly, both imperial as well as entirely outside the remit of empire. That Christianity worldwide is merely the sum of its multiple local appropriations is what risks being implied by missiologists' increasing use of the pluralised 'World Christianities'. The study of Christianity worldwide is dominated today by a multiplication of volumes collating local studies; many begin with a nod to global connections, but in truth they are at heart largely self-contained local studies that lack synthetic perspectives and comparative investigation. Historian Klaus Koschorke's perceptive criticism of World Christianity is that 'various new publications resort to juxtaposing more or less unconnected regional or local histories; they largely "add and stir" a few isolated examples from the South to traditional Western-centered syllabi' (Koschorke 2014: 180). A more nuanced account of worldwide Christianity than the 'add and stir' model might consider the extensive evidence for, say, South–South networks and connections, starting from a recognition that interactions and exchanges between residents of Melbourne, Johannesburg, Hong Kong and multiple cities and towns have been important centres of Christian enterprise. In what follows, we suggest that, alongside a more critical and nuanced perspective on culture, World Christianity as an emerging field of study also needs a more robust sense of connected, comparative and transnational histories.

World Christianities: The 'World' and the 'West'

As in the case of theology and missiology, scholars within the humanities and social sciences have long thought in global terms; in many respects, the pioneers of global studies were also the founders of the social sciences. Max Weber (1864–1920) wrote a series of works on the religions of India and China, Judaism and Protestant Christianity, and sought to identify what was distinctive and what was similar among them. Émile Durkheim (1854–1917) worked outwards from case studies of tribal society to build general theories of organic solidarity. And Karl Marx (1818–83) built his universal theories about the inevitable expansion of capitalism from a wealth of historical and early ethnographic data. Nevertheless, processes and events in the 1980s and 1990s brought about a qualitatively different 'Age of Globalisation'. The internet and satellite technologies allowed for rapid flows of capital, culture and information across national borders on a vastly different scale than had previously been possible. And the cessation of the Cold War in 1989 removed significant barriers to trade, movement and the exchange of ideas, all of which led to predictions of the demise of the nation-state. The event of globalisation focused minds, research priorities and funding bodies, and social scientists evolved new terms and concepts to describe and explain this process of bringing the world together in more intense interaction: networks, flows, scapes, and the notions of transnational and global (Juergensmeyer 2014: xiii–xvii, 3–7).

Initial studies of these processes were dominated by anthropologists and cultural theorists. Figures such as Arjun Appadurai posited that the political and theoretical narratives of modernity centred around the unit of the nation-state were now largely displaced by the emergence of a global imagination. What characterised Appadurai's work – and many future contributions on the topic – was a willingness to examine globalisation 'from below', to explore the impact of globalisation on everyday, local worlds (Appadurai 1998). Clusters of globalisation-focused research agendas within anthropology soon emerged. The study of migration and diaspora became a major interest, with numerous studies examining the creation of new identities in the diaspora – often strongly invested in ethnic characteristics, a feature that had been wrongly thought in decline as the nation-state supposedly grew in importance (Kearney 1995: 559). The prevalence of new digital and electronic media also emerged as an important focus of scholarly research into globalisation, with numerous studies pointing out that media forms such as the internet and global television networks made possible unprecedented 'imagined communities' predicated not on the anonymous reading public of the nation-state, but rather on the vast transregional public mobilised via social media sites such as Facebook or networks such as CNN (Meyer and Moors 2005).

For the most part, historians were slow to join this new scholarly enterprise. The emergence of professional academic history coincided with the formation of the modern nation-state and for that reason it became one of its major ideological pillars. Even when historians wrote diplomatic or international history, they did so with the premise that nation-states were the major units of analysis. And while historians attempted to critique their Eurocentric constructions through the study of non-Western history or area studies, they took their models of nation-states with them. Moreover, the post-modern turn and the rise of cultural history turned their attentions to the local and to constructions of texts and images, work that was strong on cultural issues and on representations but weak on the analysis of structural history and on economic and political questions that are central to discussions of globalisation (Hopkins 2002: 1–2). Nevertheless, at the turn of the twenty-first century, historians such as Chris Bayly (2004), A. G. Hopkins (2002) and Patrick Manning (2003) published the first major texts in global history. Drawing on the sub-disciplines of area studies and economic, environmental and imperial history, and on North American courses on Western civilisation, global historians have reconstructed the histories of new areas and spaces such as oceans, environments and economic regions and they have traced the movement of ideas, sciences and peoples.

Although the pace and intensity of globalisation have increased markedly since the end of the Cold War and the beginning of the electronic communications revolution, globalisation is also a deep-rooted historical process, and transnational activities have antecedents. While anthropologists have focused on contemporary instances of globalisation, historians have identified periods of 'archaic globalisation' when there was a good deal of transregional or transnational activity and exchange on economic, cultural and political levels before the nation-state and industrialisation made their appearance (Hopkins 2002: 3–4). The initial spread of Christianity happened at one such moment in the ancient Mediterranean world during the Roman and Greek empires. Another key moment was the Great Acceleration at the end of the nineteenth century, when the spread of European empires, enabled by the steam ship, railways and the telegraph, increased connections across the globe (Bayly 2004). Indeed, contemporary globalisation takes its impetus from a 'global stratum of culture, education, technology and economic activity' that commenced with European colonialism in the sixteenth century (Juergensmeyer 2014: xv).

However, with some notable exceptions, world historians have been slow to engage with religious history. This paucity of reflection on the global dimensions of religious change occurred partly because social and cultural historians within area studies were interested in processes of localisation and adaptation. Scholars were also rather too quick to relegate religious expansion to a facet of imperial or political history.[20] But historians of Christianity were even slower to think globally. In some respects, Adrian Hastings' edited collection *A World History of Christianity* was something of a milestone. Its splendid chapters on Africa, China and Latin America emphasised 'the primary truth that the writing of Christian history needs to escape imprisonment within a Europe-centred story in order ... to serve the needs of the many hundreds of millions of Christians who live elsewhere' (Hastings 1999: 5). In this sense, the volume represented a considerable advance over David Edwards' rather Eurocentric *Christianity: The First Two Thousand Years* (1997), which reduced global Christianity to single chapter of just sixty pages in a tome of more than 600 pages. Nevertheless, in his 'Introduction', Hastings confessed that there had been little attempt to write a connected, comparative or unified history of the church:

> [O]ur commitment to a territorially-based history has meant that less than justice is done to the most specifically international dimensions of modern Christian history – later papacy, the missionary movement, the Ecumenical movement and the World Council of Churches, now 50 years old. Twentieth-century Church History needs a strongly international, yet unified dimension, more than we have been able to offer here. It could be argued that a separate final chapter is needed on the global reshaping of Christianity in the nineteenth and twentieth centuries.
>
> HASTINGS 1999: 5

But Hastings' format was repeated in *The Cambridge History of Christianity* Volumes 8 and 9 – *World Christianities c.1815–c.1914* (2006), edited by Sheridan

---

20   See Manning (2003: 248). An important exception is Chris Bayly's discussion of nineteenth-century religious revival and expansion in *The Birth of the Modern World* (2004; see below).

Gilley and Brian Stanley, and *World Christianities* c.1914–c.2000 (2006), edited by Hugh McLeod – where the scholarship was again often first-rate but the notion of World Christianity taken merely to mean an expanded geographical remit. In his 'Introduction' to Volume 8, Gilley explained: '[A]t least a third of the space is given to new Christian churches outside Europe. Catholic Christianity became a global religion through the Spanish and Portuguese empires in the sixteenth century and French missionaries in the seventeenth and eighteenth.' However, the chapters remained 'self-sufficient entities' (Gilley 2006: 1, 8). In his introductory comments to Volume 9, McLeod described Christianity 'as a worldwide religion' and noted the significance of the 'revolution in communications' in electronic media in enabling religious communities to establish global connections as well as to fuel greater diversity (McLeod 2006: 6–7, 13–14), but he offered no synthesis of the material in the chapters. More recent texts could also have been more effective in tracing patterns. In the opening chapter of his *Introducing World Christianity*, Charles Farhadian does engage with issues of 'global interdependence and globalisation', but the excellent chapters are concerned with analysing the social, cultural and political effects of Christianity in discrete areas rather than identifying patterns, connections and commonalties across the globe (Farhadian 2012: 1–3). Lamin Sanneh and Michael McClymond's *Companion to World Christianity* (2016) makes a significant advance. Their introduction attempts to excavate the origins of the term, discuss alternatives, and outline useful comparative themes. The collection also contains some thematic essays in which the authors draw examples from across the globe. Although first-rate scholarship throughout, many of the essays still remain regionally focused with little attempt at transregional connection or comparison.

Nevertheless, some historians have conceived of religious expansion in frameworks besides that of the nation-state. One of the earliest attempts was W. R. Ward's *The Protestant Evangelical Awakening* (2002 [1992]), which showed how an Evangelical transnational identity in Europe and North America was sustained by personal connections, correspondence and religious print. An example notable for its more explicit conceptualisation is David Hempton's *Methodism: Empire of the Spirit* (2005), in which he fashions a 'unified conceptual apparatus within which the rise of Methodism as a transnational movement could be located'. Hempton maps the expansion of Methodism 'on the back of two expanding civilisations': Britain and America. He identifies the conditions in which it thrived – namely demographic growth and population mobility, whether forced or voluntary. And he examines the means of movement and the social categories that acted as agents of its transmission. In the British case, Methodism spread through informal and then formal empire, carried by soldiers, sailors, traders, civilisers and colonial governors. In the American case it moved via an 'expansionist commercial empire', which exported Methodist traders, educators and doctors. Methodism's success in both these empires came through a 'combination of personal zeal and corporate organization, though formal missionary Methodist missionary enterprise remained vital' (Hempton 2005: 6, 158). Hilary Carey has considered how the institutions of Christian missions sustained a notion of Greater Britain, the second British Empire, settled by people who considered themselves British and who actively maintained relationships with the metropole. In British North America, New Zealand, Australia and Southern Africa, so-called 'colonial missions' acted as conservative forces binding settlers together in shared spiritual and moral enterprise (Carey 2011). But, to date, nothing quite matches the sophistication of Chris Bayly's remarkable chapter 'Empires of Religion' in his *The Birth of the Modern World 1780–1914*, where he analyses the global linkages and conflicts that brought about the reformation of doctrine and authority in all world religions, showing how they influenced each other in a symbiosis of imitation and competition. Particularly insightful is Bayly's discussion of the use of religious print and institutional centralisation to tighten religious boundaries and sharpen identities (2004: 325–65).

It is from the disciplinary perspective of history that Klaus Koschorke's Munich School made its important contribution to the study of World Christianity. With a formation in the history of Gnosticism (1967–76), Koschorke experienced an academic conversion in 1982–83 when he was exposed to the realities of Asian Christianity via a guest professorship in Sri Lanka. On his appointment to a professorship at the University of Munich in 1993, he dedicated the chair to the study of the early and global history of Christianity, bringing the methods and theoretical insights from the historiography of global history to his work. While sharing a common goal with other scholars of World Christianity to redraw the map of Christian adherence across the globe in order to recognise shifts in the church's centre of gravity and the movement of the Christian diaspora from the South into the West, his approach underlines three other much needed emphases in the scholarship. He argues, firstly, for the importance of a polycentric understanding of the church worldwide, in which there has always been a plurality of bases and actors; secondly, for the significance of multidirectional transcontinental links between these nodes; and thirdly, for a rigorously comparative approach. For Koschorke, the church has never had one centre but many, and rather than reconstructing yet more local histories (the 'add-and-stir' approach), the challenge is to explore the connections between them. Drawing from his patristic background, he offers a deeply historicised model of World Christianity in which the East Syrian Nestorian

Church was an influence alongside the Latin and Byzantine churches, and where South–South links in the sixteenth-century Portuguese Empire united Christians in religious interaction across four continents. This historical depth counters the impression given by much of the literature that World Christianity is a modern or contemporary phenomenon. Lastly, Koschorke's comparative approach has been embodied in the regular international Munich-Freising conferences that have taken place since 1997. Organised around stimulating themes such as 'The Year 1989–90 as a Turning Point in the History of World Christianity', these conferences have provoked valuable reflection on religious connectivity and on similarity and difference in Christian experience (Hermann and Burlacioiu 2016; Koschorke 2016).[21]

It is very much within this vein of tracing global, comparative connections among and between Christians worldwide that our volume seeks to make a contribution to the field of World Christianity, returning – in part – to the earlier conception of the term as a worldwide ecumenical fellowship. Rather than 'world' merely denoting an aggregate of regional Christian area studies (in the style of many World Christianity compilations), or simply a nod to Western Christian agencies with an international reach (in the vein of the older optimism regarding the eventual evangelisation of the world), we suggest that current scholarship should take more seriously as a research phenomenon whether the universalist theological aspirations of Christians amount to robustly global phenomena, if at all. It is key to remain alert to the limits and breaks on Christian adherence as well as its advances; we are not advocating a naïve return to the interwar rhetoric of an unproblematic Christian ecumene, largely blind to its Eurocentric qualities. Instead, the following chapters provide case studies of Christianity that probe the networks of exchange, as well as the constraints upon such exchange, that characterise Christian communities across the world.

The first section of the volume therefore foregrounds the theme of 'Connections and Comparisons'. The three authors contained in this section offer historical contributions that not only focus on the saliency of connections across geographical space but also are devoted to comparatively charting how these exchanges gave rise to interlocking processes in different parts of the world, dynamics that exhibited both similarity and divergence. In various ways, all

---

21   An active board member of *The Journal of World Christianity* (2008 to the present), Koschorke was honoured in 2016 with a special edition of the journal devoted to the Munich School to mark his retirement from his chair. This provides a fulsome description of the centre's activities, including the work of his colleagues and collaborators.

the chapters in this volume focus on spatial connections, imagined and real linkages, and transregional networks. These opening chapters, however, are distinguished from the rest of the volume in their adoption of an explicitly comparative perspective in order to investigate whether the growth of Christian communities worldwide can be explained by reference to overlapping, mutually reinforcing historical and sociological processes and causes. One of the fruits of comparative work would be to discern whether Christianity engenders the same experiences and mentalities across the globe. Although not directly taken up by the authors represented in the present collection, a fertile area for future comparative research would be to explore the shared global debates – evincing both consensus and profound disagreement – around issues such as ecumenism, social justice, gender and sexuality.

Offering a broad, overarching survey of connection and comparison, the historian David Maxwell's chapter supplies a programmatic statement of how such research might be conducted. In the vein of examining both networks *and* ruptures in a notion of World Christianity – how Christians worldwide position themselves both as part of a local patria and as members of a global ecumene – Maxwell considers the extensive networks that knit together Christians in various parts of the world and the mechanisms that enabled these exchanges to take place, as well as the constraints and limits on such connections. Maxwell is interested not only in how Christianity was constructed as a 'World Religion' in the modern era, but also how, in the same period, Christianity was part of a broader intellectual movement (along with debates about population, race and the environment), which contributed towards the creation of a global consciousness. However, Maxwell argues that, while the notion of World Christianity has some utility in capturing the growing sense of planetary consciousness among Christians as embodied in global conferences and their proclamations, it remains loaded with unhelpful notions of homogeneity and uniformity.

A connected, comparative approach to the Christian religious encounter across the globe will thus highlight the antiquity of these transregional processes, and will also account for the frequent incidence of rupture and polarisation in large-scale networks. Pedro Feitoza's chapter in this volume (Chapter 2) goes some way towards answering these challenges by focusing on a nineteenth-century case study (a welcome contrast to the heavily presentist approach of much World Christianity scholarship) as well as by examining the internal nuance and diversity of flows of Protestant tract literature between Brazil, Portugal and Britain. Bible-reading publics in Brazil, developing a nascent nationalism, rejected British Bibles in favour of Portuguese ones that did not bear the controversial imprint of 'London' on their front covers, while pictures and images contained in tracts were refashioned for family altars – very much against the wishes of tract societies in Europe – echoing Catholicism's tradition of veneration of saints. In these ways, Feitoza's chapter shows us that the distribution of print literature from Western Europe to Latin America, far from following the usual unilinear narrative of Christianity's transferral from the West to the rest, was in fact marked by considerable 'pushback' from Brazilian reading publics, who shaped these documents to their own purposes, and, in doing so, influenced Bible and tract societies' policies in London and Lisbon.

In comparatively highlighting shared debates, many of our authors in the present volume underscore the fact that exchange did not always entail consensus or agreement. In his chapter on twentieth-century parachurch competition in Latin America (Chapter 3), the historian David Kirkpatrick shows how North and South American Christians within the same Evangelical tradition could profoundly disagree on the nature of biblical inerrancy and the defining values of their theology. Despite sharing a common commitment to the high standing of scripture in their traditions, Kirkpatrick demonstrates that growing discontent among Latin American intellectuals about the export of American-style evangelicalism to their region (seen as a variant of cultural neo-imperialism) caused theologians such as René Padilla and Samuel Escobar to chart a radically different course for Latin American evangelicalism, one more infused with a liberal social justice tradition and less amenable to doctrines of biblical inerrancy.

Whereas our opening chapters offer models of what a connected, comparative approach might look like, the second section of this volume provides a different set of methodological reflections. Entitled 'Locating Knowledge', the three chapters contained in this section underscore the contingent, variable and place-specific nature of scholarly interpretations of Christianity worldwide. One of the key goals of these chapters is their effort to demonstrate the continual unsettling of any body of knowledge or mode of interpretation considered 'normative' in the study of world Christianity, demonstrating that 'normativity' usually conceals undeclared vested interests. Echoing themes returned to in Emma Wild-Wood's afterword, these chapters all emphasise that 'place' and 'situated-ness' make a profound difference in the construction of knowledge in the field of Christianity worldwide; that the location of the observer shapes their findings and conclusions; and that the production of information is never neutral. It is in light of this, too, that we have titled the present volume *Relocating World Christianity*. This observation is perhaps particularly pertinent for theology and missiology – two interrelated disciplines that have long wrestled with issues of orthodoxy and heterodoxy and that are increasingly challenged to consider the difference that 'place' makes in the formulation of Christian doctrine and dogma.

Two contributions from the theologian Peter Phan and the missiologist Dorottya Nagy make this point in different ways. Phan's chapter (Chapter 4) takes on the notion of systematic or dogmatic Christian theology that is formulated in isolation from the lively 'folk' or grassroots traditions discernible beyond the borders of the academy. Echoing the older culturalist argument for World Christianity discussed above, Phan argues for 'new ways' of doing theology that account for the fact that 'the cultural context ... conditions and influences the very way in which theology is constructed'. Nagy's chapter (Chapter 5) is more specific in its focus on Central and Eastern Europe, inquiring into how doing theology in a manner that is explicitly rooted in this geographical region challenges normative notions of Christian theology and missiology. Nagy's selection of Eastern Europe as her region of focus usefully allows her to explore the complexity of what might be entailed in a rejection of a 'Eurocentric' mode of theology and missiology. Usually excluded in popular understandings of what constitutes 'Europe', a view from Eastern Europe allows Nagy to argue for the importance of locality and diversity alongside unity and connectivity. In the afterword to the volume, our co-editor Emma Wild-Wood returns to these themes, shedding light on the current theological interest in returning to older conceptions of Christian 'unity', yet without leaning on unduly homogenising notions of what constitutes tradition and orthodoxy.

Whereas both Phan and Nagy are interested in unseating normative (Western) European categories in the study of Christianity, the final chapter in this section questions the hegemonic role of Africanist scholarship in delineating the contours of the field of World Christianity. Chandra Mallampalli, a historian of Christianity in South Asia, draws our attention to the Afrocentric quality of the term (a point we have also made in this introduction), arguing that the study of Christianity takes on very different resonances in an Indian context (Chapter 6). He pays special attention to the influential ideas about Christian translatability developed by Walls and Sanneh, who, as we have seen, both drew on the notion of the translatable gospel to argue that African converts crafted new identities that were seamlessly Christian *and* African. Mallampalli investigates the limits of this concept of religious translatability for Christianity in India, whereby converts' departure from Hindu-Sanskritic culture to Christianity is not viewed – as is a similar move in many African contexts – as a positive act of 'translation', but rather as a desertion of or exile from a linguistic-religious culture deeply enmeshed with their national identity as Indians. In other words, while translatability theories avow that African identity can continue uninterrupted in a Christian mould, this model hits something of a wall in the South Asian context, where, for many people, national, religious and linguistic identities are profoundly intertwined in a single, non-separable whole. Mallampalli reminds us that a research agenda for Christianity worldwide that paid greater attention to South Asia – rather than making its starting point the influential Africanist scholarship of the last century – might thus find itself investing more heavily in idioms of breakage and rupture, rather than continuity and complementarity, as has historically been the case for this Afrocentric body of work.

The third collection of chapters ('Place and Belonging in World Christianity') changes tack in order to consider the importance of 'scale' in studying manifestations of worldwide Christianity. Despite our volume's interest in the significance of transregional connections between Christians in different parts of the globe (a concern particularly evident in the first and final set of chapters), it is crucial that the local is not sidelined. At times, Christians across the world have indisputably opted to invest in identities of indigeneity and local authenticity, often for strategic benefit. Moreover, it is surely significant that the much-noted worldwide explosion of Christianity occurred in the same century as that of the nationalist and independence movements that overtook much of the continents of Asia and Africa, and that the growth of global Christianity was simultaneous with the populist, patriotic revolutions that sprang up throughout Latin America. In constituting themselves as a worldwide ecumenia, many Christians have also been deeply attentive to the nationalist projects that were animating their compatriots at home.

The chapter offered by the historian Charlotte Walker-Said (Chapter 7) illuminates these frequently contradictory dynamics, providing insight into how twentieth-century Christians fluidly moved between varying 'scales' of religious identity and affiliation – and, in the case of her chapter, both the national and the international. By virtue of considering themselves members of a worldwide Catholic family, Cameroonians mobilised a Catholic social welfare tradition that developed in post-war France, putting these teachings to profitable work in the context of Cameroon's nationalist struggle. Walker-Said thus demonstrates that complex strategies of borrowing and reassembling new religious ideas around gender, family and marriage had both nationalist and internationalist resonance in modern Africa. And in the very different context of twentieth-century China, the literary scholar Chloë Starr's chapter explores how the strong relationship between Chinese Christianity and nationalist sentiment has served to limit the universalist aspirations of Chinese Christians (Chapter 8). She brings her linguistic and textual expertise in Chinese literature to an examination of Chinese theology via the texts of official church theologians, the writings of other Christians and pastors, and the scholarship of academic Christianity. Starr argues that, while theology may drive ideology, especially among the underground Roman or resurgent Calvinist-leaning churches, with regulatory consequences accepted as a cost of faith, political ideology also shapes theology, and results in Chinese Christians' determination to position themselves as part of an explicitly nationalist church.

The final chapter in this section, written by the anthropologist Joel Robbins, focuses on Pentecostal-Charismatic communities among the Urapmin in present-day Papua New Guinea (PNG). As well as highlighting the unique contribution that the discipline of anthropology makes to the study of World Christianity, Robbins also argues the Urapmin show us 'that we can talk about something like world or global Christianity, rather than simply about the fact that there are Christians almost anywhere one might travel'. Arguably the Urapmin offer the most dramatic example of shifting 'scales' of Christian identity in this volume. Consisting of a group of no more than 400 people residing in an extremely remote part of the island of PNG, over the course of conversion to Pentecostal Christianity the Urapmin experienced a radically enlarged sense of self and community. 'Kicked by the [Holy] Spirit' and gripped by dispensational premillennialist doctrines, the Urapmin transformed their ritual life and gender relations. Cult houses were dismantled as satanic, ancestral bones thrown down pit latrines, and taboos that separated men and women were set aside so that they might live moral Christian lives. Robbins shows us that when Urapmin pray, they now imagine themselves linked up with an entire global world of Christians, levering their newly expansive identities to critique the state of their home island, which they cast as demoralising and chaotic.

Titled 'Migration and Diaspora', the final section of our volume considers one of the most pressing topics of present-day society: the mass movement of people around the globe, both voluntarily (as in the case of economic migrants) and involuntarily (as in the case of displaced people) – although the line between these two categories is far from hard and fast. While the circulation of missionaries and print has been key to Christianity's worldwide dissemination, large-scale human movement through processes as diverse as slavery, indentured labour and displacement through conflict has also provided crucial conduits through which the transregional contours of the faith have been created and sustained. Historian Andrew Preston's chapter, for example, shows that immigration has been central to the emergence of the modern identity of the United States as a 'Christian nation'. Despite the country's reputation for religious pluralism, the successive waves of international migration from the nineteenth century to the present day have in fact largely served to confirm the country's Judeo-Christian character. Preston also points out that the country's position in the world as a 'bastion of Christianity' is also reinforced by American Christians' tendency to 'propel' themselves outwards internationally in evangelistic and missionary work – a dynamic already noted by Noll and Wuthnow.

Naures Atto is an anthropologist who studies Middle Eastern Christians' diasporic networks, and her chapter provides insight into the other side of this picture: the concerns and anxieties that animate those Christians who consider leaving their homeland for Western countries when confronted with extreme hardship. Atto's observation that the idealists *choose* to stay in the Middle East to assert rights to their homeland but the poor who lack transnational connections are *forced* to do so echoes a broader point made in migration studies – that certain social categories of refugees are more likely than others to 'get stuck' in locations of conflict (Chatterji 2017). Atto examines the fraught existence of Christian communities in the Middle East who are targeted by the Islamic State (formerly isis) and other militant Islamist groups. Atto focuses on the debates among these Christians regarding their future as indigenous Christians in the Middle East. Some aspire to settle in Western 'Christian' countries – including the United States – while others argue for their rightful role in a region cast as the birthplace of an ancient indigenous Christianity. Through these acute dilemmas over leaving or staying in the homeland, and consequent fears about loss of ethnic identity in the diaspora, Atto explores how a debate about survival is entangled in local and global identities, as well as in keen expectations of the obligations of global Christian networks to those in distress elsewhere in the world.

Our final chapter, written by theologian Kwabena Asamoah-Gyadu, examines the transregional Pentecostal churches of West Africa, and in particular their expansionist, missionary zeal. Asamoah-Gyadu reminds us that migration need not always be intercontinental, for the proselytising energies of West African Pentecostals are centred both on Europe and North America, and on closer-to-home regional evangelism within neighbouring West African countries. Focusing on popular Pentecostal symbols of mobility and worldwide expansion in the context of the large West African diasporic population, Asamoah-Gyadu shows how the frequent invocation of these icons in sermons, worship and church publicity bolsters a Pentecostal world view that imagines a triumphalist radiation of Christendom from West Africa outwards to the world. For example, Asamoah-Gyadu describes how a popular Nigerian church, the Church of the Embassy of the Blessed Kingdom of God for all Nations, has recently made major inroads into the landscape of Ukrainian Christianity, largely through the popular appeal of its message of financial prosperity and success amidst the uncertain post-communist climate of the entire region.

Indeed, Dorottya Nagy's chapter similarly argues that the ideological vacuum opened up by the end of Communism across Eastern and Central Europe has provided new opportunities for proselytising Christians from across the world, many of whom enter the region via immigrant routes and only later come to view themselves as missionaries.

The final point to be made in this introduction is thus to highlight that while the West is usually excluded from the purview of the world in much current World Christianity thinking, the chapters contained in the present volume (especially these final three) challenge any dichotomy between the West and the non-Western world. As we have seen with Asamoah-Gyadu's chapter, a common trope in contemporary Pentecostal and Charismatic discourse in regions such as Africa and Latin America is that it is the spiritually barren lands of Europe and North America that now require spiritual rejuvenation. In this respect, Asamoah-Gyadu is building on recent literature that adds a celebratory coda to Philip Jenkins' counter-secularisation account, which highlights the re-missionisation of post-Christian Europe by the international Christian diaspora and formal mission agencies from the global South (Adogame 2013). The identification of Europe as a mission field has a long tradition; the respectable elites who ran Protestant mission bodies in eighteenth- and nineteenth-century Europe and North America had already considered internal mission within their own bodies politic a key facet of their work, where the objects of their attention could be Jewish minorities or the working classes of newly industrialised cities (Bayly 2004: 345–51). In the late twentieth century, the work of the influential theologian and former missionary to India Leslie Newbigin provided a compelling theological justification for considering Western pluralist societies a mission field (Newbigin 1989). And as Maxwell observes in his chapter, American Evangelicals have viewed Europe as a mission field since the end of the Second World War.

However, the rationale and success of these new 'reverse mission' initiatives are far from apparent. Rather than following 'a thought out, reflexive, cross-cultural missionary strategy', they often amount to more of a 'historical "self-reparation", a means of coming to terms with the psychical traumas of colonialism. African diasporic communities in cities such as London and Birmingham, more often than not enclosed in fairly insular ethnic communities, make a poor missionary bridge to their wider communities' (Freston 2010: 161, 167). Moreover, the accuracy of the depiction of a post-Christian West versus a believing and enspirited South is still a subject for debate, as Jenkins has recently shown in a study of statistics affirming still considerable levels of Christian adherence in the West (Jenkins 2007: 115–20). Arguably, scholars' emphasis on the resurgence of Christian practice in the global South relies on essentialised notions of the intrinsic religiosity of the non-Western world, while perhaps it also makes too much of the supposed secularisation of Western Europe and North America. It is noteworthy that the Western media is little interested in religion and dominated by those who have scant religious commitment in a personal or professional sense (McLeod 2006: 643–4). Noting that journalists often missed the religious inspiration and organisation behind the fall of Communism in Eastern Europe, the eminent sociologist of religion David Martin observes: 'It is evident that Western reporters when they visit sites of important change do not know how to recognise the religious aspect, let alone interpret it' (Martin 1996: 17–18).

This introduction began by noting the increasingly ubiquitous nature of the term 'World Christianity' in academic circles, but, as we draw to a close, it is worth asking to what extent this represents a real paradigm shift or a passing academic fashion, rather like the scholarly industry that grew up around African Christian independent churches in the 1970s (Hastings 2000) or the current flurry of scholarship around Pentecostal-Charismatic Christianity. There has indeed been a good deal of institutional investment in the concept, with new departments, academic centres, teaching positions, book series and two journals. Nevertheless, it is noteworthy that few of the first- and second-generation academics in the field primarily self-identify as scholars in World Christianity, choosing instead to retain disciplinary and sub-disciplinary credentials as sociologists, church historians, historians of mission and missiologists, as well as to emphasise their various area studies loyalties. In light of this, 'World Christianity' might not best be termed a new discipline nor a new field of study, but rather a mode of doing research that complements existing disciplines' methodologies and concepts (see Chapter 5). As we have suggested here, when taken in its most robust sense – as attention both to local specificity *and* to broader identities and networks – World Christianity's invocation will surely deepen and enhance our study of historical and contemporary Christianity in all its manifold and subtle varieties.

References

Ade Ajayi, J. F. and E. A. Ayandele (1969) 'Writing African Church History' in P. Beyerhaus and C. F. Hallencreutz, *The Church Crossing Frontiers*. Uppsala: Gleerup.

Adogame, A. (2013) *The African Christian Diaspora: New Currents and Emerging Trends in World Christianity*. London: Bloomsbury.

Anderson, A. (2013) *To the Ends of the Earth: Pentecostalism and the Transformation of World Christianity*. Oxford: Oxford University Press.

Annis, S. (1987) *God and Production in a Guatemalan Town*. Austin TX: University of Texas Press.

Appadurai, A. (1998) *Modernity at Large: Cultural Dimensions of Globalization*. Minneapolis MN: University of Minnesota Press.

Austin-Broos, D. (1997) *Jamaica Genesis: Religion and the Politics of Moral Orders*. Chicago IL: Chicago University Press.

Barker, J. (ed.) (1990) *Christianity in Oceania: Ethnographic Perspectives*. New York NY: University Press of America.

Barrett, D. et al. (eds) (2001) *World Christian Encyclopedia: A Comparative Study of Churches and Religions in the Modern World*. Oxford: Oxford University Press.

Bayly, C. (2004) *The Birth of the Modern World 1780–1914*. Oxford: Blackwell.

Beattie, W. (2005) 'Globalization and Missiology: Some Implications for the Asian Church', *Mission Round Table: The Occasional Bulletin of OMF Mission Research* 1 (2): 3–10.

Bediako, K. (1990) *Jesus in African Culture*. Accra: Asempa Publishers.

Bosch, D. (1991) *Transforming Mission: Paradigm Shifts in the Theology of Mission*. Maryknoll NY: Orbis Books.

Burroughs, W. R. (1995) 'Needs and Opportunities in Studies of World Christianity', *International Bulletin of Missionary Research* 19 (4): 172–8.

Burroughs, W., M. Gornik and J. McLean (eds) (2011) *Understanding World Christianity: The Vision and Work of Andrew F. Walls*. Maryknoll NY: Orbis Books.

Carey, H. (2011) *God's Empire: Religion and Colonialism in the British World, c.1801–1908*. Cambridge: Cambridge University Press.

Chatterji, J. (2017) 'On Being Stuck in Bengal: Immobility in the "Age of Migration"', *Modern Asian Studies* 51 (2): 511–41.

Clarke, S. (2014) 'World Christianity and Postcolonial Mission: A Path Forward for the Twenty-First Century', *Theology Today* 71 (2): 192–206.

Comaroff, J. and J. L. Comaroff (1991) *Of Revelation and Revolution. Volume 1: Christianity, Colonialism and Consciousness in South Africa*. Chicago IL: University of Chicago.

Comaroff, J. and J. L. Comaroff (1997) *Of Revelation and Revolution. Volume 2: The Dialectics of Modernity on a South African Frontier*. Chicago IL: University of Chicago.

Cooper, F. (2010) *Colonialism in Question: Theory, Knowledge, History*. Berkeley CA: University of California Press.

Dirks, N. (ed.) (1992) *Colonialism and Culture*. Ann Arbor MI: University of Michigan Press.

Edwards, D. L. (1998) *Christianity: The First Two Thousand Years*. London: Cassell.

Etherington, N. (1996) 'Recent Trends in the Historiography of Christianity in Southern Africa', *Journal of Southern African Studies* 22 (2): 201–19.

Etherington, N. (ed.) (2005) *Oxford History of the British Empire Companion Series, Missions and Empire*. Oxford: Oxford University Press.

Farhadian, C. E. (2012) 'Introduction' in C. E. Farhadian (ed.), *Introducing World Christianity*. Oxford: Blackwell.

Freston, P. (2010) 'Reverse Mission: A Discourse in Search of a Reality', *PentecoStudies* 9 (2): 153–74.

Frykenberg, F. (2008) *Christianity in India: From Beginnings to the Present*. Oxford: Oxford University Press.

Gilley, S. (2006) 'Introduction' in S. Gilley and B. Stanley (eds), *The Cambridge History of Christianity. Volume 8: World Christianities c.1815–c.1914*. Cambridge: Cambridge University Press.

Grabill, J. (1971) *Protestant Diplomacy and the Near East: Missionary Influence on American Policy, 1810–1927*. Minneapolis MN: University of Minnesota Press.

Grimshaw, P. and A. May (eds) (2010) *Missionaries, Indigenous People and Cultural Exchange*. Brighton: Oregon Sussex Academic Press.

Gunson, N. (1978) *Messengers of Grace: Evangelical Missionaries in the South Seas, 1797–1860*. Melbourne: Oxford University Press.

Hastings, A. (1986) *'The Council Came to Africa.' In Vatican II by Those Who Were There*. Edited by A. Stacpoole. London: Geoffrey Chapman.

Hastings, A. (1989) *African Catholicism*. London: SCM Press.

Hastings, A. (1999) 'Introduction' in A. Hastings (ed.), *A World History of Christianity*. London: Cassell.

Hastings, A. (2000) 'African Christian Studies, 1967–1999: Reflections of an Editor', *Journal of Religion in Africa* 30 (1): 30–44.

Hastings, A. (2001) 'From the End of Colonialism to the "Young Churches"', *Cristianesimo nella Storia* 22: 747–74.

Hempton, D. (2005) *Methodism: Empire of the Spirit*. New Haven CT: Yale University Press.

Hermann, A. and C. Burlacioiu (2016) 'Introduction: Klaus Koschorke and the "Munich School" Perspective on the History of World Christianity', *Journal of World Christianity* 6 (1): 4–27.

Hopkins, A. G. (2002) 'Introduction: Globalization – An Agenda for Historians' in A. G. Hopkins (ed.), *Globalization in World History*. London: Pimlico.

Hutchinson, M. (1999) 'What's Wrong with Globalization, Anyway?' Cambridge: Cambridge Centre for Christianity Worldwide.

Hutchinson, M. and J. Wolffe (2012) *A Short History of Global Evangelicalism*. Cambridge: Cambridge University Press.

Hutchinson, W. (1982) 'A Moral Equivalent for Imperialism: Americans and the Promotion of Christian Civilization' in W. Hutchinson and T. Christensen (eds), *Missionary Ideologies in the Imperialist Era, 1880–1920*. Aarhus: Aros.

Irvin, D. T. (2008) 'World Christianity: An Introduction', *Journal of World Christianity* 1 (1): 1–26.

Jenkins, P. (2002) *The Next Christendom: The Coming of Global Christianity*. New York NY: Oxford University Press.

Jenkins, P. (2006) *The New Faces of Christianity: Believing in the Bible in the Global South*. Oxford: Oxford University Press.

Jenkins, P. (2007) 'Godless Europe?', *International Bulletin of Missionary Research* 31 (3).

Johnson, T. and S. Kim (2005) 'Describing the Worldwide Christian Phenomenon', *International Bulletin of Missionary Research* 29 (2): 80–4.

Juergensmeyer, M. (ed.) (2014) *Thinking Globally: A Global Studies Reader*. Berkeley CA: University of California Press.

Kalilombe, P. (1999) *Doing Theology at the Grassroots: Theological Essays from Malawi*. Gweru: Mambo Press.

Kearney, M. (1995) 'The Local and the Global: The Anthropology of Globalization and Transnationalism', *Annual Review of Anthropology* 24: 547–65.

Koschorke, K. (2014) 'New Maps of the History of World Christianity: Current Challenges and Future Perspectives', *Theology Today* 71 (2): 178–91.

Koschorke, K. (2016) 'Transcontinental Links, Enlarged Maps, and Polycentric Structures in the History of World Christianity', *Journal of World Christianity* 6 (1).

Landau, P. (1995) *The Realm of the Word: Language, Gender and Christianity in a Southern African Kingdom*. London: James Currey.

Latourette, K. S. (1937–48) *A History of the Expansion of Christianity*. New York NY: Harper.

Leiper, H. (1937) *World Chaos or World Christianity*. London: Willet, Clark.

Manning. P. (2003) *Navigating World History: Historians Create a Global Past*. New York NY: Palgrave Macmillan.

Marshall, R. (2009) *Political Spiritualities: The Pentecostal Revolution in Nigeria*. Chicago IL: University of Chicago Press.

Martin, D. (1996) *Forbidden Revolutions: Pentecostalism in Latin America, Catholicism in Eastern Europe*. London: SPCK.

Maxwell, D. (1999) *Christians and Chiefs in Zimbabwe: A Social History of the Hwesa People c.1870s–1990s*. Edinburgh: International African Library.

Maxwell, D. (2001) 'Introduction' in D. Maxwell with I. Lawrie (eds), *Christianity and the African Imagination: Essays in Honour of Adrian Hastings*. Leiden: E. J. Brill.

Maxwell, D. (2006a) *African Gifts of the Spirit: Pentecostalism and the Rise of a Zimbabwean Transnational Religious Movement*. Oxford: James Currey.

Maxwell, D. (2006b) 'Post-colonial Christianity in Africa' in H. McLeod (ed.), *The Cambridge History of Christianity. Volume 9: World Christianities, c.1914–c.2000*. Cambridge: Cambridge University Press.

McConnell, F. (1929) *Human Needs and World Christianity*. New York NY: Friendship Press.

McLeod, H. (2006) 'Introduction' in H. McLeod (ed.), *The Cambridge History of Christianity. Volume 9: World Christianities c.1914–c.2000*. Cambridge: Cambridge University Press.

Meyer, B. (1998) '"Make a Complete Break with the Past": Memory and Post-colonial Modernity in Ghanaian Pentecostalist Discourse', *Journal of Religion in Africa* 28 (3): 316–49.

Meyer, B. and A. Moors (eds) (2005) *Religion, Media and the Public Sphere*. Bloomington IN: Indiana University Press.

Mudimbe, V. Y. (1997) *Tales of Faith: Religion as Political Performance in Central Africa*. London: Athlone Press.

Newbigin, L. (1989) *The Gospel in a Pluralist Society*. London: SPCK.

Noll, M. (2009) *The New Shape of World Christianity: How American Experience Reflects the Global Faith*. Madison WI: IVP.

Peel, J. D. Y. (1968) *Aladura: A Religious Movement among the Yoruba*. London: Oxford University Press.

Peel, J. D. Y. (2000) *Religious Encounter and the Making of the Yoruba*. Bloomington IN: Indiana University Press.

Phan, P. (2012) 'World Christianity: Its Implications for History, Religious Studies, and Theology', *Horizons* 39 (2): 171–88.

Ranger, T. O. and I. N. Kimambo (eds) (1972) *The Historical Study of African Religion*. London: Heinemann Educational.

Ranger, T. O. and J. Weller (eds) (1975) *Themes in the Christian History of Central Africa*. London: Heinemann Educational.

Rausch, T. (2016) 'Roman Catholicism since 1800' in L. Sanneh and M. J. McClymond (eds), *The Wiley Blackwell Companion to World Christianity*. Chichester: John Wiley & Sons.

Robbins, J. (2004) *Becoming Sinners: Christianity and Moral Torment in a Papua New Guinea Society*. Berkeley CA: University of California Press.

Robbins, J. (2007) 'Continuity Thinking and the Problem of Christian Culture: Belief, Time and the Anthropology of Christianity', *Current Anthropology* 48 (1).

Robert, D. (1994) 'From Missions to Mission to Beyond Foreign Missions Since World War II', *International Bulletin of Missionary Research* 18 (4): 146–62.

Robert, D. (2000) 'Shifting Southward: Global Christianity since 1945', *International Bulletin of Missionary Research* 24 (2): 50–8.

Robert, D. (2009) *Christian Mission: How Christianity Became a World Religion*. Oxford: Wiley-Blackwell.

Robert, D. (2014) 'Forty Years of North American Missiology: A Brief Review', *International Bulletin of Missionary Research* 38 (1): 3–8.

Sanneh, L. (2003) *Whose Religion is Christianity? The Gospel Beyond the West*. Grand Rapids MI: Eerdmans.

Sanneh, L. (2008) *Disciples of All Nations: Pillars of World Christianity*. New York NY: Oxford University Press.

Sanneh, L. (2009 [1989]) *Translating the Message: The Missionary Impact on Culture*. 2nd edition. Maryknoll NY: Orbis Books.

Sanneh, L. (2012) *Summoned from the Margin: Homecoming of an African*. Grand Rapids MI: Eerdmans.

Sanneh, L. and M. J. McClymond (eds) (2016) *The Wiley Blackwell Companion to World Christianity*. Oxford: Wiley-Blackwell.

Shenk, W. R. (2001) 'Recasting Theology of Mission: Impulses from the Non-Western World', *International Bulletin of Missionary Research* 25 (3): 98–107.

Stanley, B. (1999) 'Twentieth-century World Christianity: A Perspective from the History of Missions'. Cambridge: Cambridge Centre for Christianity Worldwide.

Stanley, B. (2009) *The World Missionary Conference, Edinburgh 1910*. Grand Rapids MI: Eerdmans.

Stanley, B. (2013) *The Global Diffusion of Evangelicalism: The Age of Billy Graham and John Stott*. Downers Grove IL: IVP.

Sundkler, B. (1948) *Bantu Prophets in South Africa*. London: Lutterworth Press.

Turner, H. W. (1967) *African Independent Church: Volumes I–II*. Oxford: Clarendon Press.

Vail, L. (ed.) (1989) *Creation of Tribalism in Southern Africa*. London: James Currey.

Van Dusen, H. (1947) *World Christianity: Yesterday, Today and Tomorrow*. London: SCM Press.

Walls, A. (1987) 'The Christian Tradition in Today's World' in F. Whaling (ed.), *The Religious Situation of the World from 1945 to the Present Day*. Edinburgh: T. & T. Clark.

Walls, A. (1991) 'Structural Problems in Mission Studies', *International Bulletin of Missionary Research* 15 (4): 146–55.

Walls, A. (1996) *The Missionary Movement in Christian History: Studies in the Transmission of Faith*. New York NY: Orbis Books.

Walls, A. (2002) *The Cross-cultural Process in Christian History*. Maryknoll NY: Orbis Books.

Walls, A. and C. Ross (eds) (2008) *Mission in the Twenty-first Century: Exploring the Five Marks of Global Mission*. Maryknoll NY: Orbis Books.

Ward, K. (2006) 'Christianity, Colonialism and Missions' in H. McLeod (ed.), *The Cambridge History of Christianity. Volume 9: World Christianities c.1914–c.2000*. Cambridge: Cambridge University Press.

Ward, W. R. (2002 [1992]) *The Protestant Evangelical Awakening*. Cambridge: Cambridge University Press.

Welbourn, F. (1961) *East African Rebels: A Study of Some Independent Churches*. London: SCM Press.

Westermann, D. (1937) *Africa and Christianity*. Oxford: Oxford University Press.

Whiteman, D. (2016) 'Some Changes but the Same Mission Dei', *International Bulletin of Mission Research* 40 (1): 4–5.

Wuthnow, R. (2009) *Boundless Faith: The Global Reach of American Churches*. Berkeley CA: University of California Press.

Yates, T. (1994) *Christian Mission in the Twentieth Century*. Cambridge: Cambridge University Press.

PART 1

Connections and Comparisons

∵

Historical Perspectives on Christianity Worldwide: Connections, Comparisons and Consciousness

David Maxwell

Over the past two decades a new narrative in the history of Christianity has been established as scholars have caught up with the growth of Christian adherence in the southern hemisphere throughout the twentieth century. It is no longer possible to write an account of the church in the last century that places Europe and North America at the centre of the story. In his *The New Shape of World Christianity*, the well-known commentator and church historian Mark Noll describes the new world order by means of a series of powerful contrasts:

> This past Sunday it is possible that more Christian believers attended church in China than in all of so-called Christian Europe ... more Anglicans attended church in each of Kenya, South Africa, Tanzania and Uganda than did Anglicans in Britain and Canada and Episcopalians in the United States combined ... more Presbyterians were at church in Ghana than in Scotland ... there were more Roman Catholics at worship in the Philippines than in any single country of Europe, including historically Catholic Italy, Spain and Portugal ... and for several years the world's largest chapter of the Jesuit order has been found in India and not the United States, as it had been for much of the late Twentieth Century.
>
> NOLL 2009: 20–1

Beyond these demographic shifts, the remarkable growth of Evangelical religion, particularly Pentecostalism, in Latin America, Africa and the Pacific Rim has also changed the character of Christianity worldwide, bringing pneumatic practices to the fore of the Christian faith (Martin 1996; Maxwell 2006). In the West, Europeans may find themselves proselytised by a zealous South Korean or observe a courageous African evangelist preaching to crowds of uninterested shoppers more committed to the religion of consumption. Attendance at a Catholic church in Brussels will often reveal an aged Belgian priest assisted by a youthful African colleague and a choir of Rwandans, Burundians and Congolese. The examples can be multiplied across the globe. Noll reminds us that:

'Today more Christian workers from Brazil are active in cross-cultural ministry outside their homelands than from Britain or from Canada' (Noll 2009:10). The Overseas Missionary Fellowship (OMF), formerly the China Inland Mission of Hudson Taylor, now has in its membership a black South African working in Thailand, a Brazilian with a ministry in hip-hop resident in Japan, and a Korean at work in Cambodia.[1] The old distinctions between the Christian West and the pagan rest, between home and foreign missions, have withered away. OMF's appointment in 2005 of a Chinese director, Patrick Fung, who is based in Singapore, reflects these new global realities.

But there is much work still to do in the creation of a new history of Christianity. There is a lack of substance to some of the assertions that underpin a model of a decentred post-Christian West. And while the growing diversity and multi-polarity of the church does point to a remarkable set of religious transformations in global history, the process remains under-conceptualised. The recent emergence of a new sub-discipline of World Christianity gave a much-needed boost to old-style mission studies, which by the end of the 1970s were unfashionable because of their colonial associations (Robert 2014: 3–4). But rebranding did not stimulate much conceptual advance. As Michael Poon observes, some mission studies scholars simply revelled in the demographic shifts in adherence, being content to produce statistics of countries and groups with little accompanying analysis (Poon 2011: 8–9). Others continued business as usual, legitimating Eurocentric studies of mission with the label 'World Christianity'. The notion of World Christianity can also be used in a rhetorical manner. The classic account of the transformed global Christian landscape was Philip Jenkins' *The Next Christendom: The Coming of Global Christianity*, published in 2002. This enormously influential text has a triumphal tone, making a spirited rebuttal of scholarship that points to the waning of Western Christianity in the face of modernity and secularisation. It also proclaims the victory of Christianity over the rival twentieth-century ideologies of Communism and Fascism. On capitalism, Jenkins remains silent (Jenkins 2002). Subsequent literature adds a celebratory note to the counter-secularisation thesis, highlighting the re-missionisation and re-moralisation of the post-Christian West by Southern Christian diaspora and more formal mission agencies from the global South (Adogame 2013).

Yet the notion of a faithless West facing a vibrant Christian South is deeply problematic. Such a model often excludes the history and contemporary exper-

---

1   Dr Stephen Griffiths, Overseas Missionary Fellowship, Singapore, email message to author, 26 December 2014.

ience of the Orthodox East (Daughrity 2011). It also treats Europe and North America as a single Christian bloc, ignoring the fact that, since the end of the Second World War, American Evangelicals have viewed Europe, particularly its Southern Catholic nations, as a mission field (Preston 2012: 440–64). Likewise, it assumes that the so-called global South can be treated as a homogeneous field when in fact there are vast differences in wealth and power – and where, in particular, China and India loom ever larger (Hofmeyr and Williams 2011: 17). While the idea of the re-Christianisation of a supposedly post-Christian Europe helps restore the self-image of postcolonial nations and their diaspora, as Paul Freston observes, there is scant evidence of its success (Freston 2010). And it is doubtful whether the salvation of the West lies in the hands of Southern Christians. The recent history of the Anglican Church in Zimbabwe under Bishop Kunonga, or the fact that all the *genocidaires* who committed murder in Rwanda in 1994 identified as Christians, suggests that Southern believers are engaged in their own struggles with clientelism, ecclesiastical corporatism and tribalism. Christianity worldwide may be polycentric, but the Western centres still exert much influence. The relocation of the African synod to Rome in 1994 was a salutary reminder of the power of the Vatican. Similarly, American Catholics and Evangelicals wield enormous financial power, their aid to developing nations often accompanied by conditions (Hearn 2002). The history of Christianity may in part be characterised as the story of a travelling faith, but too great an emphasis on 'flows' gives the impression of ease of movement. Contrary to a central assertion of Afe Adogame and Shobana Shankar's recent book, *Religion on the Move*, 'disempowered peoples' *do not* 'transmit their faiths from everywhere to everywhere' because there are clearly places that Christianity has not reached and where it cannot go despite its universalist aspirations (Adogame and Shankar 2012: 31–2). 'World Christianities' in the plural avoids the homogenising connotations of 'world' or 'global' by stressing the locally specific nature of the faith, representing the sum of local appropriations. But the vast array of case studies illustrating vernacular or popular Christianity must now be examined within a comparative framework of patterns of reception and rejection (Lindenfeld 2005: 327–8). And attention should be paid to the ways in which local variations of Christianity have related to the historic centres of faith and to each other.

This chapter outlines a historical framework for the analysis of Christianity's global spread and contemporary character, taking examples from across the world. While much interesting work has already been done, it introduces scholarship that is suggestive of new approaches that enhance the conceptualisation of World Christianity. Attention will be given to the sites, arenas and frameworks of action to which Christianity has moved and where it has taken form. The task is not simply a matter of identifying the mechanisms that made connections, but also of highlighting the breaks and boundaries that have limited Christianity's progress (Cooper 2001). In addition, consideration will be given to how ideas travel, who and what transports them, the baggage they take with them on their journeys, and how they become localised on their arrival (Armitage 2013: 33). The transportation and localisation of Christian ideas and practices raise the issue of agency. Missionaries were not the only proselytisers; in fact, they often made poor evangelists, not least because of linguistic barriers. There is a need to identify those who acted as 'middle figures', mediating between two cultures, doing the conceptual work necessary to domesticate Christianity. Work on diverse local expressions of Christianity must be complemented by an examination of those mechanisms of homogenisation, such as texts, ritual practices and institutions, that created uniformity within denominations and stimulated a broader sense of a universal faith. It is also essential to identify large-scale events and moments that contributed to a growing consciousness of Christianity as a world religion. Lastly, historians must remain alert to the antiquity of Christianity's spread across the globe, mindful of the deep antecedents of its missionary impulse and transnational connections.

Historicising Christianity Worldwide

Christianity has always been a missionary religion with universalist aspirations. In the first century AD, it quickly evolved from an obscure sect of Galilean Jews into a religion of thousands centred upon the Mediterranean world, especially North Africa (Maxwell 2013a: 263). Robert Hefner reminds us that, prior to Christianity's 'catastrophic collapse' in the late Middle Ages, which left its centre of gravity in Europe, it had already established a 'global standing' via its long-established presence in Western Asia and the Middle East (Hefner 2012; Daughrity 2011: 19). Four of the five early Christian patriarchates – Jerusalem, Antioch, Alexandria and Constantinople, the exception being Rome – lay outside of what is today considered the West. Some of the earliest international connections persisted at the level of ecclesiastical authorities, so that while the Ethiopian Church was unable to expand in Muslim North Africa, it remained linked to the Eastern Church via the Coptic patriarch of Alexandria. The rekindling of the church's missionary ideal began with the Catholic Counter-Reformation from the mid-sixteenth century. Catholic missionary orders achieved great success in evangelising Latin America and had a significant impact on China and the Kingdom of Kongo (Thornton 1998; Gray 1990). The early modern Catholic missionary impulse prefigured the modern missionary movement in its transnationalism and cosmopolitanism. The Society of Jesus, for instance, drew together missionary priests from diverse origins in a web of connections that spanned Europe, Asia, Africa and Latin America. Jesuit missionaries created a transnational Tridentine Catholicism united by a shared catechism but locally distinguishable via modifications that occurred in its translation, production and recitation (Ditchfield 2007; Clossey 2011). But whereas the early modern Catholic impetus had been a movement closely related to the mercantile interests of Iberian states, the modern missionary impulse was less geographically limited and freer to mobilise at the popular level via its voluntarism. It also coincided with imperial and technological developments that enabled connections to rapidly multiply and global consciousness to develop.

In an important and innovative collection on the transnational dimensions of world religions, Vincent Viaene and Abigail Green argue for the emergence of the religious international. They define this new phenomenon 'as a cluster of voluntary transnational organizations and representations crystallizing around international issues, in which both "ordinary" believers and religious specialists could serve as protagonists' (Green and Viaene 2012: 1). Christian religious internationals began within Protestantism, with the German Pietistic and American and British Evangelical revivals of the early eighteenth century evolving into mass mobilisations in the nineteenth century. Supporters, donors and activists, of which the majority were women, were drawn into international civil society, galvanised by missionary expansion and humanitarianism. Protestant supporters were mobilised by a commitment to abolitionism and subsequent related human rights issues such as the Red Rubber Scandal (c.1896–1908) in the Congo Free State (Green and Viaene 2012; Hilton 2010; Thompson 2002). Catholics were mobilised by an Ultramontanist defence of the papacy in the 1860s and 1870s. Both Christian internationals were propelled forwards by painful collective memories: Protestants by a history of discrimination and disestablishment; Catholics by the trauma of the French Revolution. Religious diaspora and refugees carried their faith with them to settler colonies but formal missionary organisations were enabled by the communications revolution, sometimes called the first globalisation of print, steam and the telegraph, which increased connectivity and the space–time compression. Imperial connections could be intense, drawing far-flung outposts into close relations with metropoles. Such was the frequency of steamships carrying wool and refrigerated lamb from New Zealand to Britain that one prescient commentator writing in 1882 contended that the colony was 'as much a province of England, as easy a source of supply for the London market, as Yorkshire or Devon'.[2]

Many missionaries – though by no means all – benefited from empire, travelling along imperial arteries, finding protection in colonial rule and exploiting new opportunities in health, education and development. Although Christian internationals shared similar institutional forms and goals, they were never organisationally monolithic. While the Catholic international was strongly centralised around the papacy well into the twentieth century, Protestantism fractured along lines of denomination and doctrine. Moreover, across the globe, Evangelicals did battle with Ultramontanist Catholics over the meaning of Christian orthodoxy, the struggles being particularly fierce in Belgian and Portuguese colonies where indigenous Christians often took on missionary animosities.[3]

The second globalisation, beginning in the 1990s, continued the process of Christian diversification and democratisation across the world by providing new technologies to broadcast and receive its messages. The communications revolution of the internet, satellite television and mobile phones coincided with the fall of communist states and the commencement of the neoliberal era. As J. D. Y. Peel observes, the attempt by former communist and socialist regimes 'to control, monopolise or eliminate the expression of religious belief' was replaced by freedom of expression and a deregulation of the media, leading to a 'plurality of competing faiths' (Peel 2009: 183). With the removal of many barriers to the circulation of religious messages, transnational religious movements flourished and also de-professionalised. Dana Robert, a leading authority on mission history, writes:

> Short-term mission projects involving millions of people and millions of dollars, cross-cultural outreach from local congregations, proliferations of 'global' faith based organisations (FBOs), and migration have become so extensive that the missionary is being redefined in North America. What should be the trajectory of mission studies in an age when globe-trotting amateurs vastly outnumber career missionaries?
>
> ROBERT 2014: 6

---

2   *New Zealand Herald*, 1882, cited in Bellich (2009: 368).

3   On Belgian Congo, for instance, see R. D. Bedinger, 'The Relations between the Roman Catholic and Protestant Missions: And Contrasts between their Methods of Work' in *Congo Missionary Conference Report 1918. A Report of the Seventh General Conference of Missionaries and Protestant Societies Working in Congoland*, Baptist Missionary Society, Bolobo Mission, Haut

Global, Transnational and Local Christianity

Having constructed a narrative of growing diversity and connection within Christianity across the globe – while trying not to obscure its early precursors – it is now time to begin to conceptualise that process. Here I draw from scholarly debates about global intellectual history and transnational history (Moyn and Sartori 2013; Bayly et al. 2006). Both sub-disciplines are in their early development and there is little agreement concerning definitions, which can overlap. Nevertheless, it is possible to draw insights from this emerging field. I have made much use of the term 'transnational' and prefer this concept to 'world' or 'global'. World Christianity suggests a homogenisation that has rarely occurred. The label 'global' is most useful when it describes 'a historical methodology indicating the analysis of broad patterns and connections across time and space, rather than a comprehensive history of all regions'. Sujit Sivasundaram deploys it in this manner in his exploration of the interaction of science and religion across the globe (Sivasundaram 2010: 177). But 'global' is a capacious term and confusion can arise when its use is not clear. It can be a synonym for 'world' but it also has connotations of the globalisation of historical processes that occurred in the 1990s and supposedly led to the obliteration of the local (Giddens 1990: 64). And it is sometimes used to describe processes that are supranational. David Armitage's important study of the contagion of sovereignty that accompanied the diffusion of the American Declaration of Independence (1776) is subtitled *A Global History* (Armitage 2007). Influential as the Declaration was, the notion suggests a scale of intellectual encounter that rarely, if ever, occurs. 'Long-distance' is unhelpfully equated with 'global' (Cooper 2013). While the Bible, even more than the US Declaration of Independence, has had a remarkably wide circulation, few Christian ideas have had an effect that is worldwide. Indeed, as shown below, Christian forms are often intensely local, at times reifying the particular. The term 'transnational' suggests a more modest reach and influence and provides a better tool for constructing a concrete and plausible historical narrative. Transnational refers to movements and ideas that originate from one base and operate on a supranational level or at an intercontinental scale, but with uneven and varied effects. It is a means of studying large-scale processes, which are not global in scope. A transnational approach enables the analysis of multidirectional flows without privileging Western ones, and rather than assuming the global

Congo, Congo Belge and Archives Africaines: Ministère des Affaires Etrangères, Bruxelles, A5 Missions 625/2/1 Conflits entre les missions.

embrace of phenomena in transit, it provides a framework for the power relations that create fragmentations and exclusions (Bayly et al. 2006: 1448, 1458;
Cooper 2013: 284, 286, 291–2; Cooper 2001). The term's weakness is its modernity. The notion is anachronistic before the era of the modern nation-state, when
the vast majority of the world's inhabitants lived in empires (Saunier 2013: 8–9).
But here modifications such as translocal, transregional and transcommunal
suffice (Green and Viaene 2012: 5).

A broad transnational framework provides a set of useful tools for examining the dissemination of Christianity across the globe. Responsive to shifting
contexts, it facilitates the study of missionary itineraries, the transregional
activities of Bible societies and their colporteurs, and the linguistic regions
created by vernacular scriptures (Weidenmuller 2014). Protestant mission societies and Catholic religious orders were archetypal transnational or transregional organisations. They co-operated across national borders, took little notice
of imperial frontiers (although simultaneously benefiting from imperial patronage), and built bridges between the West and other parts of the world –
bridges that supported a two-way traffic of images, ideas and objects. And they
remain important present-day conduits of aid and development. Their memberships have often been multinational. The Basel Mission recruited Swiss,
Germans and Afro-Caribbeans and connected workers in India, China, New
Guinea and what became Cameroon and Ghana. The Congo Evangelistic Mission, a Pentecostal organisation, recruited South Africans, Americans, Swiss,
Dutch, New Zealanders and British – anyone who possessed the essential qual-
ification of baptism in the Holy Spirit. The analysis of missions as transnational bodies allows scholars to move beyond the binary of metropole and
colony, and to examine how mission organisations shaped metropolitan politics (Thorne 1999). The notion of the transnational also allows for the examination of South–South exchanges, entanglements and linkages, and of other
actors besides missionaries, such as refugees, labour migrants, local evangelists
and religious enthusiasts within their diaspora (Hofmeyr in Bayly et al. 2006:
1444; Maxwell 2006: 13–14; Nielssen et al. 2011). A transnational framework frees
scholars to conceptualise models of religious exchange where Western missionaries were absent or followed behind movements of indigenous Christians.
The Christian encounter in Melanesia is a prime example, as it was first evangelised by Polynesians (Barker 2005). Similarly, in Africa, a movement of more
than 80,000 ex-slaves spread Christian modernity along the West African coast
from missionary colonies in Free Town, where the British Navy had relocated
liberated slaves. Further south, Central and Southern Africa formed a vast pool
of migrant labour, which generally travelled towards the mines, farms and cities
of Southern Rhodesia and South Africa. In these colonies, migrants converted

to Christianity, subsequently carrying their faith back home, evangelising their families and villages in the process (Hastings 1994; Ranger 2002).

Local agents were often unnamed in missionary and colonial sources, but it is possible to identify those who acted as culture brokers, inculturating the faith to make a new, popular Christianity: Christianised freed slaves, nurses, school teachers, clerks and native pastors. These figures had been removed from a traditional milieu by force, labour migration or employment, while processes of relocation and literacy widened their horizons, introducing new ideas and experiences. Their dual perspective made them ideal mediators between old and new. Because they retained links with their former cultures, when they opposed widely held beliefs and practices, 'they did so knowingly', as Peggy Brock has argued (2005: 151). But their proximity to missionaries also meant that they were some of mission Christianity's earliest critics. The resultant forms of popular Christianity hinged upon the degree to which these middle figures were in either camp. They also depended on the degree of Christian literacy available. If the Christian canon was limited, local agents fell back on oral resources such as proverb and folk tale.[4] Occasionally, we do learn the names of important indigenous enthusiasts. They might have been the subject of missionary hagiography to demonstrate success to donors and intercessors back home; or they were the subject of a local hagiography to legitimate an African church tradition. Prominent examples here would be Apolo Kivebulaya – the Ganda evangelist who established Anglicanism in Northern Belgian Congo – and Shalumbo – the returned freed slave-cum-slaver who founded a Pentecostal church among the Songye, also in Belgian Congo.[5] Another was Arthur Wellington Clah, a Native American domiciled in British Columbia, who had only a few months schooling from an Anglican missionary. Clah kept a diary for over fifty years in which he recorded in idiosyncratic English his attempts at proselytising in a frontier zone. Tiyo Soga, a Xhosa educated in Scotland and married to a Scots woman, represented the cream of African elites in the nineteenth century, writing articles for the mission journal of the United Presbyterian Church in South Africa.[6]

All of the above were literate, or had access to literacy, and led transnational lives. But many indigenous Christian agents were unlettered or immobile, and

---

4 For instance, in Eastern Belgian Congo, only four years after the Luba New Testament was available: 'Heard from our Native Christians', *Congo Evangelistic Mission Report* 8, January–March 1925. More generally, see Hofmeyr (1994).

5 On Kivebulaya, see Lloyd (1923), discussed in Wild-Wood (2008). On Shalumbo, see Marcel (1968), discussed in Maxwell (2013b).

6 Clah and Soga are discussed in an important book by Brock et al. (2015).

a transnational approach that focuses on mobile elites can exclude them from the record. It is therefore also important to consider contact zones such as the mission station or Christian village if we are to capture the interactions of the evangelist, catechist and Bible woman.[7] These sites were not unconnected places of stasis. Mission stations sometimes functioned as small towns in the bush, employing a hierarchy of black workers comprising teachers, clerks, printers, nurses and labourers. In the twentieth century they were connected to the metropole by letter and then by radio. Villages were linked to African mines and cities by a regular flow of labour migrants who would return with the latest ideas, fashions and technologies, including newspapers, which were read aloud to large audiences keen to learn about the wider world. But mission stations and villages could also be foci of localisation (Pritchett 2011). A rich body of historical and anthropological work on the missionary encounter by scholars in area studies shows how Christianity could become popular and local through indigenous agents.[8] In the case of Eastern Zimbabwe, Terence Ranger showed how symbolically sensitive missionaries and creative local enthusiasts re-sacralised the landscape in Christian fashion by constructing Catholic grottos and Anglican cemeteries. Medals and scapulars protected Africans from witchcraft and demonic possession, and Catholic prayers proved efficacious in sending locusts in an Anglican direction. The American Methodist gospel of the plough provided a work ethic necessary to turn Shona subsistence farmers into peasants producing for a market (Ranger 1987).

Literacy and print technologies were also important for localising the Christian faith, particularly the new homogenised sacred languages created by scriptures. Missionaries brought orthography and word division to Bible translation; African members of language committees contributed vocabulary, putting their own concepts and images into the word (Lonsdale 2002: 187). The Bible Society's preference for the standardisation and unification of dialects usually led to the expansion of identities. Pre-existing terrains of gradual lexical and idiomatic change were transformed into discrete language zones, which often became the basis for new local and regional ethnicities, freezing identity around one language where there had hitherto been plurality and fluidity (Ranger 1989). Vernacular scriptures widened horizons but they felt local, and across the globe Christians delighted in discovering that God spoke to them in their own language. On receiving a copy of the Gospels and Acts in KiLuba in

---

7   The notion of the contact zone was first used by Pratt (1992) but has since been adapted by other scholars interested in cultural encounter (see Burke 2009: 72).

8   For classic studies, see Hastings (1994) and Frykenberg (2008).

1920, an early convert by the name of Abraham was reported to exclaim: '"Why ... it is my language; it talks to me". He read on, cracking his fingers with glee, wagging his head in wonderment ... "It speaks to my heart! It is my very own tongue"' (Salter 1936: 27). Commenting on the translatability of Christianity in Kenya, John Lonsdale observes: 'Among world religions it appears Christianity's peculiarity thus to sacralise the local while introducing the global' (Lonsdale 2002: 173).

Connections, Networks and Processes of Homogenisation

Nevertheless, Christianity *was* often mobile and it is important to identify the zones, circuits and networks through which it moved. It has proved productive to conceive of the Atlantic as a vast zone of both black and white missionary endeavour. Former slaves and their descendants, inspired by the notion of black manifest destiny, which drew upon Old Testament stories of exodus, exile and return, made committed missionary recruits in American Methodist and American Presbyterian denominations (Campbell 1995; Kennedy 2002). Subsequently, white American Evangelical missionaries grew in influence throughout the twentieth century, using their wealth to construct vast mission infrastructures of development, health and education. The African coast harboured important hubs such as Free Town and Cape Town, through which passed a rich assortment of missionaries, returned slaves, pan-Africanists, sailors and traders – each with a different vision for the continent, and all enriched through mutual interaction. The metropolis is another site of exchange: a crossroads of both trade and culture, like a hub but on a larger scale and with a more settled population (Burke 2009: 73). Los Angeles on the Pacific Ocean was certainly the pre-eminent source of early Pentecostalism, if not the only one; it was a meeting point for migrants and immigrants of different Evangelical and holiness traditions. Much significance has been made of Pentecostalism's antecedents in the spirituality of black Americans, who were present in large numbers in the city. Yet, Los Angeles was also home to several thousand Molokans, a proto-Protestant group of Armenians and Russians who were known for their prophecy, tongues, singing and dancing in the spirit, and who also contributed to the ecstatic practice at the famous Azusa Street Mission (Robeck 2006: 57).

Of all the types of Christian religious circuit, Catholic pilgrimage is the most important. Although pilgrimage to Rome and Padua had deep roots in Europe's past, the transport revolution and rise of tourism in the late nineteenth century allowed the Vatican to increase the numbers of pilgrims and the distances they travelled to these religious sites, drawing visitors from as far afield as Spanish America. Popular cults such as that found at Lourdes were also encouraged in Rome's battle against secularisation (Bayly 2004: 356). Protestants did not generally go on pilgrimage, although Azusa Street drew many radical Evangelicals in search of new experiences of the Holy Spirit. In place of pilgrimages, they had conferences, conventions, crusades and camp meetings, for which adherents would travel hundreds – even thousands – of miles. On the eve of the era of Zimbabwean nationalism on 12 October 1955, Southern Rhodesia's capital, Salisbury, witnessed its largest gathering to date. A crowd of 30,000 Jehovah's Witnesses assembled to listen not to an African nationalist but to a white New Yorker, Mr G. Hershel, address them on religious matters. In 1960, multiracial audiences of a similar size gathered in Salisbury and Bulawayo to hear the message of the globe-trotting evangelist Billy Graham.[9]

At the same time, there were non-human agents of Christianisation, or what Isabel Hofmeyr calls 'prosthetic missionaries', which had an effect through, but also beyond, human agency. Hofmeyr uses this term to refer to texts, foremost of which was the Bible, although she also uses her notion of the prosthetic missionary in relation to Bunyan's *Pilgrim's Progress* (she has written a history of the transnational circulation of the latter; see Hofmeyr 2004: 19). Bible societies, a much under-studied aspect of the Protestant international, produced the scriptures in vast numbers. Only fifty years after its foundation in 1804, the British and Foreign Bible Society had printed nearly 28 million copies of the scriptures in 152 languages and dialects.[10] From its foundation in 1816 until 1880, the American Bible Society issued just over 32 million Bibles from its depositories. While Chris Clark and Michael Ledger-Lomas rightly observe that such figures demand some caution in that they record the volume of production rather than acts of reading, we do know that in the early twentieth century there was widespread demand for literacy across Africa, where Christianity and literacy were often seen as synonymous (Clark and Ledger-Lomas 2012: 30). The frequent label given to Yoruba Christians was *Onibuku* – the people of the book – and for the Kikuyu of Kenya it was *athomi* or readers. It was also the case that missionary propaganda was the most widely circulated literature of the Victorian era amongst the British reading public (Gray 1990). Bible societies believed that the simple presentation of the Christian

9   *African Weekly*, 20 April 1960, 12 October 1955, 17 and 24 February 1960; *Rhodesia Herald*, 22 and 24 February 1960.

10   For data on the Bible Society, see http://www.biblesociety.org.uk/about-bible-society/ history/our-history/; http://www.mundus.ac.uk/cgi-bin/search?coll_id=292&inst_id= 38&keyword=Asia, both accessed 28 April 2012.

scriptures was enough to prompt conversion. Religious change was, of course, more complicated than this; Bible societies needed translators, mission societies, colporteurs and evangelists to produce and disseminate the scriptures, enabling the written text to 'make "moves"' in the world and so to 'reshape' it. However, Christians believed that they read religious texts in 'transcendent mode', and some readers certainly made inspired connections to the scriptures to reimagine their circumstances (Green and Searle-Chatterjee 2008: 1–2, 8–9). Fired by religious imagination, Protestant revival spread along international networks of print and correspondence. The rapidity with which Pentecostalism increased across the globe in the decade following the Azusa Street revival of 1906 looked to many of its participants like fire from heaven. But its rapid dissemination had much to do with improvements in transport, new print technologies, and the growth of a worldwide postage system, which created an international Protestant public sphere. Radical Evangelicals in churches and mission stations across the globe had read with great interest the tracts, journals and correspondence recounting Wesleyan and Keswick Holiness teachings and describing the emergence of faith healing and dispensational millennialism, and so they were primed for Pentecostalism when it emerged. Accounts of the Welsh revival in 1904 had whetted their spiritual appetites (Maxwell 2006: 23–32), and the communications revolution at the end of the nineteenth century fostered a network of connections that was impressively polycentric. Thus news of Pentecostalism first came to Chile not via America but from India. A Methodist missionary at work in South America, May Hoover, received an account of religious revival at Mukti Mission, Pune, written by a former Bible school classmate, Minnie Abrams. Abrams had been a participant in the 1905 Indian revival and keen supporter of its leader, the Hindu convert to Christianity Pandita Ramabai. Abrams' experience of the revival inspired her to write *The Baptism of the Holy Ghost and Fire* (1905) and to disseminate news of Pentecostalism as widely as possible from her Indian base (Cleary and Sepulveda 1997: 99–100).

As well as stimulating a plurality of interconnected local, ethnic and national Christianities, print was also a force for homogenisation and uniformity. Texts were one of a number of tools used to tighten religious boundaries in the late nineteenth century. The historic Protestant churches of Europe and North America, and throughout the British Empire, convened a series of congresses and doctrinal commissions that turned Anglican, Baptist and Congregational traditions into worldwide churches with more uniform organisation and doctrine for the first time. For example, a series of conferences in Lambeth Palace after 1867, a common training system and a new edition of the Book of Common Prayer created a sharper, more formal Anglican identity out of a previously loose collection of American, colonial and British bishoprics. The process was clearest, however, within the Roman Catholic Church. As the Vatican lost temporal power to the Risorgimento (the nineteenth-century movement for Italian unification), so it increased its spiritual authority, issuing the Syllabus of Errors in 1864 and the doctrine of papal infallibility in 1870. The papal journal, *L'Osservatore Romano*, founded in 1861, became the authoritative voice of the Catholic Church. The training of novices was centralised in Rome and there was tighter control of Catholic universities. Ultramontanist priests were sent out to Brazil and Argentina to fight a combination of Protestantism, Positivism and secularism (Bayly 2004: 338, 347, 357).

In the contemporary world, it has become a commonplace to assert that digital media creates post-modern Christians whose identities comprise a combination of different religious traditions. But, as Thomas Kirsch's research demonstrates, movements such as Jehovah's Witnesses can still police boundaries through the strategic, regular and intensive dissemination of their print publications. The organisation's twice-monthly publications, *Watch Tower* and *Awake*, have a circulation of 50 million copies, raising awareness of global interconnectedness by regularly addressing issues from around the world. As Kirsch observes, these transnational networks of dissemination represent an important modification of Benedict Anderson's notion of print nationalism (B. Anderson 2006; Kirsch 2008: 156–9). In a similar manner, a transnational Pentecostal movement such as the Zimbabwe Assemblies of God Africa (ZAOGA) maintains its identity by means of the regular, co-ordinated public recitation of its canonical history and a carefully constructed personality cult surrounding its founder and leader, Ezekiel Guti.[11] The remarkable growth of Pentecostal movements such as ZAOGA depends in part on their capacity to tighten boundaries around their memberships while at the same time extending connections into the wider world in order to ensure their own reproduction and expansion (Maxwell 2006). The religious communities established by these movements transcend national boundaries, but print has also helped create a broader consciousness, a global Christianity that traverses denominations. Indeed, it is in this context that World Christianity has most resonance, when the global is treated as 'a native or actor's category – a concept that belongs to the archive and is itself an object of investigation, rather than as a meta-analytical category belonging to the investigator' (Moyn and Sartori 2013: 17). Such an approach to the history of spatial imagination can examine

---

11   *The Sacred Book of* ZAOGA *Forward in Faith to the Leaders and the Saints. Parts 1 and 2* (Harare: Waterfalls, 1989 and 1995) discussed in Maxwell (2001).

mapping, world pictures and representations, the history of cosmopolitanisms, or debates that address so-called global issues.

A prime example of the globalising potential of religious publications is the journal *The Missionary Review*, founded in 1878 by the Reverend Royal Wilder as a ' "watch-tower" [over] ... [t]he whole foreign work of the churches'. In 1888, at a moment when the concept of world religions was taking root, it evolved into *The Missionary Review of the World* under the editorship of the missionary statesman A. T. Pierson.[12] Pierson was renowned for his pre-millennial teachings, exemplified by his watchword 'the evangelization of the world in this generation'. Containing statistical charts, maps, country surveys, cameos of leading missionary thinkers and a back-page feature entitled 'World Wide Outlook', *The Review* did much to stimulate a Protestant global consciousness.[13] The periodical *World Dominion: A Quarterly Review of Christian Progress*, edited by Thomas Cochrane, had a similar brief. Its publishing house, World Dominion Press, another Evangelical organisation like *The Review*, also produced extensive book series surveying the state of the church in regions and countries as diverse as Amazonia, Burma, Korea, East Africa, Manchuria, the Middle East, Nyasaland, Nigeria and the Pacific Islands.[14] The worldwide church was also given visual and auditory representation through missionary fairs, the most spectacular of which was the Protestant World Fair organised by American Methodists in Columbus, Ohio in 1919. Comprising over 16,000 exhibits from thirty-seven different countries, including 500 living natives inhabiting reconstructions of their homes, the event drew over 1 million visitors (C. J. Anderson 2006: 196).

Finally, the notion of World Christianity was much advanced by periodic international conferences that took stock of the missionary enterprise. The most prominent of these was the 1910 World Missionary Conference in Edinburgh and its successor in Tambaram, India, in 1938. But even international meetings with a regional focus such as the conferences in High Leigh, England (1924) or Le Zoute, Belgium (1926) drew missionary statesmen and church leaders from across the globe, building a sense of global communion.[15] The follow-on journal of the Edinburgh conference, *International Review of Mission* (1912

---

12   On the origins of so-called 'world religions', see Masuzawa (2005) and Clark and Ledger-
      Lomas (2012: 37–8).
13   *The Missionary Review of the World*. New York NY: Funk and Wagnalls Co.
14   World Dominion Press, London, New York and Toronto, taken from Tucker (1933).
15   Among those who attended the High Leigh conference were H. Anet, Max Yergan, Edwin
      Smith, Diedrich Westermann, Lord Lugard, J. H. Oldham, J. K. Aggrey and R. Baëta. Con-
      ference of British Missionary Societies, file 253, 'Africa Education', High Leigh Conference,
      September 1924, School of Oriental and African Studies.

to the present), became the venue for erudite articles by diplomats, dignitaries and missionaries on politics, international relations and global trends. It is an often overlooked fact that before the consolidation of the university disciplines and the rise of specialist commentators, missionaries did much to stimulate a planetary consciousness on issues of human rights and social justice.

The aspiration to be part of something bigger, a global Christian communion, has never been restricted to the cosmopolitan Christian elites who strode the stages of international ecumenical bodies and conventions. The same desire led Catholics living in the sixteenth-century Kingdom of Kongo to reach out to Rome in a web of correspondence and a commitment to place their children in European holy orders. In contemporary East Africa, that same spirit is manifested in attempts by Catholics to resist top-down programmes of inculturation. Groups of independent Catholics such as those in the Legio Maria have joined together under African popes to retain the Latin mass and iconography, which took root in an earlier era of popular Catholicism and were viewed as both efficacious and representative of a worldwide Catholicism. For these Christians, post-Vatican II attempts at inculturation are not interpreted as indigenisation but marginalisation. The same longing to be part of something that counts draws millions of young Africans, disillusioned with fading nation-states, to join city mega-churches and claim connection to a global born-again movement. As one young female Zambian pastor announced at a Harare-based meeting of the Zimbabwe Assemblies of God: 'It was the Devil who gave Africans a Third World mentality. But God did not create a Third World person, only a First World people.'[16] Aspirations to global Christian consciousness are important because they transcend the dualisms between the West and the rest, and metropole and colony. They remind us that Christians of all hues have co-operated to fashion shared identities and institutions.

However, while Christians across the world may have a sense of a universal church, Christianity has never been global in a geographical sense because there have always been barriers preventing its spread. In the modern era, both empire and nationalism have produced effective obstacles. Although British missionaries certainly benefited from the security and ease of movement that empire provided, they were nevertheless deeply ambivalent about it. They embraced empire because it appeared to be part of God's providential plan for the spread of the gospel, but the practical workings of imperial policies often horrified them (Stanley 1990). Indirect rule empowered Muslim lead-

16   David Maxwell, fieldwork notes, 3 October 1995.

ers, and in its coherent norms and conventions colonial officials found Islam a congenial religion to work with, not too dissimilar from Christianity (Motadel 2014). British officials helped lay the groundwork that made possible the mass movement of Muslims for the Hajj (Slight 2014). And prominent commentators identified the British Crown as the world's 'greatest Mohammedan power', gathering more Muslim subjects than any independent Muslim state (Devji 2014: 258–60). In a similar vein the British Empire also helped consolidate Hinduism in India, where mission Christianity fared much better outside the Hindu Raj. Since independence in 1947 India's Christians have struggled for recognition as their nation has become ever more closely defined in Hindu terms (Frykenberg 2008). The double standards that often accompanied Western imperialism did much to stimulate local nationalisms that proved resistant to Christian advance. In China, between the West's betrayal in the Versailles Treaty (1919) following the First World War and the country's recent liberalisation, its Christians have borne the slur of inauthenticity in Confucian and Maoist thought.

Although in the West it is certainly possible to discern the Christian roots of nationalism, it has stymied the advance of the church as much as facilitate it. Late nineteenth-century Ultramontanist Catholics suffered from accusations of disloyalty in European nation-states (Van der Veer 2013: 660). Nationalism, of course, flourishes today, partly in response to globalisation, but it limits any potential impact Southern missionaries might have on the West. Religious ideas and images can flow into the West from the South along with the odd football player, but, as David Armitage reminds us, 'the smoothly integrated globe predicted by Fukuyama has broken apart into a Eurozone South and North, the Asian trading enclaves and the socialist states in Latin America ... A new age of geopolitical exclusion and boundary making as rampant as the 19th century spread of national governments is upon us' (Armitage 2013: 33). In his enormously influential *Global Shadows*, James Ferguson argues that the notion of a 'planetary network of connected points', which is often evoked in the neoliberal era, does not pertain to Africa, which is often marginalised or completely excluded from such arrangements. Instead, 'Africa's participation in "globalization" ... has certainly not been a matter simply of "joining the world economy"; perversely, it has instead been a matter of highly selective and spatially encapsulated forms of global connection combined with widespread disconnection and exclusion' (Ferguson 2006: 14). While globalisation has heightened awareness of the range of goods and services available to the global rich, increasing levels of poverty and the failure of development limit the chances Africans have of attaining such lifestyles. They are excluded from the economic and institutional conditions that they consider to be modern. Thus, in Africa, the inspiring notion of being a member of the worldwide church is undermined by what Ferguson famously describes as a widespread sense of 'abjection' (Ferguson 1999).

Conclusion

While there exists a rich body of scholarship on the local appropriations of Christianity, work on religious transnationalism is in need of development. For all of its insights, work on transnational religion remains too concerned with movements in which Britain or America is the source of the missionary impulse, reinstating old occidental scholarly biases. South–South religious exchanges remain underexamined and few scholars have studied how Christian thought and practice from Africa, Asia and Latin America have transformed Christianity in the West. Moreover, there is a dearth of comparative studies identifying patterns of seizure and inculturation across the globe. In part, the proliferation of local studies with little attempt at comparison explains the rise of a new anthropology of Christianity. Anthropologists of Christianity are particularly interested in what social and cultural historians describe as mentalities, in 'exploring what it means to be a Christian for different groups and peoples' across the globe (Hovland 2013: 231). What little comparative work has been done by world historians has focused on the processes, situations and outcomes of cultural encounters. In a path-breaking essay for *Journal of World History*, David Lindenfeld usefully compares missionary encounters with West Africa and China. He highlights the presence of large-scale, sometimes violent Chinese resistance to Christianity and the inability of missionaries to dismantle the social economy of healing in Chinese traditional medicine, and missionary failure to come to terms with Chinese nationalism. The essay also shows how the massive scale of conversion in Africa relative to the number of Western missionaries was such that indigenous peoples had much latitude to inculturate Christianity (Lindenfeld 2005: 342–9). Peter Burke's enduring interest in knowledge formation and cultural encounter leads him to draw a simple but effective contrast between the techniques of early modern Catholic missionaries in China and their associates in Latin America in his book *Cultural Hybridity*. In sixteenth-century China, the missionaries were a small minority, and thus the situation favoured the 'lenders' and the Jesuits in China were forced to listen to their hosts and make cultural adaptions. In Latin America, missionaries were able to use force to impose Christianity upon the Indians (Burke 2009: 67–8). The potential for these sorts of cross-cultural comparison is enormous, and so is the opportunity for enlightenment.

It is, of course, impossible to capture the great complexity of World Christianity in one essay, but the primary goal of this chapter has been to advance ideas about the conceptualisation and methodology of studying World Christianity. By paying greater attention to issues of connection, comparison and consciousness, and processes of homogenisation and localisation, scholars should be better equipped to analyse the variety and location of Christian religion across the world and to examine its ability to travel, cross boundaries and create communities of an ephemeral or lasting quality.

References

Abrams, M. (1905) *The Baptism of the Holy Ghost and Fire.* 2nd edition. Kedgaon: Mukti Mission Press.

Adogame, A. (2013) *The African Christian Diaspora: New Currents and Emerging Trends in World Christianity.* London: Bloomsbury.

Adogame, A. and S. Shankar (2012) *Religion on the Move! New Dynamics of Religious Expansion in a Globalizing World.* Leiden: E. J. Brill.

Anderson, B. (2006) *Imagined Communities: Reflections on the Origin and Spread of Nationalism.* 2nd revised edition. London: Verso.

Anderson, C. J. (2006) 'The World is *our* Parish: Remembering the 1919 Protestant Missionary Fair', *International Bulletin of Missionary Research* 30 (4): 196–200.

Armitage, D. (2007) *The Declaration of Independence: A Global History.* Harvard MA: Harvard University Press.

Armitage, D. (2013) 'The International Turn in Intellectual History', *The Global Journal* 22 (January): 22–5.

Barker, J. (2005) 'Where the Missionary Frontier Ran Ahead of Empire' in N. Etherington (ed.), *The Oxford History of the British Empire Companion Series: Missions and Empire.* Oxford: Oxford University Press.

Bayly, C. (2004) *The Birth of the Modern World 1870–1914.* Oxford: Blackwell.

Bayly, C., S. Beckert, M. Connelly, I. Hofmeyr, W. Kozol and P. Seed (2006) 'AHR Conversation: On Transnational History', *American Historical Review* 111: 1440–64.

Bellich, J. (2009) *Replenishing the Earth: The Settler Revolution and the Rise of the Anglo-World, 1783–1939.* Oxford: Oxford University Press.

Brock, P. (2005) 'New Christians as Evangelists' in N. Etherington (ed.), *The Oxford History of the British Empire Companion Series: Missions and Empire.* Oxford: Oxford University Press.

Brock, P., N. Etherington, G. Griffiths and J. Van Gent (2015) *Indigenous Evangelists and the Question of Authority.* Leiden: E. J. Brill.

Burke, P. (2009) *Cultural Hybridity.* Cambridge: Cambridge University Press.

Campbell, J. (1995) *Songs of Zion: The African Methodist Episcopal Church in the United States and South Africa*. Oxford: Oxford University Press.

Clark, C. and M. Ledger-Lomas (2012) 'The Protestant International' in A. Green and V. Viaene (eds), *Religious Internationals in the Modern World: Globalization and Faith Communities since 1750*. New York NY: Palgrave Macmillan.

Cleary, E. and J. Sepulveda (1997) 'Chilean Pentecostalism: Coming of Age' in E. Cleary and H. Stewart-Gambino (eds), *Power, Politics and Pentecostals in Latin America*. Boulder CO: Westview Press.

Clossey, L. (2011) *Salvation and Globalization in the Early Jesuit Missions*. Cambridge: Cambridge University Press.

Cooper, F. (2001) 'What is the Concept of Globalization Good For? An African Historian's Perspective', *African Affairs* 100 (399): 189–213.

Cooper, F. (2013) 'How Global Do We Want our Intellectual History to Be?' in S. Moyn and A. Sartori (eds), *Global Intellectual History*. New York NY: Columbia University Press.

Daughrity, D. B. (2011) 'Christianity Is Moving from North to South: So What about the East?', *International Bulletin of Missionary Research* 33 (1): 18–22.

Devji, F. (2014) 'Islam and British Imperial Thought' in D. Motadel (ed.), *Islam and the European Empires*. Oxford: Oxford University Press.

Ditchfield, S. (2007) 'Of Missions and Models: The Jesuit Enterprise (1540–1773). Reassessed in Recent Literature', *Catholic Historical Review* 93 (2): 325–43.

Ferguson, J. (1999) *Expectations of Modernity: Myths and Meanings of Urban Life on the Zambian Copper Belt*. Berkeley CA: University of California Press.

Ferguson, J. (2006) *Global Shadows: Africa in the Neo-liberal World Order*. Durham NC: Duke University Press.

Freston, P. (2010) 'Reverse Mission: A Discourse in Search of a Reality', *PentecoStudies* 9 (2): 153–74.

Frykenberg, R. (2008) *Christianity in India: From Beginnings to the Present*. Oxford: Oxford University Press.

Giddens, A. (1990) *The Consequences of Modernity*. Stanford CA: Stanford University Press.

Gray, R. (1990) *Black Christians and White Missionaries*. New Haven CT: Yale University Press.

Green, A. and V. Viaene (2012) 'Introduction: Rethinking Religion and Globalization' in A. Green and V. Viaene (eds), *Religious Internationals in the Modern World: Globalization and Faith Communities since 1750*. New York NY: Palgrave Macmillan.

Green, N. and M. Searle-Chatterjee (2008) 'Religion, Language, and Power: An Introductory Essay' in N. Green and M. Searle-Chatterjee (eds), *Religion, Language, and Power*. London: Routledge.

Hastings, A. (1994) *The Church in Africa 1450–1950*. Oxford: Clarendon Press.

Hearn, J. (2002) 'The "Invisible NGO": US Evangelical Missions in Kenya', *Journal of Religion in Africa* 32 (1): 32–60.

Hefner, R. (2012) 'Foreword' in C. Farhadian (ed.), *Introducing World Christianity*. Oxford: Blackwell.

Hilton, B. (2010) '"1807 and All That": Why Britain Outlawed her Slave Trade' in D. Peterson (ed.), *Abolitionism and Imperialism in Britain, Africa and the Atlantic*. Athens OH: Ohio University Press.

Hofmeyr, I. (1994) *We Spend our Years as a Tale that is Told: Oral Historical Narrative in a South African Chiefdom*. Portsmouth NH: Heinemann.

Hofmeyr, I. (2004) *The Portable Bunyan: A Transnational History of the Pilgrim's Progress*. Princeton NJ: Princeton University Press.

Hofmeyr, I. and M. Williams (2011) 'South Africa–India: Historical Connections, Cultural Circulations and Socio-political Comparisons' in I. Hofmeyr and M. Williams (eds), *South Africa and India: Shaping the Global South*. Johannesburg: University of Witwatersrand.

Hovland, I. (2013) *Mission Station Christianity: Norwegian Missionaries in Colonial Natal and Zululand, 1850–1990*. Leiden: E. J. Brill.

Jenkins, P. (2002) *The Next Christendom: The Coming of Global Christianity*. New York NY: Oxford University Press.

Kennedy, P. (2002) *Black Livingstone: A True Tale of Adventure in the Nineteenth-century Congo*. New York NY: Penguin.

Kirsch, T. (2008) *Spirits and Letters: Reading, Writing and Charisma in African Christianity*. New York NY: Berghahn Books.

Lindenfeld, D. (2005) 'Indigenous Encounters with Christian Missions in China and West Africa, 1800–1920: A Comparative Study', *Journal of World History* 16 (3): 327–69.

Lloyd, A. (1923) *Apolo of the Pygmy Forest*. London: CMS.

Lonsdale, J. (2002) 'Kikuyu Christianities: A History of Intimate Diversity' in D. Maxwell with I. Lawrie (eds), *Christianity and the African Imagination: Essays in Honour of Adrian Hastings*. Leiden: E. J. Brill.

Marcel, N. (1968) *The Life of Shalumbo (Eshiba dya Yamena): The Beginnings of the E.P.C.O. among the Basongye*. Translated by E. Rowlands. Kipushya: Zaire.

Martin, D. (1996) *Forbidden Revolutions: Pentecostalism in Latin America and Catholicism in Eastern Europe*. London: SPCK.

Masuzawa, T. (2005) *The Invention of World Religions: Or, How European Universalism Was Preserved in the Language of Pluralism*. Chicago IL: University of Chicago Press.

Maxwell, D. (2001) '"Sacred History, Social History": Traditions and Texts in the Making of a Southern African Transnational Religious Movement', *Comparative Studies in Society and History* 43 (3): 502–24.

Maxwell, D. (2006) *African Gifts of the Spirit: Pentecostalism and the Rise of a Zimbab-wean Transnational Religious Movement*. Oxford: James Currey.

Maxwell, D. (2013a) 'Christianity' in J. Parker and R. Reid (eds), *The Oxford Handbook of Modern African History*. Oxford: Oxford University Press.

Maxwell, D. (2013b) 'Freed Slaves, Missionaries and Respectability: The Expansion of the Christian Frontier from Angola to Belgian Congo', *Journal of African History* 54 (1): 79–102.

Motadel, D. (2014) 'Introduction' in D. Motadel (ed.), *Islam and the European Empires*. Oxford: Oxford University Press.

Moyn, S. and A. Sartori (2013) 'Approaches to Global Intellectual History' in S. Moyn and A. Sartori (eds), *Global Intellectual History*. New York NY: Columbia University Press.

Nielssen, H., I. M. Okkenhaug and K. Hestad Skeie (eds) (2011) *Protestant Missions and Local Encounters in the Nineteenth and Twentieth Centuries*. Leiden: E. J. Brill.

Noll, M. (2009) *The New Shape of World Christianity: How American Experience Reflects the Global Faith*. Madison WI: IVP.

Peel, J. D. Y. (2009) 'Postsocialism, Postcolonialism, Pentecostalism' in M. Pelkmans (ed.), *Conversion after Socialism: Disruptions, Modernisms and Technologies of Faith in the Former Soviet Union*. Oxford: Oxford University Press.

Poon, M. (2011) 'Re-imagining World Christianity for the Church Universal: Andrew Walls and his legacy', *Fulcrum*, 4 April, http://www.fulcrum-anglican.org.uk/ articles/re-imagining-world-christianity-andrew-walls-and-his-legacy, accessed 23 May 2017.

Pratt, M. L. (1992) *Imperial Eyes: Travel Writing and Transculturation*. London: Rout-ledge.

Preston, A. (2012) *Sword of the Spirit, Shield of Faith: Religion in War and American Diplomacy*. New York NY: Random House.

Pritchett, J. (2011) 'Christian Mission Stations in South-Central Africa: Eddies in the Flow of Global Culture' in H. Englund (ed.), *Christianity and Public Culture in Africa*. Athens OH: Ohio University Press.

Ranger, T. O. (1987) 'Taking Hold of the Land: Holy Places and Pilgrimages in Twentieth Century Zimbabwe', *Past and Present* 117: 158–94.

Ranger, T. O. (1989) 'Missionaries, Migrants and Manyika: The Invention of Ethnicity in Zimbabwe' in L. Vail (ed.), *The Creation of Tribalism in Southern Africa*. London: James Currey.

Ranger, T. O. (2002) 'Taking on the Missionary's Task: African Spirituality and the Missionary Churches of Manicaland in the 1930s' in D. Maxwell with I. Lawrie (eds), *Christianity and the African Imagination: Essays in Honour of Adrian Hastings*. Leiden: E. J. Brill.

Robeck, M. (2006) *The Azusa Street Mission and Revival: The Birth of the Global Pente-costal Movement*. Nashville TN: Thomas Nelson.

Robert, D. (2014) 'Forty Years of North American Missiology: A Brief Review', *International Bulletin of Missionary Research* 38 (1): 3–8.

Salter, J. (1936) *Abraham: Our First Convert*. London: Victory Press.

Saunier, P.-Y. (2013) *Transnational History*. New York NY: Palgrave Macmillan.

Sivasundaram, S. (2010) 'A Global History of Science and Religion' in T. Dixon et al. (eds), *Science and Religion: New Historical Perspectives*. Cambridge: Cambridge University Press.

Slight, J. (2014) 'Islam and British Imperial Thought' in D. Motadel (ed.), *Islam and the European Empires*. Oxford: Oxford University Press.

Stanley, B. (1990) *The Bible and the Flag: Protestant Missions and British Imperialism in the Nineteenth and Twentieth Centuries*. Leicester: Apollos.

Thompson, T. J. (2002) 'Light on the Dark Continent: The Photography of Alice Seely Harris and the Congo Atrocities of the Early Twentieth Century', *International Bulletin of Missionary Research* 26 (4): 146–9.

Thorne, S. (1999) *Congregational Missions and the Making of an Imperial Culture in Nineteenth Century England*. Stanford CA: Stanford University Press.

Thornton, J. (1998) *The Kongolese Saint Anthony: Dona Beatriz Kimpa Vita and the Antonian Movement, 1684–1706*. Cambridge: Cambridge University Press.

Tucker, J. (1933) *Angola: The Land of the Blacksmith Prince*. London: World Dominion Press.

Van der Veer, P. (2013) 'Nationalism and Religion' in J. Breuilly (ed.), *The Oxford Handbook of the History of Nationalism*. Oxford: Oxford University Press.

Weidenmuller, S. (2014) 'Henry Martyn and the Circulation of Christian Scriptures in the Persianate World, c.1810–1914'. MPhil thesis, University of Cambridge.

Wild-Wood, E. (2008) *Migration and Christian Identity in Congo (DRC)*. Leiden: E. J. Brill.

CHAPTER 2

British Missions and the Making of a Brazilian Protestant Public

Pedro Feitoza

As stated in the introduction to this volume, the study of Christianity worldwide requires attention both to the development of localised and culturally specific forms of religiosity and to how these forms are connected to each other on a worldwide scale. The international dissemination of Christianity in the modern world can thus be seen as a globalising force, as migration, pilgrimage and missionary work have constantly pushed religious beliefs and actors beyond territorial and ethnic borders, connecting people and organisations in different parts of the globe. Abigail Green and Vincent Viaene, considering the scale and antiquity of these processes, coined the term 'religious international' to describe the process of globalisation and politicisation of religious identities, which they define as 'a cluster of voluntary transnational organisations and representations crystallizing around international issues, in which both "ordinary" believers and religious specialists could serve as protagonists' (Green and Viaene 2012: 1). Whereas scholars have stressed the vitality and depth of the renewal of Catholic and Evangelical Christianities in Latin America since the post-Second World War period (Hartch 2014), these processes of religious globalisation have deep roots in the nineteenth century, when waves of Christian revivals and religious mobilisation, as well as mass migration, imperialism and developments in communication and transport, invigorated missionary movements.

Missionary literacy and religious print played a relevant role in the internationalisation of Protestantism in the nineteenth and twentieth centuries by deepening and thickening connections between Christian churches and organisations. The transnational circulation of religious tracts, books and Bibles sharpened religious identities, asserted institutional authority, and created maritime markets of faith, doctrine and information (Bayly 2004: 333; Hofmeyr 2013: 33). In twentieth-century sub-Saharan Pentecostal denominations, where literacy, reading and writing were embedded in the daily practices and religious services of churches, religious print reaffirmed the converts' born-again identities against rival faiths and traditions, traced lineages of prophetic authority, and often affirmed the universal credentials of these Christian movements (Cabrita 2014; Kirsch 2008; Maxwell 2001).

© KONINKLIJKE BRILL NV, LEIDEN, 2017 | DOI: 10.1163/9789004355026_004

In keeping with these notions of transnationalism and missionary literacy, this chapter shows how the circulation of Bibles and Evangelical texts led by British missionary societies in nineteenth-century Brazil provided an emergent reading public with Christian literature and, at the same time, connected Protestant missionaries in Brazil with their counterparts in the Lusophone Atlantic world. Two London-based non-sectarian Evangelical organisations that maintained close connections with missionaries and evangelists in Brazil will be analysed: the British and Foreign Bible Society (BFBS) and the Religious Tract Society (RTS). Whereas the body of literature on the transnational circulation of books and periodicals is now well developed, Bible societies remain understudied, despite their cultural relevance. As will be shown in the course of this chapter, books, people and ideas moved in different directions throughout the transnational networks established by these societies in the Luso-Atlantic world. Attention will be paid to the distribution channels of books, encounters with Catholicism, resistance to the circulation of texts, the impact of these encounters on BFBS and RTS policies in Brazil, Britain and Portugal, and the details of the transatlantic flows of Protestant literature.

Filling the Land with Bibles: The British and Foreign Bible Society in Brazil

South America was permanently included in the domains of the BFBS in the mid-1850s, following the momentary pacification of post-independence conflicts in different countries of the continent (Bakewell 1997: 409–10). In the first half of the nineteenth century, agents and colporteurs of the BFBS worked in different parts of the Caribbean as well as South and Central America, circulating Protestant Bibles and promoting basic education, the most famous case being that of James Thomson (Dove 2016: 289). Although these early agents did not organise Evangelical communities that lasted long after their departure, they linked evangelisation with literacy. Initially, in 1855, the Society appointed one agent based in Cartagena, Colombia to oversee the work of Bible selling in Spanish-speaking countries. In the following year, the BFBS appointed another agent based in Rio de Janeiro to co-ordinate its work in Brazil.[1] However, due to financial problems and the scarcity of sales in the first

---

1   *The Fifty-Second Report of the British & Foreign Bible Society; M.DCCC.LVI. with an Appendix and a List of Subscribers and Benefactors* (London, 1856), pp. cxci, cxcii (henceforth referred to as BFBS Annual Report (year)). BFBS Annual Report (1857), pp. ccxxix, ccxxx.

years of work, the BFBS decided to reorganise its South American personnel in 1859 by placing one agent in Lima, Peru, and other in Buenos Aires, Argentina. No agent was left in Brazil and most transactions with the country after 1860 occurred intermittently through requests made by Anglican clergymen and colporteurs.[2] This situation changed in 1865 when the Episcopal Scottish missionary Richard Holden was appointed as superintendent of the Society in the Brazilian Empire and undertook the responsibility of co-ordinating the group of colporteurs, administering the depots and corresponding with the BFBS in England.[3]

By the time of Holden's nomination, the BFBS had been operating at a global level for over sixty years, connecting the British Isles to Asia, Africa and the Americas. The Society translated, printed, revised and circulated one single book – the Bible – or portions of the Bible, such as Testaments, the Gospels and the Book of Psalms separately. Due to its non-sectarian character, all prefaces, explanatory notes or interpretations of biblical texts were strictly forbidden in all versions printed by the Society. This was known as the 'fundamental principle', but it did not mean that the BFBS was immune to theological and denominational conflicts (Howsam 1991: 6–7). In 1825, after a bitter reaction from English Puritans and Scottish Presbyterians against the inclusion of Apocryphal books in the BFBS scriptures, all deuterocanonical texts were excluded from the Society's versions (ibid.: 13–15).

Founded in London in 1804 under the spirit of early nineteenth-century evangelicalism, the BFBS acted simultaneously as a publisher, a Christian organisation and a business (Sharkey 2011: 440–1). As a publisher, the Society carried out a wide-ranging process of printing, binding and circulation of books. As a Christian institution, the Society's founders believed that people should have access to the Bible in their own language and that its simple and unaided reading could lead to individual conversions. As a business, the BFBS's main objective was not to accumulate profit, but to subsidise the costly work of translation, publication and dissemination of scriptures. Throughout the nineteenth century, the BFBS acquired a complex organisational structure involving auxiliary societies at home that collected subscriptions from ordinary Christians and supported the Society financially; the central body of committees and subcommittees in London; and its work overseas, carried out by agents and colporteurs (Howsam 2004: 24–37). The fact that Bibles should be sold, always at low prices, and not given away reinforced the Society's commercial character.

---

2   BFBS Annual Reports (1859), p. 278; (1861), p. 214.
3   BFBS Annual Report (1865), pp. 252, 253.

Under these guidelines, BFBS agents and superintendents were good business-men, besides being good Christians.

Such was the case of Richard Holden in Brazil, who had previously worked as a merchant in the province of Pará in the early 1850s. By the time of his appoint-ment as BFBS superintendent, Holden was already familiar to some figures in religious and literary circles in Brazil, especially after his engagement in bitter religious debates in liberal periodicals in Pará and his defence of the circula-tion of Protestant Bibles in 1862 (Vieira 1980: Chapters 8 and 9). The insertion of British and American Protestant missions in Brazil and the establishment of the BFBS in Rio de Janeiro coincided with a period of reform and reorganisa-tion of the Catholic Church. Post-independence imperial laws subjected the Catholic Church in Brazil to the patronage of the state: the empire, not the church, was constitutionally entitled to appoint bishops and collect tithes, and the provincial assemblies, not the ecclesiastical authorities, had the right to create new parishes or divide the existing ones. These policies contributed to weaken Catholic bureaucracy and block the church's connections with Rome until the overthrow of the Brazilian Empire in 1889. These factors motivated the rise of a generation of Ultramontane priests and bishops, who, from the 1860s onwards, began to question the legitimacy of state patronage and denounce the effects of secularism, Positivism and Protestantism (Boehrer 1969; Neves 2009).

During his period as superintendent in Rio de Janeiro (1865–72), Richard Holden laid the groundwork for the BFBS transaction in Brazil. Colporteurs were central figures in his strategy of book selling; they worked in different provinces of the country disseminating scriptures, and were obliged to send him detailed information of their activities, including sales figures and reports of their travels.[4] Furthermore, Holden and his Brazilian and British contacts engaged in complicated work aimed at improving one specific version of the Portuguese Bible. Between Holden's retirement in 1872 and the end of the nine-teenth century, two other superintendents directed the BFBS's work in Brazil: José Martin de Carvalho (1872–79) and the Reverend João Manoel Gonçalves dos Santos (1879–1901). Throughout this period, the strategy of Bible selling established in the late 1860s was maintained with few variations. Table 2.1 shows the circulation figures of Bibles in Brazil during this period.

---

4   The first report to mention such working methods is BFBS Annual Report (1866). All sub-sequent reports have a similar structure, including figures and narratives, although varying in the degree of detail.

TABLE 2.1   *Sales of the BFBS in Brazil, 1870–98*

Year	Total	Bibles	Testaments	Portions	Grants
1870	7,465	1,611	3,759	2,095	
1871[1]	2,483	787	1,573	123	
1872	4,484	1,329	3,013	142	
1873	5,734	1,349	3,519	866	
1874	10,240	1,286	3,287	5,667	
1875	10,664	1,420	3,428	5,506	310
1876[2]	6,662	533	2,260	3,043	
1877	5,854	904	2,313	2,467	170
1878	6,766	936	2,769	3,061	
1879	4,202	617	1,534	2,051	
1880	8,204	595	1,767	5,842	
1881	12,183	908	2,522	8,753	
1882	17,912	1,190	3,091	13,631	
1883	10,872	1,105	2,737	7,030	
1884	13,879	1,975	4,253	7,651	
1885	12,834	2,524	4,695	5,615	
1886	9,022	1,650	4,311	3,061	
1887	12,058	1,973	2,498	7,587	
1888	8,354	1,459	2,830	4,065	
1889	10,883	1,359	3,294	6,230	
1890	12,756	1,817	2,814	8,125	
1891	21,671	2,260	5,449	13,962	
1892	24,340	2,009	3,748	18,583	
1893	14,658	3,281	4,112	7,265	
1894	19,743	2,967	6,961	9,815	
1895	12,844	2,502	6,059	4,283	
1896	24,043	3,042	2,902	18,099	
1897	23,390	2,596	6,126	14,668	
1898	20,204	2,907	5,220	12,077	
Total	354,404	48,966	103,164	201,794	480

Notes:

1. Figures for the first six months of the year.

2. There is a total of 826 books – 814 from the depots in Rio de Janeiro and Rio Claro and 12 not listed at all – not differentiated in this report.

Compared with the overall field of literary production and consumption in nineteenth-century Brazil, the fact that the Brazilian staff of the BFBS managed to put into circulation more than 350,000 books in less than thirty years was a considerable achievement. The reading public of the country was minuscule in this period, when more than 80 per cent of the population was illiterate. Only very successful books were able to reach their second or third editions, and then only several decades after publication of the first thousand volumes, a fact that constantly disappointed writers and men of letters in Brazil (Guimarães 2004: 65–6, 72).

What distinguished the BFBS's work, however, was that their staff in Brazil prioritised the selling of books from door to door, also known as colportage. Colporteurs, the most active agents in this system, became so distinguished in the Brazilian landscape that the journalist João do Rio observed how, at the very beginning of the twentieth century, the 'vendors of Protestant Bibles' were the most astute and tireless booksellers in Rio de Janeiro, 'with the pockets of their old jackets filled with edifying brochures' (Rio 1997 [1908]: 137–8). Their work was motivated by the Evangelical ideal that the scriptures possessed extraordinary power and authority. Texts, in these missionary theories of language, operated as 'noiseless messengers', non-human agents that could penetrate regions where missionaries themselves could not go (Hofmeyr 2004; 2005). These ideals, which attributed extraordinary textual agency to the Bible, also circulated across the missionary movement in the Lusophone world. A pamphlet printed in Lisbon and sold on both sides of the Atlantic entitled *Eu Não Comprehendo a Biblia* (*I Do Not Understand the Bible*) depicted the Bible as a godly book that used a 'heavenly language' to describe unintelligible matters, such as the heaven or the future. Only another inhabitant of heaven, the Holy Spirit, could help readers understand its meanings.[5]

The BFBS staff in Brazil regarded the Bible as a 'heavenly agent' in their missionary work, even when signs of conversion did not appear and churches did not grow. Comparing the state of affairs in Brazil at the time with the selling of Bibles, Richard Holden stated that, although he could not say that the Divine Truth was making visible progress in the country, 'yet it may be affirmed that some progress is perceptible to the eye of faith; and this, small as it may be, is the germ and earnest of something more commensurate'.[6] In 1891, the Reverend João dos Santos wrote in a very pessimistic report that, although the progress of Protestantism was still very slow, 'the seed of God's Word is being

---

5 *Eu Não Comprehendo a Biblia*. Lisbon: Typ. De Vicente da Silva & Co., 1900, pp. 4, 5.
6 BFBS Annual Report (1871), p. 310.

buried to rise again in the proper season. We see some of the fruits, but our duty is not to stop but to go forward, waiting for the time when God shall give the harvest.'[7] The fact that the hard and costly work of Bible selling in Brazil did not produce commensurate processes of religious change was a source of much disappointment for the BFBS staff. Still, narratives of conversions prompted by the unaided individual study of the scriptures nurtured the image of otherworldliness attributed to religious texts, relieved the staff's frustration, and fostered their faith in a 'future harvest' of believers.[8]

However, neither Protestant missionaries nor believers attributed to the Bible or other religious texts, as material objects, any agency or authority. As Thomas Kirsch noted in his study of missionary literacy in Southern Zambia, Pentecostal converts handled the Bible carelessly and, in periods of paper shortages, used the pages of religious tracts and booklets as wrapping paper and notebooks, showing how 'Christianity as a book religion can be quite a mundane affair' (Kirsch 2008: 85–8). In the case of nineteenth-century Brazil, some colporteurs' narratives described how the torn pages of Bibles and Evangelical periodicals initiated processes of religious change; the most illustrative cases were those of the Portuguese pastor José de Carvalho Braga, whose conversion process started after he read pages of the Bible used as packing paper, and of Joaquim Fernandes de Lima, the lay leader of the Presbyterian Church of Ubatuba, who subscribed to the Protestant periodical *Imprensa Evangelica* after receiving a number of religious books wrapped in pages of the journal (Frase 1975: 256; Glass 1914: 107).[9] According to these missionary narratives, it was the individual and reflexive act of reading that could bring about religious change; religious texts were not endowed with any inherent spiritual authority.

Furthermore, not only was the Bible associated with individual conversions, it was also depicted as an instrument for the moralisation and civilisation of nations. In a letter sent to the governor of Córdoba, Argentina in 1871, Holden referred to the Bible as the book that had exerted the most profound and widespread influence on the progress of humanity, nourishing the nation with vigorous moral principles such as civility and liberty.[10] Similarly, in 1889, João dos Santos informed the Society about the latest events in Brazil, specifically the

---

7   BFBS Annual Report (1891), p. 351.

8   This can be seen in BFBS Annual Reports (1870), p. 267; (1885), p. 251.

9   *Primeiro Livro de Actas da Igreja de Ubatuba*, 1880, Arquivo Histórico Presbiteriano, São Paulo.

10   BFBS, 'Copy of the Address to the Governor of Cordoba', BSA/DI/7 – 123 (Agents Book no. 123, South America).

abolition of slavery and the overthrow of the monarchy, affirming that these changes were signs of deeper transformations acting beyond the superficiality of politics. He related these events to the effects of the circulation of Bibles in Brazil, 'which concerns not only the individual, but the character, and therefore the destinies of nations'.[11] More than simply changing the readers' subjectivities, the Bible was advertised as a source of collective moralisation and civility. In this sense, its wide circulation would meet the demands of emerging Latin American nation-states.

Colportage, the selling of books from door to door, was the most common method of dissemination of scriptures employed by the BFBS in Brazil and elsewhere, and this determined the speed at which Bibles, books, pamphlets and periodicals circulated throughout the country. All scriptures published by the BFBS and shipped from either England or Portugal took on average two months to cross the Atlantic on steamships, and around two or three weeks to be released from the customs houses in the ports of Santos and Rio de Janeiro.[12] However, in many cases the journey of Bibles around the country could take longer than the lengthy Atlantic crossing. This was due to the enormous distances that separated the different regions of Brazil, the poor condition of the roads, the weakness of the mailing system, and the modes of travel adopted by colporteurs. In some cases, colporteurs travelled on horseback from Rio de Janeiro to the distant provinces of Bahia and Pernambuco.[13] In São Paulo, Southern American Presbyterian missionaries hired a colporteur who used a mule to carry the heavy load of books while he travelled on foot.[14] Others combined both methods, travelling on horseback themselves while they guided mules loaded with books (Glass 1914: 77).

Despite being a non-sectarian Evangelical organisation at home, most of the BFBS colporteurs and superintendents in Brazil were recruited from the ranks of the Congregational Fluminense Evangelical Church of Rio de Janeiro, whose pastor was the influential medical missionary Robert Kalley. Carvalho and Santos, superintendents of the Society in Brazil, were active members of the Fluminense Evangelical Church; the latter was appointed as Kalley's successor in 1876. Most of the colporteurs were also associated with that church, including Manoel Vianna, who was sent to the province of Pernambuco by the BFBS and acted as an evangelist for the Congregational church there, a fact

---

11   BFBS Annual Report (1890), p. 306.
12   BFBS, 'Rev. Lane to Mr Charles Finch, 30th of May 1876', BSA/D1/7 – 144 (Agents Book No. 144, South America).
13   BFBS Annual Report (1883), p. 225.
14   BFBS, 'E. Lane to the Society, 4th of June 1875', BSA/D1/7 – 144.

that caused a brief but stressful conflict of interests between the Brazilian staff of the BFBS and its committee in London.[15] Southern American Presbyterian missionaries also corresponded frequently with the BFBS, especially Edward Lane, founder of the International School of Campinas, who regularly requested Bibles and books for his school and for churches in São Paulo.[16] Few letters were exchanged with Northern American Presbyterians or German Lutherans. And no correspondence at all took place with Baptists or Methodists.

Most of the colporteurs acting in Brazil were men of modest training and from poor backgrounds. Robert Kalley described the Fluminense Evangelical Church as 'composed almost entirely of poor men, shoemakers, tailors and other of that class'.[17] José Carvalho wrote to the BFBS that only one of his colporteurs could send him detailed written reports of his activities; the others could barely write a report in Portuguese, and one of them, Manoel dos Anjos, could not write at all. He also stated that the ability to write was scarce among believers, showing that both the agents who circulated Evangelical literature and the publics who consumed it were overwhelmingly poor and semi-literate.[18]

Missionaries and evangelists employed various strategies to overcome these problems that permeated most of the Brazilian churches. Firstly, lay leaders usually read the Bible and other Christian texts aloud to their congregations in Sunday meetings and in family worship. Kalley regularly sent letters and sermons to the Congregational churches of Rio de Janeiro and Recife that were read before these communities during his absence. Similarly, a British colporteur called Frederick Glass affirmed that, in the countryside of Goiás, a man who was the only literate person in a village named Gameleira read the New Testament for his community in the evenings (Glass 1914: 70–1). Even illiterate people purchased religious literature. Samuel Elliot, another British colporteur, stated that on his journeys through the south of Brazil, illiteracy was an obstacle to the selling of scriptures, 'but generally there is one in each family who can read and the father is willing to buy one for him, especially if

15   Biblioteca Fernandes Braga – Igreja Evangélica Fluminense, Rio de Janeiro (BFB-IEF), 'R. R. Kalley to the Igreja Evangélica Pernambucana, Theresópolis, 25th February 1875. Correspondência Dr Kalley.' The BFBS goal was not to promote the evangelistic work itself, but to circulate Bibles. As Vianna acted as an evangelist of the Congregational Church in Pernambuco, increasing the expenses of the Society, both the Brazilian superintendent Carvalho and the Society's committee in London reacted against his modus operandi. Despite Kalley's defence of the colporteur, Vianna was removed from his post.
16   BFB-IEF Annual Reports (1873, 1876, 1878).
17   BFB-IEF, 'R. R. Kalley to unknown. Edinburgh, November 1881. Correspondência Dr Kalley.'
18   BFBS, 'J. Carvalho to Finch, Rio de Janeiro, 15th November 1875', BSA/D1/7 – 144.

he finds that his neighbour has bought one'.[19] Bibles, Christian literature and sermons were also read and heard in Protestant churches and houses. In this sense, these texts had reading publics and audiences simultaneously (Darnton 1991: 166–7).

Secondly, Bible societies and other Protestant institutions active in the nineteenth and twentieth centuries opened up possibilities of upward social mobility for believers. Some studies on Protestantism and Pentecostalism in Latin America have examined how the provision of formal education in mission schools and colleges as well as ascetic patterns of behaviour generated new economic cultures among Latin American Evangelicals, enabling them to accumulate (Brusco 1993; Martin 1990; Maspoli 2001). Similarly, the Brazilian branch of the BFBS offered opportunities for social mobility for its staff. When Richard Holden indicated José Carvalho as his successor for the superintendence of the BFBS, he wrote to the London committee that 'a little gradual social elevation will be desirable in order to strengthen the hands of discipline'.[20] Holden recommended that Carvalho's salary should be raised to 100,000 *réis* a month,[21] enough to include him in the limited group of primary electors in Brazil. Carvalho himself tried to negotiate with the Society the salaries of his colporteurs. In his first year as superintendent, he managed to increase the salary of Manoel dos Anjos, whom he described as a 'man of little instruction'.[22] In the following year he requested an increase on all colporteurs' salaries, arguing that, in contrast with other workers who did not have major personal expenses, colporteurs had to be clean and well dressed as they walked through the streets, 'in order not to be censured'.[23] According to Ronald Frase, the expansion of missionary societies and denominational institutions in Brazil, such as schools, publishing houses, churches and voluntary societies, generated vast and complex religious bureaucracies within which converts were able to participate and negotiate their salaries (Frase 1981: 184–5). Similarly, the bureaucracy created by the BFBS in Brazil served as a platform for the negotiation of salaries in the latter half of the nineteenth century.

---

19   BFBS, 'S. Elliot to the Committee, Brazil, 8th May 1875', BSA/D1/7 – 144.

20   BFBS, 'R. Holden to the Rev. Bergne. Homelands, 22nd of January 1872', BSA/D1/7 – 123.

21   BFBS, 'R. Holden to the Rev. Bergne. Homelands, 11th of January 1872', BSA/D1/7 – 123.

22   BFBS, 'Report on Bible Distribution in Brazil for the Year Ending 31st December 1872', BSA/D1/7 – 123.

23   BFBS, 'Report of Bible Distribution in Brazil for the Year Ending 31st December 1873', BSA/D1/7 – 144.

Resistance to the Circulation of Bibles and Christian Literature

As can be seen in Table 2.1, colporteurs' sales in Brazil did not follow a steady or continuous pattern, but varied due to several reasons. In some cases, the lack of internal organisation resulted in a reduction of sales. The work of colporteurs in Brazil was not an easy task. Beyond the widespread resistance against Protestant books and Bibles motivated by Catholic opposition, Brazil was scarcely populated in the nineteenth century and large distances separated cities and provinces from one another, which forced colporteurs to spend months on the road. According to João dos Santos, rough modes of travelling, poor accommodation, wretched food, the unhealthy climate and prolonged periods away from home drove away potential workers.[24] In 1886, he proposed to divide the large country into ten districts and appoint one colporteur for each, a reorganisation that would reduce not only the frequency of costly journeys to the countryside, but also the distance between colporteurs and their families.[25] This strategy was never adopted and the Society continued to have problems in recruiting its personnel.

In most cases, though, the obstacles to the circulation of Bibles were external to the Society. In 1876, José de Carvalho summarised the factors limiting the sale of books in Rio de Janeiro in four points: heavy rains in the first months of the year, religious indifference, the economic crisis with its impact on food prices, and outbreaks of yellow fever in Rio de Janeiro.[26] This last factor was a source of much concern among the BFBS's personnel. The capital of the Brazilian Empire became the centre of outbreaks of yellow fever from the late 1860s until the beginning of the twentieth century, when the disease was temporarily eradicated. In 1873 and 1876, two extremely serious epidemics represented a turning point in the history of yellow fever in Brazil, as it pushed state authorities to carry out a series of urban reforms to control its dissemination (Chalhoub 1993: 455–6). Carvalho and Santos mentioned in their correspondence with the BFBS how the disease disorganised the Society's work in the country. Carvalho's brother died after being infected by the disease in 1876 and his wife was also infected in the same year. Santos wrote in 1886 that the fever carried off some Christian workers in Rio.[27] Apart from affecting the BFBS staff, yellow fever also

---

24   BFBS Annual Report (1885), p. 249.
25   BFBS Annual Report (1886), p. 298.
26   BFBS, 'J. Carvalho to Bergne, 22nd of July, 1876', BSA/D1/7 – 144.
27   BFBS, 'J. Carvalho to Bergne, 13th of May 1876', BSA/D1/7 – 144; BFBS Annual Report (1886), p. 299. In 1885, only one colporteur of the Society worked in Rio de Janeiro.

created difficulties for the shipment of Bibles to Brazilian ports, as all steam-ships were quarantined, and impoverished the population of Rio de Janeiro.

Financial shortages occasioned either by these outbreaks or by economic crises curtailed the distribution of Bibles in Brazil. After being asked by the Society whether he could appoint more colporteurs, in 1876 Carvalho argued that the economic crisis of the 1870s had raised dramatically the cost of living in the country and as a result sales had decreased and he did not have the funds to appoint new colporteurs.[28] Manoel dos Anjos, a colporteur working in Rio de Janeiro, told the superintendent that most of his books were sold among poor fishermen and black sailors who could not afford the Bibles printed by the Society in times of scarcity but mostly purchased portions and Testaments.[29] One of the leading principles that guided the BFBS work at home and abroad was that their books should be sold as cheaply as possible (Howsam 1991: 50). This cheapness, though, was subject to variations in inflation rates and fluctuations in the cost of living in Brazil. Nevertheless, the Brazilian branch of the BFBS remained faithful to the advice that books should not be distributed freely. The saying 'livro dado é livro desprezado' ('a book given away is a book despised') was a commonplace among them (Glass 1914: 42).

The reaction of public authorities against the circulation of Evangelical scriptures in Brazil constantly worried the BFBS personnel. Protestant mission-aries and foreign visitors in nineteenth-century Brazil praised the qualities and liberalities of Emperor Dom Pedro II and the empire's constitution, especially the clauses on religious tolerance, and the post-1848 political stability (Kidder and Fletcher 1857: 229–30; Blackford 1886: 3). BFBS colporteurs, however, faced different realities in their journeys to small towns and through the countryside of Brazil. If the monarchy was represented as an enlightened institution that enforced order and the 'empire of the law' upon its most remote provinces, col-porteurs dealt with the peculiarities of local politics. João dos Santos repeatedly complained that county magistrates in the interior either prohibited the selling of Protestant scriptures or overcharged colporteurs with costly fines, which forced him to appeal to the laws of the empire or the Emperor himself.[30] Even after the overthrow of the empire in 1889 and the promulgation in 1891 of the republican constitution, which effectively disestablished Catholicism, these events continued to occur.[31] Due to these experiences, the BFBS staff rapidly noticed that resolutions and laws approved by the central government were not

---

28   BFBS, 'J. Carvalho to the Rev. C. Jackson, 8th of February 1876', BSA/D1/7 – 144.

29   BFBS, 'J. Carvalho to the Rev. C. Jackson, 7th of February 1873', BSA/D1/7 – 123.

30   BFBS Annual Report (1882), p. 282; (1886), p. 299.

31   BFBS Annual Report (1897), p. 267.

homogeneously enforced in the country, but were negotiated and reinterpreted by local authorities, which was indeed a component of the political dynamic in Brazil (Graham 1990).

British Protestants residing in Brazil were able to appeal to other authorities in a different way. If British missionaries working in the dominions of the British Empire could in many cases benefit from their relations with imperial powers (Porter 2004), outside the realm of the formal empire they could appeal to diplomats and envoys when their personal safety or their properties were under threat. For example, Kalley appealed to George Buckley Matthew, British envoy in Brazil, when the police delegate of Rio de Janeiro refused to grant protection for his family and the members of his church, who had been threatened by Catholic protesters. Kalley emphasised in his letters to Matthew that all religious meetings were in accord with the laws of the empire and that the actions of the police delegate disrespected the constitution.[32] Throughout the nineteenth century, these relations between British missionaries, British diplomats and Brazilian authorities were frequently denounced in the pages of Ultramontane periodicals, which associated missionary work with wider anti-Catholic conspiracies involving Freemasons and liberal intellectuals (Vieira 1980: 282–91).

However, besides all these factors, the central element that represented the greatest threat to the circulation of Bibles and Christian literature in Brazil according to the BFBS records was Catholicism, which experienced a period of expansion and revival in the late nineteenth century. The process of conservative modernisation of the Catholic Church, which was initiated in the 1860s, involved the training and moralisation of the clergy and the renewal of the Catholic Church's outward appearance. After the overthrow of the empire in 1889, which released the ecclesiastical hierarchy from burdensome state patronage, the Catholic Church in Brazil was able to intensify its connections with Rome and strengthen its internal structure by creating numerous seminaries, dioceses and bishoprics (Serbin 2006: 56). The Catholic Church also mobilised the laity in this process of reformation and enabled some people to engage in ecclesiastical work through charitable acts and the reconstruction of old parishes and cemeteries. These prestigious lay leaders were known as *beatos* and *beatas*. With the promulgation of the republican constitution in 1891, however, the Catholic Church lost its traditional control over public cemeteries and registrations of birth and marriage. This loss of temporal power, alongside

---

32   BFB-IEF, 'R. R. Kalley to George Buckley Mathew. Theresópolis, 14th February 1874. Correspondência Dr Kalley.'

the dissemination of Protestantism and Positivism, were depicted by the Ultramontane clergy and the engaged laity as perversions of the traditional social order (Della Cava 1968: 404–8).

In the 1860s, reacting to the circulation of Evangelical Bibles in Brazil, the Bishop of Pará, Antonio Costa, and the Archbishop of Bahia, Dom Joaquim da Silveira, issued pastoral letters warning their flocks against the 'mutilations and falsifications' of the Protestant scriptures, enumerating all the sections that differed from the authorised Catholic Bible (Vieira 1980: 182–3, 189–92). Both the content and the language of these pastoral letters had widespread and long-lasting reverberations in Brazil and Portugal.

The BFBS printed and circulated the two main versions of the Bible in Portuguese: the eighteenth-century translation from the Vulgate of the Catholic father António Pereira de Figueiredo and the seventeenth-century version by the reformed minister João Ferreira de Almeida, who translated the whole of the New Testament from the Greek texts and most of the Old Testament from Hebrew (Silva 1867: 277; Lisboa 1985: 438). Whereas the latter contained several grammatical mistakes from its very inception and was stigmatised as an Evangelical Bible by the Catholics, the first bore the seal of approval of the Archbishop of Bahia on its cover. Throughout the nineteenth century, the Society's personnel in Brazil and Portugal concentrated their efforts on improving Almeida's translation while colporteurs met with different echoes of the opposition to this version on their journeys around the country.

In some cases, public authorities intervened in the colporteurs' work, using the language of the Catholic pastoral letters.[33] In other cases, lay Catholics rejected Protestant scriptures, claiming that they contained magical powers of enchantment over the readers, which contrasted sharply with the nineteenth-century Evangelical notion of scriptural agency. In his first journey to the province of Paraíba, the colporteur Manoel da Silva was told by the people of the city of Nazaré that a twenty-year-old man had lost his reason after reading a false Bible sold by Protestants.[34] Another colporteur, Manoel de Souza, met people in São Paulo who were afraid of reading Bibles and Protestant books.[35]

As Bibles and Christian literature were circulated by BFBS staff in Brazil, representations of Protestants and their religious celebrations became increasingly associated with the Bible. But this was not exactly a positive association

---

33   BFBS, 'J. Carvalho to the Rev. Bergne. Rio de Janeiro, 26th August 1876', BSA/D1/7 – 144.

34   BFBS, 'J. Carvalho to the Rev. Bergne. Rio de Janeiro 15th May 1874', BSA/D1/7 – 144.

35   BFBS Annual Report (1894), p. 296.

for the missionaries. The Ultramontane periodical *O Apóstolo*, published in Rio de Janeiro, frequently complained about those whom they called 'Bible peddlers' or 'vendors of false and mutilated Bibles' from the British and American Bible societies.[36] The periodical referred to colporteurs working in the province of Ceará as 'disturbers of the social order and families' peace'.[37] Ultramontane leaders depicted the individual ownership and interpretation of the scriptures as destructive forces that acted against the well-being of families, the established religion and traditional society (Vieira 1980). Tellingly, the periodical used a pejorative, popular term to refer to Protestants: they were called *os bíblias*.

The BFBS personnel, in connection with their counterparts in Britain and Portugal, adopted a series of strategies to promote the Almeida version of the Bible and to increase their sales. Firstly, between the 1860s and the 1870s a group of missionaries and evangelists connected to the Society combined their efforts to improve Almeida's translation. Kalley and Holden informed the BFBS committee about the enormous number of typographical errors, grammatical errors and old-fashioned language contained in the translation.[38] Lacking a consistent strategy to review the translation, various people sent to the Society their notes and comments about the text.[39] In 1869, the BFBS published a new edition of Almeida's Old Testament and a revised version of the book of Genesis prepared in Portugal by a translator called Manoel Soares. As these editions were well received in Portugal and Brazil, the Society requested Soares to undertake a complete revision of the Almeida version, which was published by the BFBS in Lisbon in 1875 (Darlow et al. 1911: 1248–9). The revised translation divided opinion among foreign and Brazilian missionaries, being praised by Edward Lane and Robert Kalley, but criticised by José Carvalho and João dos Santos.[40]

Secondly, as popular resistance against the Bible was both strong and widespread, the Brazilian staff of the BFBS developed a new array of strategies relating to advertising and the selling of books. According to missionaries and

---

36   *O Apóstolo*, Rio de Janeiro, 29 February 1884, No. 24.

37   *O Apóstolo*, Rio de Janeiro, 7 November 1879, No. 129.

38   BFBS, 'R. Kalley to the Editorial Superintendent. Rothesay, 12th June 1869'; 'Holden to the Rev. S. Bergne. Rio de Janeiro, 6th July 1869', BSA/E3/1/4 – 7.

39   BFBS, 'A. Blackford to R. Holden. 2nd October 1869', BSA/D1/2, File C.

40   BFBS, 'Kalley to the Rev. Girdlestone. Rio de Janeiro, 20th November 1874'; 'J. dos Santos to the Rev. Bergne. Rio de Janeiro, 7th October 1875'; 'J. de Carvalho to Mr Frinch. Rio de Janeiro, 15th November 1875', BSA/E3/1/4 – 11. 'Rev. E. Lane to Rev. Bergne. Campinas, 13 September 1875', BSA/D1/7 – 144.

superintendents, having the words 'Bible' or 'London' printed on the covers of scriptures could heighten the resistance of the Brazilian public against the BFBS's publications.[41] Kalley suggested that replacing the word '*Bíblia*' with the title '*Escrituras Sagradas*' (Holy Scriptures) on the covers of the BFBS books would in all likelihood increase sales.[42] Despite these indications, however, the Society never adapted its publications along these lines. Furthermore, according to the American missionary Edward Lane, Presbyterian colporteurs were able to sell Bibles printed in Lisbon more easily than those bearing the word 'London' on their front page.[43] The appearance, outward characteristics and advertising of these material objects exerted a considerable influence on the purchasers of BFBS books.

In the face of these obstacles, BFBS staff began to employ new strategies of advertising and tried to prevent potential buyers from learning that the books sold by colporteurs were in fact Bibles. This started in 1874, when José Carvalho instructed the colporteurs of Rio de Janeiro to carry only portions of the text with them during the Holy Week and not to hold long conversations with people.[44] In the 1880s this method was extended to All Souls' day and Christmas. As the strategy proved successful, these practices of selling only portions of the Bible on Christian holidays and of avoiding the use of the words 'Bible' and 'Testament' in colporteurs' advertising were subsequently employed consistently,[45] which explains why sales of portions of the text outnumbered those of Bibles from 1874 onwards (see Table 2.1).

A Transatlantic Circulation of Protestant Books

While the Brazilian staff of the BFBS circulated an increasing number of Bibles and portions of the text in the country, the Religious Tract Society, another London-based Evangelical organisation, also played an important role in disseminating Christian literature among the Brazilian public. RTS administrators also held Evangelical notions of textual agency, representing religious texts as silent messengers whose reach was broader than that of the missionaries (Fyfe 2004: 170). Founded in 1799, and inspired by the spirit of British evangelicalism, the RTS also operated on a global level and reached transnational audiences

41   BFBS Annual Report (1882), p. 279.

42   BFBS Annual Report (1881), p. 187.

43   BFBS, 'E. Lane to Rev. Bergne. Campinas, 13 September 1875', BSA/D1/7 – 144.

44   BFBS, 'J. De Carvalho to the Rev. S. Bergne. Rio de Janeiro, 21st April 1874', BSA/D1/7 – 144.

45   BFBS Annual Report (1881), p. 186.

in the nineteenth century. Unlike the BFBS, though, the Tract Society 'did not draft a "fundamental principle" on the basis of which the various denominations could cooperate' (Martin 1983: 153). Its objective was simply to apply the funds collected through subscriptions, donations and contributions to the production and circulation of Christian literature at home and abroad.[46] As the volume of tracts submitted for the approval of the RTS increased exponentially, its committee slowly hammered out most of its regulations on the publication and examination of texts (ibid.: 154–5). Moreover, throughout the nineteenth century, the Tract Society did not appoint a subcommittee or staff in Brazil. Instead of employing agents, superintendents and colporteurs, the RTS decided to support established missionaries in the country, either from Protestant denominations or from non-sectarian organisations.

The American Presbyterian missionary Emmanuel Vanorden was the person who corresponded most frequently with the RTS committee in London, which constantly supplied him with books, tracts, illustrations, reams of paper and, later, a printing press and electrotypes.[47] BFBS superintendent João dos Santos and missionaries of the South American Missionary Society also received books and tracts, which then circulated in the country along pre-existing routes of distribution.[48] The Presbyterian periodical *Imprensa Evangelica*, published in Rio de Janeiro, frequently advertised RTS books and tracts, which were sold at low prices in Evangelical bookshops in Rio and São Paulo. Therefore, despite the absence of RTS personnel acting in Brazil, the Society was able to benefit from and support a wide range of missionary societies.

Throughout the nineteenth century, the Tract Society was more adaptable to new circumstances and individual appeals coming from Brazil than the BFBS had shown itself to be. For example, in the 1860s, the RTS withheld support from evangelistic work in Brazil on at least two occasions: firstly when Richard Holden used RTS funds to publish religious articles in a liberal periodical in the province of Pará; and secondly when the Presbyterian missionary Ashbel Simonton requested financial support for the periodical *Imprensa Evange-*

---

46   *The Seventy-Eighth Annual Report of the Religious Tract Society, Instituted A.D. M.DCC.XCIX., For Publishing Religious Tracts and Books at Home and Abroad* (London, 1877), p. xiii (henceforth referred to as RTS Annual Report (year)).

47   For some of the correspondence with E. Vanorden, see RTS Annual Reports (1879), pp. 210–12; (1881), pp. 201, 202; (1889), pp. 205, 206.

48   RTS Annual Reports (1883), pp. 220, 221; (1892), p. 211; (1896), pp. 221–3. BFBS colporteurs also carried with them books and tracts printed by the RTS. BFBS, 'S. P. Kalley to the Rev. Bergne. Petropolis, 22nd March 1876', BSA/D1/7 – 144.

lica.[49] The RTS committee declared that its funds should not be applied to the printing of texts of ephemeral use or of publications they could not personally examine and check. In the 1880s, however, the Society adapted its policy and supported the publication of *Imprensa Evangelica* by sending reams of paper to its editors.[50] Furthermore, as Richard Holden warned the committee in 1861, some images and pictures included in RTS tracts were being used on family altars for 'idolatrous purposes' in the same way as many Brazilian families utilised images of Catholic saints (Vieira 1980: 170–1).[51] This warning exerted a lasting influence on the operations of the Tract Society in the Lusophone Atlantic, which included few images in their Portuguese publications thereafter.

Significantly, the vast majority of books and tracts shipped to Brazil were not published at the Society's headquarters in London, but by a subcommittee founded in Lisbon. The transatlantic exchange of Protestant Lusophone literature between Brazil and Portugal dated from at least the early 1860s, when this Lisbon committee was formed and the RTS decided to publish texts written by Robert Kalley for circulation in Portugal.[52] From then on an increasing amount of Protestant literature flowed from Portugal to Brazil. In 1882, Santos and Kalley asked the Tract Society to expand its operations in the country, invoking successful examples of colportage overseen by the BFBS and the good prospects that awaited the RTS in Brazil. Their request, however, was not granted. The RTS committee nevertheless decided to meet the needs of Protestant churches and schools for Christian literature by granting to missionaries established in Brazil discounts of 50 per cent on all books and tracts printed in Portugal.[53]

From the early 1880s, Portugal became the main supplier of Protestant literature to the Lusophone world. Books and tracts flowed from Lisbon and Porto to various places in the Iberian peninsula, on the Atlantic islands of Azores, Madeira and Cape Verde, where the Lisbon committee established sub-depots, to African Lusophone societies and Brazil.[54] While the circulation of literature in Azores and Cape Verde did not meet the expectations of the Lisbon committee, the volume of books sold in Brazil and the resulting financial

---

49   RTS, 'George Henry Davis to the Rev. Richard Holden, 22nd October 1861'; 'Joseph Tara to A. G. Simonton, July 5th 1866', USCL/RTS/03/19–20 (SOAS Library, Special Collections Department).

50   RTS Annual Reports (1888), p. 194; (1887), pp. 194–7.

51   RTS, 'G. H. Davis to the Rev. Richard Holden, 3rd July 1861', USCL/RTS/03/19–20.

52   RTS, 'George Henry Davis to Mrs Roughton, 10th April 1860', USCL/RTS/03/19–20.

53   RTS Annual Reports (1883), p. 221.

54   RTS Annual Reports (1892), p. 53; (1893), p. 55.

return drew the favourable attention of RTS agents. In 1890, less than a decade after the arrangements between London, Lisbon and Rio de Janeiro had been established, sales of RTS books in Brazil outnumbered those in Portugal and the Atlantic islands.[55]

The circulation of Lusophone Christian literature in the Atlantic did not follow a one-directional path from North to South, however. In many cases, ideas, theological debates and Catholic reactions against Protestant evangelisation originating in Brazil reverberated in Portugal and prompted the Lisbon committee to respond. For example, in the 1870s, Richard Holden began to propagate the theological and ecclesiological ideas of the Plymouth Brethren in Lusophone Evangelical communities in Brazil, Portugal and Illinois and reacted against the establishment of ecclesiastical hierarchies and the creation of denominational confessions of faith (Léonard 2002: 82–3).[56] Robert Kalley, who disagreed with Holden's ideas, sent letters from his residence in Edinburgh to his friends and fellow pastors in Illinois and Rio de Janeiro warning and instructing them against Holden's tracts in the late 1870s. The Lisbon committee of the RTS compiled and published Kalley's letters in 1891, a few years after his death, circulating this tract on both sides of the Atlantic.[57] Similarly, and also in the 1890s, the RTS Lisbon committee decided to publish one of the most widely distributed tracts that had been circulating in Brazil since 1875: Émile de Laveleye's *The Future of the Catholic Peoples*.[58] Translated by the eminent Brazilian intellectual Miguel Vieira Ferreira, this tract argued that, while democratic values and economic modernisation flourished wherever Protestantism and its social ethic triumphed, Catholicism led societies to either despotism or anarchy (Laveleye 1875). A great many of the tracts and pamphlets published in Lisbon defended the Protestant Bibles against the critiques of Catholic bishops and theologians.[59] In 1882, Robert Stewart, a clergyman and agent of the BFBS in Lisbon, was also appointed as the RTS agent for Portugal, which intensified the connections between these two Evangelical societies in the Lusophone world and stimulated the publication of RTS tracts in defence of BFBS Bibles.[60] In a response to the pastoral letter written by the Bishop of Porto against Protest-

---

55   RTS Annual Report (1891), p. 61.

56   *Confissões de Fé, por Ricardo Holden* (Lisbon: Calçada dos Mestres, 1906).

57   *O Darbysmo, cartas do Dr. Robert R. Kalley* (Lisbon: Adolfo, Modesto & Co., 1891).

58   RTS Annual Report (1893), p. 56.

59   Some of these publications include: *Eu Não Comprehendo a Biblia*. Lisbon: Typ. De Vicente da Silva & Co., 1900; *A Biblia e o Povo*. Lisbon: Livrarias Evangelicas, 1897; *O Estudo Devoto da Biblia*. Lisbon: Livrarias Evangelicas, 1899; and Whately (1896).

60   RTS Annual Report (1883), p. 54.

ant missions in Portugal, Robert Kalley criticised anti-Protestant publications in Brazil and Portugal that stigmatised the BFBS scriptures as false and adulterated (Kalley 1879: 25–8).

Missionaries, Evangelists and religious publishers adapted the literary forms and textual genres of these Evangelical tracts as they crossed the Atlantic Ocean in the late nineteenth century. The Protestant classic book *The Pilgrim's Progress*, for instance, translated into Portuguese by Robert Kalley, was serialised and published in thirty-five articles by the periodical *Correio Mercantil* of Rio de Janeiro in the 1850s. Later, these articles were collected, published in the form of books in Scotland and Lisbon, and put into circulation in the Lusophone world (Leonel 2010: 56–7). These adaptations and reconfigurations of print matter show how the material reading contexts of each society exerted some influence on the transatlantic circulation of religious literature, and that the different textual genres permeated each other in the Lusophone Atlantic (Delap and DiCenzo 2008: 56).

Conclusion

Nineteenth-century missionary work and mass print consolidated a transatlantic public sphere that connected publishers and readers dispersed in different parts of the globe (Clark and Ledger-Lomas 2012: 30). As this chapter has shown, themes, theological debates and conflicts with Catholic leaders that originated in Brazil reverberated in different parts of the Lusophone world and activated the engines of the Tract Society's printing presses in Portugal and Britain. By means of a more decentralised administration than the BFBS, the RTS and its Lisbon committee were able to respond quickly to the impulses and incitements raised on both sides of the Atlantic, defending BFBS Bibles against the critiques of Brazilian and Portuguese Catholic bishops and reacting to the teachings of Richard Holden. In contrast to this, the BFBS committee in London was slower in attending to claims that arose in Brazil. On the one hand, they acted rapidly in raising the salaries of colporteurs and superintendents and in supplying their agents with books. On the other, pleas regarding adaptations to the printing and binding of Bibles and the organisation of the Society's working structure in Brazil were not received favourably by the London committee of the BFBS, a much larger and more complex bureaucratic organisation.

BFBS Bibles, Testaments and portions of the Bible, as well as the RTS books and tracts, circulated in Protestant churches and schools in Brazil, feeding a public that made frequent use of Evangelical literature. Most of the reading material, however, was purchased, read and heard by an anonymous public that colporteurs, superintendents and missionaries expected to become converts at some unknown point in the future. Narratives of conversions prompted by the simple intervention of these 'silent messengers' nourished the missionary imaginary that attributed to Christian texts extraordinary agency and power. In a worldly perspective, though, the most active agents who took on the responsibility of distributing and selling Bibles across the country were modestly educated and semi-literate men. Their encounters with Catholic resistance – either institutional (from bishops and priests) or popular – shaped the strategies they employed in their daily work and echoed in places as far away as Lisbon and London, where reports and narratives were carefully read and examined by the BFBS and RTS committees.

References

Bakewell, P. (1997) *A History of Latin America: Empires and Sequels, 1450–1930*. Malden MA and Oxford: Blackwell.

Bayly, C. (2004) *The Birth of the Modern World, 1780–1914: Global Connections and Comparisons*. Malden MA and Oxford: Blackwell.

Blackford, A. L. (1886) *Sketch of the Brazil Mission*. Philadelphia PA: Presbyterian Board of Education.

Boehrer, G. A. (1969) 'The Church in the Second Reign, 1840–1889' in H. Keith and S. Edwards (eds), *Conflict and Continuity in Brazilian Society*. Columbia SC: University of South Carolina Press.

Brusco, E. (1993) 'The Reformation of Machismo: Asceticism and Masculinity among Colombian Evangelicals' in V. Garrard-Burnett and D. Stoll (eds), *Rethinking Protestantism in Latin America*. Philadelphia PA: Temple University Press.

Cabrita, J. (2014) *Text and Authority in the South African Nazaretha Church*. New York NY: Cambridge University Press.

Chalhoub, S. (1993) 'The Politics of Disease Control: Yellow Fever and Race in Nineteenth Century Rio de Janeiro', *Journal of Latin American Studies* 25 (3): 441–63.

Clark, C. and M. Ledger-Lomas (2012) 'The Protestant International' in A. Green and V. Viaene (eds), *Religious Internationals in the Modern World: Globalization and Faith Communities since 1750*. Basingstoke: Palgrave Macmillan.

Darlow, T. H., H. F. Moule and A. G. Jayne (1911) *Historical Catalogue of the Printed Editions of Holy Scripture in the Library of the British and Foreign Bible Society*. London: Bible House.

Darnton, R. (1991) 'History of Reading' in P. Burke (ed.), *New Perspectives on Historical Writing*. Cambridge: Polity Press.

Delap, L. and M. DiCenzo (2008) 'Transatlantic Print Culture: The Anglo-American Feminist Press and Emerging "Modernities"' in A. Ardis and P. Collier (eds), *Transatlantic Print Culture, 1880–1940: Emerging Media, Emerging Modernisms*. Basingstoke: Palgrave Macmillan.

Della Cava, R. (1968) 'Brazilian Messianism and National Institutions: A Reappraisal of Canudos and Joaseiro', *Hispanic American Historical Review* 48 (3): 402–20.

Dove, S. C. (2016) 'Historical Protestantism in Latin America' in V. Garrard-Burnett, P. Freston and S. Dove (eds), *The Cambridge History of Religions in Latin America*. New York NY: Cambridge University Press.

Frase, R. (1975) 'A Sociological Analysis of the Development of Brazilian Protestantism: A Study of Social Change'. PhD thesis, Princeton Theological Seminary.

Frase, R. (1981) 'The Subversion of Missionary Intentions by Cultural Values: The Brazilian Case', *Review of Religious Research* 23 (2): 180–94.

Fyfe, A. (2004) 'Commerce and Philanthropy: The Religious Tract Society and the Business of Publishing', *Journal of Victorian Culture* 9 (2): 164–88.

Glass, F. C. (1914) *With the Bible in Brazil: Being the Story of a Few of the Marvellous Incidents Arising from its Circulation There*. London: Morgan & Scott Ld.

Graham, R. (1990) *Patronage and Politics in Nineteenth-century Brazil*. Stanford CA: Stanford University Press.

Green, A. and V. Viaene (2012) 'Introduction: Rethinking Religion and Globalization' in A. Green and V. Viaene (eds), *Religious Internationals in the Modern World: Globalization and Faith Communities since 1750*. Basingstoke: Palgrave Macmillan.

Guimarães, H. de S. (2004) *Os leitores de Machado de Assis: o romance machadiano e o público de literatura no século 19*. São Paulo: Nankin Editorial and EDUSP.

Hartch, T. (2014) *The Rebirth of Latin American Christianity*. New York NY: Oxford University Press.

Hofmeyr, I. (2004) *The Portable Bunyan: A Transnational History of the Pilgrim's Progress*. Princeton NJ and Oxford: Princeton University Press.

Hofmeyr, I. (2005) 'Inventing the World: Transnationalism, Transmission and Christian Textualities' in J. Scott and G. Griffiths (eds), *Mixed Messages: Materiality, Textuality, Missions*. New York NY: Palgrave Macmillan.

Hofmeyr, I. (2013) *Gandhi's Printing Press: Experiments in Slow Reading*. Cambridge MA and London: Harvard University Press.

Howsam, L. (1991) *Cheap Bibles: Nineteenth-century Publishing and the British and Foreign Bible Society*. Cambridge: Cambridge University Press.

Howsam, L. (2004) 'The Bible Society and the Book Trade' in S. Batalden, K. Cann and J. Dean (eds), *Sowing the Word: The Cultural Impact of the British and Foreign Bible Society, 1804–2004*. Sheffield: Sheffield Phoenix Press.

Kalley, R. R. (1879) *Observações á Instrucção Pastoral do Exc.mo. Bispo do Porto, D. Americo sobre o Protestantismo*. Porto: Imprensa Civilisação de Santos & Lemos.

Kidder, D. P. and J. C. Fletcher (1857) *Brazil and the Brazilians: Portrayed in Historical and Descriptive Sketches*. Philadelphia PA: Childs & Peterson.

Kirsch, T. G. (2008) *Spirits and Letters: Reading, Writing and Charisma in African Christianity*. New York NY and Oxford: Berghahn Books.

Laveleye, E. (1875) *Do Futuro dos Povos Catholicos: Estudo de Economia Social*. Rio de Janeiro: Typ. Universal de E. & H. Laemmert.

Léonard, E. (2002) *O Protestantismo Brasileiro: um estudo de eclesiologia e história social*. São Paulo: ASTE.

Leonel, J. (2010) *História da Leitura e Protestantismo Brasileiro*. São Paulo: Editora Mackenzie and Paulinas.

Lisboa, E. (1985) *Dicionário Cronológico de Autores Portugueses. Vol. I*. Mem Martins: Publicações Europa-América.

Martin, D. (1990) *Tongues of Fire: The Explosion of Protestantism in Latin America*. Oxford and Cambridge MA: Basil Blackwell.

Martin, R. (1983) *Evangelicals United: Ecumenical Stirrings in Pre-Victorian Britain, 1795–1830*. Metuchen NJ and London: Scarecrow.

Maspoli, A. (2001) *Religião, Educação e Progresso*. São Paulo: Editora Mackenzie.

Maxwell, D. (2001) '"Sacred History, Social History": Traditions and Text in the Making of a Southern African Transnational Religious Movement', *Comparative Studies in Society and History* 43 (3): 502–24.

Neves, G. P. (2009) 'A Religião do Império e a Igreja' in K. Grinberg and R. Salles (eds), *O Brasil Imperial. Volume I: 1808–1831*. Rio de Janeiro: Civilização Brasileira.

Porter, A. (2004) *Religion versus Empire?: British Protestant Missionaries and Overseas Expansion, 1700–1914*. Manchester and New York NY: Manchester University Press.

Rio, J. do (1997 [1908]) *A Alma Encantadora das Ruas*. São Paulo: Companhia das Letras.

Serbin, K. P. (2006) *Needs of the Heart: A Social and Cultural History of Brazil's Clergy and Seminaries*. Notre Dame IN: University of Notre Dame Press.

Sharkey, H. J. (2011) 'The British and Foreign Society in Port Said and the Suez Canal', *Journal of Imperial and Commonwealth History* 39 (3): 439–56.

Silva, I. F. (1867) *Diccionario Bibliographico Portuguez: Estudos de Innocêncio Francisco da Silva. Tome VIII*. Lisbon: Imprensa Nacional.

Vieira, D. G. (1980) *O Protestantismo, a Maçonaria e a Questão Religiosa no Brasil*. Brasília: Editora UnB.

Whately, E. I. (1896) *Objecções à Biblia e a Melhor Maneira de Lhes Responder*. Lisbon: Typ. De Vicente da Silva & Co.

CHAPTER 3

Parachurch Competition in the Latin American Religious Marketplace: Scriptural Inerrancy and the Reshaping of Global Protestant Evangelicalism

David C. Kirkpatrick

This chapter conceives of World Christianity as an arena in which parachurch organisations based in the North competed for influence across the globe, each seeking to export their vision of Evangelical Christian orthodoxy and mission. Taking as its case study the International Fellowship of Evangelical Students (IFES), the InterVarsity Christian Fellowship (IVCF) and Campus Crusade for Christ (CCC), the chapter examines their fixation with a belief in scriptural inerrancy among Evangelical students on Latin American university campuses. Although this assertion of the infallibility of the scriptures sprang from a desire to secure Christian orthodoxy, it also represented a North American agenda in which a belief in scriptural inerrancy was a marker of Evangelical credentials and a means of ensuring the flow of donations from the sizeable US Evangelical constituency. Although much of this debate was staged between US Evangelical leaders, prominent Latin American Evangelicals were drawn in, caught in the crossfire, especially between North American factions. Wounded by accusations of errant belief, Ecuadorian Evangelical René Padilla was prompted to assert his own agenda for Latin American evangelicalism, placing a greater emphasis on a social Christianity more attuned to the violence, poverty and injustice endemic to Latin America. Significantly, Padilla's intervention became the basis of his influential contribution to the Lausanne Congress in 1974.

The episode sheds light on the issue of agency in the making of World Christianity at the level of theological discourse. Although North American Evangelicals were backed by considerable material and intellectual resources, Latin American leaders were able to draw on the tradition of local autonomy fostered by the IFES and IVCF to reshape the global theological agenda. The chapter demonstrates that scholars should treat with caution the thesis that equates evangelicalism with US spiritual imperialism emanating from the so-called 'Religious Right'. In doing so, this case study focuses on the critical intersection of Latin America and the United States during the global Cold War and intellectual negotiation by Evangelical elites (Westad 2007: 3–4). It highlights previously unstudied oral interviews and personal correspondence between many of the main players in Latin America and the English-speaking world.

Many Evangelical parachurch ministries entered Latin America after the Second World War, injecting both energy and competition into the blood-stream. For Evangelical Protestants, 'the organizational structures that house the throbbing heart of evangelicalism are not denominations at all, but the special-purpose parachurch agencies that sometimes seem as numberless as the stars in the sky' (Hatch and Hamilton 1995: 398). Reflecting this shifting centre, the Evangelical faithful have increasingly transferred their donations from denominations to parachurch organisations. Today, while exact numbers are difficult to obtain, North American Evangelicals donate approximately the same amount of money to parachurch organisations as to churches or denominations (ECFA 2015). Today, 'it is difficult to overstate the significance of parachurch organizations ... as they structure and direct billions of evangelical dollars toward humanitarianism, political advocacy, and evangelism' (Turner 2008: 3). Thus, a critical analysis of parachurch organisations is crucial to understanding Protestant evangelicalism, especially its evangelistic and revivalistic ethos. The importance of parachurch organisations to religion in the global North is undeniable, but key questions and gaps in our understanding remain. In what sense are these parachurch organisations *global*, given their overwhelming focus in the North? Examining their role in reshaping global Evangelical theology will also shed light on the power balance between local and foreign actors. This analysis centres on the role and perspective of elites, focusing on the level of conciliar discourse.

In the late 1980s and early 1990s, several monographs signalled a wider turn towards Latin American Protestantism within the academic study of religion (see, for example, Stoll 1990; Martin 1990; Chesnut 1997). Andrew Chesnut's *Competitive Spirits: Latin America's New Religious Economy* (2003) moved this conversation forward by focusing on three communities: Pentecostals, the Catholic Charismatic renewal, and African diasporic religion in Latin America. Chesnut's study is particularly helpful because of his use of the concept of religious economy, which is best known in the work of sociologists Peter Berger and Rodney Stark (Berger 1967; Stark and Finke 2000: 18). The application of micro-economic theory to religious studies discourse is often illuminating, especially in a contested space such as Latin American religion.

Many of these works have also focused on Brazil, which is largely a linguistic, cultural, racial and political exception within Latin America. Many Brazilians do not consider themselves Latinos and prefer to be known simply as Brazilians. This scholarly focus on Brazil has also caused many to misread the diverse religious landscape of Latin America. Perhaps most importantly for our purposes here, Pentecostalism has been disproportionately emphasised across Latin America at the expense of non-Charismatic forms of evangelicalism. In the 2015 Pew Research Center study titled 'Religion in Latin America', 80 per cent of Brazilian Protestants self-identified as Pentecostal by denomination or identity. In contrast, fewer than half of Bolivians (49 per cent) and US Hispanics (45 per cent) self-identified as such. Across Latin America, nearly 40 per cent of Protestants did not identify as Pentecostal or Charismatic (Pew Research Center 2015: 8). Most of this 35 to 40 per cent identified as Evangelical Protestant, with a small percentage self-identifying as mainline Protestant.

While many have focused on competition between Protestants and Catholics or Pentecostals and conservative Protestants, there remains a gap in our understanding of *inter*-Evangelical competition – especially in the global South.[1] This chapter attempts to address a broad gap in scholarly literature on Latin American Protestant Evangelicals. In doing so, it resituates Latin American Protestant evangelicalism within the wider field of World Christianity by placing the former in conversation with its most prominent interlocutor in the North.

Evangelicals in the Americas are most clearly distinguished by beliefs articulated in the Protestant Reformation and by practices shaped by the so-called Great Awakening (Sweeney 2005: 24). More specifically, David Bebbington's fourfold classification of evangelicalism is widely accepted as the most accurate definition of worldwide Evangelicals: conversionism (the belief that lives need to be changed); biblicism (a particular regard for the Bible); crucicentrism (a stress on the sacrifice of Jesus on the cross); and activism (the expression of the gospel in effort) (Bebbington 1993: 2–3). The limits of this quadrilateral notwithstanding, these beliefs unite diverse individuals across regional boundaries in Latin America.

The Transnational Latin American Religious Marketplace

In December 1823, US President James Monroe delivered an annual address to the United States Congress that was widely overlooked by contemporary European governments and US foreign policy experts. But the content of his message set the Americas on a trajectory that would largely dictate US foreign

---

1 On competition between Catholics and Protestants, see Hartch (2014). Hartch argues that Protestant competition has revitalised rather than crippled Catholicism in Latin America.

policy in Latin America. Monroe and his Secretary of State John Quincy Adams (the son of President John Adams) expounded what later became known as the 'Monroe Doctrine', which outlined three core tenets: 'separate spheres of influence for the Americas and Europe, non-colonization, and non-intervention'.[2] Essentially, the Monroe Doctrine stated that any further European attempts at colonisation or intervention in the New World would be considered an act of war. In a sense, the United States was laying claim to being the sole influence on the Americas and would act upon this assertion with increasing vigour.

Prior to the First World War, Protestant communities in Latin America were mainly the product of early nineteenth-century immigration (González and González 2008: 184–206). As the nineteenth century progressed, two realities converged in the fields of politics and religion: the independence of Latin American nations from the colonial powers of Spain and Portugal; and the legacy of the Second Great Awakening in the United States, a Protestant revival movement that flourished from the 1790s to the 1820s. These factors gave rise to new missionary initiatives from the North, and an influx of Protestant missionaries from the United States into Latin America (ibid.: 206–7). At the turn of the twentieth century, Latin America experienced domestic and foreign policy tumult in the aftermath of the Spanish–American War of 1898 and the resulting Treaty of Paris, which gave America temporary control of Cuba, and territorial expansion in Puerto Rico, Guam and the Philippine islands (the Philippines were given Commonwealth status in 1935 and full independence in 1946). American involvement gradually gained momentum throughout the early twentieth century, dramatically accelerating during the global Cold War, when the United States began to assert a more active role in shaping Latin American socio-political life (see especially Westad 2007).

The intense ideological struggle of the global Cold War – the undeclared war between the United States and the Soviet Union that dominated international affairs roughly between 1945 and 1991 – was an extension of European colonialism and the proving ground of ideologies forged in Moscow and Washington (Westad 2007: 3–4). The United States, increasingly a global industrial power, began inserting itself in socio-political and economic life – most notably in Central American countries through Central Intelligence Agency (CIA) intervention. This included the 1954 CIA-backed coup and removal of the Guatemalan president Jacobo Arbenz, the failed attempt to overthrow Fidel Castro in

---

2 See 'Monroe Doctrine, 1823', https://history.state.gov/milestones/1801-1829/monroe, accessed 20 March 2016.

the Cuban exile-led Bay of Pigs invasion of 1961, and 'Operation Power Pack', the second US invasion and occupation of the Dominican Republic in 1965 (for more on the Bay of Pigs invasion, see Tombs 2002: 69; Hartch 2014: 99). These political developments unfolded alongside an emerging urban religious economy. Domestically, rural–urban migration increasingly shifted populations to the urban centres, stretching cities to their structural capacities (Kirkpatrick 2015; 2016).

For the first time in Latin American history, Protestantism began gaining a demographic foothold as urbanisation provided a new social context for religious life (Hartch 2014: 96, 97). Protestant churches found acceptance at the margins of this new urban environment, growing in places that traditional Roman Catholic structures largely struggled to reach. Challenges for the Roman Catholic hierarchy only increased as the post-war period commenced – communist advances, antipathy towards widespread military regimes, Protestant conversions, and low participation rates among the masses. The growth of Protestant churches thus coincided with the increasing involvement of US foreign policy in Latin America during the Cold War era, as described above.

Within an increasingly contested religious environment, the air was thick with anti-American sentiment. The United States was often blamed for persistent economic malaise and – perhaps most loudly – for daily atrocities committed by US-backed military regimes. In some cases Latin American military dictatorships were also friendlier to Protestants than to Catholics, as the Catholic hierarchy held power and influence while increasingly siding with the poor (see especially Hartch 2014: 59–61). By implication, many Latin American Protestants were seen as foreigners in their own land – labelled 'gringos' and Yankees (Mondragón 2010: 19).[3] Many Roman Catholic priests and authorities viewed Protestant evangelistic efforts aimed at so-called nominal Roman Catholics as imposing on their religious turf. Priests and religious leaders sometimes played into these fears by stoking mob violence against Protestants.[4] Latin American Evangelicals thus shared the socio-political context while negotiating a unique path as a religious minority community on an overwhelmingly Catholic continent.

I have written elsewhere about the cluster of political and social forces that were reshaping post-war Latin America: rural–urban migration flows, the resulting complications of urbanisation, and the rapid expansion of the universit-

---

3   Also, author's fieldwork throughout Latin America.

4   For example, the account of the Student Christian Movement staff worker and later general secretary Valdo Gallard in the Yale Divinity School Archives, New Haven CT, USA, World Christian Student Federation Papers, Collection 46, Box 284, Folder 2500.

ies, where Marxist ideas of revolutionary change presented a growing appeal to students (Kirkpatrick 2016). Indeed, the socio-political ferment of post-war Latin America was the primary catalyst for religious change in the region; this was perhaps seen most clearly in Catholic theologies of liberation and Protestant social Christianities such as *misión integral*. The emerging religious marketplace was not simply a Latin American one; rather, it was transnational in its currency – a wide variety of proprietors vied for customers and resources. This religious commerce increasingly moved from denominations to parachurch organisations in a shift that was similar to the one seen in Christianity in the United States (for more on this, see Wuthnow 1988): for the first decades of its existence, the InterVarsity Christian Fellowship enjoyed a near-monopoly on Evangelical university campuses in North America.

The International Fellowship of Evangelical Students (IFES) was founded in August 1947 at Phillips Brooks House at Harvard University in Cambridge, Massachusetts, and it played a key role in reshaping global evangelicalism to include national leaders and social Christianity (Lowman 1988: 79; MacLeod 2007: 251; Woods 1978: 137–41). IFES is the worldwide representative body that arose out of the Inter-Varsity Fellowship (IVF), later known as the Universities and Colleges Christian Fellowship (UCCF) in Britain, and the InterVarsity Christian Fellowship in the USA (IVCF). Behind IFES's inception was the Australian Evangelical leader Stacey Woods – the founding general secretary of IVCF in the USA (which would quickly become its largest and primary source of financial backing), and the first general secretary of IFES. IVF, an organisation originally based in Britain, had recently expanded into the United States in 1937 under the direction of Woods and the Canadian IVCF. In the same decade as it expanded into the USA, Stacey Woods dreamed of extending IFES's reach southwards. Woods first travelled to Latin America in April 1937, and he returned in 1944 to Mexico, Guatemala, Nicaragua, Costa Rica and Colombia (Stanley 2013a: 158; MacLeod 2007; Woods 1978: 32–3).[5] In February 1945, IVCF-USA staff worker Ed Pentecost enrolled as a postgraduate student in Hispanic literature at Mexico's National University. There, he began to initiate student Bible studies and meetings, mostly based in his home.

After the Second World War, Christian student organisations such as IVCF-USA grew quickly as a direct consequence of a booming university student population. Student enrolment increased dramatically, due in part to the US government's GI Bill of 1944, which provided tuition assistance to attend university (the GI Bill was known officially as the Servicemen's Readjustment Act).

---

5   For more on the Latin American Mission, see Hartch (2014: 20–1).

This increase in university student enrolment coincided with an explosion of religiosity in American culture, typified by packed stadiums for Billy Graham crusades and the insertion of 'One Nation Under God' into the American Pledge of Allegiance (see especially Kruse 2015). Yet, IFES and IVCF-USA were never truly at home in the burgeoning subculture of American fundamentalism, in contrast to their closest rival Campus Crusade for Christ.

Campus Crusade for Christ (CCC) was founded by American Presbyterian Bill Bright on the campus of the University of California-Los Angeles in 1951 and represented the subculture of American fundamentalism perhaps more than any other parachurch organisation (Bright 1999: 14). Fundamentalism was a militantly anti-modernist Protestant evangelicalism that developed in the United States in the 1920s (Marsden 1980: 4). 'Fundamentalists were evangelical Christians, close to the traditions of the dominant American revivalist establishment of the nineteenth century, who in the twentieth century militantly opposed both modernism in theology and the cultural changes that modernism endorsed' (ibid.: 4). Most Protestant missionaries to Latin America in the first half of the twentieth century were from American fundamentalist interdenominational organisations – including the Central American Mission and Latin America Mission.

In contrast to IVCF's uneasy relationship with American fundamentalism, Bill Bright applied his understanding of US culture to the university campus by targeting well-known college athletes, the Greek system (sororities and fraternities), and an emerging anti-communist sentiment in fundamentalist circles during the Cold War era (Turner 2008: 8). Bright also tapped into the American Evangelical view that they were 'a beleaguered minority but remained determined to recover their custodial leadership of American society' (ibid.: 67). Thus, Bright could speak to the unique *responsibility* of American students to recover their country and, in turn, reach the world for Christ. Bright wielded an incisive interpretation of post-war American culture, and streamlined that analysis into reproducible methods (ibid.: 67). By 1968, the ministry of CCC had expanded into thirty-two countries and had become one of the largest Christian organisations in the world (Bright 1999: 119). In 2011, CCC estimated that it had over 25,000 staff members in 191 countries – by far the largest Christian student organisation in the world (Goodstein 2011). Its 2014 annual report recorded $537.9 million in US revenue alone, while international revenue was over $150 million (Cru 2015). In contrast, the IFES's total income in 2011 (the date of its most recent annual report) was $7.5 million, and IVCF-USA's was $71.7 million for 2013–14 (IVCF 2015; IFES 2015). Rather than co-operate or simply expand alongside one another, IFES and CCC often competed fiercely for the same constituency. The existence and success of CCC threatened IFES general secretary

Stacey Woods in particular, challenging his ability to shape Christian orthodoxy on university campuses around the world.

For Latin American IFES staff members such as Ecuadorian Evangelical René Padilla and Peruvian Samuel Escobar, competition with CCC was more than a theological or methodological contrast. For them, CCC represented American fundamentalism and at times the paternalism of American organisations in Latin America. IFES, in contrast, prided itself on providing freedom for national leaders to shape the form and character of their movements. In 1967, Woods wrote to Escobar:

> I'm afraid we are going to face vicious competition from Campus Crusade all over the world. I don't think it's any use our trying to compete with Campus Crusade in terms of their method or stance. They have millions of dollars at their disposal. Theirs is another form of fundamentalist imperialism, without concern for anybody else.[6]

That same year, Woods wrote letters to his Latin American staff members decrying both the expansion of CCC and the methods that led to this increase: namely, vast evangelistic projects that IFES viewed as superficial.[7] In contrast, Woods perceived IFES as the healthy alternative to North American excess. Personal correspondence between Stacey Woods and IFES staff shows that, in the face of increasing competition, Woods emphasised what he saw as their distinctive characteristics: contextual methods, national leadership, and small group discipleship.[8] In their view, this was a stark contrast with the operating paradigm of most traditional Evangelical organisations, which operated with paternalistic oversight and imported methods from the North. The organisational structure of IFES provided intellectual freedom for Latin American leaders such as Padilla and Escobar to experiment with social Christianity and, in turn, to challenge the very heart of the Evangelical Protestant mission.

---

6 Billy Graham Center Archives, Wheaton IL, USA (BGCA), SC 49, Box 3, 'Staff: 1971: E-Z & Misc. Correspondence', Folder 'Samuel Escobar: 1971', Stacey Woods to Samuel Escobar, 13 October 1971.

7 Samuel Escobar Papers, Valencia, Spain, Woods to Escobar, 21 December 1967.

8 Ibid.

Freedom from Fundamentalism: The Inerrancy of Scripture and Latin American Evangelical Elites

For Evangelical Protestants in North America in the 1970s, biblical inerrancy was the foremost Evangelical boundary marker (Sweeney 2005: 155–80). The Evangelical Theological Society (ETS, founded in 1949), for example, gave assent to the authority of scripture, and particularly to biblical inerrancy, its only theological requirement (Youngblood 1984). This doctrine asserted that the Bible is 'wholly and verbally God-given ... without error or fault in all its teaching, no less in what it states about God's acts in creation, about the events of world history, and about its own literary origins under God, than in its witness to God's saving grace in individual lives' (ICBI 1978). In some ways, this was a carry-over from the American Evangelical heritage of fundamentalism. In his definitive history of American fundamentalism, George Marsden argues that inerrancy was 'a code word for much of the fundamentalist movement' (Marsden 1980: 56). The following case study, then, is much more than an abstract theological debate. Competition for resources provoked deep-seated frustration among Latin Americans with financial dependency on the United States. Growing Latin American discontent produced a context in which new theological ideas and renewed calls for national leadership flourished within traditional Protestant Evangelical organisations. This transnational space reinvigorated regional nationalism and identity, which were contested by paternalism from the North. One event – the battle over scriptural inerrancy – raised these diverse factors to the surface and accelerated the fracture of Evangelical theological consensus.

Battles between Western-based parachurch organisations reached a tipping point in the global South in the early 1970s. The moment when Latin American Evangelical elites began to publicly reject the importation of American ideas, methods and resources can be identified quite precisely: on the final day of the First Latin American Congress for Evangelisation in 1969. In the late 1960s, North American Evangelicals increasingly turned their attention towards their neighbours to the South, due to the competition described above, widespread fears over the communist penetration of Latin America, and concern over the World Council of Churches' radical theologies. In 1969, the Billy Graham Evangelistic Association (BGEA) planned what it boldly heralded as the First Latin American Congress for Evangelisation or CLADE.[9] René Padilla, an increasingly

---

9 See, for example, BGCA, SC 324, Box 4, Folder 3, C. Peter Wagner to Clive Taylor. For more on this conference, see Kirkpatrick (2015: 148–57).

influential Evangelical and the first IFES general secretary for Latin America, and Peruvian colleague Samuel Escobar were perhaps the two most prominent conservative Protestant Evangelicals there. (Today, Padilla is the most prominent expositor of Evangelical social Christianity from the global South.)

Each participant at CLADE I received a copy of American missionary and later Fuller Theological Seminary Professor Peter Wagner's book *Latin American Theology: Radical or Evangelical? The Struggle for the Faith in a Young Church*. Wagner divided Latin American Christians into three groups and labelled them: Evangelical Protestants (whom he also called Fundamentalists); conservative Catholics; and the 'radical left-wing group made up of both Protestants and Catholics' (Wagner 1970: 9). Wagner also posited a contextual Latin American understanding of mission, in which he rejected social action in favour of 'saving souls'. In response, Padilla wrote a scathing article outlining his most explicit case for Evangelical social Christianity to date – 'Teología Latinoamericana: ¿Izquierdista o Evangélica?' – in the magazine *Pensamiento Cristiano* (Padilla 1970). Many Latin American leaders were offended that the programme had been completely planned in North America, perceiving its content as aloof from Latin American contextual issues. On the last day of the first CLADE congress, Padilla, Escobar and Puerto Rican Orlando Costas met to discuss the need for a truly Latin American Evangelical theological organisation.

In response, the first gathering of the Fraternidad Teológica Latinoamericana (Latin American Theological Fraternity, or FTL) took place from 12 to 18 December 1970 in the town of Carachipampa, located just outside Cochabamba, Bolivia – although in later press releases, the nearby city of Cochabamba was named for clarity.[10] The motivation was, as Escobar noted in a 2013 interview, 'that we as Latin Americans decide who is *evangélico* in America Latina and what it means to be *evangélico*'.[11] René Padilla presented a paper titled 'Autoridad de la Biblia' ('Authority of the Bible'), which appeared tame at first. However, Padilla's paper stirred up a hornets' nest of controversy that neither he nor his colleagues could have anticipated.

Although not his paper's primary focus, Padilla set the inerrancy of scripture in his sights. The hypothesis of inerrant original manuscripts was irrelevant for Padilla, for the extant copies *do* contain errors. In one case, he wrote: 'The biblical writers are not historiographers; their intention is not to write a complete,

---

10   C. René Padilla Papers, Buenos Aires, Argentina, 'FTL Consulta 1', undated. See also Padilla (2009: 133).

11   Interview with Samuel Escobar by the author, Valencia, 22 October, 2013.

"objective", history that would meet all the standards of modern historiography. They write more from the point of view of faith, as people committed to their message' (Padilla 1972: 127). For Padilla, these 'minor errors' include ones of transmission, and could include errors in the 'minimal detail of geography, history, natural sciences' (ibid.: 129). Padilla quickly attempted to ward off criticism, however, saying that he did not mean to pass judgement on inerrancy. He wrote that his purpose was not to reject inerrancy, but to discuss the Bible in reference to the history of salvation, the revelation of Jesus, and the witness of the Holy Spirit. Ultimately, the paper signalled a refusal on the part of Latin Americans to submit to the theology of both British and North American conservative missionaries, organisations and mission agencies – many of whom utilised biblical inerrancy as a litmus test of orthodoxy.[12] Although Padilla certainly intended to challenge the North American Evangelical theological establishment, he could not have foreseen the subsequent controversy.

On 5 January 1971, Peter Wagner was commissioned by *Christianity Today* (*CT*) to write a first-hand summary of the FTL gathering at Cochabamba. In his article 'High Theology in the Andes', he expounded a generally positive account – much like the accounts of other North American Evangelical publications.[13] His initial description of Padilla's paper was straightforward, and accurate:

> In his position paper on authority, Padilla argued that insistence on an inerrant Bible means asking for something unavailable – since no present edition or version is free from difficulties of transmission and/or translation. The result, said Padilla, is the danger of ending up with no Bible and no authority. Exaggerated insistence on inerrancy, he added, in effect saws off the limb that supports evangelical theology.
>
> WAGNER 1971: 28

While Wagner's description may have been benign, his organisational identification set off a firestorm of criticism. Wagner identified Padilla's paper with 'what some called the "Inter-Varsity bloc"'. Wagner also tipped his hand by contrasting Padilla's position with that of British Anglican Evangelical Andrew Kirk. Wagner wrote: 'Not all were convinced by Padilla and his backers. Holding uncompromisingly to an inerrant Bible and verbal inspiration Andrew Kirk

---

12   For a British example, see Padilla's discussion with IVF general secretary Oliver Barclay: IFES Papers, Oxford, England, Barclay to Padilla, 15 February 1972.

13   See, for example, 'Report on Latin American Theologians', *Pulse* 6 (1) (1971).

of Union Seminary in Buenos Aires declared in his closely reasoned paper on hermeneutics, "What the text of the Bible says, God says without reservation and without reduction"' (ibid.: 28). Wagner's contrast was misleading – it went beyond belying Padilla's personal views on inerrancy. Padilla did hold to 'verbal inspiration' and later protested vehemently against a supposed division between himself and Kirk (ibid.). Wagner, however, accurately described the fault lines that arose between those who wanted to include inerrancy in the final Cochabamba declaration (Dispensational Evangelical Emilio Nuñez, Andrew Kirk, Peter Wagner) and others who wanted it left out (Peruvian IFES staff member Pedro Arana, Escobar, Padilla).[14] In the end, the response to Padilla's paper, as summarised by Wagner, from CT's primarily North American readership was swift and overwhelmingly negative.

Soon after Wagner's article appeared, Padilla told the Peruvian-born British missionary Peter Savage that IFES had received 'una lluvia de cartas' (a downpour of letters), many asking that Padilla be formally disciplined for his view on the Bible.[15] Woods, for his part, remained adamant in his support for his Latin American staff and lambasted Wagner.[16] Yet, fearing an even greater backlash, Woods requested fifty copies of the Cochabamba Declaration in English. Woods then wrote to Arana, Escobar and Padilla, requesting further documentation of their views on scripture. In his letter, he also continued to excoriate Wagner: 'I really believe the wretched Wagner is malicious. If this sort of thing continues to spread, it could have a bad effect upon the work and its support. I want to do what I can, public relations wise, honestly and sincerely, to bury the ghost.'[17]

Woods continued to receive negative letters from around the world, and responded by implementing a strategy of damage control. Padilla also sought to minimise the damage, while remaining defiant in the face of criticism:

> I make no apologies for what I said in Cochabamba. The position expressed there was carefully thought through beforehand and when I stated it I very well knew that I was sticking out my neck and opening myself to all sorts of accusations and misunderstandings. Yet I felt that I would not be honest if I did not express my deep convictions that the big

---

14   Interview with Samuel Escobar by the author, Valencia, Spain, 22 October 2013.
15   BGCA, 358, Box 8, Folder 1, Padilla to Savage, 14 April 1971. See also Woods to Padilla, 4 March 1971.
16   Padilla Papers, Buenos Aires, Argentina, Woods to Padilla, 4 March 1971.
17   Ibid.

fuss that most evangelicals raise over inerrancy reflects a serious misun-
derstanding of the nature of Biblical revelation, tied up with a reduction-
ist concept of truth.[18]

Padilla's statement acknowledged that he understood that he would cause
controversy by his rejection of inerrancy. Wagner, for his part, attempted a
reconciliation with Padilla, writing an open letter through the FTL in June 1971,
defending church growth theory in the process.[19] Wagner resigned from his FTL
responsibilities that year and left Latin America to return to the United States,
where he was hired by Donald McGavran at Fuller Theological Seminary in
Southern California.[20]

Although major theological issues were at stake, this prolonged FTL inerrancy controversy must be seen in light of one primary factor: competition for
financial resources. Global Evangelical networks connected Latin American
Evangelicals through mission agencies and, in the case of Padilla and Escobar, the global Evangelical student movement. IFES staff member Alec Clifford
wrote a handwritten note to Wagner on 19 June 1971, decrying the financial
impact of the inerrancy controversy:

> The repercussions of your CT report have been most unfortunate and
> far reaching. The whole program of IFES and IVF (USA) seems to have
> suffered through a loss of financial support and confidence thanks to the
> article ... I don't know what can be done to undo the harm at this stage.[21]

The financial situation certainly motivated Stacey Woods to implement dam-
age control measures. That year, 1971, IVCF-USA contributed 67 per cent of the
IFES's overall income and budget.[22] Any drop in funds from donors in the
United States would reverberate around the world. Although IFES had move-

---

18   Padilla Papers, Buenos Aires, Argentina, Padilla to Woods, 15 March 1971.

19   Padilla Papers, Buenos Aires, Argentina, C. Peter Wagner, 'Carta Abierta a Rene Padilla Para
     "Noticiero de la Fraternidad"', 15 June 1971.

20   BGCA, SC 358, Box 8, Folder 1, Wagner to Padilla, 13 May 1971. For more correspondence
     regarding this controversy, see BGCA, SC 358, Box 8, Folder 1, Wagner to Savage, 1 June 1971;
     BGCA, SC 358, Box 8, Folder 1, Wagner to Padilla, 31 March 1971.

21   BGCA, SC 358, Box 8, Folder 1, Alec Clifford to Peter Wagner, 19 June 1971.

22   BGCA, SC 49, Box 'I.F.E.S. Minutes', Folder 'General Committee (9th) 8/20–9/1/75', 'Minutes
     of the Meeting of the Ninth General Committee, 20 August–1 September 1975', p. 13.
     Special thanks to IFES general secretary Dr Daniel Bourdanné for access to this restricted
     file.

ments in over ninety countries, financial generosity from the United States supported the overwhelming burden of funding its operations. Thus, Latin Americans were necessarily concerned with their perception in the North, even with regard to foreign theological concerns. The transnational nature of post-war evangelicalism tied their fates together, even as they sought to expand their independence.

In hindsight, Clifford's fear of a decrease in American donations was only partially founded. Donations from the United States to IFES fell by 17 percentage points from 1971 to 1974, from 67 per cent in 1971 to just over half in 1974. The overall income of IFES, however, rose from $243,279 in 1971 to $347,440 in 1974. Minutes from the Executive Committee also make clear that IFES had been planning to wean itself off American financial dependency for some time. Thus, it is unclear whether this drop should be credited primarily to the Padilla controversy or to active fundraising outside the United States. Regardless, this competition did not remain at the intersection of Latin America and the United States. Instead, Latin American Evangelicals took their perspectives to global conciliar gatherings, shifting the trajectory of Evangelical discourse.

Transnational Competition and the Reshaping of Global Evangelicalism

The repudiation of forms of Christian theology fashioned in the United States was more than a theological statement: it was a reflection of broad Latin American antipathy towards US foreign policy in the region, a rejection of missionary paternalism, and a rejection of Latin American Protestant Evangelical sensitivity being associated with certain colleagues in the North. Ultimately, this attention to transnational competition sheds light on key moments in the history of evangelicalism in the twentieth century – especially the Lausanne Congress of 1974. In 1974, *Time* magazine called the Billy Graham-funded Lausanne Congress 'a formidable forum, possibly the widest-ranging meeting of Christians ever held', with nearly 2,500 Protestant Evangelical leaders from over 150 countries and 135 denominations participating (*Time* 1974). A growing body of literature has also begun to note its importance (Wacker 2014: 229; Noll 2012: 287; Stanley 2013b). Perhaps most notably, the Lausanne Congress signalled the refusal of non-white and non-Western Christians to accept Western-planned agenda for the rest of the world, where issues of social justice often remained marginal (Stanley 2013a: 155; 2013b: 534). Rather than a wholesale *shift southwards*, this marked the beginning of a multidirectional conversation with a wide variety of interlocutors.

Lausanne's loudest and most controversial voices came from Latin Americans, whose proximity to the United States and fraught history with aggressive Cold War foreign policy positioned them to challenge a paternalistic Evangelical context. In his scathing plenary speech, René Padilla decried the equating of Christian orthodoxy with political conservatism and the export of the 'American way of life' to the global South (Padilla 1975: 130). Padilla also argued for a wider definition of Christian salvation: 'A comprehensive mission corresponds to a comprehensive view of salvation. Salvation is wholeness. *Salvation is total humanization*. Salvation is eternal life – the life of the kingdom of God – life that begins here and now ... and touches all aspects of man's being' (ibid.: 130). Padilla's controversial speech became the centre of theological negotiation at the congress, and largely set the trajectory for debates that carried on throughout the next two decades.

At Lausanne, Latin Americans led the charge for two key components. First, they negotiated a place at the table for leaders from traditional mission fields. Second, they negotiated space for widening Evangelical discourse to include social Christianity. The controversial nature of social Christianity within Evangelical circles can only be understood against the background of the theological landscape of the post-war period. In the late nineteenth and early twentieth centuries, Evangelical social action was largely justified theologically either through the removal of 'obstacles to the progress of the gospel', or through the elimination of social sins that contravened divine commands (Bebbington 1983: 10–13). In terms of theological methodology, this fitted squarely within a 'two-mandate approach', which predominated in Evangelical theological circles prior to the 1970s (Bosch 1991: 403). This method bifurcated Christian mission into a primary, spiritual mandate and a subordinate social mandate. Padilla and others at Lausanne led the charge to synthesise these two 'mandates', giving priority to neither evangelism nor social action. Padilla called this approach *misión integral*, or an 'integral mission' – a phrase derived from his home-made *pan integral* (wholewheat bread). Today, the language of integral mission is utilised by over 500 Christian mission and relief organisations – including US-based parachurch organisations Compassion International and World Vision. In 2015, World Vision was the eleventh largest charity in the United States, with a revenue of over $1 billion that year alone (Forbes 2015).

Latin American negotiation widened not only Evangelical leadership and theology but also the language of their mission. This had clear implications for humanitarian parachurch organisations, which leveraged this wider Evangelical discourse on social Christianity to raise funds from the Evangelical faithful. Now, Evangelical organisations with an explicitly social mission could be considered *family* rather than *foe*, like the Social Gospel of the late nineteenth and early twentieth century.

Much has been written about the surprising, sharpened rhetoric of Latin Americans at Lausanne. Personal letters reveal that René Padilla, however, was already *persona non grata* in various conservative Evangelical circles prior to the Lausanne Congress of 1974. Why, then, was Padilla still chosen as a plenary speaker by conservative Evangelicals in the North? It was IVCF-USA staff member Charles Troutman who spoke on behalf of Padilla and Escobar. Troutman wrote to Jack Dain, Lausanne convener and assistant bishop in the (particularly Evangelical) Sydney Anglican diocese, urging Lausanne leaders to avoid the paternalistic mistakes of the American-exported CLADE I (described above).[23] Troutman had attended the Billy Graham-led CLADE I and had witnessed the backlash against BGEA's paternalistic methods. Troutman's realisation, however, was simply one example in a wider conversation among Northern Evangelical leaders. Many were increasingly aware of the vast growth of Christianity in the global South. By implication, they set a larger table that included seating for diverse leaders, even though this resulted in a correspondingly complex conversation. With Billy Graham's blessing, Padilla and Escobar were ultimately invited by Dain to speak at Lausanne – an invitation that had manifest implications for the future trajectory of global Evangelical conciliar discourse. The power of Evangelical parachurch networks and resources therefore surfaced at Lausanne and influenced the trajectory of its legacy.

The structure of IFES and its competition with 'sibling' organisations such as CCC should be credited with stirring the pot that spilled over at Lausanne in 1974. Latin Americans such as Padilla and Escobar had been exercising their own leadership and exploring theological ideas within parachurch organisations since the 1960s. Thus, attempts to reassert paternalistic influence over theological formulation was met with fierce resistance. The emergence of holistic and contextual theologies in global Evangelical Protestantism was the direct result of these conflicts and negotiations. The intersection of North American influence and Latin American dependency was increasingly salient for the emergence of Protestant Evangelical social Christianities.

---

23   BGCA, SC 46, Box 30, Folder 3, Troutman to Dain, 28 February 1972. See also Troutman to
     Bürki, 11 February 1974.

Conclusion

This brief case study sheds light on the issue of agency in the making of World Christianity at the level of theological discourse. Latin American and Northern Evangelical leaders negotiated resources, ideas and power, even as their mission overlapped in significant ways. Rather than co-operate or simply expand alongside one another, they often competed fiercely for the same constituency. Although North American Evangelicals were backed by considerable material and intellectual resources, Latin American leaders were able to draw on the tradition of local autonomy fostered by IFES and IVCF to reshape a global theological agenda.

Competition for resources provoked deep-seated frustration among Latin Americans with financial dependency on the United States. Growing Latin American discontent then produced a context in which new theological ideas and renewed calls for national leadership flourished within traditional Protestant Evangelical organisations. As Latin American Evangelical theologians awoke to the issue of dependency on the US, they set the trajectory for a new, contextual brand of social Christianity.

Theological battles that played out on the pages of Christianity Today were, in some ways, a trial run for the negotiation that would arise over the role of social Christianity in Evangelical discourse. This controversy over inerrancy also clarifies the well-known events of the Lausanne Congress of 1974. In particular, Padilla was already persona non grata in certain conservative circles prior to his influential speech at the congress. This helps to explain the tenor of his controversial speech and his explicit reference to the 'American way of life' that was poisoning mission fields around the world. Padilla's inclusion on the Lausanne docket also reveals two realities that existed in tension. First, many Evangelical leaders maintained a stark realism regarding the need for complex postcolonial conversations. While increasingly controversial, Padilla (among others) represented a growing and sizeable constituency of young leaders from the global South. Rejecting him and his emerging brand of social Christianity risked fracture on a global scale. Second, many in the conservative Evangelical establishment remained largely unaware of the growing frustration regarding US influence in the global South. At Lausanne, however, few could ignore that the simmering pot of global evangelicalism appeared ready to boil over. Padilla's repudiation of forms of Christian theology fashioned in the United States was therefore more than a theological statement – it was a reflection of broad Latin American antipathy towards paternalistic oversight by North American missionaries, US foreign policy in the region, and Latin American Evangelical sensitivity to being associated with certain colleagues in the North.

Scholars, then, should treat with caution the thesis that equates evangelicalism with US spiritual imperialism emanating from the so-called Religious Right. As Latin Americans negotiated space for social Christianity, they played a crucial role in widening Evangelical discourse and building the intellectual scaffolding of the Evangelical Left as a foil to the Religious Right in the United States.

References

Bebbington, D. (1983) 'Evangelicals and Reform: An Analysis of Social and Political Action', *Third Way* 10–13.

Bebbington, D. (1993) *Evangelicalism in Modern Britain: A History from the 1730s to the 1980s*. London: Routledge.

Berger, P. L. (1967) *The Sacred Canopy: Elements of a Sociological Theory of Religion*. Garden City NY: Doubleday.

Bosch, D. J. (1991) *Transforming Mission: Paradigm Shifts in Theology of Mission*. Maryknoll NY: Orbis Books.

Bright, B. (1999) *Come Help Change the World*. Orlando FL: NewLife.

Chesnut, A. (1997) *Born Again in Brazil: The Pentecostal Boom and the Pathogens of Poverty*. New Brunswick NJ: Rutgers University Press.

Chesnut, A. (2003) *Competitive Spirits: Latin America's New Religious Economy*. Oxford and New York NY: Oxford University Press.

Cru (2015) *Cru 2014 Annual Report*. Orlando FL: Cru, http://www.cru.org/content/dam/cru/about/2014-cru-annual-report.pdf, accessed 27 March 2016.

ECFA (2015) '2014 ECFA Annual State of Giving Report'. Winchester VA: Evangelical Council for Financial Accountability (ECFA), http://www.ecfa.org/Content/2014-ECFA-Annual-State-of-Giving-Report, accessed 15 March 2016.

Forbes (2015) 'The 50 Largest US Charities', http://www.forbes.com/companies/worldvision/, accessed 24 March 2016.

González, O. E. and J. L. González (2008) *Christianity in Latin America: A History*. Cambridge and New York NY: Cambridge University Press.

Goodstein, L. (2011) 'Campus Crusade for Christ Is Renamed', *New York Times*, 20 July.

Hatch, N. O. with M. S. Hamilton (1995) 'Epilogue' in D. G. Hart (ed.), *Reckoning with the Past: Historical Essays on American Evangelicalism from the Institute for the Study of American Evangelicals*. Grand Rapids MI: Baker Books.

Hartch, T. (2014) *The Rebirth of Latin American Christianity*. Oxford Studies in World Christianity. Oxford: Oxford University Press.

ICBI (1978) *The Chicago Statement on Biblical Inerrancy*. Oakland CA: International Council on Biblical Inerrancy (ICBI).

IFES (2015) *Annual Report, 2011.* Oxford: International Fellowship of Evangelical Students (IFES), http://ifesworld.org/sites/all/libraries/ckfinder/core/connector/php// files/2011_IFES_annal_report_en.pdf, accessed 24 March 2016.

IVCF (2015) *Annual Report, 2013–2014.* Madison WI: InterVarsity Christian Fellowship (IVCF), http://www.intervarsity.org/page/annual-report-2013-2014, accessed 24 March 2016.

Kirkpatrick, D. (2015) 'C. René Padilla: Integral Mission and the Reshaping of Global Evangelicalism'. PhD thesis, University of Edinburgh.

Kirkpatrick, D. (2016) 'C. René Padilla and the Origins of Integral Mission in Post-War Latin America', *Journal of Ecclesiastical History* 67 (2): 351–71.

Kruse, K. (2015) *One Nation Under God: How Corporate America Invented Christian America.* New York NY: Basic Books.

Lowman, P. (1988) *The Day of His Power: A History of The International Fellowship of Evangelical Students.* Downers Grove IL: InterVarsity Press.

MacLeod, D. (2007) *C. Stacey Woods and the Evangelical Rediscovery of the University.* Downers Grove IL: InterVarsity Press Academic.

Marsden, G. (1980) *Fundamentalism and American Culture: The Shaping of Twentieth Century Evangelicalism, 1870–1925.* New York NY: Oxford University Press.

Martin, D. (1990) *Tongues of Fire: The Explosion of Protestantism in Latin America.* Oxford and Cambridge MA: Blackwell.

Mondragón, C. (2010) *Like Leaven in the Dough: Protestant Social Thought in Latin America, 1920–1950.* Madison NJ: Fairleigh Dickinson University Press.

Noll, M. A. (2012) *Turning Points: Decisive Moments in the History of Christianity.* Grand Rapids MI: Baker Academic.

Padilla, R. (1970) 'Teología Latinoamericana: ¿Izquierdista o Evangélica?', *Pensamiento Cristiano* 17 (66): 133–40.

Padilla, R. (1972) 'La autoridad de la Biblia en la teología Latinoamericana' in P. Savage (ed.), *El debate contemporáneo sobre la biblia.* Barcelona: Ediciones Evangélicas Europeas.

Padilla, R. (1975) 'Evangelism and the World' in J. D. Douglas (ed.), *Let the Earth Hear His Voice. International Congress on World Evangelization Lausanne, Switzerland: Official Reference Volume: Papers and Responses.* Minneapolis MN: World Wide Publications.

Padilla, R. (2009) 'My Theological Pilgrimage', *Journal of Latin American Theology* 4 (2): 91–111.

Pew Research Center (2015) 'Religion in Latin America'. Washington DC: Pew Research Center, http://www.pewforum.org/files/2014/11/Religion-in-Latin-America-11-12-PMfullPDF.pdf, accessed 27 March 2015.

Stanley, B. (2013a) *Global Diffusion of Evangelicalism.* Nottingham: InterVarsity Press.

Stanley, B. (2013b) '"Lausanne 1974": The Challenge from the Majority World to Northern-Hemisphere Evangelicalism', *Journal of Ecclesiastical History* 64 (3): 533–51.

Stark, R. and R. Finke (2000) *Acts of Faith: Explaining the Human Side of Religion*. Berkeley CA: University of California Press.

Stoll, D. (1990) *Is Latin America Turning Protestant?: The Politics of Evangelical Growth*. Berkeley CA: University of California Press.

Sweeney, D. A. (2005) *The American Evangelical Story: A History of the Movement*. Grand Rapids MI: Baker Academic.

Time (1974) 'A Challenge from Evangelicals', *Time*, 5 August.

Tombs, D. (2002) *Latin American Liberation Theology*. Boston MA and Leiden: E. J. Brill.

Turner, J. G. (2008) *Bill Bright & Campus Crusade for Christ: The Renewal of Evangelicalism in Postwar America*. Chapel Hill NC: University of North Carolina Press.

Wacker, G. (2014) *America's Pastor: Billy Graham and the Shaping of a Nation*. Cambridge MA: Harvard University Press.

Wagner, O. (1971) 'High Theology in the Andes', *Christianity Today*, 15 January.

Wagner, P. (1970) *Latin American Theology: Radical or Evangelical? The Struggle for the Faith in a Young Church*. Grand Rapids MI: Eerdmans.

Westad, O. (2007) *The Global Cold War: Third World Interventions and the Making of Our Times*. Cambridge: Cambridge University Press.

Woods, S. (1978) *The Growth of a Work of God: The Story of the Early Days of the Inter-Varsity Christian Fellowship of the United States of America as Told by its First General Secretary*. Downers Grove IL: InterVarsity Press.

Wuthnow, R. (1988) *The Restructuring of American Religion: Society and Faith since World War II*. Princeton NJ: Princeton University Press.

Youngblood, R. (ed.) (1984) *Evangelicals and Inerrancy: Selections from the Evangelical Theological Society*. Nashville TN: Thomas Nelson.

PART 2

Locating Knowledge

••
•

CHAPTER 4

Doing Theology in World Christianities: Old Tasks, New Ways

Peter C. Phan

It is intriguing that the last two volumes of the monumental nine-volume *The Cambridge History of Christianity* bear the subtitle 'World Christianities'. Volume 8, edited by Sheridan Gilley and Brian Stanley, covers the history of Christianity in the nineteenth century (*c.*1815–*c.*1914) (2006), and Volume 9, edited by Hugh McLeod, that of the twentieth century (*c.*1914–*c.*2000) (2006). What happened, one wonders, to Christianity in these two centuries that justifies describing it with the new sobriquet of World Christianities, qualifying this Christianity as 'world' and using 'Christianity' in the plural? By giving this unusual title only to the last two volumes of the series, does *The Cambridge History of Christianity* imply that the Christianity that is narrated in Volumes 1 through 7 was neither 'world' nor 'Christianities'?

The answer to the above question depends, of course, on what is connoted by both 'world' and 'Christianities'. If by 'world' one means that Christianity is universal and open to all peoples and to all regions of the world – another expression for this is 'catholic' – and if by 'Christianities' is meant that Christianity is variegated in self-definition, cultural and confessional ethos, doctrinal formulation, liturgical worship and organisational structure, then Christianity has undoubtedly been so since its very beginnings. Indeed, the goal of the first volume of *The Cambridge History of Christianity*, entitled *Origins to Constantine*, as stated by its editors Margaret M. Mitchell and Frances M. Young, is to emancipate past historiography from a schematised view of early Christianity as a uniform and invariant institution. Indeed, as the editors put it tersely, 'the recognition of diversity within Christianity from the very beginning has transformed [the] study of its origins' (Mitchell and Young 2006: xiii).

While catholicity ('world') and diversity ('Christianities') are arguably constant features of Christianity as a whole, a persuasive case can be made that Christianity of the nineteenth and twentieth centuries is so different from that of the previous eighteen centuries in geographical expansion and internal diversity that it alone deserves to be dubbed 'World Christianities'. Curiously, neither Sheridan Gilley in his introduction to Volume 8 nor its other contributors use the expression themselves. But the fact that, as Gilley notes, contrary to most other histories of nineteenth-century Christianity, this volume dedicates nearly a third of its 600 pages to the new Christian churches outside Europe is an eloquent testimony to the transformation of nineteenth-century Christianity into a truly 'world', or global, and highly diversified religion.

While still implicit in Volume 8, the concept of World Christianities is elaborated at length in the next volume. Noting 'the development of Christianity from a mainly European and American religion to a worldwide religion', its editor Hugh McLeod points out that one of the book's five major themes is that 'Christianity becomes a worldwide religion' (McLeod 2006: 6). Indeed, the entire volume can be viewed as offering a documentation of this global expansion of Christianity ('Part II: Narratives of Change') and of the resulting variations and multiplicities within Christianity as it sought to respond to the many and diverse challenges of the modern and postmodern age ('Part III: Social and Cultural Impact').

Of course, *The Cambridge History of Christianity* is not the only work, nor the first, that highlights the global and multiple character of contemporary Christianity. There has recently been a plethora of scholarly and popular studies in church history as well as – and perhaps especially – in missiology, new journals and periodicals, courses and programmes, and centres and institutes at both universities and seminaries that make World Christianities or Christianity in the non-Western world the object of research and teaching.

The immediate impact of the concept of World Christianities is, of course, on the discipline of church history – or, more accurately, the history of Christianity, as evidenced by *The Cambridge History of Christianity*.[1] Another academic discipline that has been significantly impacted by this view of World Christianities is missiology. Works by renowned missiologists such as David Bosch, Andrew Walls, Lamin Sanneh, Robert Schreiter and Stephen Bevans, to cite only a few, have shifted the focus of mission from evangelisation by foreign missionaries to the building of local churches by native Christians, thereby contributing to the indigeneity and variety of Christianities.

In their comprehensive survey of World Christianity, Sebastian Kim and Kirsteen Kim spell out six aspects in which Christianity as a 'world religion' can be studied. Topographically, the mapping of Christianity takes into account its local varieties and types throughout the globe. Theologically, Christianity's claim to be both universally applicable and locally inclusive needs to be taken

---

1   On the distinction between 'church history' and 'history of Christianity', see Phan (2012). On how the concept of World Christianities demands new ways of doing church history, see the insightful and challenging work by González (2002) and Kollman (2004).

seriously. Geographically, its presence and impact in all parts of the globe must be recognised. Socio-politically, its diversities and multiplicities can be seen mainly as the result of attempts by indigenous and grassroots communities – and not by expatriate missionaries – to contextualize the Christian faith. Historically, Christianity's global expansion was never carried out by and from a single geographical and ecclesiastical centre, exporting and imposing a homogeneous and identical form; rather, Christianity was polycentric from its very beginnings, expanded in different directions and in diffuse fashion, and adapted itself to each locale and context. Lastly, structurally, Christianity is shown to be a transnational and transcontinental movement constituted by complex networks of diverse kinds (Kim and Kim 2013).

A parallel focus on the impact of World Christianities on systematic theology is also emerging, especially on the way in which theology should be done (methodology) and on how the various *loci theologici* are to be reformulated (systematics). Regrettably, theology has not yet dealt with the concept of World Christianities with the same vigour and intensity as the history of Christianity and missiology. One reason for this relative paucity of interest is that systematic theologians, whose field is doctrine, generally tend to be more concerned with permanence and less sensitive to historical changes than their colleagues in history and missiology. Furthermore, it comes as no surprise that most of the theological effort to respond to the challenges of World Christianities so far has taken place in the so-called Third World (or Two-Thirds or Majority World): that is, Africa, Asia and Latin America, where new types and forms of Christianity are proliferating. However, Third World theologians generally do not enjoy the same academic status as their Western colleagues and, for the most part, their writings are unknown, unless they come under scrutiny and censure by ecclesiastical authorities, especially in the Catholic Church.

In what follows I focus on the challenges World Christianities pose to the theological enterprise, and, more specifically, to dogmatic/systematic/constructive theology, leaving to others the task of reflecting on its implications for other sub-disciplines, such as biblical, historical, moral and practical theologies. I first examine, under the rubric of 'Theology in World Christianities: Old Task, New Ways', the new methods in which theology is being performed in World Christianities. Next, to flesh out this methodological section, I illustrate these new ways of doing theology with concrete examples of some key *loci theologici* taken from different parts of the Christian world ('Theologies *in* World Christianities'). Finally, I indicate how World Christianities entails a new understanding of Christianity itself ('Theology *of* Christianities').[2]

---

2 For a more extensive explanation of the concept of World Christianities, see Phan (2012).

Critics of the notion of World Christianities point out that Christianity has always been diverse and indigenised and therefore one must not overstate its alleged novelty. This might well be the case, since nothing is utterly new under the sun, and the caution against overstatement is well taken. However, it is beyond doubt that the change from Christianity as Christendom during the so-called Constantinian era to Christianity as World Christianities in the sense indicated above is so radical that it is perfectly legitimate to use the overwrought, but in this case exquisitely accurate, expression 'paradigm shift' to characterise it. Nowhere is this paradigm shift more evident, I contend, than in systematic theology.

Theology in World Christianities: Old Task, New Ways

Theology as faith seeking understanding – *fides quaerens intellectum*, to use Anselm's celebrated definition – is as ancient as Christianity, but this old task has been carried out in ever new ways throughout the course of Christian history, searching for understandings and practices of the faith that are appropriate to different socio-political, economic, cultural and religious contexts, as any historical survey of Christian theology readily shows. All theologies, without exception – just like rationality itself – are therefore unavoidably context-dependent, and any theology's pretensions to universal applicability and permanent validity can easily be unmasked as symptoms of either intellectual naïveté or hegemonic ambition. The question, then, is not whether World Christianities can or should shape theological method, but rather *how* they actually do so. One convenient way to see the impact of World Christianities on theology in recent decades is to examine how they have affected the deployment of the six 'sources' of theology – or, to use John Macquarrie's expression, 'formative factors'. Let us briefly consider each.

Experience

Since theology is, to use Gustavo Gutiérrez's celebrated phrase, 'critical reflection on praxis' that 'rises only at sundown' (Gutiérrez 1991: 9), its matrix must be the various concrete contexts in which World Christianities are located. In the West, at least since the eighteenth century, the primary experience for theology consists of such cultural shibboleths as secularism, atheism, agnosticism and relativism, against which Christian thinkers have devised a whole array of philosophical arguments in defence of theism and objective truth. No doubt these Enlightenment-inspired ideologies are also present outside the West, but in these non-Western countries the pervasive reality from which theology arises is not centred on these epistemological and metaphysical issues but on massive and dehumanising material poverty and oppression bolstered by economic and political structures. Elsewhere, in Africa and Asia, the destructive legacy of Western colonialism has been enormous, and now insidious and manifold forms of neo-colonialist capitalism, with its Western models of economic development through monetisation and technological modernisation, are reducing millions of people who used to live on a subsistence economy to abject poverty because they have no role and are of no use in a global market economy. These new forms of economic domination challenge World Christianities to find new ways to speak about God and things pertaining to God.

Besides poverty, other forms of oppression, such as racism, classism and patriarchalism, confront theology in as well as outside the West. Ecological degradation is another pressing worldwide issue. Other problems of global character include stateless terrorism and violence, and national and international migrations. By contrast, some problems are peculiar to certain countries, such as the caste system, tribalism and communalism. In light of these very diverse contemporary experiences, many theologians in non-Western Christianities have abandoned an introspective, spiritualistic and individualistic conception of experience as the context for theology. Instead, they expand the nature of theology as *sapientia* (wisdom) and *sacra scientia* (rational knowledge) by doing theology as a critical reflection on praxis that is animated by the 'option for the poor' (*orthopraxis*). The basic questions for theology in World Christianities are therefore about *which* and *whose* experiences should be both its source and its hermeneutical lens.

Revelation

God's self-communication in the history of Israel and supremely in Jesus of Nazareth remains, of course, the definitive norm (*norma normans*) for Christian theology. However, more than ever World Christianities are encountering other religions that also claim to be recipients of divine revelation, such as Hinduism with its *sruti* (that which is heard), Islam with its Qur'an, and the Church of the Latter Day Saints with its *Book of Mormon*, not to mention a host of other recent religious movements and sects with their respective founders' religious experiences and recorded utterances (for example, the Unification Church or the Moonies with its *Divine Principle*). Whereas Christian theology has until recently limited itself to considering divine revelation exclusively in Israel and in Christianity, especially in the context of Jewish-Christian dialogue, theologians in World Christianities are today challenged to consider the possibility of divine revelation as the inbreaking and disclosure of Holy Mystery in religions other than Judaism and Christianity and relate it to God's self-gift in Jesus Christ. This in turn leads to a systematic reconceptualisation of God, Christ, the Holy Spirit, church, and other *loci theologici*.

Scripture

Intimately connected with the possibility of divine revelation outside Judaism and Christianity is scripture. As alluded to above, many religions other than Judaism and Christianity possess scriptures whose origins are also attributed to divine communication and that are venerated as the inspired 'Word of God'. Furthermore, even religions that do not claim divine origin have sacred texts, such as Buddhism (the Tripitaka), Jainism (the *Agamas*), Sikhism (the *Guru Granth Sahib*), Zoroastrianism (the *Avesta*), Confucianism (the Four Books and Five Classics), and Daoism (the *Daodejing*). In World Christianities, particularly in Asia, where Christians regularly encounter the followers of other religious traditions, it is imperative to re-examine the Christian doctrine of biblical inspiration and canonicity in light of the existence of non-Christian scriptures and sacred texts, especially in interreligious dialogue and shared religious rituals and prayer services.

The issue of biblical hermeneutics often comes up for discussion in this connection. Whereas in the West biblical scholars for the most part have adopted the historical-critical method and interpret the Bible as a standalone text, and, in some cases, only intratextually, theologians in other World Christianities are urged to practise an intertextual and even interreligious reading of sacred texts. This is the project of the emerging disciplines of cross-cultural and interreligious hermeneutics and 'comparative theology'. On the other hand, an almost opposite hermeneutical approach is widespread in several World Christianities, particularly those associated with Pentecostalism, the fastest-growing Christian church in Africa and Latin America and in some Asian countries such as China. It privileges biblical elements that are largely dismissed in mainline churches, such as prophecy, exorcism, glossolalia and miraculous healing.[3] Thus, theologians in World Christianities can no longer assume the historical-critical method that is dominant in Western academy as the standard, nor limit themselves to practising an exclusively intratextual hermeneutics.

Tradition

Also under intense debate in World Christianities is the nature of tradition, and, above all, what should count as tradition. Rejection of tradition takes the

---

3   This point is strongly made by Jenkins (2006).

form of *sola scriptura*, especially in Pentecostal churches of World Christianities. By and large, however, the necessity of tradition is readily acknowledged, particularly in cultures such as those of Asian societies where tradition is generally given a normative role. Rather, the debate centres on what should count as normative tradition. Ironically, Vincent of Lérins' triple canon formulated in his celebrated dictum 'That which has been believed everywhere (*ubique*), always (*semper*), and by all (*ab omnibus*)', which is commonly appealed to in conservative circles in defence of tradition, is given a new and surprising twist in light of World Christianities.[4] Geographical ubiquity, temporal antiquity and numerical universality, which are often attributed to Western tradition as proof of its universality and normativity, are now turned on their heads. For the first time, it is argued, these three Vincentian criteria of Christian orthodoxy have been met – albeit never perfectly and unambiguously. Only in World Christianities is 'everywhere' found, 'always' instantiated, and 'by all' realised. In World Christianities, the Western tradition of the past as well as the present is not given a privileged status, much less a normative one. Western Christianity is not related to World Christianities as centre to periphery, with all the privileges associated with the centre; rather, it is only one Christianity among other Christianities, no more no less, and its traditions, often maintained through power and imposed by force, legal and otherwise, must be seen for what they really are: local, context-dependent and culture-bound historical particularities.

Needless to say, it is in local traditions that World Christianities embody their specific differences and peculiarities. These traditions embrace each and every aspect of church life: Bible translation, liturgical language, sacramental celebration, worship, prayer, sacred objects, art and architecture, music, canon law, organisational structure, theology, spirituality, and so on. In World Christianities, variety in tradition is not simply the result of adapting previously existing – mainly Western – traditions to different local contexts through the process of translation, linguistic and cultural, although admittedly this did happen extensively thanks to the work of expatriate missionaries. Rather, in World Christianities, new traditions are constantly 'manufactured', especially in Pentecostal and independent churches, with staggering variety and dazzling ingenuity, in a process of 'globalisation from below'. This independent and unrestrained proliferation of traditions, often the work of charismatic leaders and without local, national or international consultation and agreement, poses

---

4   The best critical edition of Vincent of Lérins' *Commonitorium* is by Demeulenaere (1985). An older edition, with a very informative introduction, is Moxon (1915).

a serious threat to faithfulness to the Christian faith and church unity. How to achieve this faithfulness and unity without falling into uniformity and fostering 'the tradition of the dead' is one of the most difficult tasks for theology in World Christianities (Farhadian 2007).

Culture

Nothing is more conspicuous in World Christianities than the fact that the gospel is expressed in a mind-boggling variety of languages and cultures, at times even within the same country, such as Indonesia with its more than 700 spoken languages.[5] Beneath the language lies a world view or a common pattern of thought and behaviour into which the Christian faith is contextualised, indigenised or inculturated. Culture, in contrast to nature, is a human construction, and in the process of cultural creation, the powerful often arrogate for themselves the right to determine what belongs to culture and what does not, what is true and normal and what is false and deviant, and thus only what serves their interest is acceptable as culture. Furthermore, even where there is no conscious attempt at domination, certain cultural achievements by the elite are elevated to the status of 'classical' or 'high' culture, which alone deserves propagation and preservation. As a result, 'popular' culture and the cultures of minority and tribal groups are neglected and even marginalised.

In inculturation – that is, the encounter between Christianity and local cultures – the same dynamics are at work. In the past, cultural indigenisation has been conducted between official Christianity and 'world religions' with their canonical classics, hierarchical leaders and approved theologians (for the most part, expatriate missionaries). This was the case, for instance, with Matteo Ricci and the Confucian literati in China, and with Roberto de Nobili and the Hindu Brahmins in India. In contemporary World Christianities, however, the dialogue between Christianity and cultures (note the plural) has eschewed this elitist bias, and much attention is now being paid to the local, regional, ethnic and tribal 'small traditions'. For instance, in India, local Christianities are made up largely of Dalits and Tribals, and in China, Catholic, Protestant and Pentecostal churches gain the largest following in rural areas where Chinese folk religion is widely practised. In Africa, African Independent or Initiated Christianity, whose membership increased from 50,000 in 1900 to 99 million in 2010, has incorporated many beliefs and practices of African traditional

---

5   For Christianity in Indonesia, see the over 1,000-page work edited by Aritonand and Steenbrink (2008).

religion.[6] In general, it is the adoption of these 'small traditions' that is the distinguishing mark of Christianities in the Third World.[7]

In this context, an issue that is being hotly debated is popular religiosity or popular devotions. In the past, a good number of these popular devotions were condemned as superstition, idolatry and magic, and conversion to Christianity required a total renunciation of these practices. Witness the repeated proscription of ancestor worship by Roman authorities in the Catholic Church until 1939 (the so-called Chinese Rites controversy). In World Christianities, especially in the Catholic Church, there has been a vibrant renaissance of popular piety, especially devotion to Mary and the saints, veneration of ancestors, and pious practices such as novenas, procession and pilgrimage, particularly in Christianities influenced by Iberian spirituality such as those in Latin America, the Philippines and Vietnam. Furthermore, 'popular Catholicism' has become an important source for Catholic theology. In general, the relation between Christianity and local cultures has been widely discussed in contemporary theology, especially in missiology, and an abundant literature has been produced on the issue, which is known under various names such as contextualisation, indigenisation, localisation or inculturation of the Christian faith.

---

6 On African Christianity in general, see Hastings (1994). Hastings' book should be brought up to date with his own *A History of African Christianity 1950–1975* (1979), Isichei (1995) and Bediako (1995). On African Independent/Initiated Churches (AICs) and their bewildering varieties and multiplicities, the literature is growing rapidly (see Barrett 1968; Sundkler 1961; Anderson 2000a; 2000b; Daneel 1987; Pobee and Ositelu II 1988). It is extremely difficult to obtain the exact number of AIC members. According to a report from the World Council of Churches (WCC), in 1981 AICs constituted 15 per cent of the total Christian population in sub-Saharan Africa. Assuming a growth estimated at more than 2 million per year, their adherents probably numbered close to 100 million in 2010, thus constituting a significant section of African Christian demography.

7 With this statement, I am making only a historical and phenomenological observation on the way in which Third World churches have dealt with local cultures, and not a value judgement on their ecclesial character: that is, whether they are more or less authentic than mainline churches. Such a doctrinal judgement is, of course, predicated on a set of mutually agreed criteria for orthodoxy which may not be available. With regard to AICs in particular, they no doubt had strong connections with Pentecostal missionary movements from the West, but they have consciously severed these connections through their attitude – generally by no means uniformly positive – toward African traditional religion and culture. Motivations for ecclesial independence are varied and include considerations that are political (freedom from Western imperialism), denominational (the Protestant tendency to divide and separate in situations of conflict), and cultural (adoption of the African world view).

Reason

The last formative factor in theology in Macquarrie's list is reason. Although it originated from divine revelation and thus is not rational in the sense of being derived from pure philosophy or autonomous reason, Christianity claims to be reasonable, not merely in the sense that it is not absurd or contrary to reason (*pace* Tertullian) but also in the sense that at a minimum it must give a justification for its hope. This is done not by appeal to divine authority and authorised tradition but by means of reasoned arguments with publicly available criteria of truth (apologetics and fundamental theology). Moreover, beyond this apologetical task, Christian theology has engaged in conversation – at times in friendly alliance, at other times in hostile confrontation – with various philosophies, other human sciences such as history, anthropology, psychology, sociology and natural sciences. This, of course, has been the main way in which Western Christianity has interacted with reason.

In other Christianities, however, the dialogue between Christian faith and reason takes on unfamiliar forms. In many countries, such as India, China, Japan, Korea and Tibet, to cite just a few Asian countries, there are centuries-old and well-developed philosophies. Here, Hindu, Buddhist, Confucian, Daoist and Islamic philosophical systems are in full vigour, expressed in sophisticated conceptual frameworks and in a huge number of multilingual writings, such that no one scholar can claim mastery of even one philosophical tradition.[8] Interestingly, many Asian philosophers are well versed in Western philosophy, which may facilitate the dialogue between Asian philosophy and Christianity, but the same cannot be said of Western theologians, for the majority of whom Asian philosophy still remains a closed book.

Furthermore, for the majority of people in World Christianities outside the West, where orality is predominant, philosophical world views are expressed not in philosophical texts but in myths, stories, proverbs, koans, songs, dance, rituals, festivals and dramas. Here, the dialogue between Christianity and these forms of rationality is no less theologically complicated and pastorally even more urgent.

Thus far I have shown through a cursory examination of the six formative factors in theology how doing theology has become vastly complex in World Christianities, much more so than in Western theology. Both the resources of theology and their deployment have changed and multiplied as Christianity has become global, requiring widely divergent approaches and methodologies

---

8   A helpful one-volume guide to Asian philosophies is Carr and Mahalingam (1997).

and entailing new and different articulations of the basic Christian beliefs. In the following section, I highlight some of the ways in which the main *loci theologici* have been reconceptualised in World Christianities.

Theology in World Christianities

New contexts, new experiences, new resources, new methodologies and a new generation of theologians inevitably bring forth new theological insights, and this is especially true of Christianities in the non-Western world. A rapid survey of theological developments since the second half of the twentieth century shows that, apart from some significant trends in Germany and France, and to a lesser extent, Britain and the United States, the most challenging, and even revolutionary, innovations in theology have taken place in Latin America, Africa and Asia. In the Catholic Church, this general assessment is confirmed by the fact that, under the leadership of then-cardinal Joseph Ratzinger as Prefect of the Congregation for the Doctrine of the Faith, and later as Pope Benedict XVI, the two theologies that were attacked, and their key proponents censured, were liberation theology and theology of religious pluralism, both of which originated in the Third World, the former in Latin America and the latter in Asia.

This does not mean that these two theological trends (and others) developed by themselves, in isolation and without an extensive dialogue with and learning from Western theologies. On the contrary, in recent decades there has been an extensive and constant contact and exchange among various World Christianities. The Catholic Church with the Second Vatican Council (1962–65), the World Council of Churches with its numerous general assemblies and committees, and the World Evangelical Fellowship have all greatly fostered communication and collaboration among theologians in all parts of the world. In addition, the Ecumenical Association of Third World Theologians (EATWOT), founded at Dar es Salaam, Tanzania in 1976, has been a fertile venue for worldwide theological exchange. Furthermore, thanks to innumerable academic conferences, church gatherings, international networks and online communications, theological ideas and movements circulate the globe with a speed unimaginable only a couple of decades ago.

The theologies in World Christianities have been given different names in which the relation between Christianity and culture is described by various prefixes. If culture is deemed positive, these theologies are said to be *trans*cultural, *multi*cultural, *cross*-cultural and *inter*cultural, each denoting a particular aspect of the dynamics of the encounter between faith and culture (Küster 2011:

16–17).[9] The theologian's task is to mediate between faith and culture, and the goal is to express the contents of the faith in categories that are understandable to the people of a particular time and place, and, if necessary, to jettison the traditional, even ecclesiastically sanctioned, formulations of Christian beliefs and practices to meet the needs of the age. On the other hand, theologies are dubbed *counter*cultural and *anti*-cultural if a particular culture is judged godless and hostile to the gospel ('culture' standing in for 'world' in the Johannine sense of being opposed to God). In the latter case, the main task of theology is to critique – and, when necessary, resist and reject – cultural trends that are judged to be inimical to the Christian faith, rather than seeking ways to accommodate it to culture.

By and large, however, the terms 'intercultural' and 'contextual', as well as the underlying positive perceptions of culture, are more common in World Christianities. 'Intercultural' highlights the fact that contemporary theology is inevitably a culture-dependent and culture-bound intellectual production arising out of and at the same time shaping the encounter between the gospel and a particular culture. 'Intercultural' makes it clear that this encounter is not between a culture-free, 'pure' gospel and another culture (which the words 'inculturation' or 'incarnation', commonly used in Catholic circles, might misleadingly suggest), but always between an already culture-laden gospel (Jewish and Hellenistic) and a particular culture – or more likely cultures – in a given place that usually contains both values and disvalues. 'Contextual', on the other hand, accentuates the fact that the cultural context is not a neutral geographical venue in which World Christianities are implanted but rather something that conditions and influences the very way in which theology is constructed.[10] Let us now review the main re-articulations of Christian beliefs in World Christianities.

God

Whereas most Third World theologians emphasise the need to start from an accurate social analysis of concrete socio-political, economic, cultural and religious contexts in which theology is done – the first part of the three-stage process of 'see judge act' – the primary object of their theologies is not human experience as such but God and all things insofar as they pertain to God. This should be stated in response to the criticism, often voiced by conservative theologians, especially those under the sway of Karl Barth, that Third World theolo-

---

9   See also Cartledge and Cheetham (2011).
10   This connotation of 'context' is implied in the subtitle of Tennent (2007).

gies, allegedly heirs of modernity and liberal theology, are anthropocentric and immanentist in orientation and have lost sight of the real object – or rather the subject – of theology, namely God as the Absolute Transcendent and the Totally Other.[11] On the contrary, it must be acknowledged that God remains the central focus of many currents of theology in World Christianities, and therefore it is appropriate to begin the discussion of theology in World Christianities with God. However, what is new and distinctive in these theologies is that they take the vastly different experiences in World Christianities, as outlined above, and not the Bible or church teachings, as their starting point, perspective and hermeneutical lens for a reconstruction of the traditional understanding of God. Broadly speaking, their method is more inductive than deductive.

Interestingly, this critique of the doctrine of God was undertaken first in Western Christianity, where it took the form of a wholesale rejection of what is termed 'classical theism'. It means by this a philosophy and theology of God in which, following the legacy of Hellenism, God's perfection is understood to imply aseity, self-sufficiency, immutability, impassibility, and total detachment from the change, pain and suffering of the world. Leading this charge are Process philosophers and theologians such as Alfred North Whitehead, Charles Hartshorne, John Cobb Jr, Joseph Bracken, and a host of others. Akin to Process theology, in Evangelical theology, proponents of Open Theism such as Clark Pinnock argue for a view of God that presents God as freely and intimately involved in a dynamic relationship of love with human beings, which makes God vulnerable to temporality, change and suffering, and in which God affects creatures and creatures affect God.[12]

Third World theologies of God would resonate sympathetically with the basic understanding of God proposed by Process theology, especially its concept of a suffering God. However, their starting point, resources and methodology, and hence their resulting theology of God, are substantially different. As mentioned above, their immediate context is not dissatisfaction with 'classical theism'. Nor is their goal an elaboration of a speculative metaphysics in which God as 'responsive love' (God's 'consequent nature'), to use Process thought's

---

11   This criticism is often voiced by proponents of the so-called 'Radical Orthodoxy', especially John Milbank.

12   See Pinnock et al. (1994) and Sanders (2007). In its early phase, from the 1930s to the 1960s, Process theology focused on God. After the 1970s, it turned its attention to other topics such as liberation (Schubert Ogden), feminism (Marjorie Suchocki), science (Ian Barbour, Philip Clayton, Ann Pederson), interreligious dialogue (John Cobb Jr, David Ray Griffin, Clark Williamson, Joseph Bracken), evil (Griffin, Suchocki, Bracken) and ecology (Jay McDaniel).

expression, is subject to change, and in which God as a 'fellow-sufferer who understands' acts in the world by persuasion and lure, not by coercive power. By contrast, as has been alluded to above, the context of Third World Christianities is massive systemic impoverishment and exploitation. Seen in this context, and reading the Bible through this hermeneutical lens, God is understood primarily as a liberator of the oppressed who has created an option for the poor, and, because of this option, 'has shown strength with his arm; has scattered the proud in the thoughts of their hearts; has brought down the powerful from their thrones and lifted the lowly; has filled the hungry with good things, and sent the rich away empty' (Luke 1: 51–3).

For liberation theologies, it is these acts of God in 'lifting the lowly' and 'filling the hungry with good things' that define the nature of God. What and who God is are known in and through what God does – not in generic actions in the world such as creation, providence and consummation (the customary categories in Western theology to describe God's activities in the world) but in specific, highly partial and politically charged interventions that liberate those who are treated as non-persons by the rich and the powerful, and that in this way overturn the social order. Thus, in Third World theologies of God, there has been a shift not merely from the immanent Trinity to the economic Trinity, as exemplified by the two paragons of First World theology, Karl Barth and Karl Rahner, but from a generic understanding of the economic Trinity as the immanent Trinity self-actualising in human history to an economic Trinity self-actualising in God's identification and solidarity with a specific group of people designated with the umbrella term 'the poor'.

Needless to say, these poor in turn reconceptualise God from their particular form of oppression. This is not because, as a black woman in Sue Monk Kidd's novel *The Secret Life of Bees* tells a white girl who wonders why there is a black Madonna, 'Everybody needs a God who looks like them' (Kidd 2002: 141); rather, it is because it is precisely in these people with their specific forms of oppression that God has revealed what and who God is and for whom God 'has shown strength with his arm'. Thus, there is black theology (against racism), African theology (against cultural colonialism), Latin American theology (against economic oppression), feminist theology in its various forms (against patriarchy and androcentrism), Dalit theology (against the caste system), tribal theology (against marginalisation and the exploitation of minorities), *minjung* theology (against dictatorship and capitalism), theology of struggle (against state security ideology), ecological theology (against environmental degradation), and so forth. Because of their focus on particular forms of human oppression, these theologies run the risk of being perceived as anthropocentric, and of being accused of reducing salvation to the socio-political and economic dimensions.

Furthermore, because these theologies are a critical reflection on praxis, they may be liable to the charge that they foment class struggle and even violent revolution. In light of these misunderstandings, it is necessary to point out that when these theologians articulate their theologies of God, they are not indulging their 'need to have a God who looks like them' (Feuerbachian and Marxian theories of projection); rather, they are seeking to reveal the real face of God as God has truly appeared in the world (the economic Trinity) and the specific ways in which God saves humanity and the cosmos (grace as freedom, salvation as liberation). In sum, in World Christianities, God is one who is world-relational, all-inclusive, co-suffering, and saving-by-liberating.[13]

Christ

Because Jesus is the human face of God, it is in Christology that the distinctiveness of Third World theologies is most evident. Indeed, it is in Christology that the efforts of World Christianities to contextualise the Christian faith have produced the largest amount of literature. Again, as in the theology of God, although the Bible still functions as the *norma normans*, it is the context that serves as the starting point, the perspective and the hermeneutical lens for Christological construction. As K. K. Yeo puts it concisely:

> Global Christologies seek creative dialogues toward: (1) a *catholic* faith based on biblical Christologies that honor multiple and interacting worldviews; (2) a global theology that respects cross-cultural and shifting contexts in which faithful communities embody real-life issues; (3) a translatability of the Scripture that upholds various dynamic vernaculars and hermeneutics; and (4) a round-table symposium of proclaiming and worshiping a biblical Christ portrayed in varied Christologies.
>
> YEO 2014: 168

Add to Yeo's list of missiological ('proclaiming') and doxological ('worshiping') goals the praxiological dimension (the overturning and transformation of oppressive societal structures) of Third World theology, and we have a glimpse of the dazzling variety of non-Western Christologies. Within this framework, it is possible to classify Christology in World Christianities according to the various concerns relating to race (black), ethnicity (Chinese, Indian, Latino/a, etc.),

---

13   An example of this theology of God can be found in the works of the Taiwanese Presbyterian professor of theology Choan-Seng Song. Among his many writings, see Song (1982). Of course, this theology of God is not exclusive to Third World theologians. Among First World theologians, Jürgen Moltmann can be considered its foremost proponent.

gender (white, womanist, *mujerista*, etc.), class (Dalit), tribe (American Indian, Tribals in north-east India), geography (continents and countries), culture and religion.

My point here is not to offer a bibliographical survey of these Christologies; any competent overview of contemporary Christologies will present their significant trends, their guiding concepts, and the writings of their prominent proponents. Rather, I would like to examine the basic ideas that provoke, challenge and shape the bewildering variety of Christological reflections in World Christianities. One helpful way to understand their basic orientations is to group them under the three major concerns of World Christianities: namely, liberation, inculturation and interreligious dialogue. It is, however, important to remember that these three tasks are not distinct and unrelated; rather, they are deeply intertwined and overlap with each other so that one task cannot be fully achieved without the other two, although each can be given a particular emphasis depending on the local context.

Under the first category – liberation, which was developed first and foremost in Latin America – the focus is on the historical Jesus as the Liberator, with his message on the reign of God as reported primarily in the Synoptic Gospels. Jesus's words and deeds during his ministry, death and resurrection are mined to highlight his preferential option for the poor and the liberative force of his actions against all kinds of oppression in all aspects of life, including the environment. Here lie the major contributions of Latin American, black, feminist and ecological Christologies.

The second category includes inculturation Christologies, which find a congenial home in Africa, where colonialism has wrought extensive cultural pauperisation, and which centre on the retrieval and adoption of certain elements of indigenous cultures to present Christ as a universal person, 'without borders' and cross-cultural, and, precisely for that reason, capable of being 'African'. Here, the images that emphasise kinship and community take pride of place and are used to present Jesus as mother, elder brother, ancestor, chief, and healer. Again, the Synoptic Gospels as well as the other writings of the New Testament, especially the Pauline letters, provide ample materials for inculturated Christologies.

Religious Pluralism and Interreligious Christology

The third category of Christology, which falls within the ambit of interreligious dialogue, is so complex, vast and controversial that it merits discussion under a separate heading. Of all the Christologies developed in World Christianities, interreligious Christology has the potential to be the most revolutionary trend, shaking Christianity to its foundations. In a real sense, interreligious encounter is not new, of course, as Western theologians from the earliest times had to present Christ in relation to – or, more precisely, *over against* – Judaism, pagan religions and Islam.

What is novel and is causing deep reverberations in Christology in World Christianities is, firstly, that interreligious dialogue is now taking place in all World Christianities, but, for obvious reasons, particularly in Asia, the cradle of all world religions. Thanks to globalisation and migration, religious pluralism is now a global phenomenon, with large and complex socio-political, economic, cultural and religious implications and calling for interreligious dialogue, not least for the sake of world peace and harmony. Secondly, the encounter between Christianity and other religions is now conceived, at least by the majority of Christians, not as confrontation but as *dialogue*, requiring a set of intellectual and moral virtues that make mutual understanding and co-operation among believers of different faiths possible.[14] Thirdly, this interreligious dialogue now involves new partners, not only Judaism and Islam, with which Christianity has family resemblances and a common heritage, but also religions with which Christianity has little or no connection, such as Hinduism (non-personal theism), Buddhism (non-theism), Confucianism and Daoism (immanentism and humanism), and a host of other no less global religious traditions, such as Jainism, Sikhism and primal religions. Fourthly, this dialogue has led to a radical and thorough re-examination of all the major Christian *loci theologici*; indeed, none of the reputed non-negotiables of the Christian faith have been left undisturbed. These include not only Christology but also the doctrine of God and the Trinity, pneumatology, revelation, inspiration, biblical hermeneutics, church, worship, spirituality and ethics, and, of course, as mentioned above, the six formative factors in theology.

Again, it is not my intention to provide here an overview of the ways in which Christian theology has been challenged by religious pluralism; informative surveys of interreligious dialogue are plentiful.[15] What I would like to do is outline the various challenges that religious pluralism poses to Christology and set out the two main types of interreligious Christology in World Christianities.

---

14   This is not to say that dialogue occurs everywhere in World Christianities. Conflicts with, violence against, and persecutions of Christians in countries such as China, India, Sudan, Nigeria and many Middle Eastern countries have been widely reported. What I intend to say is that even in these conflictive situations, the only means to achieve peace, justice and reconciliation is dialogue, especially in its fourfold mode: namely common life, practical collaboration, interreligious conversation, and sharing of spiritual experiences.

15   See, for instance, Cornille (2013), Cheetham et al. (2013) and Becker and Morali (2010).

First, regarding theological challenges, as alluded to above, the very found-ation of traditional Christology has been shaken. With regard to Judaism, one major issue concerns supersessionism: that is, the doctrine that Christ – and hence Christianity – has 'fulfilled' Judaism, and therefore the covenant or test-ament that God has made with the Jews has become obsolete or 'old' and has been replaced by the 'new', Christian covenant. It is now asked, with deep moral anguish, especially in light of the Holocaust, whether this anti-Jewish and anti-Judaic 'teaching of contempt', albeit widespread in Christian tradition and claimed to be based on a number of statements in the New Testament, especially the gospels of Matthew and John and Hebrews, is biblically groun-ded in view of God's eternal faithfulness to his word and of what Paul says about the Jewish covenant (see Romans 9–11). If this supersessionism is rejected, and in my judgement it must be, disturbing questions are raised about the number of covenants and 'peoples of God' (note the plural) outside the historical Jesus and Christianity and their mutual relation, and about the appropriateness of the Christian mission to 'convert' the Jews.

Furthermore, traditional claims regarding Jesus as the unique, universal and eschatological Revealer and Saviour have been challenged. Troubling questions are raised regarding the salvific function of non-Christian religions. Are they, as missionaries of generations past and, in our time, Karl Barth have held, merely human, mostly superstitious, idolatrous and vain attempts to reach God? Or are they God-intended and God-initiated 'ways of salvation' in themselves? And, if the latter, how do we relate them to Christ and Christianity? Are they parallel and independent, or mutually complementary? Contemporary theologies of religions, commonly categorised as exclusivism, inclusivism, pluralism and a variety of combinations of these, are too well known to require exposition here.[16]

Connected with this Christological issue is biblical hermeneutics and the role of sacred books of non-Christian religions. It is not merely a question of how to interpret exclusive-sounding texts that categorically affirm the unique-ness of Christ, such as Acts 4: 12, 1 Timothy 2: 5; and John 14: 6 (critics would say interpret away). It has been suggested that their apparent exclusiveness can be overcome by contextualising them within an all-inclusive and universalistic orientation of the whole biblical tradition, expressed powerfully, for example, in John 1: 9. However, the more challenging task is how to interpret the Bible in light of non-Christian sacred scriptures. It is here that Third World biblical scholars and theologians such as Samuel Ryan, George Soares-Prabhu, R. S. Sug-

---

16   A very helpful introduction to these issues is Knitter (2002).

irtharajah, Archie C. C. Lee and Kwok Pui Lan, to mention just a few, have made innovative contributions to interreligious hermeneutics. Furthermore, in some places, for example in India, experiments have been made to include selected texts from these non-Christian scriptures into worship and prayer. Implicit in this hermeneutical practice and liturgical usage is a theology of revelation and inspiration that acknowledges the activity of the Holy Spirit ('in-*spiration*') in the origination and composition of these sacred texts.

Secondly, concerning its basic approaches, contemporary interreligious Christology has pursued two lines of research. The first explores how Christ and Christianity have historically been viewed in non-Christian sacred texts and by non-Christian thinkers themselves. This task is somewhat straightforward in the case of Judaism and Islam, given the fact that, like Christianity, they are 'religions of the Book', and given the long history of encounter among theologians of the three faiths. It is a commonplace, for example, that the Qur'an contains narratives about Abraham, the prophets, the Jews, Jesus and Mary; that the Christian Bible includes the Tanak; and that there has been a lively conversation among Jews, Christians and Muslims concerning their common theological heritage. Of course, the challenge is how to remove mutual misunderstandings, suspicions and hostility embodied in these texts and to bring to full flowering the common heritage and shared convictions among these three Abrahamic religions.

The second line of research in interreligious Christology is much more arduous and controversial than the first, seeking to relate the figure of Jesus to other religious founders and moral teachers such as the Buddha and Confucius, and to read the Bible in light of sacred texts that have little historical or literary commonality with it, such as the Vedas, the Upanishads, the Tripitaka, the *Guru Granth Sahib* and the Chinese classics. Fortunately, Christian theologians are neither the first nor the only ones to embark upon this task. Various Hindu, Buddhist and Confucianist thinkers have attempted this comparative work, often out of a sincere admiration for Jesus, his life and his teaching, but without converting to Christianity. Thus, in this type of Christology, similarities as well as differences between Jesus and other religious figures are highlighted, allowing Jesus to be spoken of as the Sage, the Way, the Guru, the Avatara, the Bodhisattva, the Satyagrahi, the Servant, the Compassionate, the Dancer, and the Pilgrim.[17] Obviously, these new Christological titles, notwithstanding their linguistic strangeness, resonate with those ascribed to Jesus in the New Testament, but clearly they also expand and enrich our traditional understanding

---

17   See Brinkman (2007), Barker (2005) and Amaladoss (2006).

of Jesus and speak meaningfully to Third World Christians. At the same time, this interreligious Christology causes much anxiety among guardians of orthodoxy for its alleged downplaying of the uniqueness of Jesus and its syncretistic tendency.[18]

The Holy Spirit

Another momentous development in contemporary theology in World Christianities is the emergence of a vigorous and vibrant pneumatology, thanks in part to theological attempts to account for the activity of God outside Jesus and Christianity. Appealing to Irenaeus's arresting metaphor of God the Father's 'two hands' working in the world – namely, the Word of God and the Holy Spirit – a number of theologies of religion invoke the activities of the Holy Spirit before, during and after the incarnation of the Word of God in Jesus of Nazareth. The Holy Spirit, it is argued, functions not independently from (much less in opposition to) but in collaboration and harmony first with the 'Logos not yet made flesh' (Logos asarkikos) and then with the 'Logos made flesh' (Logos sarkikos). But this collaboration between the Spirit and the Word of God should not be understood as dependence of the former on the latter, which the traditional Western theology of the Trinity, with its conception of the linear procession of the Spirit from the Father and the Son (Filioque), might misleadingly suggest. On the contrary, as the 'two-hands' metaphor implies, the Son and the Spirit work 'autonomously' or 'single-handedly', albeit in mutual collaboration, in different places and times, in diverse modalities, and with varying degrees of impact.

The venue in which the Spirit is actively present outside the historical Jesus and Christianity is pre-eminently non-Christian religions, with their beliefs and practices. In interreligious dialogue there have been attempts at finding analogues for the Spirit in the teachings of non-Christian religions, similar to those made in Christology mentioned above. Again, this task is relatively straightforward in the case of Judaism and Islam, although the challenge to express the 'personality' of the Spirit remains considerable. The task is much more complex in the case of Asian religions, given the great differences in conceptual frameworks. Contemporary research has singled out the concepts of prana (in Hinduism) and Qi or Chi (in Chinese thought) – that is, the

---

18   Within the Roman Catholic Church, this anxiety is well known, especially in the Congregation for the Doctrine of the Faith, and the latter's attempts to censure writings by theologians such as Jacques Dupuis, Jon Sobrino, Roger Haight, Michael Amaladoss and a host of others have been well chronicled.

energy or life force circulating in all things – as being particularly illuminating analogues for the Spirit as immanent grace and life-giving power.[19]

However, the main catalyst for the current resurgence of pneumatology in World Christianities is not interreligious dialogue but the phenomenal growth of evangelicalism or Pentecostalism – a new Pentecost – in Third World Christianity, especially in Africa, Asia (especially South Korea, India and China) and Latin America (especially Brazil and Guatemala). As a result, a different type of Christianity, quite different from the mainline churches of the First World, is spreading like wildfire, with a more literal understanding of the Bible and an exuberant panoply of the gifts of the Spirit.[20]

Theology of Christianities: Different Ecclesiologies

This mention of the astounding global expansion of Pentecostal churches is a natural transition point to the last part of my chapter. With all the developments in World Christianities today hinted at above, what is being produced is not a new 'Christendom' but a new Christianity – or, better, the birth of Christianities that explode the categories of traditional ecclesiology. Earlier, I mentioned how the three Vincentian canons for orthodoxy – namely, antiquity (*semper*), ubiquity (*ubique*) and unanimity (*ab omnibus*) – have been given a surprisingly new and ironic twist. It is not that these criteria are no longer valid or helpful; rather, it would seem that only in contemporary World Christianities do they apply, albeit not fully, for the first time.

At the same time, these criteria are upended. Whereas Vincent of Lérins deployed them not only as marks of orthodoxy but also as a means to foster ecclesiastical uniformity, or at least conformity, in today's World Christianities precisely the opposite effect occurs if they are applied consistently. When the 'always', 'everywhere' and 'by all' are given their full scope in global Christianity, what comes into view is not similarity, much less uniformity, but mind-boggling multiplicity and even profound discordance. Of course, in churches where there is a powerful central control mechanism, such as the Catholic Church, doctrinal and structural uniformity can be enforced, as was done under the pontificates of John Paul II and Benedict XVI. But even here appearances

---

19 See, for instance, Kim (2007), Kim (2011) and Lee (2014).

20 See Miller et al. (2013). Jenkins (2011) has drawn the contrasts between the Christianity of the global North and that of the global South in his book *The Next Christendom: The Coming of Global Christianity*. At times, Jenkins has overstated these contrasts, but his general point about the difference between these two types of Christianity is well made.

are deceptive. Perhaps one of the reasons for the latter's abdication was his inability to deal not only with the scandals of various kinds that were buffeting the church but also with the manifold and serious discrepancies between grassroots and hierarchical leaders that were cracking the foundations of the ecclesiastical edifice – and this in spite of restorationist policies he had established to slow down the reforms initiated by Vatican II and to quash ideas and practices he judged to be misinterpretations of the council. In World Christianities, however, attempts to revert to central control to ensure uniformity are doomed to failure.

Of course, variety, multiplicity and polycentricity in global Christianity raise the question of Christian identity, ecumenical unity, and, more basically, the nature of being 'church', since the Christian faith is essentially a social reality. In essence, there is no Christian faith without Christianity and church. But what makes Christianity and church 'Christian'? The urgency of this question in World Christianities can be gauged by noting how the breaking up of Christianity today, should it occur, would be far more devastating in scope and depth than the eleventh-century division between the Greek and Latin churches and the sixteenth-century separation between Roman Catholics and Protestants within the Latin church combined.

For one thing, the eventual disunity would be truly global for the first time – 'ecumenical' in the etymological sense of the term. This time, instead of the Middle East and Europe only, Africa, Asia, Latin America and Oceania – the so-called global South – would be active partners in the dispute, part of the world where, according to some demographic projections, four out of five Christians will live by 2050.[21] Secondly, there would be no centre that held, at least in the way it did when divisions occurred in the past, since the dividing lines now run not merely among churches, but in the midst of each church and denomination, especially where there is no central authority or recognised authoritative inter-church bodies. Thirdly, there would be no checklist of universally agreed-upon doctrinal non-negotiables that could serve as a litmus test for Christian

---

21   Whereas in 1900 over 80 per cent of all Christians lived in Europe and Northern America, by 2005 this proportion had fallen to under 40 per cent; it is likely to fall below 30 per cent before 2050. In *The New Faces of Christianity: Believing the Bible in the Global South*, Philip Jenkins, on the basis of various statistical projections, notes that, in 2015, 60 per cent of the estimated 2 billion Christians in the world lived in Africa, Asia or Latin America. By 2050, there will be an estimated 3 billion Christians, 75 per cent of whom will live in what is the 'global South'. The two most helpful statistical studies of global Christianity are Johnson and Ross (2009) and Johnstone (2011).

identity, such as a commonly formulated creed. Fourthly, relations with other religions would enter into discussions on intra-church matters, especially in areas where Christians are in a minority, such as Asia and North Africa, since it is impossible to be religious without being interreligious in these parts of the world. Finally, political factors such as government intervention would play a more invasive role, especially where religious freedom is severely curtailed.

Lest it be thought that the above rumination is an alarmist doomsday scenario, let's consider the case of Pentecostal Christianity, especially in China. In his informative study of Chinese Christianity, *Redeemed by Fire*, Lian Xi, Professor of World Christianity at Duke University, focuses on what he terms Chinese 'popular Christianity': that is, the Christian movements that developed in China outside mainline Protestant Christianity and the Catholic Church after the Taiping Uprising (1850–64) and that continue today in the explosive and bewildering mushrooming of unregistered 'house churches' (Xi 2010). 'Popular Christianity' is an attempt by Chinese Protestants to indigenise Christianity by drawing inspiration from anti-foreign nationalism, Pentecostal revivalism, Chinese rural and grassroots utopian millenarianism, and beliefs and practices of Chinese popular religion to form an indigenous Christianity.

Lian Xi traces the roots of popular Christianity back to the Christian-inspired millenarian and utopian Taiping Heavenly Kingdom and its founder Hong Xiuquan (1814–64). Other charismatic leaders of attempts at autonomous, 'self-supporting' churches in late Qing coastal China include Xi Zichi, known as Xi the Overcomer of Demons, founder of the opium refuge churches; Xie Honglai, organiser of the Chinese Christian Union; Yu Guozhen, founder of the China Christian Independent Church; Cheng Jingyi, who eloquently urged non-denominational Christianity at the 1910 Edinburgh World Missionary Conference; Ding Limei, founder of the Chinese Student Volunteer Movement for the Ministry; and Yu Cidu, a Methodist revivalist itinerant preacher. Following the Boxer Uprising, these Chinese Christians felt that the survival and growth of Christian communities in China now appeared to hinge on their ability to separate themselves from Western missions. However, due to their lack of personnel and financial resources, these movements towards autonomy succeeded only in fulfilling the missionary vision of a native church safely within the limits of mainline Western Protestantism.

What was still required for successful and lasting independent Protestant churches to develop was a millenarian vision of an impending end of the world and of the imminence of the Second Coming of Christ. Lian Xi traces the origins and chronicles the development of six such 'churches' with their founders: the True Jesus Church (Wei Enbo, 1876[?]–1919); the Jesus Family (Jing Dianying,

1890–1957); the Shandong Revival and the Spiritual Gifts Society (Zhaorui Ma, Yang Rulin and Sun Zhanyao); the Christian Tabernacle (Wang Mingdao, 1900–91); the Bethel Worldwide Evangelical Band (John Sung/Shangjie Song, 1901–44); and the Little Flock (Watchman Nee/Ni Tuosheng, 1903–72). In the two decades from 1930 to 1950, these churches experienced unprecedented growth. Once the communist government orchestrated the Three-Self movement to unify the Protestant churches in China, their phenomenal growth came to an abrupt end, but their apocalyptic, pre-millenarian fire was smouldering, waiting for the right time to burst into new Pentecostal flames.

Lian Xi ends his study with a survey of the stupendous explosion of unregistered, independent 'house churches' after the Cultural Revolution (1966–76). In his assessment, it is 'in the unofficial churches where one would find the heartbeat of the Christianity of China's masses and glimpse the future of Chinese Protestantism, which, at the turn of the twenty-first century, was already poised to rival the CCP [Chinese Communist Party] in total membership' (Xi 2010: 206). These house churches mostly grew out of the six pre-1949 churches mentioned above, but they have taken on lives of their own, spinning off into dizzying numbers of idiosyncratic and uncontrollable sects under charismatic leaders. True to their Pentecostal origins, these churches prize glossolalia, visions, trances, miracles and exorcisms.

There is no doubt that Christianity in its apocalyptic, pre-millenarian form is experiencing an explosive revival in China, so much so that some Western observers, such as David Aikman, have breathlessly predicted a 'Christianised China' that will, together with Christian America, promote global evangelism and contribute to world peace. Lian Xi is rightly sceptical of the likelihood of such a scenario: 'Persecuted by the state, fractured by its own sectarianism, and diminished by its contempt for formal education (theological or otherwise), it [Chinese contemporary popular Christianity] will probably also remain, as sectarian religious groups in the past, in the state of "intellectual decapitation"' (Xi 2010: 242). Lian Xi also astutely notes that as long as Chinese politics, Chinese society and Chinese life in general evolve towards the rule of law, stability and greater equality and harmony, Chinese Christianity is unlikely to foment popular uprising, and that, even if it does, it is unlikely to succeed 'given the historical tendency of messianic movements in China toward utopian radicalism, internal strife, a plebeian estrangement of the elite, and, ultimately, political incompetence' (ibid.: 247).

Of course, contemporary Chinese Christianity is sui generis, and many of its features, especially those related to its cultural and political contexts, are not found outside China. But its basic ecclesial characteristics are derived from the Evangelical/Pentecostal movement and are common to innumerable communities throughout the globe, including in Africa, Latin America and the United States. Together they form the fastest-growing Christian group today, with an estimated membership of more than half a billion.

There is no doubt that most of these 'independent churches', though they have some common networks among themselves, do not have a central authority and lack many of the essential attributes that traditional ecclesiology considers constitutive of 'church'.[22] Consider, for instance, the Faith and Order Paper No. 214 of the World Council of Churches, entitled *The Church: Towards a Common Vision*, the final fruit of nearly twenty years of intense ecumenical discussions, consultations and conferences on the nature and mission of the church.[23] It has been presented 'to the churches as a common point of reference in order to test or discern their own ecclesiological convergences with one another and so to serve their further pilgrimage towards the manifestation of that unity for which Christ prayed' (WCC 2013: 46). Thus, the ultimate validation and success of the document are measured by its ability to promote in churches 'a mutual recognition of each other as churches, as true expressions of what the Creed calls the "one, holy, catholic and apostolic Church"' (ibid.: vii).

In light of the criteria for genuine 'ecclesiality' proposed by the document, especially historical episcopacy and valid Eucharist, clearly the independent churches are not 'church in the proper sense', to use the terse expression of the declaration *Dominus Iesus* of the Congregation for the Doctrine of the Faith of the Catholic Church.[24] Add to the independent churches the churches that issued from the Reformation, including the Anglican Church, which, according to *Dominus Iesus*, are also not 'church in the proper sense', without them World Christianities would be neither 'world' nor 'Christianities'.

There would therefore be something wrong with either our current ecclesiology or with World Christianities. But if there is no denying the abundant presence of the fruits of the Spirit among independent and Pentecostal churches, a different ecclesiology is needed to honour their ecclesial character. Such ecclesiology should be formulated from grassroots experiences of church – from

---

22   Although AICs have formed ecumenical organisations among themselves and some are members of national councils of churches and of the WCC, most lack some of the features, such as apostolic succession and the Eucharist, that are considered essential to authentic 'ecclesiality' by historical mainline churches.

23   For a history of this document, see WCC (2013: 41–6).

24   *Dominus Iesus* (2 August 2000). Note that, according to *Dominus Iesus*, only the Catholic Church and the Orthodox churches are 'church in the proper sense', excluding all the churches originating from the Reformation and the Anglican Church.

below – and not deductively, from above, on the basis of a priori conceptions of the four marks of the true church. Connected with this issue of ecclesial identity is how ecumenical unity is to be envisaged in World Christianities. It may be asked whether a certain conception of apostolic succession, and with it historic episcopacy and the validity of the Eucharist, and the very understanding of church unity itself are too restrictive to do justice to the reality of World Christianities.

In sum, from what has been said above about the formative factors of theology, the re-articulations of fundamental *loci theologici*, such as the theology of God, Christology, pneumatology and the need for a different ecclesiology, the reality of World Christianities today presents an enormous challenge as well as rich opportunities for systematic theology. We are just beginning to see the complex contours of such a theology, but we must try to discern their forward movement to respond to what God is saying to the churches.

References

Amaladoss, M. (2006) *The Asian Jesus*. Maryknoll NY: Orbis Books.

Anderson, A. (2000a) *African Reformation: African Initiated Christianity in the 20th Century*. Trenton NJ: Africa World Press.

Anderson, A. (2000b) *Zion and Pentecost: The Spirituality and Experience of Pentecostal and Apostolic/Zionist Churches in South Africa*. Pretoria: University of South Africa Press.

Aritonand, J. S. and K. E. Steenbrink (eds) (2008) *A History of Christianity in Indonesia*. Leiden: E. J. Brill.

Barker, G. A. (ed.) (2005) *Jesus in the World's Faiths: Leading Thinkers from Five Religions Reflect on His Meaning*. Maryknoll NY: Orbis Books.

Barrett, D. (1968) *Schism and Renewal in Africa: An Analysis of Six Thousand Contemporary Religious Movements*. Nairobi: Oxford University Press.

Becker, K. and I. Morali (eds) (2010) *Catholic Engagement with World Religions: A Comprehensive Study*. Maryknoll NY: Orbis Books.

Bediako, K. (1995) *Christianity in Africa: The Renewal of a Non-Western Religion*. Maryknoll NY: Orbis Books.

Brinkman, M. E. (2007) *The Non-Western Jesus: Jesus as Bodhisattva, Avatara, Guru, Prophet, Ancestor or Healer*. London: Equinox.

Carr, B. and I. Mahalingam (eds) (1997) *Companion Encyclopedia of Asian Philosophies*. London: Routledge.

Cartledge, M. J. and D. Cheetham (eds) (2011) *Intercultural Theology: Approaches and Themes*. London: SCM Press.

Cheetham, D., D. Pratt and D. Thomas (eds) (2013) *Understanding Interreligious Relations*. Oxford: Oxford University Press.

Cornille, C. (ed.) (2013) *The Wiley-Blackwell Companion to Inter-religious Dialogue*. Oxford: Wiley-Blackwell.

Daneel, M. L. (1987) *Quest for Belonging: Introduction to a Study of African Independent Churches*. Gweru: Mambo.

Demeulenaere, R. (1985) *Corpus Christianorum Series Latina* 64: 127–95.

Farhadian, C. (ed.) (2007) *Christian Worship Worldwide: Expanding Horizons, Deepening Practices*. Grand Rapids MI: Eerdmans.

Gilley, S. and B. Stanley (eds) (2006) *The Cambridge History of Christianity: World Christianities c.1815–c.1914*. Cambridge: Cambridge University Press.

González, J. L. (2002) *The Changing Shape of Church History*. St Louis MO: Chalice Press.

Gutiérrez, G. (1991) *A Theology of Liberation*. Translated by Sister Caridad Inda and J. Eagleson. Maryknoll NY: Orbis Books.

Hastings, A. (1979) *A History of African Christianity 1950–1975*. Cambridge: Cambridge University Press.

Hastings, A. (1994) *The Church in Africa 1450–1950*. Oxford: Clarendon Press.

Isichei, E. (1995) *A History of Christianity in Africa: From Antiquity to the Present*. Grand Rapids MI: Eerdmans.

Jenkins, P. (2006) *The New Faces of Christianity: Believing the Bible in the Global South*. Oxford: Oxford University Press.

Jenkins, P. (2011) *The Next Christendom: The Coming of Global Christianity*. 3rd edition. Oxford: Oxford University Press.

Johnson, T. M. and K. R. Ross (eds) (2009) *Atlas of Global Christianity 1910–2019*. Edinburgh: Edinburgh University Press.

Johnstone, P. (2011) *The Future of the Global Church: History, Trends and Possibilities*. Downers Grove IL: InterVarsity Press.

Kidd, S. M. (2002) *The Secret Life of Bees*. New York NY: Penguin Books.

Kim, G. J.-S. (2011) *The Holy Spirit, Chi, and the Other: A Model of Global and Intercultural Pneumatology*. New York NY: Palgrave Macmillan.

Kim, K. (2007) *The Holy Spirit in the World: A Global Conversation*. Maryknoll NY: Orbis Books.

Kim, S. and K. Kim (2013) *Christianity as a World Religion*. London: Bloomsbury.

Knitter, P. (2002) *Introducing Theologies of Religion*. Maryknoll NY: Orbis Books.

Kollman, P. V. (2004) 'After Church History? Writing the History of Christianity from a Global Perspective', *Horizons* 31 (2): 322–42.

Küster, V. (2011) *Einführung in die Interkulturelle Theologie*. Göttingen: Vanderhoeck & Ruprecht.

Lee, H.-D. (2014) *Spirit, Qi, and the Multitude: A Comparative Theology for the Democracy of Creation*. New York NY: Fordham University Press.

McLeod, H. (ed.) (2006) *The Cambridge History of Christianity: World Christianities c.1914–c.2000.* Cambridge: Cambridge University Press.

Miller, D. E., K. H. Sargeant and R. Flory (eds) (2013) *Spirit and Power: The Growth and Global Impact of Pentecostalism.* Oxford: Oxford University Press.

Mitchell, M. M. and F. M. Young (eds) (2006) *The Cambridge History of Christianity: Origins to Constantine.* Cambridge: Cambridge University Press.

Moxon, R. S. (1915) *The Commonitorium of Vincent of Lérins.* Cambridge: Cambridge University Press.

Phan, P. C. (2012) 'World Christianity: Its Implications for History, Religious Studies, and Theology', *Horizons* 39 (2): 171–88.

Pinnock, C. et al. (1994) *The Openness of God: A Biblical Challenge to the Traditional Understanding of God.* Downers Grove IL: InterVarsity Press.

Pobee, J. S. and G. Ositelu II (1988) *African Initiatives in Christianity.* Geneva: World Council of Churches (WCC) Publications.

Sanders, J. (2007) *The God Who Risks.* Revised edition. Downers Grove IL: InterVarsity Press.

Song, C.-S. (1982) *The Compassionate God: An Exercise in the Theology of Transposition.* Maryknoll NY: Orbis Books.

Sundkler, B. (1961) *Bantu Prophets in South Africa.* London: International African Institute.

Tennent, T. C. (2007) *Theology in the Context of World Christianity: How the Global Church Is Influencing the Way We Think about and Discuss Theology.* Grand Rapids MI: Zondervan.

WCC (2013) *The Church: Towards a Common Vision.* Geneva: World Council of Churches (WCC) Publications.

Xi, L. (2010) *Redeemed by Fire: The Rise of Popular Christianity in Modern China.* New Haven CT: Yale University Press.

Yeo, K. K. (2014) 'Biblical Christologies of the Global Church: Beyond Chalcedon? Toward a Fully Christian and Fully Cultural Theology' in G. L. Green, S. T. Pardue and K. K. Yeo (eds), *Jesus without Borders: Christology in the Majority World.* Grand Rapids MI: Eerdmans.

CHAPTER 5

World Christianity as a Theological Approach: A Reflection on Central and Eastern Europe

*Dorottya Nagy**

Introduction

This chapter argues that the term 'World Christianity' represents a multidiscip-linary theological approach in researching Christianity worldwide. This is instead of regarding it as a new field, discipline or phenomenon, as is more usually done by scholars. In order to sketch out the ways in which a theological World Christianity approach could be understood, the chapter takes Central and Eastern Europe as its field of reference, particularly Hungary and Romania. In doing so, it seeks to problematise both normal scholarly perspectives in existing studies in World Christianity and a number of ecclesial and theolo-gical assumptions commonly made about Christianity in Central and Eastern Europe. Furthermore, this chapter's focus on Central and Eastern Europe illus-trates the complexity inherent to the study of Christianity worldwide. In a scholarship densely populated by theories of 'global South shift' (Robert 2000; Jenkins 2011 [2002]), literature on Christianity worldwide tends to neglect Cent-ral and Eastern Europe, with only a few exceptions (see, for example, Farhadian 2012; Goodwin 2009). Before delving into a proposed new World Christianity approach, however, the chapter explains the problems of terminology that have made this rethinking so necessary.

The Need for an Approach

The study of Christianity worldwide under the name 'World Christianity' is densely populated by religious studies scholars, church historians and theo-logians. The term appeared in academia during the last twenty years or so and reflected a dissatisfaction about our current state of knowledge of Christian-

---

* I wish especially to thank Martha Frederiks for challenging me to engage in discussions on World Christianity.

ity worldwide. Researchers now interrogate questions of whether an abstract notion of 'Christianity' adequately reflects the complexity of the faith's expression worldwide, and whether our knowledge of World Christianities includes both dominant and subordinate voices. New methods are required to support research on Christianity and to provide new ways of doing anthropology. New historiographies and genealogies of Christianity are needed (Koschorke 2009; 2014), and even new ways of doing theology may be necessary, such as Kollman's 'world-Christian turn' (2014; see also Phan 2008; Bevans 2009). Scholars identify the necessity of researching Christianity in its global implications, with comparative perspectives across time and space, with an inclusive attitude, and with attention to the interconnected nature of Christianity. Yet the same scholars who call for a new approach continue to use the term 'World Christianity' as if it merely captures a single unitary phenomenon (Kollman 2014; Koschorke 2014; Phan 2012).

A related or similar problem is also evident in studies that continue to adopt a basic division of the world according to the so-called Western/non-Western dichotomy, and either implicitly or explicitly prioritise the so-called non-Western world as the object of their study (for example, Akinade 2010; Walls 1995; 2001; Jenkins 2011 [2002]; Koschorke 2014; Yong 2014; Burrows 2014). Even such outspoken scholars as Sathianathan Clarke, who are forthright in expressing the need for a shift away from Western-derived categories, seem to drift easily between advocating for the need to define more rigorously the term 'World Christianity' and at the same time somewhat taking for granted its straightforward meaning as 'an international movement fuelled by the local embrace of the gospel in indigenous cultural forms' (Clarke 2014: 195). As Namsoon Kang contends, even progressive views of the diversity of non-Western Christianity continue to build arguments around the division between 'Christianity-the West' and 'world Christianity-the rest' (Kang 2010: 35). Attempts to distinguish between World Christianity – as an indigenous response to Christianity outside the European Enlightenment frame – and Global Christianity – as a 'faithful replication of Christian forms and patterns developed in Europe' (Sanneh 2003: 22) – do not necessarily aid our comprehension. This is not least because the 'two forms often mutate and merge into each other' (Jenkins 2007: xiii).

This chapter proposes discarding 'World Christianity' as a term claiming to represent the empirical reality of Christianity worldwide, and suggests instead that the label is invoked merely as a way of indicating a broad theological project for researching Christianity across the world, requiring a global awareness and a wide perspective. This broad project needs to consider four factors: it must address both the *interconnected* and *diverse* nature of Christianity, while still envisioning *unity* and being concerned with the importance of *localities* (Phan 2008; 2012; Robert 2000; Irvin 2008; Stanley 2011). The remainder of this chapter explains how these concepts form a World Christianity approach as well as it argues for its interdisciplinary utility. First, however, I briefly clarify key terms and the theological discipline before offering a short discussion of Eastern Europe and its significance for a World Christianity approach.

Terms, Disciplines and Regions

The terms 'Christianity' and 'world' both require further explanation. 'Christianity' indicates the plural and diverse confessions of faith relating to the person of Jesus Christ, which have been manifest in communities, organisations, networks, groups, churches and individuals since the early first century AD and in a continuous geographical reconfiguration. It implies agents – 'Christians' – and everything to which the adjective 'Christian' is applied, including broader ideological, political and historical discourses. The term indicates that there is a 'central (albeit mutable) core', around which any diversity and plurality 'must circle' and through which core believers can speak about and live out their faith (Berglund and Porter-Szűcs 2013: 12). This expansive definition of Christianity includes groups often excluded by traditional theological definitions, as noted throughout this chapter. The term 'world' indicates the inclusion of all regions around the globe that can profitably be studied in their relation to Christianity. This global perspective rejects previous interest in only the 'non-Western world', 'Third World' or 'majority' world, and includes European regions typically not taken into consideration when the analytical lens of 'world' is employed. There is also an implication that the term 'world' can be used to describe conceptual, ritual and virtual domains: the digital world, or the overlapping 'worlds' of particular confessions or movements, for example. Furthermore, this holistic 'world' approach includes interdisciplinarity, and anticipates extensive communication and cross-fertilisation between multiple theories and disciplines. A World Christianity approach, then, is interested in everything that relates to Christians and their relation to their surroundings, over time and throughout the globe, as well as in their study, both within and beyond disciplinary borders.

A brief definition of my own discipline of theology needs to be given as well. In common with a historical theological tradition, I assert that 'theology is the business of all God's people' (Moltmann 2000: ii). Theology is an act of faith and faith is dynamic. Theologising can take place on many levels, with academic theology being but one form of the discipline. Theology studies the beliefs of

Christians throughout the ages, the demonstrations of these beliefs in daily life, and the relationship and interaction of beliefs with all other aspects of human existence and social organisation. Theology is 'faith seeking understanding' (Sölle 1990; Norman 2007; Bevans 2009), where faith is not a fixed category resting on definite knowledge; where understanding is iterative; where its motivation is the ultimate concern formulated as 'love God and love your fellow human being' (Tillich 1951); and where its praxis is existential (Moltmann 2000; Kritzinger 2008). As will become apparent, my theology is influenced by the missiological and ecumenical traditions that have played an important role in informing the study of Christianity worldwide.

Theologians studying Christianity worldwide most often begin their enquiries with an analysis of lived experience – 'a context' – which is further examined in the light of scripture, philosophical tradition, ethics and so forth. These theologies are often interdisciplinary but they could be more intentionally so by using a threefold schema (Tötösy de Zepetnek and Vasvári 2011). Firstly, theologians should place issues relating to Christianity worldwide into dialogue with the large spectrum of approaches within theology, asking which theological sub-disciplines (systematic, biblical, church history, missiology, practical theology, for example) should be consulted to more adequately answer specific research questions (intra-disciplinarity). Secondly, theologians should consult the social sciences, cultural studies, literature studies, philosophy and religious studies to broaden their understanding of research questions (multi-disciplinarity). Thirdly, theologians should actively work together with scholars from different disciplines (pluri-disciplinarity). In the case of Central and Eastern Europe, this would involve different languages, thereby adding much needed nuance to World Christianity studies mainly conducted in English.

This chapter's reference to Central and Eastern Europe invokes the region not merely as a straightforward geographical label for fixed territorial units, but rather as a term to denote complex social worlds. The usual tendency in World Christianity studies is to use 'Central and Eastern Europe' as simply the counterpart of 'Western European', a term as problematic and heavily contested as the former (see, for example, Farhadian 2012). However, 'Central and Eastern Europe' provides a conceptual framework in which questions of identity can be articulated, although this does not obviate the need to rigorously examine the exact content of the term. 'Central and Eastern Europe' has meant different geographical areas at different times for different people. 'Central and Eastern Europe' – or its variations 'Eastern Europe', 'East Central Europe' and 'Central Europe' – goes beyond any topographical definition, has no legal status, and remains a quasi-geographical category 'often employed to contextualize and establish cultural, political and ideological narratives'

(Tötösy de Zepetnek and Vasvári 2011: 23). Whether one agrees with Larry Wolff's theory about the invention of Eastern Europe by Western Europe in the supposed Age of Enlightenment (Wolff 1994: 4) or takes earlier controversial sources such as Oskar Halecki (1944) as evidence for a fundamental East–West division, 'Central and Eastern Europe' continues to be a contested idea in both academic and popular discourse (Esterházy 1993: 11–12). Since the political turbulence of 1989–1991, Central and Eastern Europe has once again gained new layers of meaning, both for those within the region and for those outside it. For example, the so-called West continues to reinforce the notion of Central and Eastern Europe as a region with an independent existence through debates on its role in the extension of the European Union (EU). Central and Eastern European migrants are increasingly invoked in discussions about migration in Europe (see, for example, Mole et al. 2014). The ten Eastern and Central European nation-states that recently joined the EU are grouped under one regional label and are viewed with suspicion in other European countries. Similarly, Central and Eastern Europe functions as a technical term when it comes to the issue of refugees within the EU. A World Christianity approach needs to give attention to the complex layers of meaning attached to any geographical label.

The Approach

Having clarified the conceptual apparatus for using World Christianity as an approach, I now turn to the four concepts mentioned above. Locality, diversity, unity and connectivity are terms that are often present in the theologically informed literature of World Christianity. They form a contrast with older missiological terms such as 'culture', 'indigenous', 'ethnicity', 'mission' and 'identity', labels that have not always proved helpful in the creation of a new research agenda for the study of Christianity worldwide. These concepts are all interrelated, creating overlapping webs of meaning. For example, unity and diversity gain meaning only through their connection to specific locations where these characteristics are expressed. In this sense, a single locality may contain multiple worlds, demonstrating complex change over time (chronology is also a key factor). Furthermore, these interactions are moderated through various types of power relations, which regulate all interactions in which humans are involved. Perceiving the world as constituted by multiple contexts in which humans interact with each other and with God (Nagy 2009: 6), the researcher can define the context of a concrete research area only by pinning down the specific locality.

Locality

Space, location and context are at the heart of a World Christianity approach. Their analysis runs counter to usual ideas of locality within the discipline of theology that prioritise territorialisation. A specifically theological analysis of locality might emancipate the church from an overriding concern with 'territorialising' space and make it more sensitive to the exclusionary processes that often accompany this act of claiming space.

Territorialisation refers to the process of humans occupying particular locations over time, thereby transforming pieces of earth into territories over which human ownership is declared. Territorialising the earth in this sense means creating places that bear the mark of certain dynamics of human co-existence – above all, reflecting humans' endeavours to build communities reflecting certain beliefs and values. Territorialisation – both building up and destroying localities (places) – has been present throughout the history of Christianity worldwide. The long history of Christian empires and kingdoms (Lupieri 2011) or of Christian nations and nation-states[1] thus stands in continuity with more recent traditions of Charismatic movements proclaiming ownership over or 'conquering' ungodly lands through prayer and exorcism. Territorialisation also implies humans' desire to pin God down to a piece of land that is identified as a 'holy' space, and is thus contrasted with other sites that are cast as profane. Territorialisation, therefore, became an ecclesiological matter and was introduced in reflections on the nature and work of the church. To counter assumptions that the church required territory to carry out God's work, Dietrich Bonhoeffer underlined the ethical importance of critical theological reflection on what I have here called locality and territorialisation.

> The space of the church is not there in order to fight with the world for a piece of its territory, but precisely to testify to the world that it is still the world, namely, the world that is loved and reconciled by God. It is not true that the church intends to or must spread its space out over the space of the world. It desires no more space than it needs to serve the world with its witness to Jesus Christ and to the world's reconciliation to God through Jesus Christ.
>
> BONHOEFFER 2005: 64

---

1   See the ideas of Johann Gottfried Herder (1744–1803).

Bonhoeffer emphasises the importance of perceiving locality in ways that go beyond a simple desire on the part of religious groups to stake out their exclusive ownership over a territory.

A World Christianity approach would seek to contribute to such an ethical endeavour by making explicit the processes by which such territorialisation occurs. It does so by first widening the concept of locality: it includes geographical location or place but it is not restricted to this. Christians find their place in villages, states, regions, cities, or indeed throughout the entire globe, in the case of institutions with worldwide reach. But the scale of Christian presence can also be much smaller as well as territorially unmoored, being located in the realm of the private, a small institution, a family network, a loose movement of individuals, or a formal organisation such as a church. Localities never stand alone; they are connected and interconnected with other localities. Mission theologians have often referred to localities as 'context'.

Secondly, a World Christianity approach contests the meaning of any named locality. For example, when studying Christianity worldwide in light of the seismic political events of 1989–90 (Koschorke 2009), the location under study is usually the unit of the nation-state. Nation-states underwent significant political change in this period – for example, the satellite states of the former Soviet Union – and yet their names often evoke an assumed knowledge. The same can be said for particular cities or rural settings. The fact that this knowledge is not coherent for everyone, that all geographical places witness unsettled histories, is usually not addressed. Examining a region known by the ambiguous term 'Central and Eastern Europe' foregrounds the shifting social world in which identities are contested. Furthermore, making Central and Eastern Europe into a locality entails consideration of the theological and political discourses of the Cold War, hitherto marginalised in studies of Christianity worldwide.

Thirdly, the proposed World Christianity approach focuses on both the visible means of claiming a particular space as God's own – for example, religious architecture or published material such as billboards – and invisible means such as the various ideologies circulating about the sacrality of a particular location. It also seeks to comparatively analyse this process by examining evidence of the ways in which other religions also evince such acts of spiritual territorialisation (for example, folk traditions identifying a particular spirit with a village, a mountain or a forest).

An example of a World Christianity approach would be to focus on the revitalised acts of territorialisation that occurred in post-communist Central and Eastern Europe (Krawchuk and Bremer 2014; Hryniewicz 2007), as competing groups attempted to claim particular sites as their own, and as God's. These acts included competition between Greek Orthodox churches and Romanian

Orthodox churches for public visibility as well as the recent boom in missionary enterprise in Central and Eastern Europe – missionaries have arrived from
all parts of the world (not only from the so-called West) and are attempting
to reclaim the former heartland of Communism for God. These dynamics go
far beyond the obvious division into Christian and non-Christian camps. A
close examination of the interactions between Christian groups and post-1989
political leadership is instructive. In an interview given twenty-five years after
the political changes in Romania, Gheorghe M. Stefan, the former minister of
education, retrospectively legitimated his choice of introducing religious education into public schools. Stefan, who claims to be 'fundamentally atheist', was
convinced that in the post-communist ideological vacuum, the church (primarily the Romanian Orthodox Church) would be able to act as an agent of moral
education for the young.[2] Stefan saw the church as an institution with which
the state could co-operate for social well-being. The reintroduction of religion
into schools, however, was contested because, while the state was expecting
purely moral education from the church, the church could not and was not
willing to provide education free of doctrinal content. In some cases, allowing
the church re-entry into public schools meant that former lessons on communist ideology were now simply replaced by instruction on Orthodox moral
values. This reclaiming of secular 'territory' on the part of religious educators
was accompanied in many schools by the replacing of official portraits of the
former dictator, Nicolae Ceausescu, by a Christian cross and later by the country's restored coat of arms, in which the cross also figures. This phenomenon
led to political and legal proceedings in Romania, some of which are still not
settled. Drawing insights from the discipline of political studies, in this case
the World Christianity approach could help analyse disputes between competing ideologies as debates for visibility in public space in the so-called post-
communist Central and Eastern Europe.

Furthermore, using insights from the area of urban studies, the phenomenon of new religious space springing up throughout the region could be
theologically analysed as a process of territorialisation. This would include
the booming religious construction business, and in particular major church-
building enterprises in Central and Eastern Europe. Romania takes the lead
in this area, with more than 4,000 churches newly constructed since 1989, at

---

2   See 'School, After Twenty-five Years: The Minister Who Introduced Religion. "Catechism
    You Are Doing in the Church!"' (English translation of article title), http://www.realitatea.net/
    scoala-dupa-25-de-ani-ministrul-care-a-introdus-religia-catehizare-faceti-la-biserica-i_
    1445205_foto_1396331.html, accessed 28 January 2015.

least half of which belong to the Romanian Orthodox Church (Andreescu 2007; Stan 2014). In Protestant communities in Hungary, the expression 'scaffolding-worshipping clergy' (Guóth 2010) fittingly captures the territorialising business of Christian communities in building new properties and renovating old ones over which they have regained possession. It is important to note that such processes of territorialisation frequently exclude certain groups of people. Countless missionaries, both Christian and non-Christian, and not only from the 'West' but also from the East, North and South, flooded into Central and Eastern Europe after the political changes of 1989–90. To counter this perceived intrusion into their territory, many of the older churches in the region simply claimed that missionaries did not belong in a particular area, or that they had no rights to the canonical territories of the parishes and dioceses of the multiple national churches. Nevertheless, missionaries persisted in their efforts to plant churches in these areas because they themselves saw good reason to 'occupy' territory they perceived as marked by religious decline and characterised by the loss of piety. Understanding locality in this way underscores the importance of conflict, competition and debate in religious groups' efforts to assert themselves and gain followings and public legitimacy.

Diversity

Diversity is best demonstrated by returning to two examples of Christianity in post-1989 Central and Eastern Europe. The first connects locality with diversity. A single public square in Budapest offers one visually arresting example of how different religious groups compete for visibility and presence. The square is dominated by a historic building, topped by a biblical figure of Mary carrying the child Jesus in her arms. But rather than being a church, this structure is in fact the largest Buddhist meditation centre in Budapest. The centre was started by Lama Ole Nydahl (born in Denmark), who, in 1969, together with his wife, became one of the first Buddhist missionaries to Hungary sent from the Western school of the sixteenth Gyalwa Karmapa of the Karma Kagyü School. This community in Budapest bought a listed historic building for their headquarters. The building's façade required restoration, and therefore the statue of Mary and Jesus just above the main entrance, along with a statue of Saint Florian and a cross on the top of the chapel, were all preserved. The square in which the Buddhist meditation centre is based also features a Greek Catholic church and a Lutheran school. This relatively small, confined 'locality' would provide a rich research site for a study of Christian diversity in competition and co-existence conducted using a World Christianity approach. Data relating to the square, and even the city's architectural and planning strategies, as well as the commentaries of residents and passers-by could all function as primary sources.

The second example examines public discourse and Christian movements. In many ways, communist ideology aimed at total social homogenisation and levelling (Bíró 2013). Some scholars have argued that the communist regimes silenced the unsettled ethnic and cultural conflicts that had long characterised the region throughout earlier centuries (Louthan et al. 2011). Even during and shortly after the 1989 collapse of Communism, diversity was usually perceived as highly problematic, conformity was valued, and there was unease about the relativism of pluralistic societies. Yet socio-religious diversification had already occurred during the communist system. Evidence of this could be seen in the so-called underground churches and movements, which, after the fall of the communist system, 'suddenly' became visible to the broader public – although, in reality, they had long existed in the region. The post-communist diversification of Christianity in Central and Eastern Europe only intensified through increased migration to these areas. After 1989, former communist countries became simultaneously regions of emigration, immigration and migration, in which new religions, religious groups and forms of Christianity rapidly appeared (Borowik 1997). Existing Christian bodies reacted to and interacted with these multiple new arrivals.

Religious diversity – and Christian diversity in particular – has captured the attention of social scientists but remains theologically under-researched. In Central and Eastern Europe at least, this is because the churches regard with suspicion any diversity in their life and doctrine. A theological World Christianity approach has first to acknowledge this mistrust within its discipline. Academic theology in Central and Eastern Europe is usually practised in institutions closely related to or even owned by churches. Provided that academic theology implies serving the church, its close relationship to churches should not be a problem for its involvement in methodology and transformation. The issue, however, as is the case in all academic contexts, becomes sensitive when theologies enter into conflict with each other, and especially when theologies represented by church leadership and theologies from the academic context use divergent resources, concepts and intellectual traditions, frequently resulting in mutual misapprehension.

One recent example of mutual miscommunication was the proposed introduction of feminist theology into the curriculum of a Protestant faculty of theology in Hungary. It was rejected by the leadership of the church, who argued that the inherently inclusive nature of the Hungarian language made feminist theology irrelevant for Hungary, not recognising the very different theoretical background and concerns of those who argued for its inclusion (Kovács and Schwab 2014). Another example of miscommunication between different intellectual traditions is the refusal to ordain women in the Evangelical Church of the Augsburg Confession in Poland, despite a seventy year-long discussion of the subject. A World Christianity approach could put this question in a comparative setting by also investigating, for example, the processes that led the Georgian Evangelical Baptist Church to elect a female bishop in the person of Rusudan Gotsiridze. A theological World Christianity approach could address this example of diversity by adopting a threefold methodology (Meissner and Vertovec 2015) from migration studies. This begins with a description of the phenomenon and its context, followed by an iterative method that critically revisits existing ecclesiological practice, and culminates in an orientation towards policy change. For theological research practice and policy, this would also imply changes made to the theological curriculum of institutions such as seminaries.

Unity

Christian movements often anticipate some level of common accord or bond in their worship of God. This commonality has been expressed historically through doctrinal agreements, institutional membership and ecclesial practice. This goes some way to explain the theological nervousness (identified above) that sometimes surrounds diversity. Two broad strands of theological thought influence theologians studying Christianity worldwide, and in particular their reflections on the issue of Christian unity.

First, World Christianity studies are part of an ecumenical tradition that has prized unity within the Christian tradition alongside diversity. Ever since the Faith and Order Movement's 1927 Lausanne Conference, ecumenical dialogues and encounters have sought to spell out unity in diversity and have aimed for the realisation of visible fellowship among adherents of different traditions within Christianity. Indeed, the first use of the term 'World Christianity' arose within this context of ecumenical dialogue. Henry P. Van Dusen, for example, dedicates his book *World Christianity: Yesterday, Today and Tomorrow* (1947) to 'Colleagues in Every Phase of World Christianity', implying that, in time, the 'unity in diversity' project would unfold worldwide. Van Dusen optimistically believed that diversity would inevitably be resolved into a harmonious state of unity: when the 'movement of Christian missions and the movement for Christian unity' came together, the 'one single world Christian movement' would become visible (ibid.: 106–7). One of the ways used by theologians to approach

the issue of Christian unity has been to search for a minimal common denom-
inator upon which all agree. Yet the tension – hopefully a productive one –
in the World Christianity approach lies between the extent to which Christian
unity is realised at the grassroots, in terms of organic fellowship among diverse
groups of Christians, and the extent to which there is a need for organised
engagement in order to achieve unity among formal, institutionalised forms of
Christianity. A new approach would regard unity as a dynamic process – shot
through with continuous diversity and even disagreement – rather than as an
end result to be necessarily achieved. For this approach, the early twentieth-
century Pentecostal revival of pneumatology is relevant: the Spirit, 'blowing
where it wills', is the dynamic, creative coherence of diverse ecumenical movements (Körtner 2012: 466). Theology, engaged in World Christianity discourses,
becomes a method for perceiving the Spirit and for listening to and rethinking
articulations of faith in terms of grassroots practice rather than official recommendations for church unity.

The second strand that is relevant to a World Christianity approach emerges
as a critique of theology that has historically prioritised ecclesiology as a rubric for the being and behaviour of the institutional church. Within current
World Christianity discourses, some call for caution, at least in historical studies, in considering the concept of 'church' as central in the study of Christianity worldwide (Kollman 2004; Thangaraj 2011; Phan 2011). Instead, they wish
to provide a more holistic approach to the history of Christianity worldwide
than that offered by the church history framework. These scholars rightly argue
that an exclusive focus on institutionalised forms of 'being church' may result in a somewhat blinkered view of the diversity and richness of forms of
Christian life occurring outside institutional settings. The meaning of 'Christianity' is broader than the meaning of the church, states Catholic theologian Peter Phan (see Chapter 4 in this volume), arguing that there are Christ-
confessing communities that do not identify themselves as 'church' (Phan 2012:
179). Phan's approach suggests that all those who self-identify as Christian
have a place in the study of Christianity worldwide. Many theologians working
within World Christianities increasingly focus on grassroots, non-institutional
forms of Christian identity. In an interesting contrast with this position, the
anthropology of Christianity school makes a case for the ongoing relevance of
'church' in the World Christianity approach. The scholarly study of churches,
denominations and schisms is undergoing something of a revival within the
discipline of anthropology. Joel Robbins, for instance, expresses his dissatisfaction with 'idealist definitions of Christianity as something like a culture to tie
together disparate ethnographic cases in a single bundle ... focused on Christian cosmological conceptions and values more than on Christian institutions'

(2014: 162). For Robbins and other anthropologists, the concepts of 'church' and other church-related Christian institutions, such as schools, universities, hospitals and homes for the elderly, continue to function as important units of analysis. There may be a fruitful interaction of these insights with Bonhoeffer's idea of a worldwide church mingling with all dimensions of social life. Furthermore, 'indigenous' theological understandings of 'church' provide primary sources for such anthropological and non-theological engagements with the concept.

A World Christianity approach in Central and Eastern Europe, then, is primarily interested in the envisioning, understandings and experiences of unity of everyday Christians, where discrepancies between everyday Christianity and the formal doctrines and teachings of the churches point to different realities. Furthermore, the issue of unity in Central and Eastern Europe also brings us to the often denied disunity – one may even say conflict – within one's own tradition. The theologian Stanley Hauerwas (2013: 266) has observed simultaneous unity between representatives of different Christian traditions and disunity within individual traditions; these conflicts are everyday experiences in Central and Eastern Europe. One of the most striking phenomena in discussions of unity in post-1989 Central and Eastern Europe is the strong populist divide between communists and non-communists, which creates an imagined Christian unity through 'we anti-communist' slogans. Often it is the convergence between populist political discourse and institutionalised forms of Christianity that propagates anti-communist slogans. In 2013, during a church service in the historical Reformed church in the city of Debrecen (nicknamed the 'Calvinist Rome' or 'Hungarian Geneva'), the Prime Minister of Hungary offered 10 billion Hungarian forints (approximately €30 million) for the restoration and maintenance of the Reformed College in Debrecen and its educational units. The gift was to be provided as preparation for celebrating the five hundredth anniversary of the Reformation worldwide. The Prime Minister's justification for offering such generous financial aid to the church was that his government was only returning what the communists had stolen from religious institutions. This example shows how the state and the institutional church collaborate within a shared moral agenda by asserting their unity in the face of a communist past. However, populist unity formations based on the communist versus anti-communist divide are not as sharp in the minds of the public as their proponents would like to assume. In place of these simplistic dichotomies, Central and Eastern Europe needs a more profound understanding of the ways in which theology and church leaders have interacted with socialist ideologies, both during and after the period of so-called communist regimes worldwide.

'Unity' within a World Christianity approach is thus about experiences of unity in everyday Christianity, expressed through diversification in particular ecclesiologies limited to concrete places and visible in the complex webs of interconnections between these places. A pragmatic, grassroots focus on ongoing tensions and conflicts that co-exist alongside the more official push for institutional unity is pertinent to a World Christianity approach seeking to better understand specific examples of Christians crossing confessional or religious boundaries.

Connectivity

The final concept of connectivity enters theological discourse through network and complexity theories, which propose that systems (real-world systems as well as intellectual systems) are more than a simple set of multiple parts. It is the connectivity, or the interrelatedness, between the multiple parts that gives identity to a system. These theories, together with various globalisation theories, have become increasingly influential due to the worldwide political changes of the years 1989 and 1990, as well as the ever more networked and connected nature of societies across the globe, the latter development in no small part due to the role of the internet. There has been a rediscovery of the world's interrelatedness, making it evident that knowledge formation happens through relationships, through connections over shorter or longer distances (physical or otherwise), which, when transposed to temporality (or chronology), can be called genealogies or histories of connectivity.

The concepts of diversity, locality and unity as elaborated in this chapter have already touched on the issue of connectivity in time and space. Connectivity therefore invites us to study Christianities worldwide in their geographical and chronological embeddedness within the larger context or locality. Wilbert Shenk observes that 'every Christian community ought to perceive and affirm its relationship with every other Christian community around the globe' (Shenk 1996: 50), noting too that the Christian movement needs to be examined within 'the vast network of multilateral connections that operate at local, regional, national and global levels' (Shenk 2002: xv). The World Christianity approach adds to this observation that connectivity also needs to be explored beyond the Christian-to-Christian context, in the whole complexity of worldwide connections. It is through connections and interrelations that diversity changes, places are created or destroyed, and fragile experiences of unity occur.

The dynamics of migration have created new kinds of connectivities between Christians in Central and Eastern Europe and elsewhere in the world.

Christians who once imagined the worldwide unity of their denomination have questioned the nature of that unity after encountering believers of the same Christian tradition elsewhere on the globe, many of whom espouse radically different doctrinal positions. In many cases, imagined unities seem to be undermined by experiences revealing profound differences in Christian ethics. Issues such as homosexuality, euthanasia and abortion, to name only the most discussed, have become major topics through new connections brought about by the increased flow of people across borders via migration. Furthermore, the complexity produced by connectivity allows researchers to formulate fresh and important avenues of enquiry into the transnational nature of Christianity worldwide. For example, how did Billy Graham connect with communist leaders in Central and Eastern Europe? And how did those connections provide him with contacts with Orthodox clergy? How was the very concept of Central and Eastern Europe shaped by Evangelical discourses on the Cold War in the United States of America? Through which connections did Bishop Ting from the People's Republic of China receive an honorary degree at a Reformed theological university in Hungary during communist times? What effects did that connectivity have on Reformed Christians in the country?

A focus on connectivity in a World Christianity approach avoids essentialising the characteristics of any locale by examining the intrinsically interrelated nature of locality. For example, it does not ask what is unique about Christianity in Central and Eastern Europe. Rather, it asks through which connections, in the region and outside it, are continuity, difference and change all observable.

Conclusion

This chapter began with the observation that the increasing popularity of World Christianity as an area of study for theologians and missiologists demonstrates the necessity of elaborating new methods through which its complexity could be addressed. This chapter has argued that the term 'World Christianity' is too hastily being made into a field of study, or even a new discipline, allowing for confusion about its definition and the persistence of unhelpful dichotomies between the West and the non-West. In order to address these methodological problems, this chapter has proposed to use the term as an approach, rather than as an empirical area of study. Locality, diversity, unity and connectivity are the keywords of this approach. Locality here refers to the scholar's engagement with a particular context of Christian practice. Within this locality, the issues of diversity, unity and connectivity address complexity and create awareness of issues connected to power relations and exclusionary tactics. The World

Christianity approach proposed is also interdisciplinary in character. While dialogue with other theologian-missiologists (intra-disciplinarity) and scholars from other disciplines (multi-disciplinarity) has been prioritised throughout the chapter, its pluri-disciplinarity also invites us to actively work with a range of colleagues from multiple disciplines, both within and outside the academy. Multidisciplinary engagement is promising because it asks how the disciplinary 'other' – that is, a colleague from another discipline – analyses Christianity, and by using which premises. The proposed World Christianity approach discovers how unity and connectivity appear in other disciplinary analyses of Christianity and which other social worlds can be discovered or detected through the practice of multi-disciplinarity.

This chapter has proposed an agenda for theologians that allows us to learn from others interested in Christianity worldwide. It has done so by identifying a methodological direction that critiques theological certainties developed over generations and provides new perspectives on our interaction with God and with each other (Nagy 2009: 6). Those who deploy the proposed World Christianity approach will engage in new methods of knowledge construction about Christianity worldwide. They will do so with a desire to know the Christian other and the other who interacts with, reacts to and acts on Christianities or Christianity and Christians, and to see how this knowledge can bring about a transformation within academia – and, through this, in and beyond Christian communities worldwide.

References

Akinade, A. E. (ed.) (2010) *A New Day: Essays on World Christianity in Honor of Lamin Sanneh*. New York NY: Peter Lang.

Andreescu, L. (2007) 'The Construction of Orthodox Churches in Post-communist Romania', *Europe-Asia Studies* 59: 451–80.

Berglund, B. R. and B. Porter-Szűcs (eds) (2013) *Christianity and Modernity in Eastern Europe*. Budapest: Central European University Press.

Bevans, S. B. (2009) *An Introduction to Theology in Global Perspective*. Maryknoll NY: Orbis Books.

Bíró, G. (2013) 'Advancing the Mandate in Post-communist Countries' in H. Malloy and U. Caruso (eds), *Minorities, their Rights, and the Monitoring of the European Framework Convention for the Protection of the National Minorities*. Leiden: E. J. Brill.

Bonhoeffer, D. (2005) *Ethics*. Minneapolis MN: Fortress Press.

Borowik, I. (ed.) (1997) *New Religious Phenomena in Central and Eastern Europe*. Zaklad Wydawn: NOMOS.

Burrows, W. R. (2014) 'World Christianity and the Ecumenical Frontier' in C. B. Essa-muah (ed.), *Communities of Faith in Africa and the African Diaspora: In Honor of Dr. Tite Tiénou with Additional Essays on World Christianity*. Eugene OR: Wipf and Stock.

Clarke, S. (2014) 'World Christianity and Postcolonial Mission: A Path Forward for the Twenty-first Century', *Theology Today* 71 (July): 192–206.

Esterházy, P. (1993) *The Book of Hrabal*. Evanston IL: Hydra Books and Northwestern University Press. Originally published in 1990 as *Hrabal könyve*. Budapest: Magvető.

Farhadian, C. (ed.) (2012) *Introducing World Christianity*. Oxford: Wiley-Blackwell.

Goodwin, S. R. (ed.) (2009) *World Christianity in Local Context: Essays in Memory of David A. Kerr*. Volume 1. London: Continuum.

Guóth, E. (2010) 'Ügynökkérdés, tényfeltárás vagy valóságismeret?' ('Agent's Question, Fact-finding or Real-world Knowledge'), *Keresztyén Igazság* 88: 35–9.

Halecki, O. (1944) 'The Historical Role of Central-Eastern Europe', *Annals of the American Academy of Political and Social Science* 232: 9–18.

Hauerwas, S. (2013) 'Which Church? What Unity? Or, an Attempt to Say What I May Think about the Future of Christian Unity', *Pro Ecclesia* 22: 263–80.

Hryniewicz, W. (2007) *The Challenge of Our Hope: Christian Faith in Dialogue*. Polish Philosophical Studies. Washington DC: Council for Research in Values and Philosophy.

Irvin, D. T. (2008) 'World Christianity: An Introduction', *Journal of World Christianity* 1: 1–26.

Jenkins, P. (2007) *The Next Christendom: The Coming of Global Christianity. Revised and Expanded Edition*. Oxford: Oxford University Press.

Jenkins, P. (2011 [2002]) *The Next Christendom: The Coming of Global Christianity*. 3rd edition. Oxford: Oxford University Press.

Kang, N. (2010) 'Whose/Which World in World Christianity: Toward a World Christianity as Christianity of Worldly Responsibility' in A. E. Akinade (ed.), *A New Day: Essays on World Christianity in Honor of Lamin Sanneh*. New York NY: Peter Lang.

Kollman, P. (2004) 'After Church History? Writing the History of Christianity from a Global Perspective', *Horizons* 31: 322–42.

Kollman, P. (2014) 'Understanding the World-Christian Turn in the History of Christianity and Theology', *Theology Today* 71 (July): 164–77.

Körtner, U. H. J. (2012) 'Towards an Ecumenical Hermeneutics of Diversity: Some Remarks on the Hermeneutical Challenges of the Ecumenical Movement', *Theology Today* 68: 448–66.

Koschorke, K. (ed.) (2009) *Falling Walls: The Year 1989/90 as a Turning Point in the History of World Christianity / Einstürzende Mauern: das Jahr 1989/90 als Epochenjahr in der Geschichte des Weltchristentums*. Wiesbaden: Harrassowitz.

Koschorke, K. (2014) 'New Maps of the History of World Christianity: Current Challenges and Future Perspectives', *Theology Today* 71 (July): 178–91.

Kovács, Á. and Z. S. Schwab (eds) (2014) *In Academia for the Church: Eastern and Central European Perspectives*. Carlisle: Langham Monographs.

Krawchuk, A. and T. Bremer (eds) (2014) *Eastern Orthodox Encounters of Identity and Otherness: Values, Self-reflection, Dialogue*. New York NY: Palgrave Macmillan.

Kritzinger, J. N. J. (2008) 'Faith to Faith: Missiology as Encounterology', *Verbum et Ecclesia* 29: 764–90.

Louthan, H., G. B. Cohen and F. A. J. Szabó (eds) (2011) *Diversity and Dissent: Negotiating Religious Difference in Central Europe, 1500–1800*. New York NY: Berghahn Books.

Lupieri, E. (2011) *In the Name of God: The Making of Global Christianity*. Grand Rapids MI: Eerdmans.

Meissner, F. and S. Vertovec (2015) 'Comparing Super Diversity', *Ethnic and Racial Studies* 38: 541–55.

Mole, R. C., V. Parutis, C. J. Gerry and F. M. Burns (2014) 'The Impact of Migration on the Sexual Health, Behaviours and Attitudes of Central and East European Gay/Bisexual Men in London', *Ethnicity and Health* 19 (1): 86–99.

Moltmann, J. (2000) *Experiences in Theology: Ways and Forms of Christian Theology*. Minneapolis MN: Fortress Press.

Nagy, D. (2009) *Migration and Theology: The Case of Chinese Christian Communities in Hungary and Romania in the Globalisation Context*. Zoetermeer: Boekencentrum.

Norman, R. (2007) 'Abelard's Legacy: Why Theology is not Faith Seeking Understanding', *Australian eJournal of Theology* 10, http://aejt.com.au/__data/assets/pdf_file/0011/378074/AEJT_10.3_Norman_Abelard.pdf, accessed 23 September 2014.

Phan, P. C. (2008) 'Doing Theology in World Christianity: Different Resources and Methods', *Journal of World Christianity* 1: 27–53.

Phan, P. C. (ed.) (2011) *Christianities in Asia*. Malden MA: Wiley-Blackwell.

Phan, P. C. (2012) 'World Christianity: Its Implications for History, Religious Studies, and Theology', *Horizons* 39: 171–88.

Robbins, J. (2014) 'The Anthropology of Christianity: Unity, Diversity, New Directions', *Current Anthropology* 55: 157–71.

Robert, D. L. (2000) 'Shifting Southward: Global Christianity Since 1945', *International Bulletin of Missionary Research* (April): 51–8.

Sanneh, L. (2003) *Whose Religion is Christianity: The Gospel beyond the West*. Grand Rapids MI: Eerdmans.

Shenk, W. (1996) 'Toward a Global Church History', *International Bulletin of Missionary Research* 20: 50–7.

Shenk, W. (ed.) (2002) *Enlarging the Story: Perspectives on Writing World Christian History*. Maryknoll NY: Orbis Books.

Sölle, D. (1990) *Gott denken: Einführung in die Theologie*. Stuttgart: Kruez Verlag.

Stanley, B. (2011) 'Edinburgh and World Christianity', *Studies in World Christianity* 17: 72–91.

Thangaraj, T. (2011) 'An Overview: Asian and Oceanic Christianity in an Age of World Christianity' in H. Y. Kim (ed.), *Asian and Oceanic Christianities in Conversation: Exploring Theological Identities at Home and in Diaspora*. Amsterdam: Radopi.

Tillich, P. (1951) *Systematic Theology*. Volume 1. Chicago IL: University of Chicago Press.

Tötösy de Zepetnek, S. and L. O. Vasvári (2011) 'The Study of Hungarian Culture as Comparative Cultural Studies' in S. Tötösy de Zepetnek and L. O. Vasvári (eds), *Comparative Hungarian Cultural Studies*. West Lafayette IN: Purdue University Press.

Van Dusen, H. P. (1947) *World Christianity: Yesterday, Today and Tomorrow*. New York NY: Abingdon-Cokesbury Press.

Walls, A. (1995) 'Christianity in the Non-Western World: A Study in the Serial Nature of the Christian Expansion', *Studies in World Christianity* 1: 1–25.

Walls, A. (2001) 'From Christendom to World Christianity: Missions and the Demographic Transformation of the Church', *Crux* 37: 9–24.

Wolff, L. (1994) *Inventing Eastern Europe: The Map of Civilization on the Mind of the Enlightenment*. Stanford CA: Stanford University Press.

Yong, A. (2014) *Renewing Christian Theology: Systematics for a Global Christianity*. Waco TX: Baylor University Press.

CHAPTER 6

The Orientalist Framework of Christian Conversion in India: Three Venues of 'Inducement' from Colonial Times to the Present

Chandra Mallampalli

In his inaugural lecture of April 1861, the Oxford Sanskritist Monier-Williams stressed the importance of the study of Sanskrit to missionary work in India. As the 'sacred and learned language of India', Sanskrit, he claimed, was not only the source of 'all the spoken dialects of India' but was the 'only safe guide to the intricacies and contradictions of Hinduism, the one bond of sympathy, which, like an electric chain, connects Hindus of opposite characters in every district of India' (Monier-Williams 1861: 39). Despite the small number of people in India who could actually read or understand Sanskrit, Monier-Williams was convinced that India's 'national character is cast in a Sanskrit mould' and that a grasp of Sanskrit language and literature was the 'one medium of approach to the hearts of the Hindus' (ibid.: 41).

For Monier-Williams, 'Sanskrit' did not simply refer to the classical language, which recorded the sacred Vedas and the epic literature of ancient India, but was far more generative in its scope and meaning. In keeping with earlier Orientalist ethnography, Monier-Williams regarded Sanskrit as designating a race of people, their derivative dialects, and their cultural institutions. He devoted a significant portion of his lecture to ethnographic descriptions of the Sanskritised upper castes and their fundamental difference from low-caste and untouchable communities, whom he labelled 'Semi-Hindus' and 'Non-Hindus' respectively (ibid.: 2–5).

Monier-Williams lamented that only a small minority of Christian converts 'belong to the Hindu race properly so called'. His 1861 address drew attention to the fact that barely 3,000 of the 112,000 converts who had been made in the whole of India belonged to the 'true Sanskritic race', and that the vast majority of converts had come from South India.[1] Only by learning Sanskrit,

---

1 He made no reference to so-called 'Dravidian people', who, according to another thread of Orientalism, the Madras School, derived their identity from a different family of languages (Trautmann 2006).

© KONINKLIJKE BRILL NV, LEIDEN, 2017 | DOI: 10.1163/9789004355026_008

he maintained, could missionaries hope to gain access to the heart and soul of the Indian nation.

Monier-Williams represents a tradition of Orientalism, rooted in the colonial period, that identified Sanskritic texts and institutions as forming the basis of a cohesive Hindu society. Regardless of how we might respond to his categories or ambitions – a clear example of Orientalism in the service of missionary work (Oddie 1994) – it is difficult to deny their enduring relevance to debates about conversion in India, not only during the colonial period but also extending to the Hindu nationalist politics of the present day. The majority of Christians in today's India are drawn from classes that are considered to be the farthest removed from Sanskritic influence. These include, but are not restricted to, low caste, Dalit and Tribal communities (which are primarily from southern or north-eastern India). In spite of the fact that India's Christian population amounts to no more than 2.5 per cent of a population of 1.2 billion, conversion among Dalits and Tribals continues to sound the alarm bell of 'Hinduism in danger'.[2] Converts from these communities continue to suffer violence at the hands of Hindu nationalists. Recent campaigns to 'reconvert' Dalit and Tribal Christians to Hinduism enliven a long-standing debate about their historic place within 'the Hindu fold'.

This matter of religious conversion in the 'Hindu' world acquires added relevance when set against a wider literature concerning the dramatic rise in Christian numbers in parts of Africa, Asia and Latin America.[3] Recent scholarship concerning this emerging 'world' or 'global' Christianity raises critical questions about agency, motives and structural factors affecting religious choices. In their pioneering work, Andrew Walls and Lamin Sanneh have stressed the role of Bible translation and local agency in driving the conversion process in much of sub-Saharan Africa. Such factors have placed Africans at the centre and foreign missionaries at the margins of the conversion process.[4]

---

2   Andre Beteille describes the fear of an endangered Hinduism as a 'hysteria' affecting not only extremist groups but also more liberal and enlightened Hindus. This stems in large part from their disillusionment, since independence, with secular modernity (Beteille 2003).

3   For Monier-Williams, the Sanskritic world refers to those sections of South Asian society whose values and identities have been shaped by Sanskrit literature, laws and institutions. Sheldon Pollock's examination of the 'Sanskrit cosmopolis' envisions the scope of such influence as extending from the Afghan region to Java (Pollock 2006).

4   This 'demographic shift' in the world's Christian population to the global South is producing new centres of Christian vitality and a changing ethnic complexion of the global church. For a discussion of these developments, see Andrew Walls (1997), Dana Robert (2000; 2009) and Philip Jenkins (2002).

Their articulations of a 'World Christianity paradigm', however, have been challenged in the work of John and Jean Comaroff (1997), Robert Wuthnow (2009) and David Maxwell (2006), who draw attention to the global forces emanating from American capital that continue to influence Christian growth and experience in the global South.

Whether we embrace the notion of World Christianity as rendered in the work of Sanneh and Walls or problematise it as others have done, we can at least appreciate that a debate about local agency is alive and kicking relative to Christian growth in places such as Zimbabwe, Guatemala or Brazil (Hartch 2014). In India, however, Hindu nationalists are staging a popular debate about conversion in which an 'indigenous discovery of Christianity' by Dalits and Tribals merits no consideration. Rather than considering their own choice, voice or agency in becoming Christian (or Muslim), the debate is centred almost entirely on their 'inducement' out of the Hindu fold by foreign capital and on the need to retain them within Hinduism through state policies and reconversion drives. On the face of it, this debate may appear to resemble debates about local agency versus global capital in World Christianity literature. The Indian debate over conversion, however, has a deeper history anchored in many of the assumptions voiced by Monier-Williams in his 1861 lecture. This unique history and its distinct idiom for framing the topic of religious conversion, I argue, have had the effect of isolating studies of South Asia's Christians from broader discussions of World Christianity.

Underlying India's conversion debate are assumptions about a coherent Hindu fold from which people are extracted or where they are retained. The Orientalist study of Sanskritic texts and institutions (such as caste) has played an important role in reifying notions of this 'Hindu fold', as has the implementation of Hindu law under colonial rule. My aim in this chapter is to discuss three distinct venues in which the theme of inclusion in and exclusion from Hinduism has shaped official policies towards Christian converts. In all three venues, we can observe the deployment of some version of the concept of inducement. 'Inducement' here refers to the production of incentives for abandoning one religious identity and adopting another for reasons that are unrelated to the intrinsic claims of religion. The language of inducement presents conversion in purely instrumental terms. Converts are 'agents' only in their pursuit of material resources, not in their embrace of the message of another religion.[5] Extremely disadvantaged groups such as Dalits or Tribals

---

5   Related to the language of 'inducement' is the tendency to deny the 'authenticity' of conversions allegedly arising from a desire for material resources. In her revealing study of

may be said to lack any agency at all, since their conversion arises from conditions of extreme deprivation. Missionaries become the real agents of conversion when they are able to provide such groups with much needed assistance.[6]

The first venue I will discuss is set in early colonial India and involves the state of exile suffered by converts under Hindu law and their related 'civil disabilities'. Here I discuss the role of Protestant missionaries in advocating for the rights of converts after their Hindu families had disinherited them. The discussion of missionaries as patrons of converts is immediately followed by a discussion of Protestant missionary discourse about caste. This, as we shall see, played an important role in shaping the debate about the social advantages or disadvantages that follow conversion. The second venue moves us into the affirmative action policies of the postcolonial Indian state, specifically its denial of benefits to Dalits who convert to Islam or Christianity. The third venue concerns attempts by Hindu nationalist organisations to reconvert Christians and Muslims to Hinduism. These snapshots of India's conversion debate arise from distinct historical contexts, but a common thread runs through them: namely, the cost of leaving Hinduism. By examining them side by side, my aim is to isolate the discursive framework they share in common and demonstrate the role of that framework in: (1) silencing the voices of Dalit and Tribal converts; and (2) marginalising South Asia's Christians from discussions of key tropes of World Christianity.

Civil Disabilities of Converts

I begin in early colonial India, because I believe that it was colonial policies that defined the terms of India's conversion debate, even for the other two venues. Believing that Indians would best be governed according to their own religion-based family laws, the first Governor General of Bengal, Warren Hastings, developed a plan of applying Hindu law to Hindus and Muslim law to Muslims. The separate courts for each religious community adjudicated 'civil' as distinct

---

pariah labourers in colonial Madras, Rupa Viswanath identifies two sources of the language of authenticity. In their attempt to explain Indian indifference to the Christian message, missionaries often complained that Indians were more oriented to 'material' than 'spiritual' benefits. This made conversion for material reasons less than authentic. Indian elites also deployed the language of authenticity as a way of protesting against the departure of *pariahs* from their traditional, servile roles upon conversion (Viswanath 2013).

6   This was Gandhi's argument for conversion by inducement (Gandhi 1941: 146–9).

from 'criminal' matters.[7] The dilemma the Hastings Plan created for so-called 'native Christians' stemmed not only from their marginal status relative to the two dominant 'communities' of India, but also from the loss of rights they suffered within their families upon conversion.

Under Hindu law, converts to Christianity underwent a 'civil death' whereby they forfeited inheritance and other familial rights. Gauri Viswanathan describes this civil death as a state of exile or excommunication, which entails a loss of both community and entitlement. The legal fiction of a civil death portrays the convert as 'deracinated and, as an outcaste, no longer recognized by scriptural law as a functioning member of his or her former community' (Vishwanathan 1998: 79). Under *Mitakshara* law, the outcaste convert no longer qualified to perform the funeral rites that were deemed necessary for the salvation of the deceased. Unable to perform such rites, the convert forfeited inheritance within the Hindu joint family.[8]

Seen through the lens of Hindu law, the story of Christian conversion in India thus begins with an eviction, an act of severance, or, as Vishwanathan has noted, a state of 'exile from [the Hindu] community'. This starting point is problematic precisely because it begs the questions of whether a single 'Hindu community' actually existed, what relationship – if any – such a community had to textual Hindu law, and whether someone could be said to have belonged to this community before converting to another religion. Out-casting and disinheritance were meaningful only if someone possessed caste status or access to ancestral property to begin with. The strictures of Sanskrit law are inapplicable to Dalits and Tribals precisely because of their cultural distance from Sanskritic institutions, and yet their conversion to Christianity is framed in terms of a departure from Hinduism.

Disenfranchised under Hindu law, converts lived in a state of legal limbo. They eventually would appeal to a different legal device in order to secure their rights. In 1850, a law known as the Caste Disabilities Removal Act, or *Lex Loci* Act, came to their rescue. According to the Act, no one could be deprived

---

7   Under Hastings' Judicial Plan of 1772, civil matters included property, inheritance, marriage, caste, debt and rent. Details of this plan, including the division of civil and criminal courts, the state appointment of native experts (*pundits, qazis* and *muftis*) in Hindu or Muslim law, and the authority of the courts relative to that of district collectors are provided in Monckton Jones (1918).

8   Elsewhere, I have argued that colonial courts provided a laboratory in which social ramifications of religious conversion were analysed and addressed. Litigation often revolved around the highly evocative language of desertion, degradation and severance (Mallampalli 2004: 83; Rocher 2010).

of their civil rights on account of their change of religion. Christian converts appealed to this law so that 'they would not be deprived of property, guardianship of children, conjugal rights or other familial rights' because of their conversion (Mallampalli 2004: 23). Not surprisingly, the *Lex Loci* evoked strong reactions from missionaries and Hindu families within various provinces of British India.[9]

Missionaries came to regard the Act as reflecting an imperial commitment to freedom of conscience and religion. They believed that the Act would eliminate a major disincentive for conversion, particularly among propertied classes. The Hindu gentry of Madras, however, attacked the Act as a breach of religious neutrality and as evidence of the East India Company's Christianising agenda. The Act evoked similar opposition from Hindus in Bengal. The subtext of the arguments of both sides was that colonial policies were creating powerful incentives either to remain 'Hindu' or to convert to another religion (Ali 1965: 117–32; Suntharalingam 1974: 44–5). Because the incentives in such instances pertained to either the maintenance or the forfeiture of familial rights and not to the intrinsic claims of religion, I contend that this colonial debate laid the structural foundations for the language of inducement. In its earliest incarnation, however, the debate was framed in terms of the state's interest in either promoting freedom of conscience or preserving Hinduism.

Protestant missionaries played an important role in advocating for the rights of converts. During the nineteenth century, they enumerated various 'civil disabilities' arising from the convert's state of disenfranchisement. Originally, these disabilities were tied to the convert's polluted status (*patita*) under Hindu law, and their potential forfeiture of inheritance, guardianship of children, or conjugal rights. As missionaries assumed more prominent roles as the legal advocates of converts, however, they infused the conversion debate with the language of freedom of religion and conscience, derived from the rights-based discourse of European liberalism. Gradually, missionaries moved the discussion of 'civil disabilities' beyond the parameters of the Hindu joint family (i.e. the domain of Sanskritic textual law) to include other types of disenfranchisement occurring within an evolving public domain.

An important aspect of the civil disabilities of converts concerned their difficulty in finding employment in government posts. Two regulations of 1814

---

9 These reactions reflected disparate ideological commitments of the Company's Raj, with individual rights and freedom of conscience on the one hand, competing with commitments to religious neutrality on the other. In princely states, the Company was more explicitly committed to 'preserving Hinduism', and so was all the more reluctant to introduce the Act (Mallampalli 2004: 25–7).

barred native Christians from holding positions in the evolving legal profession. The regulations stated that the office of the *munsiff* (a judge in a small claims court) and *vakil* (a native pleader) should be either Hindu or Muslim. As much as this restriction reflected the aims of the Hastings Plan of creating courts for Hindus and Muslims, the petitioners saw no reason why all personnel had to be either Hindu or Muslim. The petition also cited restrictions to military service imposed on Christians, such as being excluded from the cavalry and from promotion in the infantry. Christians shared such disadvantages with 'all other persons of certain low castes'.[10]

The Church Missionary Society missionary to Tirunelveli, C. T. E. Rhenius, claimed that 'native Christians' in the Madras presidency were excluded from employment as writers in the *cutcherries* (administrative offices) and as translators or interpreters in the courts. Additionally, he claimed that hiring practices favoured persons who spoke Hindustani, while marginalising speakers of South Indian vernaculars. This, he explained, was largely because district collectors and magistrates who were most proficient in Hindustani tended to hire Hindu and Muslim interpreters, who could hear complaints in a local language such as Tamil, and relay them in Hindustani to their superior officers (Rhenius 1841: 394).

While acknowledging the rationale behind reserving certain offices for Hindus and Muslims, Rhenius insisted that native Christians were Hindus: that is, persons of 'pure Hindoo blood'. The regulations, however, deracinated Christians by assigning a religious meaning to the term 'Hindu', or, in Rhenius's words, by taking 'Hindu' to mean 'heathen' (ibid.: 392). 'A Christian government,' he charged, 'supports the natives whilst they are Heathens, but withholds that support when they become Christian' (ibid.: 393)! During the 1830s, Rhenius shared the views of an increasingly vocal Evangelical lobby that the government was violating its commitment to neutrality through its sponsorship of Hindu festivals, temples and ceremonies. Such rhetoric construed the disabilities of converts as stemming from the state's hand in an expanding public domain that privileged Hindu institutions and left converts in a state of legal invisibility (Carson 2012: 52–69).

Ironically, Rhenius made these claims as the East India Company, under its renewed charter of 1833, was withdrawing its support of Hindu temples and more actively supporting Evangelical interests. The role of the Governor General, William Bentinck, in abolishing sati and defending the inheritance

---

10   *Appendix to the Report from the Select Committee of the House of Commons on the Affairs of the East India Company*, 16 August 1832. London: J. L. Cox and Son, pp. 121–2.

rights of converts was widely (although somewhat inaccurately) perceived as evidence of his support for the Evangelical cause (ibid.: 201).

Missionaries tended to portray themselves as underdogs relative to Company power and as advocates for converts, who had become marginalised because of Company policies. As much as missionary rhetoric drew references to the converts' disenfranchisement within the Hindu family, it also emphasised the advantages of joining the alternative society that Christianity represented. Upon conversion, the convert was evicted from the Sanskrit-based caste society, but attached himself or herself to a purportedly 'casteless' one.

The Castelessness of Christianity

In theory, Christian conversion carried starkly contrasting implications for the Sanskritised caste Hindu and the so-called untouchable. For the former, becoming Christian was ritually polluting and entailed an immediate loss of status, but for the untouchable it was construed as a vehicle for social advancement. The untouchable, after all, joined a religion that denounced caste distinctions and offered him or her access to missionary institutions. As much as this may appear to be an instance of inducement, it becomes most poignantly charged with such connotations when we locate Dalits and Tribals within Hinduism originally: that is, when we project the Sanskritic paradigm of the polluted convert – applicable to caste Hindus – onto classes of people whose relationship to Sanskritic institutions were highly varied and contestable.

Protestant missionary discourse played an important role in bifurcating Sanskritic and Christian domains. This was due in large part to their attack on caste as both a religious *and* a civil institution, and their claim that Christianity was inherently opposed to caste. The normative discourse of Protestantism, ironically, seems to have made it more difficult for Dalit Christians (and their missionary patrons) to make a case for their enduring disabilities. A closer examination of nineteenth-century Protestant missionary attitudes towards caste brings these cross-cutting developments into sharper focus.

Missionary ethnography during the 1830s and 1840s was hostile to India's caste system but conceded the persistence of a caste mentality within the new churches. The very missionaries who advocated for the legal rights of converts played an active role in denouncing caste as a religious residue that had to be effaced upon conversion. By the 1850s, nearly every Protestant missionary society in India, according to D. M. Forrester, had reached a consensus in their opposition to caste (Forrester 1980: 40). Caste, they insisted, was both a civil and a religious institution, and to retain any aspect of it was to remain steeped in 'heathen' practices. Caste impeded the spread of the gospel by imposing draconian penalties for any form of apostasy and by inhibiting the social admixture that conversion presumably encouraged. It consolidated the power of Brahmins by placing them at the top of the social order and consigning lower castes and untouchables to a life of 'slavery'.[11] Moreover, caste impeded the social progress experienced in Western societies, by fixing at birth one's station in life.

Familiar arguments such as these informed a theoretical opposition to caste, but resulted only in a limited experience of equality. Missionary reports frequently lamented the prevalence of a 'caste mentality' among converts. Enduring prejudice tied to notions of purity inhibited comingling and was part of a more general tendency of converts to 'backslide' into former habits and customs (Billington Harper 2000: 251–9). Later reformers such as B. R. Ambedkar would note that, in spite of their role in uplifting the untouchables, Christian churches continued to manifest caste prejudice.[12]

During the 1840s, a group of high-ranking clergy from South India formulated their views on Christianity and caste in a series of letters, reports and pamphlets. As part of their deliberations, they interviewed a number of converts in order to measure the degree to which they had retained their caste identity. Despite the pressure applied on them to renounce caste, converts continued to view their place within the church in terms of their caste identity. The larger story told by these interviews – which assumed the form of legal depositions – is that of churches only partially achieving their goal of eradicating caste among converts. An important litmus test used by missionaries was whether a caste convert was willing to mingle with *pariahs* (which had become a generic, colonial designation for untouchables in the south). The following interview with an unnamed Tamil from the Vepery Mission in Madras illustrates the liminal space occupied by converts relative to their former rules of association:

> Q: To what caste do you belong?
> A: To the cultivator's caste.
> Q: In what sense do you consider yourself different from a Pariah?

---

11 For a discussion of how the language of 'slavery' was deployed in missionary and state rhetoric, see Viswanath (2010) and Irschick (1994: 176–90). For a nineteenth-century Catholic–Protestant exchange on the viability of conversion of the Hindus vis-à-vis the power and corruption of Brahmins, see Dubois (1823) and Hough (1824).

12 For a concise discussion of Ambedkar's attitudes towards Christianity relative to other 'non-Hindu' religions, see Jaffrelot (2005: 120–9).

A: There is no difference in religious performance; but there is a difference in the inter-marriages and eating.

Q: Would you marry a Pariah Christian woman?

A: No.

Q: Would you eat with a Pariah Christian man?

A: No.

Q: Would you go into a Pariah Christian's house?

A: Yes, freely.

Q: Would you permit a Pariah Christian man to enter your house?

A: He might come to the entrance, but he has no business to go further.

Q: Would you partake food, bread, or water, with any European Christian gentleman?

A: What advantage is there?

Q: That is not an answer to the question.

A: I do in the church.

Q: If a Pariah Christian, having been ordained, should preach in Vepery church, would you stay and hear him?

A: Yes, I would.

Q: Why, then, did you leave that church when Rev. N. Parenjody read the lessons there?

A: I never heard that Parenjody put his foot on the reading desk, or went into that place.

Q: Did he read the lessons, then, from some other part of the church?

A: I saw him sitting in a certain seat; but I never saw him read the lessons, nor the prayer, nor preach there.

Q: Do you think it scriptural to do as you do in the matter of Caste?

A: Whatever is reasonable is scriptural; but scriptural maxims are quite different from worldly customs.

ROBERTS 1847: 46–7

This exchange shows how eager the witness was to differentiate himself from a *pariah* even though he was a person of low status himself. It also reveals the detailed attention to spaces within the church that denoted the relative status of persons of various castes. It was important to the witness that Reverend Parenjody, presumably a *pariah*, read lessons only from a sitting position, away from the 'reading desk' of the church.

The interview with Annapen, a schoolmaster in the Vepery Mission, similarly highlights the differentiated spaces of *pariahs* and others in the school, but additionally explores changes to occupation and dress that accompany conversion:

Q: Are there differences between persons of the Pariah class?

A: No, all Pariahs are the same.

Q: Of what class are barbers, chucklers, toties, and washmen?[13]

A: They are the lowest kind of Pariahs.

Q: Then how are all Pariahs the same?

A: I mean they are all the same if they are Christians.

Q: Are there any Christian barbers, chucklers, toties, or washmen?

A: No, I never saw any.

Q: If a barber becomes a Christian, does he continue a barber?

A: No, we make him a gardener, or some similar trade.

Q: Why may not a barber continue a barber after conversion?

A: Because that is a mean business.

Q: Supposing a person of one of these lowest trades determines to continue a barber, chuckler, toty, or washman, as the case may be, and gives notice of this before baptism, would you permit him to be baptized?

A: Yes, but we would not eat with him, nor give him our daughter in marriage, if he continued in either of these trades.

ROBERTS 1847: 48

Annapen proceeded to explain that no 'Tamil boys' (which here denoted Tamil-speaking caste Christians) attended his school, but only 'Heathens, Moor boys, and Pariah Christian boys' (ibid.: 48). Another mission school in Black Town, however, integrated *pariah* Christian, Muslim, Hindu and Tamil boys, and they all sat together. Annapen did not explain the basis for caste integration at the Black Town school. His discussion of Jesudasen, the master of the school, however, shed further light on the relationship between dress, identity and rules of association observed in the mission schools. Jesudasen, he said, was a 'native [Tamil] or a Malabar man' but dressed like a 'country-born' or European man. Because of his adoption of European clothes, he lost his caste, and, according to Annapen, he would not be admitted into the homes of Tamil Christians. Jesudasen had also married a *pariah* woman, but it was his dress, not his *pariah* wife, that formed the basis of his exclusion from Tamil Christian homes (ibid.: 49).

Whereas the assumption of Western clothes in this instance indicates Jesudasen's deviation from the norms of his caste and his subsequent loss of status, change of dress accompanied a more favourable trajectory for *pariah* con-

---

13   A *chuckler* is a native shoemaker. A *toty* is a low-caste labourer, sometimes acting as a messenger.

verts. A pattern of seeking patrons from among *farangis*, or foreigners, reaches back to eighteenth-century Portuguese–Indian interactions (Spear 1963: 62). *Paraiyar* labourers converted to Christianity to escape the debilitating stigma of untouchability, an event that inclined them to change their dress. 'Eating meat, drinking liquor and wearing Western clothes' thus became a phrase linked to Europeans and the converts who associated with them (Mallampalli 2011: 36).

Protestant attitudes to caste, of course, were neither static nor monolithic but varied according to time and context. Towards the turn of the twentieth century, Protestant missions became more reconciled to the reality of caste in the lives of Christians, especially as they encountered the phenomenon of group or mass conversions. Debates about conversions en masse highlighted not only the increasingly Dalit composition of the Indian church, but also the transformative implications of their ties to foreigners and their resources.

Accounts of missionary labour among Dalit communities placed a stronger emphasis on their ensuing upward mobility and cultural transformation. This was the case in the nineteenth-century transformation of the toddy-tapping Nadar (once labelled pejoratively 'Shanar') into the upwardly mobile, entrepreneurial Nadar, documented in the work of Robert Hardgrave (1969). This emphasis is also evident in the work of the Baptist missionary John Clough, who became part of the conversion of Madiga leather workers in Ongole during the 1870s.

Clough required converts to abstain from eating carrion, working on Sundays, and worshipping Hindu deities. These requirements, he claimed, struck at the very heart of 'Dravidian village life', revolutionising relations the Madigas had with their Sudra employers, meat vendors, and Brahmin leaders at temple establishments (Clough and Rauschenbusch-Clough 1914: 159–60). The humanitarian aid his mission provided for Madigas during the great famine of 1876–78 played a critical role in turning people, in his words, from 'idols' to the God of the English and American people (ibid.: 265–6). Local newspapers, however, invoked the phrase 'rice Christians' to describe these developments, portraying these conversions as the direct result of foreign aid in a time of need (ibid.: 267).

Nineteenth-century missionary ethnography never seemed to reconcile its normative opposition to caste with its awareness of the prevalence of caste distinctions within churches. Somehow, it was the image of what the church *ought to* be, not what it actually *was*, that informed the categories and policies of the emerging ethnographic state (Dirks 2001: 130–4). A normative discourse of opposition to caste would eventually reify legal notions of a 'Christian community' as a casteless domain. This disjunction between normative, or text-based, notions of religious identity versus lived experience belongs to the legacy of the Hastings Judicial Plan of 1772, a plan that divided Indian society into clearly differentiated religious domains. It would form the basis of intense disagreements over the disadvantages faced by Dalit Christians. Were they less in need of assistance because of their embrace of a 'casteless' religion, or were they, as John Webster (1996) has argued, doubly marginalised as Christians and as Dalits? Such questions lie at the heart of the debate over affirmative action for Dalit converts to Christianity.

Amending the 1950 Order

The current debate over affirmative action (or 'reservations') for Dalits who convert to Christianity is freighted with assumptions inherited from the colonial period. To this day, the government refuses to recognise Dalit Christians as members of India's scheduled castes (scs). Those who count as scs qualify for state assistance and quotas in education and employment under existing affirmative action schemes. The policy can be traced back to the Constitutional (Scheduled Castes) Order of 1950, which established state-specific lists of communities that could be classified as scs. The Order stipulates that 'no person professing a religion different from Hinduism shall be deemed to be a member of a Scheduled Caste'.[14] This was amended in 1956 to include Sikhs and again in 1990 to include neo-Buddhists. Despite persistent appeals to make reservations completely 'religion blind', Dalit Christians (and Muslims) find themselves excluded from sc status on the basis of their religious identity. Their repeated protests against the policy have stressed the high degree of ritual discrimination that persists in their lives as Christians. Such advocacy appears to have landed on deaf ears, even during the long reign of the Congress Party, which purports to uphold secularism.

The debate over reservations for Dalit Christians bears a structural similarity to the colonial debate concerning the 'civil disabilities' of converts. Knowledge production in the nineteenth century shaped the identity politics of the centuries that followed. In the debate over Dalit Christian reservations, the image of the convert's eviction from the Hindu family and ensuing 'disabilities' is re-enacted on the grand stage of the Indian nation. Eviction from the 'little society' of family or caste foreshadows the forfeiture of state benefits within the 'big society' of the nation. In advocating for the extension of those benefits to Dalit

---

14   The text of the original Order is provided at http://socialjustice.nic.in/writereaddata/ UploadFile/scorder1950636011777382153618.pdf, accessed 23 May 2017.

converts, church leaders are essentially asking for a modern-day equivalent of the Caste Disabilities Removal Act, which precluded anyone from being punished on account of his or her change of religion or loss of caste status.

In the debate over reservations, the language of exile from community is applied to classes of people whose historical ties to a 'Hindu community' are highly disputed. In his provocative essay *Why I Am Not a Hindu*, Kancha Ilaiah (1996) drew sharp distinctions between the 'Dalit Bahujan' community from which he hailed and the 'Hindu community' into which he believes his community was co-opted. Whereas many regard his essay as polemical, it taps into a larger pool of literature that maintains the non-Hinduness of Dalits. This includes a tradition of non-Hindu confessionalism championed by men such as B. R. Ambedkar and E. V. Ramaswamy Naicker (to which I will return). It also includes ethnographic studies that distinguish cultural practices and beliefs of Dalits from those of caste Hindus.[15] Finally, it includes a body of 'advocacy scholarship' that highlights the paradox that those who suffered centuries of discrimination and exclusion relative to Hindu institutions are now claimed for Hinduism in order to secure India's Hindu majority.

Attempts to change the 1950 SC Order to extend SC status to Dalit Christians seem repeatedly to encounter the same conceptual barriers. According to Zoya Hasan, the policy framework of independent India separated the needs of religious minorities from those of disadvantaged caste communities. Whereas the government had an interest in promoting the 'cultural preservation' of religious minorities, it framed its policy towards Dalits and Tribals in terms of their development and empowerment (Hasan 2009: 42–3). Constitutional protection for religious minorities placed such a strong emphasis on religious identity that it ignored the inequality and deprivation often faced by Muslim or Christian converts (ibid.: 47). This sharp bifurcation of religion and caste also seemed geared

---

15   One stream of writing that asserts the non-Hinduness of Dalits and other low-caste peoples is traceable to a distinctively South Indian 'school' of Orientalism, which Thomas Trautmann has called the Madras School. This tradition of Orientalist scholarship posited a distinctively Dravidian family of languages, which in turn informed an anti-Brahminical, anti-Sanskrit politics of identity (see Trautmann 2009; on Dravidianism, see Geeta and Rajadurai 1998; Ramaswamy 1998). A recent collection of essays, which documents the pre-modern basis of untouchability and other forms of subordination, is provided in Parasher-Sen (2004). Contributors to the 'subaltern studies' project also have produced accounts of subordinate groups who have differentiated themselves from Hinduism (see Guha 2009; Chatterjee 1993: 187–94). More recent studies that posit the autonomy of untouchable communities and their differentiation from Hinduism can be found in Lee (2015) and Baumann (2008: 44–6). These studies problematise the understanding of conversion as a clear shift from one religion to another.

towards barring anyone from 'double dipping' into minority rights and aid for the disadvantaged. The state's denial of intersectionality between religion and untouchability lies at the heart of the omission of Christian and Muslim Dalits from sc lists.

Another reason for excluding Dalit Christians from the award is grounded in the idea that Christianity is a casteless religion. When Dalits join a religion that does not teach caste distinctions, they exit a Sanskritic domain and forfeit benefits targeting those who continue to suffer caste discrimination. By becoming Christian, not only do Dalits become 'casteless', but they also gain access to an infrastructure of resources – schools, orphanages, hospitals and other charities – which obviates state assistance. So the argument goes. Hence, the denial of sc status to Dalit Christians is anchored not only in their alleged castelessness but also in a belief in their higher degree of social mobility relative to other Dalits.

In their advocacy for a change to the Constitutional Order of 1950, Dalit Christian leaders are under a burden to show that: (1) they continue to retain a caste identity even after conversion; and (2) they continue to suffer invidious discrimination on the basis of this identity after conversion. In spite of producing convincing evidence of both fronts, their appeals have been unsuccessful.

In 1985, Soosai, a Tamil Christian convert, challenged the sc Order in court, only to be met with the enduring logic of the state in excluding Christians from the award. He was a cobbler who worked at a roadside near an intersection in Madras. In May 1982, local officers surveyed the sites where the cobblers were working and subsequently granted many of them free bunks from the Khadi and Village Industries Board. Soosai did not receive one because he was a Christian. In his petition, he argued that he was a member of the Adi Dravida community, which was listed in the original sc list of 1950, and had remained a member of that community after conversion. He argued that the Order of 1950 was invalid because it penalises his change of religion, contrary to Articles 14 and 15 of the Indian Constitution, which ensure equal protection under the law and freedom of religion respectively. Conversion, he argued, in no way eliminated the deprivations faced by members of his community.[16]

In its decision, the court did not deny the continuity of one's caste identity after conversion, but contended that this by itself was insufficient to classify someone as sc:

---

16   *Soosai and Others v. Union of India and Others* [1986] AIR 733, SCR Supl. (3), 24, 242–3.

To establish that paragraph 3 of the Constitution (Scheduled Castes) Order, 1950 discriminates against Christian members of the enumerated castes it must be shown that they suffer from a comparable depth of social and economic disabilities and cultural and educational backwardness and similar levels of degradation within the Christian community necessitating intervention by the State under provisions of the Constitution. It is not sufficient to show that the same caste continues after conversion. It is necessary to establish further that the disabilities and handicaps suffered from such caste membership in the social order of its origin – Hinduism – continue in their oppressive severity in the new environment of a different religious community. No authoritative or detailed study dealing with the present conditions of Christian society have been placed on the record in this case.[17]

The court's acknowledgement of the persistence of a caste identity after conversion is a marked change from earlier decisions, tracing back to the colonial period, which simply regarded Christianity as a religion that did not teach caste distinctions and concluded from this that Christians possessed no caste identity.[18] What the courts were willing to concede in 1985, however, would not be sufficient for overturning a long history of disassociating Christians from untouchable communities.

In 2005, the ruling United Progressive Alliance (UPA) government established a commission headed by Ranganath Mishra, the former Chief Justice of India. One of the main aims of this commission was to identify the criteria that define backwardness among linguistic and religious minorities and to recommend remedial measures on the basis of those criteria. Unlike the 1985 decision of *Soosai*, the Mishra Commission not only recognised caste as a pervasive institution in Indian society, irrespective of religion, but clearly acknowledged the persistence of ritual discrimination faced by Christian converts:

The position of persons of Scheduled Caste origin converted to Christianity remains the same as before. They continue to be forced into the most demeaning occupations. Their position both in the Church as well as amongst fellow Christians is no better than that suffered by their counterparts in other religious denominations. They continue to be both poor

---

17   *Soosai and Others v. Union of India and Others* [1986] AIR 733, SCR Supl. (3), 24, 250.

18   The Madras High Court, for instance, voiced this position in *K. Michael Pillai v. J. M. Barthe and Others* [1917] AIR, Madras, 432–4.

and socially and educationally backward. Inter-marriages between them and upper caste Christians are rare. In the Churches they are segregated from the upper caste Christians. Even after death they are buried in different burial grounds.

Ministry of Minority Affairs 2007: 140

Dalit Christians could ask for no better statement for legitimising their claims to SC status that what was offered in the Mishra Report. When it was submitted to the government in 2007, it had the backing of several parties within the UPA. It was the Congress Party, however, that was reluctant to act. Its members appear to have been pressured by certain MPs and ministers in the UPA who opposed the measure. Some of these members had expressed fears that extending SC status to Christian and Muslim Dalits would encourage Hindu Dalits to convert to those religions (Hasan 2009: 215).

These challenges to the 1950 SC Order reveal three recurring themes in the debate about religion and caste disability in India. First, they illustrate how both sides of the debate have deployed the language of 'inducement', which belongs to anti-conversion legislation. Opponents of the 1950 Order regard it as inducing Muslim or Christian converts to revert to Hinduism to qualify for state assistance. Defenders of the Act, including proponents of Hindutva ideology, regard the extension of SC status to Muslims and Christians as providing an inducement for conversion to those religions.

Secondly, these challenges show how the policy remains unchanged despite strong arguments on the ground for the persistence of caste-related disabilities among Christian converts. The evidence put forth in the Mishra Report has been joined by scholarly works by anthropologists and social scientists, and an official report by the National Minorities Commission enumerated the social disabilities faced by Christian and Muslim communities (ibid.: 218). Finally, responses to these challenges fail to adequately explain why Sikhs and Buddhists have been included in the SC lists, while Muslims and Christians have not. Like Islam and Christianity, after all, Sikhism and Buddhism are egalitarian religions, which disavow caste distinctions. The policy seems to invoke a long-standing distinction between religions of India versus those of foreign origin, a distinction that proponents of Hindutva are voicing with new vigour in their efforts to make India Hindu.

Ghar Vapsi and Inducement

Current attempts to reconvert Dalits and Tribals to Hinduism are predicated on the notion that these communities have been forced or induced to convert to 'foreign religions' and must somehow be brought 'home' to mother Hinduism.[19] This particular campaign belongs to a larger project of making India an officially Hindu nation, a project co-ordinated by a cluster of organisations known as the Sangh Parivar. The *Ghar Vapsi* (or Homecoming) campaign, led by the Vishwa Hindu Parishad (VHP, or World Hindu Federation), operates within the same discursive framework as that found in the debate over the convert's plight under Hindu law and Dalit Christian reservations. The campaign to bring people home to the Hindu fold presumes a stable 'Hindu community' from which they were extracted, and offers a mechanism for bringing them back.

In December 2014, the VHP reportedly reconverted thirty-seven families to Hinduism in Elappara, Kerala. As many as 100 of those reconverted belonged to the Pentecostal Church, which is quite prominent in Kerala, but had formerly been Hindus. The VHP claimed that on the same day it had also reconverted twenty-seven other Christians from five families in Kayamkulam. In both cases, priests at local temples performed the rites of re-entry (*shuddhi kalashakriya*).[20] VHP spokesmen claim that these Christians had actively sought their assistance, citing 'neglect from authorities in the name of caste and religion'.[21]

Gaining the most press coverage was a reconversion drive in December 2014 in the outskirts of Agra, in which 200 Muslims were reconverted to Hinduism. There, fifty-seven Muslim families, mostly poor migrants from Bihar or Bengal, claimed that members of two militant Hindu organisations, the Dharma Jagran Manch and the Bajrang Dal, had employed both force and inducement to reconvert them.[22] A Muslim slum dweller named Farhan claimed that Hindu activists had forced him to participate in a *puja*, wash the feet of Hindu gods, and wear auspicious marks with vermilion on his forehead. 'If forty people in saffron come and stand on your head,' he charged, 'you will do just as they

---

19   Goldie Osuri (2014) traces current reconversion drives to developments of the late colonial period, in which Hindu activists drew their inspiration from European fascists to advance their agenda.

20   '"Ghar Vapsi" in Idukki, Alappuzha', *The Hindu*, 19 January 2015.

21   Ibid.

22   'Agra Reconversion Row: Uproar in Parliament as Opposition seeks Prime Minister's reply; UP cops on high alert', *Hindustan Times*, 11 December 2014, http://www.hindustantimes .com/india-news/agra-conversion-that-muslims-say-wasn-t-rocks-parliament-bsp-cong -target-bjp/article1-1295082.aspx, accessed 3 May 2017.

want.'[23] Whereas Farhan insisted that his compliance was simply to get the saffron-clad activists 'off his back', others who were reconverted claimed that they were offered ration cards and access to the local water supply in exchange for the decision to reconvert.[24]

The idea that India's poor had been 'induced' to leave Hinduism, and hence must be reclaimed for Hinduism, has a history that predates today's *Ghar Vapsi* campaign. During the nineteenth and twentieth centuries, the Arya Samaj, a reformist organisation founded largely to stem the tide of Hindu conversion to other religions, employed the Vedic purification ceremony of *shuddhi* to read-mit converts back into Hinduism. As Cassie Addock has observed, however, Arya Samajist campaigns of the 1920s were not simply about 'making Hindus' but were also occasions for 'adjusting' caste relations between Hindu com-munities. The readmission of Muslims or Christians into the Hindu fold required that high-caste elites recognise the new status of reconverts and extend them the privileges due to them (Addock 2014: 124–6). Mohandas Gandhi himself became an outspoken critic of conversion among the untouch-ables. He distinguished conversions resulting from an appeal to the intel-lect from those that merely appealed to 'the stomach'. The vast majority of untouchables who converted to Christianity, he claimed, had done so because of the material inducements offered by foreign missionaries. So convinced was Gandhi of the falseness of their motives that, when asked whether reconverts should undergo the ritual of *shuddhi*, Gandhi replied that there was no need for the rite, since the conversions were not 'real' ones (Gandhi 1941: 83).

The Hindu nationalist *Ghar Vapsi* campaign shares with Gandhi a belief in the illegitimacy of Dalit and Tribal conversion out of Hinduism. But instead of becoming an excuse to eliminate the rite of *shuddhi*, today's Hindu nationalists assert that *ghar vapsi* is not conversion but 'homecoming'. Because of this dis-tinction, they do not believe that their methods violate current anti-conversion laws, which prohibit conversion by force, fraud or inducement.[25] In fact, finan-cial contributions from Indians in the UK, US and various parts of Europe play an important role in funding *Ghar Vapsi* campaigns in India. A pamphlet cir-culated in Bihar and Uttar Pradesh by the Dharma Jagran Manch claimed that it costs one lakh rupees (approximately $1,500) to convert a Muslim. It costs

---

23   Ibid.

24   This was the claim of Haji Jamiluddin Qureshi, president of the Rashtriya Sarvdaliya Muslim Action Committee (ibid.).

25   Such laws are in place in Odisha, Madhya Pradesh, Gujarat, Rajasthan, Chhatisgarh and Himachal Pradesh.

three times this amount to convert a Christian, however, because of the financial resources that circulate through churches and Christian organisations.[26]

In addition to raising important questions about methods, reconversion requires the negotiation of caste identity. To which caste will those readmitted to Hinduism belong? According to one report, the VHP promised that reconverts will be allowed to choose their caste, a claim that clearly challenges the notion of caste as an immutable, hereditary identity (Harris 2014).

Conclusion

This chapter has discussed three venues – the colonial, postcolonial and contemporary – that employ a common framework, derived from Sanskritic law, for staging a debate about conversion. That framework establishes conversion first and foremost as a moment of eviction or exile from an imagined Hindu community. In all three contexts, the language of 'inducement' displaces that of 'choice' as the logic that drives conversion. In colonial times, conversion out of the Hindu family resulted in the convert's 'civil death' and forfeiture of familial rights. Hindu gentry decried the passing of the Caste Disabilities Removal Act of 1850 for providing state-based incentives for conversion (and for breaching the Raj's commitment to religious neutrality). In the debate over Dalit Christian affirmative action, the loss of rights within the 'little society' of family and caste is re-enacted within the 'big society' of the nation. Having left Hinduism, converts no longer qualify for assistance aimed at rectifying the historical abuses of Hinduism. Church leaders view the denial of SC status to Dalit Christians as inducing Dalits to identify with Hinduism, whereas their opponents view the possible extension of that status as providing an inducement for conversion. Finally, the *Ghar Vapsi* campaign sustains the myth of a 'Hindu fold' from which members of 'foreign religions' have extracted Dalits and Tribals through force and inducement. The irony of bringing Dalits and Tribals back 'home' is that these groups have lived on the fringes – if not beyond the pale – of Sanskritic influence, as Monier-Williams observed in his 1861 address. The language of homecoming not only eclipses any discussion of their original identity, but also absolves Hindutva activists of any responsibility for violating the very anti-conversion laws they have promoted.

In conclusion, two implications of the Orientalist framework for Christian conversion are worth considering. First, the framework has had the effect of

---

26   'Project Hindutva', *Frontline*, 22 December 2014.

pre-empting an important aspect of Dalit assertion: namely, a politics of non-Hindu confessionalism. Conversion to Christianity or Islam may be regarded as one dimension of the assertion of difference. During the early twentieth century, anti-Hindu and anti-Brahminical ideology and politics were centrepieces of Dalit activism. This is evident in Ambedkar's assertion that dignity for Dalits could only come outside Hinduism and that 'he would not die a Hindu' (Mendelsohn and Vicziany 1998: 114–15).[27] 'Conversion,' he once claimed, 'is as important to the untouchable as self-government is to India' (Ambedkar 1981: 17). E. V. Ramaswamy Naicker launched a similar politics in his championing of a Dravidian identity (which applied to non-Brahmins more broadly), which countered Brahminical and/or Sanskritic hegemony in the south. Steadily, the disadvantages of being 'non-Hindu' tamed the politics of non-Hindu confessionalism. Scholars have noted how the politics of the census, affirmative action schemes and electioneering have created stronger incentives for Hindu elites to preserve and mobilise their majority in India. The Hindu nationalist, Bharatiya Janata Party (BJP)-led government's promotion of Sanskritic values and a revisionist 'Hindu history' further marginalised the roles of non-Hindus in India's past and present (Guichard 2010).[28] The new traction Hindutva has gained among India's middle class has also made southern political parties such as the Dravida Munnetra Kazhagam (DMK) and All India Anna Dravida Munnetra Kazhagam (AIADMK) less effective in maintaining their historical opposition to Sanskritic hegemony.

Finally, what might India's conversion debate imply for the place of South Asian Christians within broader discussions about World Christianity? Thus far, South Asia's Christians have been somewhat isolated from this literature and its themes of agency, appropriation and power. This is due in part to their enclosure in an internal debate about religious conversion in India, which has been framed in the Orientalist categories described here. Another factor, however, has also contributed to this insularity. Macro-studies of World Christianity tend to be driven by a fascination with changing demographics of the global church. If demographics continue to drive scholarship and if Christian growth in India continues to be challenged by the range of disincentives discussed in this chapter, the main stories likely to emerge from India are those of resistance or hostility, not those of numerical 'growth', and India's

---

27   This was Ambedkar's famous declaration at the Yeola Conference of 1935. See the discussion of this in Mallampalli (2004: 164–5).

28   Guichard (2010) provides an extremely thorough summary of this project of rewriting Indian history along Hindutva lines.

Christians will continue to factor minimally in discussions of Christianity in the global South.

If, however, we move away from a preoccupation with numbers, we can better appreciate an emerging scholarship addressing ethnographic, historical and theological dimensions of Indian Christianity. As much as votaries of Hindutva may silence any discussion of an 'indigenous discovery' of Christianity among Dalits and Tribals, secular scholarship is making this narrative more audible. Important work by scholars such as John Webster, Sathe Clarke, James Massey, Chad Baumann, Nathaniel Roberts, David Mosse and Arvind Nirmal brings to light social, historical and theological dimensions of Dalit conversion within various parts of India. This stream of literature is matched by a wave of scholarship focused on the Indianness of Christianity and cross-cultural interactions between Christians and their Hindu–Muslim environments.[29] The question of Christianity's marginality relative to India's Hindu majority need not imply any marginality relative to World Christianity if studies of the latter move beyond their fascination with church growth and draw attention to other important cross-cutting themes.

References

Addock, C. (2014) *The Limits of Tolerance: Indian Secularism and the Politics of Religious Freedom.* Oxford: Oxford University Press.

Ali, M. (1965) *The Bengali Reaction to Missionary Activities, 1833–1857.* Chittagong: Mehrub Publications.

Ambedkar, B. R. (1981) *Why Go for Conversion?* Bangalore: Dalit Sahitya Academy.

Baumann, C. (2008) *Christian Identity and Dalit Religion in Hindu India, 1868–1947.* Grand Rapids MI: Eerdmans.

Beteille, A. (2003) 'Hinduism in Danger?', *The Hindu,* 3 January.

Billington Harper, S. (2000) *In the Shadow of the Mahatma: Bishop V. S. Azariah and the Travails of Christianity in British India.* Grand Rapids MI and Richmond, Surrey: Eerdmans and Curzon Press.

Carson, P. (2012) *The East India Company and Religion, 1698–1858.* Woodbridge: Boydell Press.

Chatterjee, P. (1993) *The Nation and its Fragments: Colonial and Postcolonial Histories.* Delhi: Oxford University Press.

---

29   Much of this literature addresses in some shape or form the question of Indian Christianity's continuity or discontinuity relative to local culture.

Clough, J. and E. Rauschenbusch-Clough (1914) *Social Christianity in the Orient: The Story of a Man, a Mission and a Movement.* New York NY: Macmillan.

Comaroff, J. and J. L. Comaroff (1997) *Of Revelation and Revolution. Volume 2: The Dialectics of Modernity on a South African Frontier.* Chicago IL: University of Chicago Press.

Dirks, N. (2001) *Castes of Mind: Colonialism and the Making of Modern India.* Delhi: Permanent Black.

Dubois, J. A. (1823) *Letters on the State of Christianity in India, in which the Conversion of the Hindus is Considered as Impracticable.* London: Paternoster Row.

Forrester, D. M. (1980) *Caste and Christianity: Attitudes and Policies on Caste of Anglo-Saxon Protestant Missions in India.* London: Curzon.

Gandhi, M. K. (1941) *Christian Missions: Their Place in India.* Ahmedabad: Navajivan.

Geeta, V. and S. V. Rajadurai (1998) *Towards a Non-Brahmin Millennium: From Iyothee Thass to Periyar.* Calcutta: Samya.

Guha, R. (2009) 'The Career of an Anti-God in Heaven and on Earth' in R. Guha and P. Chatterjee (eds), *The Small Voice of History: Collected Essays.* Ranikhet: Permanent Black.

Guichard, S. (2010) *The Construction of History and Nationalism in India: Textbooks, Controversies and Politics.* London: Routledge.

Hardgrave, R. (1969) *The Nadars of Tamilnad: The Political Culture of a Community in Change.* Berkeley CA: University of California Press.

Harris, G. (2014) 'Reconversion of Religious Minorities Roils India's Politics', *The New York Times,* 23 December, http://www.nytimes.com/2014/12/24/world/asia/india-narendra-modi-hindu-conversions-missionaries.html?_r=0, accessed 3 May 2017.

Hartch, T. (2014) *The Rebirth of Latin American Christianity.* New York NY: Oxford University Press.

Hasan, Z. (2009) *Politics of Inclusion: Castes, Minorities, and Affirmative Action.* Delhi: Oxford University Press.

Hough, J. (1824) *A Reply to the Letters of the Abbe Dubois on the State of Christianity in India.* London: L. B. Seeley & Sons.

Ilaiah, K. (1996) *Why I Am Not a Hindu: A Sudra Critique of Hindutva Philosophy, Culture, and Political Economy.* Calcutta: Samya.

Irschick, E. (1994) *Dialogue and History: Constructing South India, 1795–1895.* Berkeley CA: University of California Press.

Jaffrelot, C. (2005) *Analyzing and Fighting Caste: Dr. Ambedkar and Untouchability.* Delhi: Permanent Black.

Jenkins, P. (2002) *The Next Christendom: The Coming of Global Christianity.* New York NY: Oxford University Press.

Lee, J. (2015) 'Jagdish, Son of Ahmad: Dalit Religion and Nominative Politics in Lucknow', *South Asia Multidisciplinary Academic Journal* 11.

Mallampalli, C. (2004) *Christians and Public Life in Colonial South India, 1863–1937: Contending with Marginality*. London: Routledge Curzon.

Mallampalli, C. (2011) *Race, Religion and Law in Colonial India: Trials of an Interracial Family*. Cambridge: Cambridge University Press.

Maxwell, D. (2006) *African Gifts of the Spirit: Pentecostalism and the Rise of Zimbabwean Transnational Religious Movement*. Athens OH: Ohio University Press.

Mendelsohn, O. and M. Vicziany (1998) *The Untouchables: Subordination, Poverty and the State in Modern India*. Cambridge: Cambridge University Press.

Ministry of Minority Affairs (2007) *Report of the National Committee for Religious and Linguistic Minorities*. Delhi: Government of India.

Monckton Jones, M. E. (1918) *Warren Hastings in Bengal, 1772–1774*. Oxford: Clarendon Press.

Monier-Williams, M. (1861) *The Study of Sanskrit in Relation to Missionary Work in India*. London: Williams and Norgate.

Oddie, G. (1994) '"Orientalism" and British Protestant Missionary Constructions of India in the Nineteenth Century', *South Asia* 17 (2): 27–42.

Osuri, G. (2014) 'Foreign Swadeshi', *Frontline*, 24 December, http://www.frontline.in/thenation/foreignswadeshi/article6715524.ece?homepage=true&css=print, accessed 3 May 2017.

Parasher-Sen, A. (ed.) (2004) *Subordinate and Marginal Groups in Early India*. Delhi: Oxford University Press.

Pollock, S. (2006) *The Language of Gods in the World of Men: Sanskrit, Culture and Power in Premodern India*. Berkeley CA: University of California Press.

Ramaswamy, S. (1998) *Passions of the Tongue: Language Devotion in Tamil India, 1891–1970*. New Delhi: Munshiram Manoharlal Publishers.

Rhenius, J. (1841) *Memoir of the Rev. C. T. E. Rhenius*. London: James Nisbet and Co.

Robert, D. (2000) 'Shifting Southward: Global Christianity Since 1945', *International Bulletin of Missionary Research* 24 (2): 50–8.

Robert, D. (2009) *Christian Mission: How Christianity Became a World Religion*. Malden MA: Wiley-Blackwell.

Roberts, J. (ed.) (1847) *Caste, in its Religious and Civil Character, Opposed to Christianity: Being a Series of Documents by the Right Reverend Bishops Heber, Wilson, Corrie, and Spencer and by Eminent Ministers of Other Denominations, Condemnatory of the Observance of Caste among the Native Christians in India*. London: Longman, Brown, Green, and Longmans.

Rocher, R. (2010) 'The Creation of Anglo-Hindu Law' in T. Lubin, D. R. Davis Jr and J. K. Krishnan (eds), *Hinduism and Law: An Introduction*. New York NY: Cambridge University Press.

Spear, P. (1963) *The Nabobs: A Study of the Social Life of the English in Eighteenth Century India*. London: Oxford University Press.

Suntharalingam, R. (1974) *Politics and Nationalist Awakening in South India, 1852–1891.* Tucson AZ: University of Arizona Press.

Trautmann, T. (2006) *Languages and Nations: The Dravidian Proof in Colonial Times.* Berkeley CA: University of California Press.

Trautmann, T. (2009) *The Madras School of Orientalism: Producing Knowledge in Colonial South India.* Delhi: Oxford University Press.

Vishwanathan, G. (1998) *Outside the Fold: Conversion, Modernity and Belief.* Princeton NJ: Princeton University Press.

Viswanath, R. (2010) 'Spiritual Slavery, Material Malaise: "Untouchables" and Religious Neutrality in Colonial South India', *Historical Research* 83 (219): 124–45.

Viswanath, R. (2013) 'The Emergence of Authenticity Talk and the Giving of Accounts: Conversion as Movement of the Soul in South India, ca. 1900', *Comparative Studies in Society and History* 55 (1): 120–41.

Walls, A. (1997) *The Missionary Movement in Christian History: Studies in the Transmission of Faith.* Maryknoll NY: Orbis Books.

Webster, J. (1996) *The Dalit Christians: A History.* Delhi: ISPCK.

Wuthnow, R. (2009) *Boundless Faith: The Global Outreach of American Churches.* Berkeley CA: University of California Press.

PART 3

Place and Belonging in World Christianity

∴

Christian Social Movements in Cameroon at the End of Empire: Transnational Solidarities and the Communion of the World Church

Charlotte Walker-Said

Introduction

On 14 November 1956, an estimated 3,000 African Christians assembled in Douala, Cameroon's port city and economic centre, to attend the Pan African Conference of the Jeunesse Ouvrière Chrétienne (JOC). Catholics from across French West and Equatorial Africa – with the largest contingents from Cameroon, as well as Senegal and Ivory Coast – had planned the conference for a year with their JOC *équipes* and diocesan leaders, including African and French priests and nuns. By the end of 1956, they were ready to open the three-day forum to discuss the obligations of religious activism in the midst of turbulent political movements and ideologies troubling France's African territories and particularly the Catholic Church: nationalism, Communism and anti-colonialism. Along with scheduled ceremonies, speeches, parades and worship services, Michel Tenke, a JOC *militant* from Cameroon, along with Abbé Jean Noddings, the territory's chief French JOC organiser, led a mass dedicated to 'praying that the human family be remembered in the work of social organising for the future in Africa'.[1]

The 'human family', or, more specifically, the African family, had been a principal concern of Catholic as well as Protestant religious life in Cameroon from the early twentieth century, as thousands of African catechists, pastors and priests, alongside foreign missionary workers, professed a faith that promised to renew not only individual souls but also African community life by nurturing monogamous coupling, individualised households, and marriages without bridewealth (Walker-Said 2015b). At the 1956 Douala conference, speeches by JOC youth group leaders, organisers for the JOC women's league, and other volunteers, *militants* and seminarians referenced marriage, family and Chris-

---

tian communalism in Africa as sources of 'moral energies' through which Communism could be fought. In preparation for the conference, and in the years following it, the JOC leadership in Cameroon focused heavily on joining young Christian couples in sacrament and law and founding religious associations that fostered interdependency, professional networks and social outlets for African Christian families. Together with the church and its organisations, African Christians would become the motor of local social and economic development in the new nation as well as critical sponsors of international Christian solidarities that could mobilise and realise the spiritual goals of the postcolonial era in Africa.[2]

At the 1957 international JOC conferences in Dakar and Rome, Catholics from Cameroon sent delegations from social work organisations, Catholic Action groups, Catholic hospitals, and blocs from the Christian trade union, the Confédération Africaine des Travailleurs Croyants (CATC), to communicate their vision of locally and internationally oriented Christian values to the broader audience of African and international Christian youth.[3] Messages articulated in transnational forums and circulated to local publics within the territory in the last decade before Cameroon's independence demonstrate alternative forms of both nationalism and internationalism that generated new aspirations among the Cameroon territory's nearly 1 million Christians. Importantly, the religious ideologies that inspired value-driven social mobilisations at the end of French rule provide an alternative vantage point from which the historian can perceive a form of conservative modernism that was emerging globally, and perhaps most sharply in Africa.

Christian conservatism was a popular sentiment among Cameroon's rural and urban classes, and, in many ways, its intellectual trajectory was not too dissimilar from that of trade unionism, Communism or anti-colonialism. European and African church hierarchies and local parishes exchanged conservative Christian ideas via transnational organisations, much as European labour organisations and political confederations corresponded with African workers' cadres and emerging political parties. However, in contrast to leftist groups, African Christians brought forth a particular vision of modernism that was rooted in narratives of tradition, constancy and stability, rather than rupture, revolution or innovation. European and African diocesan leaders, members of the clergy, youth ministers and engaged laity participated in dialogues on a

---

2   ACSSp., 2J1.1.15b9 Conférénce JOC, Douala, 1956.

3   ACSSp., 2J1.7a2 Congrès JOC à Rome. See also 'Echos Camerounais du rassemblement mondial de la JOC à Rome', *L'Effort Camerounais* 102, 15–21 September 1957; Pierrard et al. (1984: 167–74).

vision of modern conservatism that focused heavily on the family and community, and especially its bonds of marriage, kinship strategies, reproduction and education. In doing so, these leaders combined a 'social values' discourse with theories of nationalism that were current in Cameroon and Africa in the late colonial era. The result was a clearly defined articulation that appropriately cultivated gender relations and family and community models could determine social welfare, and that this objective was as critical to political progress in the nation as administrative autonomy and economic development.

Reconsidering Religion and Politics in African Nationalism

In Cameroon, African priests and pastors were critical interlocutors of world events. Jean Zoa, who would become Archbishop of Yaoundé after independence, aimed to articulate the paradoxical message that Africans' full inclusion and participation in the world community of Christian believers was essential for forging a national church. African Christians were not to be 'excluded from an ecclesial reality' by being forever subject to missionaries, Zoa argued; rather, they would 'speak the common language of Christians' and 'become aware of their exceptional role in the Church and in the world by clarifying their social, political, and economic engagement using the light of the Gospels' (Zoa 1961). Zoa's widely circulated tract 'Pour un nationalisme chrétien au Cameroun', published in 1957 when he was the vicar of the church of Sacré-Coeur in Mokolo, urged Cameroonians to 'awaken to a consciousness of national rights' but warned them that: 'Political emancipation alone is not a panacea for our problems ... Guided by the Social Doctrine of the Church, we must seek a nationalism guided by Christian principles ... we must act like one family' (Zoa 1957). Protestant pastor Eugene Mallo, who was the head of the Fédération des Églises et Missions Protestantes, likewise called for prayers for 'a sane nationalism', through which Africans would gain full autonomy but 'maintain the flame of Christian devotion' (Mallo 1954). African Catholic and Protestant leaders' careful delineations of the appropriate forms of nationalism demonstrate their empathy with political movements that opposed oppression and subjugation. Their statements also reflect their need to prove, as fellow members of the African faithful, that they were not dominated by the French missionary episcopacy or the colonial state, which were hostile to African self-governance. Zoa, Mallo and other African priests, bishops and pastors were, however, also genuinely afraid that 'the spirit of combat' and the spectre of Marxism would overwhelm the bonds of Christian solidarity that the churches had worked so hard to instil in the interwar and post-war decades (Mallo 1965: 34–6; Zoa 1960; Etoga 1956).

After the Second World War, the launch of new French development projects through the Fonds pour l'Investissement en Développement Économique et Social (FIDES) and the simultaneous founding of African anti-colonial political parties and labour movements organised through the Confédération Générale du Travail (CGT) expanded professional possibilities for Africans throughout the French-administered territories. Africans seized the opportunities these and other transnational administrative, political and labour organisations provided to actively shape the structure of the empire, and, eventually, to participate in determining the outcomes of its end. Scholars have carefully traced the emergence of secular, statist reform programmes in Africa in the post-war period, illuminating the roles of French and Francophone social theorists and administrators in crafting grand reformist visions for colonialism that would eventually set decolonisation in motion (Cooper 1996; Morgenthau 1964; de Benoist 1982; Gifford and Louis 1982). Many have also emphasised the agency of African politicians from across the political spectrum in articulating new development frameworks for Africa's territories by organising labour, mobilising political claims, and expanding access to government, industry, health and education for everyday Africans (Joseph 1977; Allman 1993; Lindsay 1999; Cooper 2014). However, while the considerable range of this scholarship has included native and non-native agents in the history of crafting postcolonial citizenship and rights, most scholars have also largely limited the scope of their investigations to political initiatives and the mobilisations of political groups and civic leaders who crafted secular laws, constitutions and communities (Chatterjee 1993; Mamdani 1996; Terretta 2014; Wilder 2015). Karen Fields and David Maxwell are two notable exceptions to this, as they illuminate not only how religious doctrines influenced and addressed political struggles during and after colonialism but also how African religious leaders could eschew nationalism in search of the cathartic possibilities of supranational spiritual human bonds (Fields 1985; Maxwell 2006). Religious visions of independent Africa are notable because they typically transcended the nation-state and sought sustainable solidarities that were not purely instrumental to the achievement of independent nationhood, but rather were essential to continuous membership in another form of community.

Religious Organising and the Life of the Church in Cameroon

In French-administered Cameroon in 1946, the territory's roughly 3 million inhabitants included 500,000 baptised Catholics and catechumens and nearly 200,000 Protestants, whose fidelity to the tenets of the faith was made evident in their zealous promotion of pious practices, including worship, performance of devout works, and a high level of commitment to the clergy and consecrated life (Guernier and Briat 1951: 95–6; Messina and Van Slageren 2005; Ngongo 1982; Pokam 1987).[4] Active members of the Christian churches in Cameroon were led by growing numbers of African priests, pastors, nuns and deaconesses, with African men increasingly joining the ranks of the high episcopacies of Catholic and Protestant denominations, where they wielded considerable authority on matters of social and civic importance (Akoa-Mongo 2011; Tiandong 1973; Messina et al. 2000). Histories addressing the evolutions of particular Christian denominations in Cameroon are numerous and emphasise how, over the first half of the twentieth century, foreign missions became powerful indigenous institutional structures whose leadership systems and administrative networks arose from local socio-cultural frameworks that compelled recognition of church authority (Van Slageren 1972; Messina 1988; Laburthe-Tolra 2005; Etaba 2007). By the end of the Second World War, Christian congregations were mobilising to address issues of forced labour, punitive taxation, autocratic native authority, reified customary law, elementary and adult education, land rights and religious freedom (Zoa 1959; Kibénél Ngo Billong 2009; Njougla 1950).

Importantly, movements for social reform led by religious principles in the post-war era contrasted sharply with those led by the radical anti-colonial Union des Populations du Cameroun (UPC) party and its allies in the CGT, which enjoyed considerable support (Joseph 1977; Mbembe 1996; Gardinier 1963). The nationalist UPC party was motivated primarily by a desire to shed the constraints of European rule and drew from pan-Africanist, black internationalist and global Marxist ideologies that emphasised self-determination, the political unification of Cameroon, and anti-imperialism (Terretta 2014: 4–8). Many Africans in Cameroon who considered themselves devout Christians did not necessarily share the same vision of revolutionary anti-colonialism; many who were active in their congregations espoused alternative visions of solidarity based on intimate reciprocities fostered between French and African

---

4   Statistics for this era vary slightly, but generally point to the territory's Christian population equalling roughly one-quarter to one-third of the total African population of Cameroon.

parishes, dioceses and religious orders. The clergy and laity nurtured a vision of human rights based not – or not only – on the achievement of civil and political rights, but rather on a culture of local charity and the religious responsibility to heal, educate, minister, counsel and alleviate suffering. In general, foreign and local ecclesiastical leaders urged their flocks to seek liberation in forms not limited to political independence (Etaba 2007: 86–94; Messina et al. 2000: 90–108). African priests and pastors, as well as Christian youth movement leaders and health and education workers, were acutely aware of Franco-African interdependency and mutuality and these bonds shaped distinctive kinds of communal networks in which hopes for the future were pinned on the achievement of spiritual and social goals.

European church leaders and French and Francophone colonial administrators anxious about Marxist political influences and anti-colonial radicalism in post-war Africa sought to expand social and economic development on a model similar to that proposed by Pius XI in 1927, in which he called for 'political charity', or a vast social investment and evangelism that could fight against 'remote and foundational causes' of evil and injustice throughout the world.[5] After the Second World War, Catholic anti-communist strategies focused on economic development that was imbued with Christian social objectives such as family assistance and maternal and child health for those in the colonies (Chamedes 2015).

The initiation of state-led development projects in the health, governance and education sectors further galvanised Christian lay and clerical leaders and their respective publics to launch parallel and reciprocal efforts for social welfare, including rural development, youth education and professionalisation, poor relief and local charity, as well as legal reform in the areas of personal and family law, including laws concerning abortion, polygamy, bridewealth, child marriage, widow inheritance and forced marriage (Walker-Said 2015a; Binet 1953; Abitbol 1966). Both foreign and indigenous bishops and pastors expressed eagerness to co-operate in political reform, promoting the 'human interest' dimension of post-war colonial initiatives.[6]

---

5 Pius XI, 'Rerum Ecclesiae: Encyclical of Pope Pius XI on Catholic Missions', 1926, http://w2 .vatican.va/content/pius-xi/en/encyclicals/documents/hf_p-xi_enc_28021926_rerum -ecclesiae.html, accessed 5 May 2017; 'Address to the Italian Catholic University Students' Federation, FUCI', 1927.

6 Société des Missions Évangéliques de Paris/Service Protestant de Mission-Défap (hereafter SMEP/DEFAP), Papiers Jean Keller, Carton V, Fédération Évangélique du Cameroun et de l'Afrique Equatoriale, P.V. de réunion du Conseil à Ngaoundéré, 17–20 January 1953, 1–2.

In 1941, at the suggestion of the American Presbyterian Mission and the Société des Missions Évangéliques de Paris (SMEP), the Féderation des Missions Évangéliques du Cameroun et de l'Afrique Équatoriale was founded with the explicit intention of facilitating relations between the Protestant missions and the French administration to prevent 'political disorders' among African Christians, to promote civic education, and to orient social action towards religious goals.[7] Louis-Paul Aujoulat, white *colon* settler, Social Catholic, member of the Mouvement Républicain Populaire (MRP) party, and deputy for the Cameroon territory between 1945 and 1956, persuaded the territorial government and the overseas ministry to invest more in Catholic philanthropies and humanitarian projects, drawing from FIDES funds as well as private French Catholic endowments to pursue social and economic reform within the French Union in Africa (Turpin 1999: 171–2; Lachenal and Taithe 2009).

What is essential is that for many Catholic and Protestant Africans in the post-war years, as well as for many French Catholic leaders in the laity and clergy, Cameroon was not only emerging as a national space, it was acquiring a reality as a culture and a society. In their idealisations, Cameroon was not only to be shaped as a distinct geographic and political entity; it would constitute part of a broader human community. For Africans, their vision of their community was one of strong believers whose aspirations reflected the Universal Church and included constituents from beyond the boundaries of the Cameroonian nation-state.[8]

Transnational Organisations and the Flow of Conservative Ideals

Global transformations had made possible the imagining of Cameroon as a place of religious enfranchisement and Christian progress in the post-war period. The unique atmosphere of international colonialism prevalent in the League of Nations mandate for Cameroon during the interwar years allowed for many more opportunities to engage with Christianity than was the case in many of France's other colonies (Austen 1971). Later, during the period of

---

7   SMEP/DEFAP, Papiers Jean Keller, Carton V, Fédération Évangélique du Cameroun et de l'Afrique Equatoriale, P.V. de réunion du Conseil à Ngaoundéré, 17–20 January 1953. See also Grottelli (1984).

8   In both Catholic and Protestant teachings, the Universal Church is the name given to the church worldwide. The New Testament uses the term 'church' in myriad instances to refer to a community of believers beyond a singular, bounded space. See Acts 8: 3; Acts 9: 31; 1 Corinthians 12: 28; 15: 9; Matthew 16: 18; Ephesians 1: 22–23; Colossians 1: 18.

United Nations trusteeship, a host of powerful religious institutions, including Catholic and Protestant missionary societies and their affiliated pious brother-hoods, benevolent societies, relief organisations, youth groups and even Chris-tian labour unions such as the Cameroon chapter of the Confédération Fran-çaise des Travailleurs Chrétiens (CFTC), deepened their ties to African com-munities and rural villages and to dioceses and religious organisations in the French *métropole* and Rome.

Cameroonian bishop Albert Ndongmo reflected that, in the 1950s and 1960s, the 'good efforts' of the African churches 'could not survive without the Ponti-fical Missionary Works', as local seminaries, youth centres, experimental farms, orphanages and clinics depended nearly entirely on foreign financial support (*La Croix* 1969). Religious organisations such as the JOC, the Union Chrétienne des Jeunes Gens (YMCA/UCJG), the Croix Bleue and the Légion de Marie, among many others, were both deeply rooted in village and parish networks in Cameroon but also internationally active, linking councils and dioceses at local, regional and global levels. These densely woven networks of spiritual exchange shared a common interest in the particular locality of Cameroon, but they promoted socio-religious organisations and activities – and hence a concept of community – that were not solely territorially based (Sappia and Servais 2010: 329; Privat 1992; Mallo 1954; Brutsch 1950b; Bouchaud 1954; Aujou-lat 1947). While African Christians in Cameroon articulated their commitment to the national polity – indeed, the African Catholic and Protestant high cler-gies often expressed consternation at the frequent and fervent demands for national sovereignty from their flocks – they simultaneously held the belief that they also belonged to a community that surpassed the geographic refer-ent of Cameroon.

Simultaneous expressions of nation-state nationalism and Christian inter-nationalism among Cameroon's Catholics and Protestants in the last decade and a half of French rule reveal that there were complementary visions of a political future of national sovereignty and a social future of international solidarity, reciprocity and interdependence. Histories of Cameroon at the end of empire have tended to focus on the contentious and often violent con-frontations between cadres and leaders with contending visions of the coun-try's political prospects (Joseph 1977; Terretta 2014; Mbembe 1984). However, incorporating accounts of the value-driven social activism of African Chris-tian clergymen, consecrated laypersons and everyday believers in the final years of French administration demonstrates that Africans believed in multiple and diverse postcolonial futures and, as such, historians must, in the words of Manu Goswami, 'index shifting horizons of collective aspiration' in order to more carefully chronicle the 'heady mix of utopian aspiration and pragmatic reckoning, collective action and conceptual improvisation' that constituted the actions taken to forge a non-imperial tomorrow (Goswami 2012: 1462–3).

The Contradictions of Conservatism: Political Leadership in Cameroon

It is critical to note that ostensibly 'secular' French colonial reform efforts in Africa in the wake of the Second World War were infused with Christian – and notably Catholic – social thought (Nettelbeck 1998; Shepard 2008: 224–8; Nord 2012: 357–70).[9] Colonial administrators from the MRP such as Paul Coste-Floret and Louis-Paul Aujoulat and other Christian democrats including René Pleven, along with social conservatives such as Félix Éboué, set the new terms of colonial policy beginning with Éboué's assumption as governor-general of French Equatorial Africa in 1941. In the decade that followed the 1944 Brazzaville Conference, he and other administration officials on the ground innovated political methods that reflected a family-oriented and traditional-istic vision of social betterment for Africa's people (M'Bokolo 1982). The revised *Code Penal Indigène* for French Equatorial and West Africa, Cameroon and Togo of 1944, authored by Pleven, Charles de Gaulle's *Commissaire aux Colonies*, out-lawed native abortion, adultery, gambling and usury.[10] As governor of Chad, and later governor-general of all French Equatorial Africa, Éboué expressed nostalgia for 'traditional institutions' such as chieftaincy and favoured policies that reinforced patriarchal and local authority rather than accelerated paths to development that might 'disrupt' customary institutions.[11] In Cameroon, Aujoulat, the territorial parliamentary representative and the founder of Cath-olic Action in Cameroon in 1937, sought to more deeply instil Christian ideals

---

9   See also Archives Nationales de France (hereafter AN), Fonds MRP 350, AP 124.

10   Archives Nationales d'Outre-Mer (hereafter ANOM), Affaires Politiques (hereafter AFF-POL) 2098/7 Code Penal Indigène en AOF-AEF, Cameroun et Togo, Decret du 17 juillet 1944 instituant un Code Penal Indigène pour l'Afrique Occidentale Française, l'Afrique Equat-oriale Française, le Cameroun et le Togo.

11   In 1941, Éboué asserted: 'If we do not bolster the foundations of native political institu-tions, these foundations will give way to unbridled individualism, and how could we act upon an unorganised mass of individuals?' (Félix Éboué, Circulaire général du 19 janvier 1941, *Journal Officiel de l'Afrique Occidental Française*, 1 février 1941, p. 89). Even in 1944, Éboué envisioned a predominantly 'peasant' Africa, and believed any industrial develop-ment should be 'prudent' (Éboué 1941); Félix Éboué, Circulaire général de 19 janvier 1941, *Journal Officiel de l'Afrique Occidental Française*, 1 février 1941, pp. 86–90.

in post-war French colonial policy and espoused a humanist vision for social and economic reform. His leadership of Catholic Action, as well as of the Catholic medical foundation Ad Lucem, guaranteed funding for clinics, hospitals and leprosariums throughout Cameroon, and for training facilities for African Catholics to promote their integration into the public health and social work corps (Lachenal and Taithe 2009; Aujoulat 1947).

Although French administrative measures envisioned harmonious development, they also ignored many local dimensions of inequality and social conflict. For the rural, small-town and urban Christians of Cameroon, the post-war period was defined not so much by a political awakening as by a broadening of their understanding of their local grievances, many of which concerned corrupt chiefs, greedy patriarchs, obtuse tribunal judges (both French and African), and those who manipulated colonial political and economic policies for profit (Guyer 1980; 1984; Eckert 1999). According to many religious leaders on the ground, these adversaries required a co-ordinated response that granted greater individual liberties to those seeking contracts, employment, marriages and other rights on their own terms (Zoa 1959). Other afflictions included alcoholism, prostitution, polygamy and divorce, which would be forcefully combatted through organised social movements, notably among the youth.[12] Actions taken against local malevolence – rather than simply French hegemony – sharpened perceptions of the relationship between the local and the national and how Africans' futures were linked by the moral, legal and social decisions they and their fellow Africans would make in the near future. The deployment of church organisational structures to combat widespread societal ills was a politically complex task in a period of anti-colonial nationalism, as the budgets for catechists, newspapers, pamphlets and meeting places relied on French assistance as well as on French chaplains for guidance and transnational co-ordination (Foster 2015; Pokam 1987). Nevertheless, many African religious leaders believed that the foreign Protestant and Catholic leadership was a critical voice in articulating and criticising colonial policy so that realities on the ground might be better understood.

Problematically, even though the French administration was aware that many African chiefs perverted customary law to enrich themselves and favoured their allies in court, and even though French tribunal overseers dis-

---

12   SMEP/DEFAP, Section Église Évangélique du Cameroun (hereafter EEC), Inventaire du Fonds Brutsch (hereafter FB) 2/2, Eugène Mallo, Rapports: 'Formalités du mariage et donations nuptials', 1951; 'Mariage par échange (beaucoup de troubles)', 1956; ACSSp., 2J1.7a7 Ad Lucem: Milieux sociaux africains, Cameroun fev–mars 1946, no. 7; ACSSp., 2J1.7b4 'Journée d'Étude: Les Jeunes Face au Mariage', Nkongsamba, 5 juin 1955.

cussed how fathers and patriarchs manipulated colonial laws on bridewealth to drive up the price of marriage for young grooms, post-war legal reforms continued to glorify 'legitimate chieftaincy' and to underscore the importance of the African tribal and family patriarchate as the 'leader in politics'.[13] Bishop Pierre Bonneau urged the French administration to reconsider their support of chiefs and asked that taxes be reduced and that African Christians be granted their own 'personal law' status, but to little avail (Delavignette 1946: 91–103; Bouchaud 1954: 47–56). In direct contradiction to the stance of religious leaders, Éboué even sought to limit the influence of the upwardly mobile educated class of African farmers, traders and teachers, writing in 1941: 'Even when besotted with strong drink and women, or when he employs poison in order to govern arbitrarily, the legitimate chief commits fewer abuses than a native civil servant, and his coercion of the citizens is no more onerous than that of the modern state.'[14] Jean Aubame, the Gabonese politician, criticised Éboué and the Brazzaville reforms for 'distorting' native institutions and giving chiefs too much power (Thompson and Adloff 1960: 46–7). Similarly, African catechists and pastors in Cameroon were vocal in their denunciation of African elders and chiefs and those who governed through them for inhibiting the 'moral progress' they deemed necessary in the territory. Nevertheless, colonial administrators continued to pursue economic and social policies that favoured outmoded and reified forms of leadership, rather than fully handing power to the increasingly activist African professional classes and religious cadres, for fear that their zealousness would disrupt traditional institutions.[15]

Internal Divisions: Growing from a Mission into a Church

Achille Mbembe has analysed how young converts were incorporated into the prestigious church hierarchy and clergy, challenging generational cleavages of privilege that had been previously organised by headmen or elders (Mbembe

---

13 ANOM SJ 2 Rapport II: Application des mesures relatives à la suppression de la 'justice penal indigene'. La period critique: (1946–1947): Une Colonisation provisoire; Archives Nationales du Cameroun (hereafter ANC), 2AC/2043, Lettre Personnelle du Thomas Nyangon Nnanga, 27 avril 1942, Chef du Groupement à Ekowong, Subdivision de Ebolowa à l'Administrateur-Chef de la Subdivision de l'Ebolowa.

14 Félix Éboué, Circulaire général du 19 janvier 1941, *Journal Officiel de l'Afrique Occidental Française*, 1 février 1941, 4, 89.

15 ANC, 1AC 3523 Robert Delavignette rapport, 1947; ANC, 1AC 3523 Rapport sur le Mission Presbytérienne Américaine, 1950; ANC, APA 11016/D liste de pasteurs, 1941.

1988: 31–50). In addition to claiming their status as learned men within their local societies, Africans in the Catholic and Protestant clergies also asserted themselves against other eminent men: European church leaders.

Asserting the right to administer the rites of the faith and guide religious praxis within church institutions was a struggle for Africans in Cameroon. While Africans and Europeans in the clergy and the laity in Cameroon shared sympathies regarding the nature and purpose of progress, they often differed over how it should be achieved and over what forms of social work and religious ministry would lead the budding nation to spiritual emancipation (Myazhiom 2001: 67–80; Messina and Van Slageren 2005: 178–90). Moves by European church leaders to shield pious villagers and farmers from leftist politics often inadvertently politicised rural peoples and mobilised them to resist both the politics of the radical UPC party and the paternalist policies of the high clergy in the Catholic Church and the Protestant congregations. Concerns among white bishops and pastors that Africans in Cameroon were 'easy prey' for Moscow, as they were 'a half-formed proletariat' with aspirations to revolution, aggrieved African ecclesiastics, seminarians and lay teachers who worked tirelessly among the poor, unemployed and disenfranchised to evangelise and sustain their faith.[16]

Eager to adopt new social welfare agendas for Cameroon, many African Catholic clergymen, including Monsignor (Mgr) Thomas Mongo and Mgr Paul Etoga, nonetheless clashed with European Catholic leaders such as Mgr René Graffin, the French Bishop of Yaoundé, over who would lead humanitarian and development initiatives such as the Catholic *villages pilotes* (independent religious communities with experimental farms and religious schools) or how movements including the JOC, which sought greater economic freedom and social progress for African Christians, would take shape (Pasquier 1997; Walker-Said 2015a). Moreover, members of the African Catholic laity increasingly sought to articulate their own spiritual objectives in the post-war years, encouraged by their experiences leading local initiatives in the territory after advancing to positions of administrative authority when French priests and government officials were called to the front in Europe.[17] African laypersons offered a vision which was distinct from that of the European high clergy, who, amidst the spectre of global Communism, espoused parochial objectives

---

16   Hermann F. Witschi, 'Compte-Rendu d'une visite au Cameroun', *Journal des Missions Évangéliques*, 1950, p. 428.

17   ACSSp., 2J1.8.a1 District de Douala, L'Église pendant la guerre, annonce de la mobilisation générale, 1939.

to combat 'Marxist atheism' and to reinforce the power of church institutions.[18] African ecclesiastics often disagreed even more sharply with French and African political leaders, who frequently clung to traditionalistic regulations and precedents in an attempt to mitigate the rapid pace of social change. By contrast, the African lay leadership faced up to the challenges of unstable local conditions and directly confronted the issues of African custom and tradition in a rapidly evolving time and space, and often brazenly challenged practices such as polygamy, prostitution, chiefly corruption, youth exploitation and a host of other social ills plaguing city and countryside using social activism (Brasseur 1986; Bouchaud 1958). The Protestant churches in Cameroon included a significantly higher number of Africans (as a proportion of believers) in its clerical ranks and also envisioned social progress through spiritual catharsis, benevolent works and forthright confrontation in the spaces of everyday life (Brutsch 1950a).

Religious Activism and Adaptation

In 1946, Jean Bosco Mama and Gilbert Essala, two young Bané Christians, founded the Association de la Civilisation et Réalisation du Pays, a Christian social group in the town of Mbalmayo whose mission was the radical reform of marriage custom and bridewealth exchange among all Bané.[19] The association sought to create an autonomous and self-policing marriage code for Bané Christians in order to 'fix custom' and remedy what they perceived as 'a crisis in which we will all die single because of this greed'. Mama, Essala and their allies publicly vented their disgust with Bané families' 'milking of the fiancé' and sensed the magnitude of what they were proposing, as they knew it 'did not support the customs of the country'. This fiercely reformative group organised locally but expressed an interest in abolishing bridewealth – or, at the very least, fixing it at a nominal sum to symbolise custom but prevent abuses – in laws that would affect the entire territory. The association's president, Jean Bosco Mama, obtained the consent of chiefs and local police in Mbalmayo to enforce strict bridewealth maximums and to ban its exchange outside the parameters set out

---

18   ACSSp., 2J1.6.2 Rapports annuels des diocèses: Cameroun, 1940–1965; *Cameroun Catholique*, issues 1950–60. See also Messina and Van Slageren (2005: 400–10). For comparative histories, see also Keith (2012) and Foster (2013).

19   ACSSp., 2J1.15.b2 Statut de civilisation, Jean Bosco Mama, L'Association de la Civilisation et Réalisation du Pays, 28 mars 1950.

in the association's charter, which were restrictively low at 5,000 francs and ten goats per bride, making the limits more prohibitive than those in French law.[20]

The Association de la Civilisation et Réalisation du Pays registered first as an official association in Mbalmayo and later became active in Yaoundé in 1950, and was comprised of young Bané men who had first met in the Catholic congregations of Mbalmayo and Akono or had attended the *petit seminaire d'Akono*, which had opened in the 1920s. The Association de la Civilisation worked closely after 1955 with the local Akono JOC chapter to form a *foyer de jeunesse*, where the association's principles regarding bridewealth and marriage ethics could be transmitted to young Christians.[21] Mama responded to complaints against the group's reactionary code by stating:

> In these times, bridewealth is 300,000 francs, thirty goats, five pigs, a cow, wine, bicycles, and many more things ... and fathers charge 2,000 francs just to see the girl, 1,000 francs to hold her hand, 1,000 francs to have her appear well-dressed, 2,000 francs to speak with the mother-in-law to make arrangements, and the entire family exploits the fiancé ... we must extinguish evils like this.[22]

The exasperation of other young African men with local approaches to bridewealth and marriage contracts is evident when reading the testimonials of the men who attended Christian social meetings as part of JOC *journée d'études* or meetings of local *foyers de jeunesse* and Action Catholique Familiale (ACF) in the 1940s and 1950s. In these spaces, complaints like that of Laurent Effa – who was proud to say that his devout family had given his sister in marriage without demanding bridewealth, but, in doing so, had rendered him dependent on finding a pious family who would accept him as a groom without bridewealth to give – were frequent and bitter.[23] Feeling the need to bolster solidarity among young couples facing challenges to their marital autonomy, the JOC and ACF launched the Société des Jeunes Ménages in several cities in Cameroon and

---

20   ACSSp., 2J1.15.b2, Bané de Mbalmayo, L'Association de la Civilisation et Réalisation du Pays, 1951.

21   ACSSp., 2J1.13b1 Jean Noddings, Akono Association Chrétienne des Foyers, *Laiccam*, 6, 1 décembre 1954, 'Bulletin trimestriel de liaison pour la formation d'un Laicat d'Action Catholique au Cameroun'.

22   ACSSp., 2J1.15.b2 Statut de civilisation, Jean Bosco Mama, L'Association de la Civilisation et Réalisation du Pays, 28 mars 1950.

23   ACSSp., 2J1.7b4 Témoignage de Laurent Effa, Témoignage de l'Action Catholique d'Outre Mer, 1955, par Abbé J. Noddings.

circulated slogans such as 'Love is the essence and the base of marriage' and 'Loving marriage will guard against the abuses of capitalism and the trap of syndicalism'.[24]

By 1946, Christians and catechumens across Cameroon networked through 258 religious associations and 2,200 villages with a Catholic affiliation to organise, deliberate and execute necessary actions for the improvement of social welfare.[25] French religious leaders such as Aujoulat and Protestant mission leader Pastor Jean-René Brutsch worked closely with African Christian activists such as Henri Effa, a Catholic journalist, Marguerite-Marie Mensah, a Christian women's organiser, Baptist pastors Paul Jocky and Modi din Jacob, and numerous others to establish new chapters of men's and women's religious collectives and to open new schools, hospitals, *foyers de jeunesse* and other spaces and groups where pious solidarities could be forged to create a greater sense of Christian community.

From their inception in the interwar period, this sense of community was not solely bound to Cameroon, or even to Africa. Ad Lucem, or the Association des Ligeurs Universitaires et Missionnaires, was born in 1931 out of the Ligue Universitaire Catholique et Missionnaire (LUCEM) and the Ligue Missionnaire des Étudiants de France (LMEF), which were founded by French priests in collaboration with students at the Université Catholique de Lille as a plan to encourage graduates to evangelise in universities and through youth groups as well as to pursue careers in medicine, social work and philanthropy in France's overseas territories (Ribaut 1997; Monchanin et al. 1985: 18). At the 1932 Ad Lucem national congress, Aujoulat called for the organisation's orientation towards France's colonies as a means of rooting the work of '*la plus grande France*' in '*la plus grande Église*' (Jacquin 2005: 398). Its revised statute stated that it was an '*Association Auxiliaire d'Action Catholique pour la Chrétienté Universelle*' and added the subtitle '*Union Fraternelle des Races* (UFER)' in order to underline its ecumenical ethos. Mgr René Graffin, who would become the head of the Catholic Church in Cameroon after the Second World War, also attended the 1932 Ad Lucem congress as the coadjutor of François-Xavier Vogt, Bishop of Yaoundé, and expressed his great interest in sponsoring Ad Lucem and Catholic Action endeavours in Cameroon (Messina and Van Slageren 2005: 170–80; Turpin 1999).

Ad Lucem, Catholic Action and the Diocese of Lille financially endowed as well as provided significant clerical personnel for the project of expand-

24   ACSSp., 2J1.7b4 Rapport sur le Laicat apostolique indigène, 1953.
25   ACSSp., 2J2.1a. Journal de la Mission de Nlong, 1925–38.

ing Catholic social organising in Cameroon. By 1946, Christian social organisation had exploded across rural, small-town and urban Cameroon through the
introduction of scout and youth movements, as well as benevolent societies
and pious brotherhoods known as *cercles* and *confréries*.[26] The Protestant congregations affiliated with the SMEP soon also granted large sums to Christian
fraternities and social work organisations in Cameroon, which, like Catholic
alliances for social renewal, spread between towns and from cities to villages
following pre-existing networks of commerce and regional family and lineage
networks.[27]

The most widespread Protestant-based socio-religious collective in Cameroon was the Croix Bleue, a temperance society devoted to eliminating alcohol
use and dependence among African men for the benefit of African marriages
and families, which was sponsored by the Evangelical and Baptist churches
of the French Protestant Mission. Founded in 1876 in Bern by Louis-Lucien
Rochat, a pastor with the Swiss Reformed Church, the Croix Bleue was brought
to Cameroon by Pastor Pierre Galland as a branch of the Société Française
de Tempérance de la Croix-Bleue (Daulte 1927; Schaffner 1958).[28] Known as
Mbas'a Blu in Duala, it quickly gained ground in Cameroon as a brotherhood
that aimed to contribute to the 'history of communities doing good' (*mwemba
ma myango ma bwam*) among Christians, primarily in metropolitan areas such
as Duala and the Yabassi region.[29]

Like the Catholic *confréries*, Croix Bleue chapters (*Mwemba ma Mbas'a Blu*)
were led by young Africans eager to assume leadership of associations with
reformist inclinations. Protestant pastors Gotliep Soppo and Ebonji led the
Croix Bleue in expanding their presence in coastal Cameroon during the interwar years and believed that marriage practices had changed with urbanisation

---

26   ACSSp. 2J1.7b4 Ekoan Maria, Confrérie de Sainte Marie, Confrérie des Cinq Plaies de Jésus,
      Confrérie de l'Enfant Jésus, Confrérie de Saint Joseph, Confrérie de Sainte Anne, Confrérie
      de Sainte Angès.

27   SMEP/DEFAP, EEC, FB 2/2 Premier congrès des femmes protestants du Cameroun, 1958;
      Farelly (1946: 7–16); Brutsch (1950a: 16–18).

28   The Croix Bleu Camerounaise is currently active in seven out of the ten provinces of
      Cameroon. It receives financial subvention and support from the government, as well as
      from non-governmental organisations (NGOs) and religious organisations. It hosts con-
      ferences, seminars and round tables and works in youth education to fight alcoholism, as
      Cameroon's national alcohol consumption is one of the highest on the African continent,
      with an estimated 2 million litres consumed annually (see Koum'enioc 2009).

29   SMEP/DEFAP, EEC, FB 2/2, Statut de la Société de Tempérance de la Croix-Bleue des églises
      chrétiennes du Cameroun à Yabassi, 1930.

in large part because of men's exposure to alcohol, bars and nightlife – tempta-
tions that were practically non-existent in rural villages. They believed that
alcohol's effects on men's morals resulted in prostitution and men's isolation
from family life, which the Croix Bleue had a duty to remedy by 'creating unanimity in the anti-alcoholic struggle'.[30]

These largely male Catholic and Protestant social associations were led by
Africans who channelled the power of ecclesiastical discipline and used it to
position themselves as persons in charge of helping their flocks achieve their
moral destiny. African Christian leaders provided an alternative to the leadership of corrupt chiefs and restrictive elders, as well as that of white priests and
African politicians, who many believers thought were not sufficiently sensitive to their particular struggles. However, African Christian leaders knew too
well that their vibrancy depended on the financial support of foreign missions – and even, at times, co-ordination with the political elite. Catholic Action
and related organisations such as the Association Chrétienne des Foyers and
the Mouvement de l'Enfance, as well as the Protestant Union Chrétienne des
Jeunes Gens, received funding from religious networks in France as well as from
FIDES.[31] This engendered a strong sense of ecumenism in specific moments,
such as when Paul Soppo Priso, a Cameroonian Protestant politician, worked
with Mgr Pierre Bonneau to acquire FIDES funds to finance the construction of
the Catholic Collège Libermann in 1954.[32]

With growing political agitation in post-war Cameroon came an even more
vibrant organisation of congregational social structures that mobilised various
initiatives that sought to renew the social and moral foundations of African
society in the country and to initiate a new conversation about national independence and the true meaning of liberation. The organisational foundation
for collective action had been put in place during the interwar period, and later,
after 1946, it responded to new stimuli emanating from Eastern and Western
Europe, from neighbouring territories of West and Central Africa, and locally
from the hotbeds of union organisation and political radicalism in Douala and
Yaoundé. Socio-religious associations' organisational networks and reformist
repertoires made for a swift and co-ordinated transition to youth movements
and collective calls for social and moral considerations as part of nationalist
imaginings. As political life and institutions were in flux in the period between
the institution of the Brazzaville reforms and the declaration of independence,

---

30   Ibid.
31   ACSSp., 2J1.6.6 Réunion des Ordinaires du Cameroun à Yaoundé, 20–21–22 mars 1956.
32   ACSSp., 2J1.5b6 Rapport sur l'Assemblé Territoriale du Cameroun, 1954.

congregations, parishes and religiously based social clubs formed the substantive base of cadres of devout, philanthropic and socially conscious Catholics who were committed to forging national institutions. Among these cadres, personal and associational priorities largely centred on enshrining rights and objectives surrounding marriage and family life to ensure the stability and decency of the modern Cameroonian nation-state.

Conclusion

By the time of the onset of nationalist mobilisations in Cameroon in the post-war years, Christianity had been an intrinsic part of spiritual and cultural life in the territory for several decades. Enculturated expressions of African Christian devotion merged with nationalist aspirations as well as tangible prescriptions for transnational religious unanimity. African Christians' close identifications with both the local (at the level of village and ethno-social group) and the supra-national helped form their idealisations of the nation, which both influenced and were informed by indigenous ministers in the leadership.

Recently, historians have asserted that, within reformist conceptions of governance and of pathways for social and political progress in post-war Africa, nation-state nationalism lacked appeal for many African visionaries, who aspired to forms of solidarity beyond borders (Cooper 2014; Wilder 2015). Buttressed by international reciprocities for development and for military and industrial assistance, certain political designs imagined balancing sovereignty with continuity and economic inclusion. Envisioning a less bounded 'community' than the nation-state was indeed a radical political project, but it was not one that existed solely in the domain of politics and governance. Histories that have made their principal enquiries in the political realm have failed to perceive the long-standing spiritual, organisational and affective ties that bound Africans and Europeans together throughout the period of colonial administration and endured after national independence. This chapter has endeavoured to demonstrate that community could also be a communion of faith with a broad enough range of interests that it could include Africans from a diverse set of ethnic groups, from rural and urban zones, and from distinct denominations, as well as European clergy, lay ministers and humanitarians. Far from being a microcosm of all of Cameroonian society, it was embedded in larger social aggregates such as ethnicities, political parties, social classes and regional groups. As such, it sought to bring aid and advantage to these other groups by affiliating them with the Christian community and by demonstrating the value of fostering notions of a collective that could be forged beyond the boundaries of Cameroon.

Cameroon had been staunchly Gaullist and was the headquarters of Free France in Africa during the war, which consequently nurtured aspirations among some in the African political class of future co-dependent development. After the Second World War, African political leaders expressed their preoccupations with greater native participation in legal and educational reform, urban development, and the provision of new social and economic benefits, which they believed would bring about necessary emancipation from various forms of oppression, including ignorance, disease, forced labour and poverty (Joseph 1977: 87–91). Other politicians, as well as emerging labour leaders in Cameroon, however, argued for social welfare together with more profound liberation in the form of autonomy and self-governance (Mbembe 1985).

African Christians had experienced the effects of religious education and social transformation between the onset of German colonialism and the introduction of the Brazzaville reforms at the end of the Second World War. Catholic and Protestant conversion and community building among African societies had engendered more sweeping and intimate changes in the social and moral order than the French mandate administration could have imagined, and the new trusteeship government wished to both capitalise on and rein in the influence of Christianity in African societies in Cameroon. As a result of new moral frameworks that were instructed and moulded by congregational participation, tribunal adjudication and religious schooling, Africans adopted new sympathies and shaped new ethical codes and were fully ready to confront the charged struggles of choosing a political ideology, a religious identity and a civilisational imperative. Indeed, it was African Christians' leadership in and zealous appropriation of the post-war social welfare programme that caused some anxiety among French administrators that Africans would create national political and economic institutions that were perhaps too influenced by the church.[33]

In sum, studying the processes of national and societal meaning making via religious relationships allows the historian to perceive Africans' identification with communities that surpassed the territorial boundaries of Cameroon. Moreover, what it reveals refutes assumptions that cultural and national reform initiatives emanate from the centre, when in fact many were organic move-

---

[33]   The Catholic Church in Cameroon was accused by the French colonial government of being the 'antechamber of Communism' and part of the 'progressive parties' because of its opposition to extractive colonial capitalism.

ments led by indigenous Christian leaders who possessed a keener idea of what kinds of progress Africans envisioned in the movement towards national sovereignty.

References

Abitbol, E. (1966) 'La Famille Conjugale et le Droit Nouveau du Mariage en Côte d'Ivoire', *Journal of African Law* 10 (3): 141–63.

Akoa-Mongo, F. (2011) *Le Pasteur François Akoa Abômô: l'homme et l'oeuvre*. Bloomington IN: Xlibris Corp.

Allman, J. (1993) *The Quills of the Porcupine: Asante Nationalism in an Emergent Ghana*. Madison WI: University of Wisconsin Press.

Aujoulat, L.-P. (1947) 'Les Problèmes Sociaux de l'Afrique Noire', *Chronique Sociale de France* 4 (4): 413–23.

Austen, R. A. (1971) 'Varieties of Trusteeship: African Territories under British and French Mandate' in P. Gifford and W. R. Louis (eds), *France and Britain in Africa: Imperial Rivalry and Colonial Rule*. New Haven CT: Yale University Press.

Binet, J. (1953) 'Le Mariage et l'évolution de la Société Sud-Camerounaise', *L'Afrique Française* 62 (6): 40–2.

Bouchaud, J. (1954) *Monseigneur Pierre Bonneau: Evêque de Douala: Rapport du Diocèse de Yaoundé*. Yaoundé: Éditions de l'Effort Camerounais.

Bouchaud, R. P. (1958) 'Cameroun: Église et Communisme', *Spiritains: Missions des Pères du St. Esprit* 31 (1).

Brasseur, P. (1986) 'L'Église Catholique et la Décolonisation en Afrique Noire' in C.-R. Ageron (ed.), *Les Chemins de la Décolonisation de l'Empire Colonial Français, 1936–1956: Colloque Organisé les 4 et 5 Octobre 1984*. Paris: Éditions du Centre National de la Recherche Scientifique (CNRS).

Brutsch, J.-R. (1950a) 'Impressions d'un Premier Séjour au Cameroun', *Journal des Missions Évangéliques*: 16–18.

Brutsch, J.-R. (1950b) 'A Glance at Missions in Cameroon', *International Review of Missions* 39 (155): 302–10.

Chamedes, G. (2015) 'The Catholic Origins of Economic Development after World War II', *French Politics, Culture and Society* 33 (2): 55–75.

Chatterjee, P. (1993) *The Nation and its Fragments: Colonial and Postcolonial Histories*. Princeton NJ: Princeton University Press.

Cooper, F. (1996) *Decolonization and African Society: The Labor Question in French and British Africa*. Cambridge: Cambridge University Press.

Cooper, F. (2014) *Citizenship between Empire and Nation: Remaking France and French Africa, 1945–1960*. Princeton NJ: Princeton University Press.

Daulte, H. (1927) *Le Livre du Jubilé 1877–1927. Histoire des Cinquante Premières Années de La Croix-Bleue*. Lausanne: Agence de la Croix-Bleue.

de Benoist, J. R. (1982) *L'Afrique Occidentale Française de 1944 à 1960*. Dakar: Nouvelles Éditions Africaines.

Delavignette, R. L. (1946) *Service Africain*. Paris: Gallimard.

Éboué, F. (1941) *La Nouvelle Politique Indigène pour l'AEF*. Paris: Office Français d'Édition.

Eckert, A. (1999) 'African Rural Entrepreneurs and Labor in the Cameroon Littoral', *Journal of African History* 40: 109–26.

Etaba, R. O. (2007) *Histoire de l'Église Catholique du Cameroun de Grégoire XVI à Jean-Paul II*. Paris: Éditions L'Harmattan.

Etoga, P. (1956) 'Il n'y a pas de Race Supérieure', *Echo des Missions*, 'A propos du sacre de Monsegneur Paul Etoga', 2 (March).

Farelly, M. (1946) 'Les Églises Indigènes au Cameroun', *Journal des Missions Évangéliques*: 7–16.

Fields, K. (1985) *Revival and Rebellion in Colonial Central Africa*. Princeton NJ: Princeton University Press.

Foster, E. A. (2013) *Faith in Empire: Religion, Politics, and Colonial Rule in French Senegal, 1880–1940*. Stanford CA: Stanford University Press.

Foster, E. A. (2015) 'Theologies of Colonization: The Catholic Church and the Future of the French Empire in the 1950s', *Journal of Modern History* 87 (2): 281–315.

Gardinier, D. E. (1963) *Cameroon: United Nations Challenge to French Policy*. Oxford: Oxford University Press.

Gifford, P. and W. R. Louis (1982) *The Transfer of Power in Africa: Decolonization 1940–1960*. New Haven CT: Yale University Press.

Goswami, M. (2012) 'Imaginary Futures and Colonial Internationalisms', *American Historical Review* 117 (5): 1461–85.

Grottelli, K. (1984) 'La Fédération Évangélique du Cameroun et de l'Afrique Équatoriale: Mise en Situation Politique, 1940–1969'. Thesis, UER d'histoire, Université d'Aix-en-Provence.

Guernier, E. and R. Briat (1951) *Cameroun, Togo: Encyclopédie de l'Afrique Française*. Paris: Éditions de l'Union Française.

Guyer, J. I. (1980) 'Head Tax, Social Structure and Rural Incomes in Cameroun, 1922–37', *Cahiers d'Études Africaines* XX (3): 305–29.

Guyer, J. I. (1984) 'Family and Farm in Southern Cameroon'. Boston MA: Boston University, African Studies Center.

Jacquin, F. (2005) 'Naissance du Laïcat Missionnaire: L'exemple d'Ad Lucem (1930–1939)' in J. Comby (ed.), *Diffusion et Acculturation du Christianisme (XIXe–XXe s.): Vingt-cinq Ans de Recherches Missiologiques par le CREDIC*. Paris: Éditions Karthala.

Joseph, R. A. (1977) *Radical Nationalism in Cameroon: Social Origins of the U.P.C. Rebellion*. Oxford: Oxford University Press.

Keith, C. (2012) *Catholic Vietnam: A Church from Empire to Nation*. Berkeley CA: University of California Press.

Kibénél Ngo Billong, G. T. (2009) *Noces de Grâce de la Congrégation des Soeurs Servantes de Marie de Douala: 70 Ans d'Existence*. Douala: Congrégation des Soeurs Servantes de Marie de Douala.

Koum'enioc, K. (2009) 'Cameroun: Les Autorités en Difficulté avec les Débits de Boisson', *Journal du Cameroun*, 15 September.

Laburthe-Tolra, P. (2005) 'La Mission Catholique Allemande du Cameroun (1890–1916) et la Missologie' in J. Comby (ed.), *Diffusion et Acculturation du Christianisme (XIXe–XXe s.): Vingt-cinq Ans de Recherches Missiologiques par le CREDIC*. Paris: Éditions Karthala.

Lachenal, G. and B. Taithe (2009) 'Une Généalogie Missionnaire et Coloniale de l'Humanitaire: Le Cas Aujoulat au Cameroun, 1935–1973', *Le Mouvement Sociale* 227: 45–63.

La Croix (1969) 'Mgr. Ndongmo: "L'Église d'Afrique ne Pourrait Subsister sans les Oeuvres Pontificales Missionnaires"', *La Croix*, 17 October.

Lindsay, L. (1999) 'Domesticity and Difference: Male Breadwinners, Working Women, and Colonial Citizenship in the 1945 Nigerian General Strike', *American Historical Review* 104 (3): 783–812.

Mallo, E. (1954) 'L'Église Évangélique du Cameroun', *Le Semeur* 3–4 (December): 67–9.

Mallo, E. (1965) *Sermons de chez nous: sermons pour les temps de l'Eglise*. Yaoundé: Éditions CLE.

Mamdani, M. (1996) *Citizen and Subject: Contemporary Africa and the Legacy of Late Colonialism*. Princeton NJ: Princeton University Press.

Maxwell. D. (2006) *African Gifts of the Spirit: Pentecostalism and the Rise of a Zimbabwean Transnational Religious Movement*. Oxford: James Currey.

Mbembe, A. (1984) *Le Problème National Kamerunais: Ruben Um Nyobé*. Paris: Éditions L'Harmattan.

Mbembe, A. (1985) 'La Palabre de l'Indépendence: Les Ordres du Discours Nationaliste au Cameroun (1948–1958)', *Revue Française de Science Politique* 35 (3): 459–87.

Mbembe, A. (1988) *Afriques Indociles: Christianisme, Pouvoir, et État en Société Postcoloniale*. Paris: Karthala.

Mbembe, A. (1996) *La Naissance du Maquis dans le Sud-Cameroun, 1920–1960: Histoire des Usages de la Raison en Colonie*. Paris: Éditions Karthala.

M'Bokolo, E. (1982) 'French Colonial Policy in Equatorial Africa in the 1940s and 1950s' in P. Gifford and W. R. Louis (eds), *The Transfer of Power in Africa: Decolonization 1940–1960*. New Haven CT: Yale University Press.

Messina, J.-P. (1988) 'Contribution des Camerounais à l'Expansion de l'Église Catholique: Le Cas des Populations du Sud-Cameroun, 1890–1961'. Thesis, Université de Yaoundé.

Messina, J.-P. and J. Van Slageren (2005) *Histoire du Christianisme au Cameroun: Des Origines à nos Jours: Approche Oecuménique*. Paris: Éditions Karthala.

Messina, J.-P., O. Mimboé and B. Gantin (2000) *Jean Zoa, Prêtre, Archevêque de Yaoundé: 1922–1998*. Paris: Éditions Karthala.

Monchanin, J., E. Duperray and J. Gadille (1985) *Théologie et Spiritualité Missionnaires*. Paris: Éditions Beauchesne.

Morgenthau, R. S. (1964) *Political Parties in French Speaking West Africa*. Oxford: Clarendon.

Myazhiom, A. C. L. (2001) *Sociétés et Rivalités religieuses au Cameroun sous domination Française (1916–1958)*. Paris: Éditions L'Harmattan.

Nettelbeck, C. W. (1998) 'The Eldest Daughter and the Trente Glorieuses: Catholicism and National Identity in Postwar France', *Modern and Contemporary France* 6 (4): 445–62.

Ngongo, L.-P. (1982) *Histoire des forces religieuses au Cameroun*. Paris: Éditions Karthala.

Njougla, F. (1950) *La Dot Africaine*. Leverville: Bibliothèque de l'Étoile.

Nord, P. (2012) *France's New Deal: From the Thirties to the Postwar Era*. Princeton NJ: Princeton University Press.

Pasquier, R. (1997) 'La Jeunesse Ouvrière Chrétienne (JOC) et la Formation d'une Élite en AOF' in C. Becker, S. Mbaye and I. Thioub (eds), *AOF: Réalités et Heritages: Sociétés Ouest-Africaines et Ordre Colonial, 1895–1960*. Dakar: Direction des Archives du Sénégal.

Pierrard, P., M. Launay and R. Trempé (1984) *La J.O.C.: Regards d'Historiens*. Paris: Éditions Ouvrières.

Pokam, K. (1987) *Les Églises Chrétiennes Face à la Montée du Nationalisme Camerounais*. Paris: Éditions L'Harmattan.

Privat, A. (1992) *Coup de coeur pour l'Afrique: 1956–1957*. Geneva: Éditions du Pressoir de Montalègre.

Ribaut, J.-P. (1997) 'Le Cardinal Liénart et Ad Lucem (Journée d'Étude du 25 Septembre 1993 à l'Université Catholique de Lille)', *Mélanges de Sciences Religieuses* 54 (3): 37–56.

Sappia, C. and O. Servais (2010) *Mission et engagement politique après 1945: Afrique, Amérique latine, Europe*. Paris: Éditions Karthala.

Schaffner, H. (1958) *Im Dienst an Menschen und Völkern: Das Blaue Kreuz, Ein Missions- und Liebeswerl von Weltweiter Bedeutung*. Bern: Blaukreuzverlag.

Shepard, T. (2008) *The Invention of Decolonization: The Algerian War and the Remaking of France*. Ithaca NY: Cornell University Press.

Terretta, M. (2014) *Nation of Outlaws, State of Violence: Nationalism, Grassfields Tradition, and State-building in Cameroon*. Athens OH: Ohio University Press.

Thompson, V. and R. Adloff (1960) *The Emerging States of French Equatorial Africa.* Stanford CA: Stanford University Press.

Tiandong, J.-H. (1973) *L'autobiographie du Pasteur Jean-Henri Tiandong de l'E.E.C.* Douala: Douala, S.N.

Turpin, F. (1999) 'Le Mouvement Républicain Populaire et l'avenir de l'Algérie (1947–1962)', *Revue d'Histoire Diplomatique* 2: 171–203.

Van Slageren, J. (1972) *Les Origines de l'Église Évangélique du Cameroun: Missions Européennes et Christianisme Autochtone.* Leiden: E. J. Brill.

Walker-Said, C. (2015a) 'Science and Charity: Rival Catholic Visions for Humanitarian Practice at the End of Empire', *French Politics, Culture and Society* 33 (2): 33–54.

Walker-Said, C. (2015b) 'Wealth, Law, and Moral Authority: Marriage Markets and Christian Mobilization in Interwar Cameroon', *International Journal of African Historical Studies* 48 (3): 393–424.

Wilder, G. (2015) *Freedom Time: Negritude, Decolonization, and the Future of the World.* Durham NC and London: Duke University Press.

Zoa, J. (1957) *Pour un nationalisme chrétien au Cameroun.* Yaoundé: Imprimerie Saint-Paul.

Zoa, J. (1959) 'La Dot dans les Territoires d'Afrique' in L'Union Mondiale des Organisations Féminines Catholiques (ed.), *Femmes Africaines: Témoignages de Femmes du Cameroun, du Congo Belge, du Congo Français, de La Côte-d'Ivoire, du Dahomey, du Ghana, de La Guinéa, de La Haute-Voita, du Nigéria, du Togo, Réunies à Lome par l'Union Mondiale des Organisations Féminines Catholiques, 1958.* Paris: Éditions du Centurion.

Zoa, J. (1960) 'Les Chrétiens et la Communauté Nationale', *Nova et Vetera* 1: 12–14.

Zoa, J. (1961) 'Valeurs Ancestrales et Valeurs Modernes', *Nova et Vetera*, 15 December.

CHAPTER 8

Maintaining Faith in the Chinese World

Chloë Starr

One of the sayings of the Confucian *Analects* that has remained active in the collective imagination in China is the concept of naming names, or rectifying names, so that name and reality accord, and social harmony ensues. This notion provides an entry point to a discussion of the contemporary religious scene in China: if we take the state-administered Chinese Catholic Patriotic Association (CCPA) as an example, the name and the organisation imposed in 1957 designates a Chinese Catholic Church, not a Roman Catholic Church, and in this distinction proclaims its allegiances and ideological centre. In the equivalent Protestant organisation, the Three-Self Patriotic Movement (TSPM), the triple iteration of self (in self-governing, self-financing and self-propagating) speaks equally strongly to the ideals of autonomy and freedom from outside ('imperialist') interference. Another more recent theological movement in Chinese academic and intellectual circles also announces its sphere in its name – *Hanyu shenxue* (汉语神学) – a 'Chinese-language theology' whose reach proclaims a linguistic territory, not a state boundary. In each of these three, the relationship between the Chinese church and the rest of World Christianity is signalled.

For the greater part of the twentieth century, the Chinese church contended to define itself as a *Chinese* church, and to distinguish itself from the legacy of foreign missions that provoked so much resistance in society as well as within the church. An ambivalent relationship with 'the foreign' has shaped the development of the church in China and its relations with the world church. The taint of 'imperialism' damned the church in the secular world, while the inheritance of multiple denominations from the heyday of Victorian mission tarnished the church in the view of many Protestant Christians. A theological desire among Chinese Christians and mission partners in the early twentieth century to create a 'Chinese church' became a social imperative during the anti-Christian movements of the 1920s, and later a political necessity, as the new People's Republic of China (PRC) attempted to remove all foreign personnel and influence from the church after 1949. The enforced separation from the outside world in the second half of the twentieth century gave the Chinese church a particularly sharp insight into the relationship of the universal to the local: all too many died rather than relinquish their ties to Rome or concede that the state held higher authority than the church.

© KONINKLIJKE BRILL NV, LEIDEN, 2017 | DOI: 10.1163/9789004355026_010

The problematic of the relationship between church, nation and the wider church in Chinese Christian thinking is the focus of this chapter. The basis of the argument is simple: that it is impossible to understand the Chinese churches' relations with the rest of the world or their respective senses of a church universal without first grasping something of China's complex relationship with itself as a nation and as a people. This is not to claim that the Chinese case is unique, or that its particular construct of nation is vastly different from, say, that of its global hegemonic competitor the US (or that Chinese Christians' patriotism differs from Christian patriotism elsewhere); rather, I argue that the particularities of the Chinese case are important in understanding its view of the world and of its place in the world church. In an age when a fifth of the world's population lives in China or in a Chinese-speaking territory, and given the year-on-year increase in China's Christian population (perhaps to 70 million or more),[1] it is clearly important that the role of Chinese Christians in determining their vision of the local and global church – as both a practical entity and a spiritual force – is given more prominence. The second premise is also obvious: that the Chinese church is many different bodies and organisations, which hold different ecclesiologies and which exist in different networks and patterns of overseas connections. The differences between groups are often related to the very question of church–state relations, and understandings of the nature of the local and universal churches are shaped by historical exigencies and by political conditioning in tandem with theological thinking. Chinese views may offer an important counterpoint to other experiences and ways of conceiving 'World' Christianity.

There is a fine tension between the role that the state has played in the recent history of the Chinese church and narratives of nationhood that the churches have adopted. The relation between church and state is evidently not a one-way street, and old models of 'state control' of religion have ceded to more nuanced accounts of the agency of individuals and various religious organisations, with the focus shifting from 'conflict' to adaptation and co-operation between the multiple groups involved (Ashiwa and Wank 2009). At certain points in twentieth-century church history, however, the relationship to the state became a theological and political crux for millions of Chinese Christians. For Roman Catholics in the mid-twentieth century, there was a stark choice: join a Chinese Catholic Church and forge a new type of localised Catholicism, or align with Rome and become an illegal, underground organisation. For a sizeable number of Protestants, the perceived choice was equally clear: remain

---

1   See, for example, Pew Report (2011) for one authoritative estimate of 67 million in 2010.

part of a transcendent, universal kingdom of God, and risk prison and earthly privation, or align with an atheist state and deny the ultimate authority of God. Forced by government directives to take a stance on nation and identity, understandings of the church universal have been a key differentiating factor within the different sectors of each church – and these divisions from the early decades of the PRC have remained with the churches into the present. While the state's claim to authority was a prime factor in the splits, what is perhaps surprising is how widely a common rhetoric of 'China' has since been embraced within Christianity, even among groups antagonistic to the state.

This chapter offers a three-stage argument: the first section explores how historical circumstances have shaped understandings of 'China' for citizens of all religious persuasions; the second examines briefly how differing understandings of state and authority were key to church developments and to relations with 'the foreign' and with the world church; and the third section presents a case study drawing on contemporary Protestant house church materials, to examine how narratives of 'China' are being expressed in hymns and theological essays in one part of the church. In their diverse engagements with national directives and local context, the different sectors of the Christian church in China have forged a variety of different networks with external or global bodies. Since theological engagement with political forces was a major factor in the creation of Christian sectors (within an ostensibly post-denominational, unified church), the result has been a complex set of ecclesial structures and theologies of belonging. Different Chinese understandings of church and of world church co-exist; however, the unusually strong impact of government ideologies on the church's development in mainland China means that local political context forms a significant part of the discussion of how these understandings were shaped and how they continue to channel global engagement.

Creating a Chinese Christianity

China's changing relations with the outside world have inevitably influenced Christians' spiritual outlook on their place in, and the meaning of, the world church. Commentators have linked China's religious growth in the last three decades not just to global religious revival, but also to China's own cultural revival (Li Xiangping 2015).[2] Some academics have placed Chinese Christianity

---

2   As Li notes, the term 'faith' or 'belief' in China incorporates not just faith in God or gods, but

in a broader setting by embracing the idea of a Chinese religious sphere determined by language use and not by state boundaries, or by studying migrant flows and religious affiliations from south China across South-East Asia and in the newer communities of Chinese in Africa, or by focusing on the theologies of Chinese-American churches (Lee 2001; Yang 1999); however, the ambiguities of the scope of 'China' in a global era have often masked the thrum of nation in much internal discourse, and have highlighted the fact that the notion of globalisation is also culturally localised. Commentators debating what a 'Greater China' might mean politically, economically and culturally in the 1990s showed how the term differed according to location and political intent (see Harding 1993). Differences between PRC and Taiwanese maps and concepts of 'China' are one obvious example, but here the focus is on mainland perspectives, in which China's relation to the outside world may differ from other analyses.[3] China has embraced the language of globalisation, and its economic integration with the world has increased markedly since its accession to the World Trade Organization in 2001, with greater political openness encouraging Chinese to study abroad, and allowing Hong Kong and overseas Chinese in Taiwan, the US and elsewhere to fund religious buildings and groups in China, yet China's views on its role in a globalised world have naturally not always tallied with other transnational perspectives.

Anti-foreign feeling is now more ideological than active in China, and certainly not as strident as in the 1920s or at the height of the Maoist era in the 1960s. However, as recently as spring 2015, Chinese officials under President Xi Jinping were promoting a campaign to ban the teaching of Western values in academia,[4] and a curriculum of 'national learning' or traditional Chinese culture (*guoxue* 国学) was introduced for civil servants, to counter a diet of too much 'Western' learning. In a country where the imperialist aggression of the nineteenth century and the war against Japan in the 1930s are still regularly recalled in news media and played out in endless television soap operas, the

---

faith in the state, in local customs, and in cultural morality, encompassing both religious and secular aspects, and in this it differs from global revival (Li Xiangping 2015: 614).

3   For a relatively trivial example, see the eclipse of Xi Jinping's visit to the US (in September 2015) by that of the Pope in US media coverage, while the Chinese press blanket-reported Xi's successful visit. The Chinese leaders' gamble on the schedule clash suggests that what matters more is internal prestige, but they may also have misjudged the strength of a religious leader's popularity and meaning elsewhere in the world.

4   See, for example, Xinhua News Agency, '袁贵仁: 高校教师必须守好政治、法律、道德三条底线', 29 January 2015, http://education.news.cn/2015-01/29/c_1114183715.htm, accessed 7 May 2017; also, for example, Anderlini (2015).

intertwining of 'foreign' and 'Christian' remains an issue, and religious studies scholars in China regularly pose the question of which faith is most Sinicised and therefore most 'appropriate' for China.[5] Christians have long been engaged in two types of bridge building: an internal apologetics, to explain and (re-)produce the gospel within Chinese culture, and a defensive, sometimes critical, interpretation of 'the foreign', with which Christians are aligned (or maligned) due to their religious adherence.

Two formative influences on the contemporary church derive from the historical circumstances of Chinese mission: the fact that the identity of the Chinese churches was shaped during intense national discussions on the meaning of 'China' as a nation; and the historical perception of 'the foreign' as an obstacle to be overcome. The two greatest periods of theological flourishing in China in the twentieth century (the 1920s and 1930s, and the 1990s onwards) have coincided with times of greater openness to the wider world – and also with periods of strenuous debate on China and its role, from the need for an autonomous and independent nation in the 1920s, to the discourse of 'China's Rise' and a 'Harmonious Nation' in the 1990s.

The need to create Chinese-run church structures, a Chinese-language theology and a Chinese Christian literature weighed heavily on the first generation of Christians educated abroad in the early twentieth century. For many, the new Chinese nation was to be the unit through which the church conceived itself and through which it understood its relation to the world. For Protestants in the historical denominations, the nascent pan-Chinese church was to be progressive and appropriately inculturated into a pluri-religious setting: true to human nature, open to science and invention, affirming Chinese ethics and a true moral life for all, but also centred on resolving its own individuality. In a speech to the inaugural National Church Council in 1923, set up in part to counter mission divisions, Zhao Zichen set out his vision for the relationship of the infant Chinese Protestant Church to the one church universal:

> The Chinese church, like other churches that compose the Church Universal, is a national church, she is national not because she has her roots in Chinese soil, nor because her constituency is entirely Chinese, but because she has a special message for the nation and the special task of spiritualizing the civilization of the Chinese people ... She understands that as a national church she must not champion any national cause

---

5   For example, the discussion panel on 'Sociology of Faith' at the Twelfth Annual Chinese Religions Social Science Forum conference, 'Religion in Global Politics', 18 July 2015, Beijing.

which is wrong, but must protest against the wrongs that other nations are doing and may do to the Chinese Republic. She shall hasten the development of a national consciousness among the people so that through such national awakening the Chinese people may soon discover their true self and make their special contribution to the world.[6]

ZHAO 2009: 121

The elision of the cultural and the political in the task of building a national (Protestant) church in the early years of the Republic is clear, as are the background notes of revolutionary and Social Gospel movements. The interchange between 'local' and 'national' is made almost unconsciously; inculturation into Chinese culture also meant addressing the Chinese nation and its well-being.

In their book *The Religious Question in Modern China*, Vincent Goossaert and David Palmer employ an anthropological model to suggest that a 'broad social ecology' is needed to understand religion in China. Religion cannot be isolated as a distinct institution, they argue, but has been embedded in dynamic relations with political and economic structures in China, at both local and macro levels (Goossaert and Palmer 2011: 4–6). One reason for this relates to the integrated nature of religion, politics and society in traditional China. When, during the reforms and revolution of the early twentieth century, the religious and cosmological foundations of society were dismantled, a new place had to be found for 'religion' outside the imperial and local social framework. A new term (*zongjiao* 宗教), imported from the Japanese, was predicated on Western, Christian understandings of how a 'religion' functioned (Meyer 2014). Whereas the 'three teachings' (*san jiao* 三教) of Confucianism, Daoism and Buddhism had denoted a merged horizon, if not a single field of belief, religious adherence was now defined in terms of private dogmatic belief and discrete institutional structures (Goossaert and Palmer 2011: 10). Religious activities that failed the institutional test, or were not seen as rational purveyors of morality, came to be defined as superstition, and religions, including Buddhism and Daoism, reformulated themselves to be more consistent with these new understandings, forming church-like structures and national associations where none had existed previously (Nedostup 2009; Kuhlmann 2014).

The timing of events in the early Republic brought church and national identity to the fore as a question of modern China. The new understanding of the role of religion in China represented a local instantiation of a global-

---

6   Zhao Zichen, who trained at Vanderbilt, was a university professor and later an Anglican priest; he is one of the most prolific and well-regarded theologians of his era.

ised religious discourse. It was not just 'religion' that was being defined by the new Republic, but 'China' itself. As Arif Dirlik (2015) has argued, China's self-identification owes much to Western definitions of 'China', and the choice of 'Zhongguo' as a name for the new state by late Qing political thinkers signified a very different conception of China politically, spatially and culturally than that of dynastic China – one that reimagined 'China's' past as a continuous entity, and that laid the groundwork for twentieth-century Sino-centric and Han-focused national narratives. Theologians entered identity debates just as enthusiastically as other young intellectuals. Many of the most internationalised (Protestant) theologians, active in Edinburgh in 1910 or at the World Council of Churches, were among those most fervently seeking an indigenous Chinese church. As the church was experiencing rapid expansion, a growing anti-foreign attitude, catalysed by the Versailles Treaty of 1919, began to elicit a profound identity crisis among Chinese Christians. Questions that theologians were asking about what a Chinese theology should look like, and how to produce an indigenised theological literature, were also questions about how Christianity could save the nation and contribute to a strong China (Starr 2016a). A shared desire among foreign missionaries and Chinese Christians for a strong, truly Chinese church came together with pressure in society to dissociate from 'the foreign'. For many, a more genuinely 'Chinese' church was to be found in the proliferating Chinese-led independent churches (Bays 2012; Lian 2010).

If the theology of the Chinese church was shaped by both the social embedding of religion in traditional China and the modernising changes of the early twentieth century, nationalist discourses were only heightened under the Marxist–Leninist–Maoist ideology of the People's Republic. As the Chinese government oversaw the negotiated, but ultimately compulsory, uniting of Protestant denominations, the forced severance from foreign financial support and personnel for all denominations, and the creation of national patriotic associations during the 1950s, questions of allegiance became not just matters of church choice or ideological aspiration, but articles of faith. The tearing down of churches and curtailment of church activity in the 1950s and 1960s affected all, but certain church groups garnered more favour with the authorities than others. Protestant champions of an indigenous church and of the 'Three-Self' aims were, in many cases, those who approved of the social aims of the Communist Party in poverty alleviation or land reform. Leaders such as Wu Yaozong (Y. T. Wu), who drafted the 'Christian Manifesto' condemning imperialism, openly acknowledged the 'evils' of Christianity's relations to foreign imperialists, and cultivated support for a more patriotic church. As the Korean War increased nationalist fervour in the 1950s, the language of (liberal)

Protestant publications such as *Tian Feng* magazine became ever more insistent in their calls for a wholly Chinese church. 'Love the country and love your church' (*aiguo aijiao* 爱国爱教) became a core slogan, propagated by the government and adopted by believers – a slogan that remains current in today's state-managed Protestant church body and its theology. Those who opposed the elision of church and state and the growing Communist demands on the church were liable to harassment and imprisonment.

For most Protestant denominations, the existence of a national church did not preclude belief in a universal church, whereas Roman Catholics such as Beda Chang SJ (Zhang Boda, martyred 1951) argued strongly that no patriotic Catholic could ever accept 'Three-Self' ideals, and Pope Pius XII's 1954 '*Ad Sinarum Gentem*' ('To the Chinese People') reiterated that a 'national church' would be the negation of universality.[7] The Vatican rejection of Communism and explicit threats of excommunication for those who accommodated, or collaborated with, Communist rulers presented believers with a clear choice.[8] On the Chinese government side, 'imperialism' remained a heinous crime against the state, and relations with 'imperialists' were cause for sanction. The result of these twin pressures was that some faithful remained 'loyal to Rome' while others acclaimed the need for a Chinese Catholic Church. When this new Chinese Catholic body began its own episcopal ordinations, a deep split was inevitable, and the reverberations – and the complications of reintegration – have remained with the church to the present, affecting relations with the Vatican, with each other (especially in areas with dual bishops) and with other dioceses and sees worldwide.[9] Although relations between the underground and the open church may now be good locally, and diocesan bishops may work with both congregations in such matters as Bible supply, the institutional divide remains a problem and a key task for Pope Francis's Secretary of State, Pietro Parolin.

Choosing to relate to outside religious bodies has been a fraught, and at times dangerous, matter for Chinese believers into the twenty-first century. Because of the perceived overlap between the recent history of Western imper-

---

7   See http://w2.vatican.va/content/pius-xii/en/encyclicals/documents/hf_p-xii_enc_07101954
    _ad-sinarum-gentem.html, accessed 7 May 2017.

8   On the Vatican's anti-Communist stance, see Madsen (1998: 36); on the dangers to the church
    in promoting a climate of martyrdom and the intransigence and self-righteousness it can
    foster, see pp. 83–4.

9   An important juncture was Benedict XVI's reconciliatory letter to the Chinese faithful in
    2007 (see http://w2.vatican.va/content/benedict-xvi/en/letters/2007/documents/hf_ben-xvi
    _let_20070527_china.html, accessed 7 May 2017).

ialism and of Western mission, and the Marxist repudiation of religion, the question of Chinese religious relations with the rest of world cannot be separated from that of the Chinese state's relations with the outside world. Throughout the church's recent history, links to the world church have been a deeply political question, as well as a theological one.

Ongoing Divisions in Chinese Christianity

The experiences of the churches between the eras of mission and Marxism are manifest in current divisions in Chinese Christianity, and have shaped different groups' relations with the outside: passively through policy and actively through theological beliefs. Those with close ties to 'imperialists', whether Roman Catholics or unregistered Protestant groups, were the recurrent target of government legislation throughout the second half of the twentieth century, and saw much greater restrictions on their activities.[10] Theological beliefs guided groups' links to outside bodies, even at the cost of their own continued existence as a recognised church body. During the period of Reform and Opening Up (1978 onwards), the church can effectively be categorised via its relations with the state: Catholic churches registered with the CCPA; unregistered or 'underground' Catholics; Protestant churches registered with the TSPM; and unregistered or 'house church' Protestants. (The only recognised Christian denominations are Roman Catholicism and Protestantism, with historic Russian Orthodox churches able to operate in the north-eastern province of Heilongjiang.) This gives three functional divisions within Chinese Christianity: members of state-recognised and authorised Christian churches; members of unauthorised churches (with a distinct subcategory of those deemed more heretical and labelled evil cults, *xie jiao* 邪教); and a separate group of academic scholars of Christianity.[11] Theologies, relations with the state and relations with the outside world are all interlinked, and broadly follow these divisions.

---

10   Document 19 urged the redress of injustices against believers but also set out measures to be taken against 'criminal and anti-revolutionary' activities, including 'infiltration by hostile foreign religious forces' (Article XI; see, for example, MacInnis 1989: 23).

11   Chinese academics such as Zhuo Xinping, director of the Institute of World Religions at the Chinese Academy of Social Sciences, have argued that theology in China forms three separate streams – Chinese theology, Sino-Christian theology and academic theology – streams that represent a sliding scale from confessional to 'faith-neutral', but that leave unofficial publications (i.e. those from unregistered church theologians) off the scale.

After the churches and state-sponsored seminaries (Three-Self and Roman Catholic) started to open up again in the early 1980s, leaders reconnected with former friends and colleagues, and exchange delegations began, such as that between the British Council of Churches and the China Christian Council (the church arm of the Protestant TSPM). Former China missionaries were often instrumental in creating links, as with David Paton's creation of the Friends of the Church in China group in 1984, a group that has organised visits and clergy exchanges, and has supported Chinese charity work. In 1991, the China Christian Council re-entered the World Council of Churches, after some wrangling over the naming and status of the Taiwanese church in the council – a body it had last walked out of during the Korean War in disgust at support for the USA in the conflict. Early international connections were naturally between the official, or registered, churches and official bodies overseas, while the easing of travel restrictions for Chinese citizens and of overseas support for churches in the last decade or so has meant greatly increased liaison between overseas Chinese Christians and underground churches. The growth in Chinese émigrés has also led to the important corollary question of which group 'represents' the Chinese church abroad – as in the debates over which image of Our Lady of China should hang in the National Cathedral in the US, and whether this should be the choice of Chinese Catholics, or of Chinese Roman Catholics locally (see Madsen and Siegler 2011: 232).

Two factors modulated the reopening of the church in China and its relations with the world: firstly, according to official perspectives, the church was now on a different footing, as independence brought a more co-equal relationship with the church worldwide; and, secondly, overall theological direction would be within a frame of aligning theology with socialist life.[12] In his opening address to the third national Christian conference in 1980, Bishop Ding Guangxun set the tone for much Protestant official church theology over the next two decades. Lauding the efforts of the TSPM in fulfilling (Republican-era) aims of ridding the church of imperialism and allowing the Chinese public to disassociate Christianity from 'the foreign', Ding wrote:

---

12 The 'Theological Reconstruction' programme of the 1990s (神学思想建设) included the deepening of the 'Three-Self' approach and of running the church well, together with the aligning of theology to life in a socialist China. There were other streams that interacted more with elements of traditional Chinese philosophy, such as Wang Weifan's 'Unceasing Generation' theology, or Shen Yifan's incarnational theology, but these were less prominent.

> While affirming the universality of Christianity, we understand that Chinese Christianity cannot talk of making contributions to world Christianity unless it rids itself of its colonial nature, ceases to be a replica of foreign Christianity, does not antagonize or dissociate or alienate itself from the cause of the Chinese people, but joins them in that cause, plants its roots in Chinese culture, forms a Chinese self, and becomes a Chinese entity.
>
> TING 1985

Other than removing China's 'dependent' status, one of the core successes of the TSPM was, argued Ding, in 'making Chinese Christians patriotic Christians'. Patriotism, he reiterated, need not be the warped nationalism that many foreigners held it to be: one could be patriotic in the mould of Moses or Daniel.

The ideological commitment of the Chinese Catholic Church to working with the government parallels that of the registered Protestant Church, and here too the guiding model (that of 'Running Church Affairs in a Democratic Way', part of the 'Three Documents and Systems' programme instituted in 2003) shows how the policy framework has been expected to set the agenda for theological thought, at least in official rhetoric. 'Running church affairs democratically' is explicitly linked to the national good and to a sense of global Catholic belonging, as evidenced by a range of recent essays and articles coming from official church presses.[13] As in TSPM rhetoric, the independence of the Chinese church is acclaimed.[14] As state officials describe, 'Running Church Affairs in a Democratic Way' incorporates the dual ideals of 'love of country' and 'anti-imperialism', while being consonant with Vatican II directions on greater local autonomy.[15] For both Protestant and Roman Catholic church leaders, the theological ideal of autonomy in the Chinese church (which coincides with state narratives) should govern relations with the outside.

---

13   See, for example, articles by bishops Li Shan (李山) and Shen Bin (沈斌) in volume 4 (2013) of the journal *Zhongguo Tianzhujiao* (中国天主教 or *Chinese Catholicism*), entitled respectively 'Consistently Raise High the Flag of "Love Country Love Church": Firmly Develop the System of a Democratically Run Church' and 'The Local Implementation of a Democratically-run Church is a Development Trend in the Universal Church'.

14   Some foreign commentators have read matters differently: Criveller (2003) argues that '"democratic running" means simply the total control of the Church by the Party and political authorities'.

15   See, for example, Cai Yongsheng's speech given in July 2013 and published on 20 August 2013 as '蒋坚永副局长在中国天主教民主办教"三项制度"颁布十周年座谈会上的讲话', http://www.chinacatholic.cn/html1/report/1405/2729-1.htm, accessed 7 May 2017.

While the state-sponsored churches have adopted state or Party narratives on 'the foreign' to a considerable degree, the house churches have operated on the basis of a very different relation with the state. For Roman Catholics this evidently relates to the supranational authority of Rome, and links have been maintained with Rome via diverse sources. Many house church Protestants, meanwhile, have held freedom of belief and unconditional independence to be fundamental to the church's existence. As commentator Liu Tongsu contends: 'If the government has already chosen the theological interpretations or form of worship for all Christians, then how can we still talk about freedom of belief?' He adds that 'a soul decided by political power is only a pseudo-soul, and a pseudo-soul can only produce a pseudo-faith' (Liu 2001). In line with various urban house church pastors in China, Liu has argued in print that, as Chinese society opens up, the house church needs to participate more fully in public life and worship openly.[16] For others in the Protestant house church movement, the decades of oppression and the sacrifices of those who resisted the Communist Party's subjugation of religion have left a wariness of deeper engagement with 'the world'.

In the three decades since Bishop Ding railed against foreign Christians for their support of the 'so-called underground churches' and the 'anti-China' organisations abroad raising money for them, house churches have moved from illegal to extra-legal, from hidden to operating out of malls and office blocks, and from secretive Bible shipments to inviting Chinese-American pastors to preach and teach. Just as the Protestant house churches have received large inflows of money from overseas Chinese, the underground Roman Catholic Church has also received substantial support and remittances from expatriate Roman Catholics. As Madsen and Siegler note, when the underground church in China sees buildings that they have funded torn down by the government, this 'only strengthens the resolve of outraged communities living in New York' (Madsen and Siegler 2011). Both 'underground' churches have leveraged foreign connections to maintain an international spotlight on government suppression of religion.[17]

Meanwhile, a third sector in Chinese Christianity, the academic study of religion, has enjoyed a very different trajectory to that of the churches. While intellectuals and academics studying Christianity have no necessary connection to

---

16   See, for example, Yu and Wang (2010: 230–1). Liu also argues that purity (a key term for older house church believers) should no longer involve a separation from the world, and that social seclusion was only ever a temporary expedient to preserve faith.

17   See, for example, Wenzhou activists connecting with Radio Free Asia over arrests during the campaign to remove crosses from the tops of churches (Phillips 2015).

the churches, the growth of the study of Christianity in Chinese universities has had a role in bringing credibility to religion and in spreading Christian ethical values more widely in society, and leading academics have acted as consultants to the government. Academic Christianity has had an important voice in the construct of Chinese Christianity and how it relates to the world.[18] Academics have enjoyed relative freedom vis-à-vis church theologians in their internal activities and international relations – although, as He Guanghu points out, a socialist state system also governs the study of religion structurally, in terms of the questions asked and resources provided (see He 2014).[19] Given the restrictions on seminaries, on their intake of students and research scope, some have gone so far as to claim that theological research in 'the past thirty years has not burgeoned from a seminary system, but from the humanities and social science departments in universities' (Yang 2014: 123). Sino-Christian theology has established one of its aims as bringing theology, or theological methods, into the academy and from there into wider society. For Yang Huilin, theology unrestricted by religious belief has a broader social function, where it 'can create the intellectual space for considering fundamental issues of cultural identity, value systems, and meaning generation' (ibid.: 123).[20]

Two of the earliest writers in the Sino-Christian theology movement, He Guanghu and Liu Xiaofeng, a well-known public intellectual, discuss Christianity and national identity. He Guanghu's construct of a 'native language theology' or 'mother-tongue theology' presents a non-nation-based alternative to indigenous or contextual theologies (and was appropriately introduced via two articles in a Canadian Chinese-language journal in the mid-1990s). Liu Xiaofeng has decried the use of faith as an instrument of nationality, arguing that, by refusing to identify with Chinese culture, Christianity can serve rather as an agent of rupture or transformation, through its perspectives on the nature of individual existence or divine autonomy (see Chin 2011: 146–7). Liu's work – and that of the many young scholars in fields from philosophy to church history to biblical studies – supported by state universities and linked to global academic networks, offers a challenge to China in its deconstruction of received

---

18   For a fuller discussion, see, for example, Starr (2014).

19   Other problems He lists in the study of Christianity include a backlog of international works not translated into Chinese; risks for publishers in taking on topics that may be blacklisted; and the small number of undergraduate courses in religious studies, which limits those coming into the field.

20   Yang draws links between Žižek's investigation of theology beyond the Christian system, John Milbank's Radical Orthodoxy and French critical theorists in his explorations of why and how a non-religious Christianity can enlighten the humanities.

thought, to the church and to the meaning of theology in its creation of a non-church theology, and to this volume in its renegotiation of Chinese theology's relation to World Christianity.

Across a Spectrum of Unregistered Beliefs

The spectacular growth in the number of unregistered churches or house church meeting points in China over the last three or four decades offers a fascinating insight into the relationship between legislation, persecution and church expansion, and how questions of faith may thwart government intentions or disprove secular expectations. A notable aspect of house church development, as suggested above, is the breadth of the churches' links within China and abroad; there has been no attempt to follow the self-sufficiency model of the Jesus Family communes of the 1930s. The house churches that have mushroomed since the late 1970s have forged a variety of networks within China and to the outside world: the genesis of some of these networks, their growth and their overseas' links are described by Xin Yalin (2009), David Aikman (2003) and others. The trend is even more striking among the new urban house church movements, whose leaders are frequently well-connected and openly engaged in dialogues with national church leaders, with academic theologians, with wider society and with international partners.

One might imagine that the theologies of the Protestant house churches, or 'underground' churches, the inheritors of the defiantly anti-Communist and holiness-oriented rhetoric of Wang Mingdao, Samuel Lamb (Lin Xiangao) and other bastions of faith and suffering, would be attuned towards the kingdom to come, and would display a pan-Evangelical global vision in the present. The message of defiance – the core scriptural texts of obeying God and not human ordinances, and of ultimate authority transcending all worldly powers – is certainly present and commented upon in contemporary house church writings, but alongside this there is also an enduring strand of China-nation rhetoric, seemingly more in keeping with other, pro-government, sectors of the church. Contemporary house church networks receive considerable financial and material aid from overseas Chinese and foreign church groups, their seminary and church teaching materials may be based on American or Korean Evangelical pedagogical materials, and they may regard themselves as part of one true, global, Evangelical movement, but for many there is no contradiction between this and a strong pro-China sentiment.

This final section considers how certain voices within the house churches have recently addressed the themes of China as a nation and the Chinese church in the world. Some, such as Wang Yi, a Chengdu pastor of a 'Reformed Church', address the relationship between Christian patriotism and nationalism directly in their theological thinking, while for others nationalist yearnings are woven seamlessly into Christian sermons, essays and hymn texts. Long essays on the topic have also appeared in web and print media from mainland and overseas Chinese writers, but some of the most emotional and ingenuous pleas for the nation come in the hymns and song tunes of the popular hymn-writer and itinerant evangelist Lü Xiaomin. Lü's life story is well-known among house church Christians: how she dropped out of high school through illness, converted, and joined the ranks of rural evangelists moving from village to village during the period of great church growth in the early 1980s. The composer of more than a thousand hymn tunes and lyrics, Lü's lively hymns and songs set to variations of Chinese folk melodies are widely sung in Christian gatherings and churches. Her ministry and hymns speak to the suffering of a generation of rural Christians, who put their livelihoods, and sometimes their lives, on the line for the gospel. The hardships of life on the road are alluded to in various songs, and brief spells in prison attest to the clashes with local authorities that Lü and other evangelists encountered as a result of their witness. As the fervent but simplistic faith of the rural Chinese house church movement of the 1970s and 1980s was transformed as faith spread to the urban and intellectual centres in the 1990s, Lü's own life underwent its own changes.

Internationally known as Xiaomin (or Xiao Min), Lü's global fame has come in the twenty-first century through her links to the US-based China Soul for Christ organisation, whose director Yuan Zhiming is a well-known figure in US Christian circles as a prominent post-1989 dissident and pastor, and on the mainland as one of the young intellectual scriptwriters on the provocative Chinese documentary series *Heshang* (*River Elegy*, 1988).[21] China Soul for Christ has acted as Xiaomin's agent and has produced DVD, karaoke and CD recordings of her hymns, including recordings made in Sydney Opera House, as well as hosting a permanent web collection of the hymns and enabling free and paid downloads. Lü's life story is included as an episode in the acclaimed 2003 documentary on the Chinese house church movement produced by China Soul for Christ, *The Cross – Jesus in China*, and the faithfulness of her life has been used as an encouragement to others across the world. Lü does not read Western

---

21   *Heshang* caused a national political debate in China for its trenchant criticisms of Chinese culture and traditions. Yuan is currently on sabbatical from his organisation, as allegations of sexual misconduct dating back prior to Yuan's conversion are investigated; the allegations were brought by another well-known 1989 dissident and Christian convert, Chai Ling.

musical notation and composes orally; the sumptuous orchestral arrangements represent an intriguing marketing, promotion and internationalisation of Lü's work.

The content and theological parameters of Lü's compositions have changed little over the years. Praise is a dominant note in the collection, alongside the theme of hope in difficult circumstances. In line with much rural preaching and the dispensationalist heritage of the earlier independent house churches, the end times and an imminent judgement form the focus of several hymns, adding impetus to the strong calls to mission that sound throughout the collection. This mission begins in China, but since 'the gospel has no national boundaries', 'we will continue, laughing joyfully, until the whole of humanity turns to God' (Lü 2001: vol. 1, no. 42). Like many house church proponents of her generation, Lü's hymns suggest a mission westwards, through central Asia towards Jerusalem, in keeping with the house churches' 'Back to Jerusalem' movement.[22] More striking, however, is the close link between mission and national revival. The depths of loyalty to the nation and of identification with China and its fate are immediately evident across the hymn collection. The lyrics to 'China Belongs to the Lord' include the lines: 'If I only had one drop of blood, one drop of sweat left/ I would shed it for China/ ... If I only had one breath left, one ounce of strength left/ I would dedicate it to China.'[23] The love of one's neighbour and love for China are both Chinese attributes and Christian ones, even to the point of martyrdom: 'If we don't love our compatriots/ it is a reproach to the heroic spirits of our ancestors/ a reproach to the many heroes/ ... O Lord, you alone know how much we long for the revival of the church in China/ even if our lives on earth are cut short by you' (ibid.: vol. 1, no. 18).[24] In some hymns, such as 'Fire of Revival', the call is for a Christian presence in China, where reviving fires spread through the land and 'every inch of land rejoices', welcoming

---

22   See https://backtojerusalem.com/home/; cf. Hattaway et al. (2003). This is echoed in Lu's hymn linking mission north-west through the Gobi: for example, 'The gospel doesn't distinguish between nationalities/ it must surely be transmitted to all nations/ we are a blessed generation/ the envoys of Heaven/ the camel bells of the Gobi Desert/ the cry of sheep in mountain valleys/ the Holy Spirit constantly moves us/ urges us forward/ to go throughout the whole world/ to spread the gospel' (*Jia'nan shixuan*, vol. 1, no. 6, '万国的大使命').

23   Canaan Hymn Selection, no. 551, '中国属于上帝' ('China Belongs to the Lord'). The entire collection can be found at https://www.chinasoul.org. For a discussion, see Starr (2016a: 264–8).

24   '因为我们先听见' ('Because We First Heard'). Other hymns in this particular selection with a focus on China include nos. 26, 28, 45, 48, 82 and 90.

Jesus to China (ibid.: vol. 1, no. 16). In others, prayers for the people of China and the conversion of China seem to equate to prayers for China itself. The full lyrics to 'China Has Great Hope' run, in a literal translation:

> China has great hope, China has great hope
> Servants of God, you must be steadfast, you must be steadfast,
> Use eyes of faith to pass through the dark nights, tomorrow will be filled
>   with light.
> With your fervent prayers, China has great hope
> The great momentum of the flow of the Holy Spirit, momentum cannot
>   be blocked
> Flowing east, flowing east towards China, China has great hope
> The long months and years of the past saw much hardship; tomorrow
>   we head towards glory,
> Workers of the era, God is watching you; China has great hope.[25]

While the hope here could be read merely as a Christian hope for China, rather than in any sense of secular or nationalistic gain for the nation, it is clearly couched within a national framework. In other hymns, the nation and the people of the nation are elided, as in 'Ah, Father, I Kneel Before You', where eschatological imminence signalled by ecological disaster blurs the distinction between a Christian salvation and the survival or salvation of the nation:

> Father, ah Father, I now kneel before you
> And beseech you to give my compatriots a heart of repentance; because
>   Jesus will soon come again.
> The ice rivers of the South Pole are melting, disasters are ever more
>   frequent.
> In troubled times, look up to Jehovah, do not fear, no matter how great
>   the hardship.
> My conscience tells me, do not sin against Jehovah.
> Lord, I kneel and face you, I kneel now, and ask you to save China.[26]

Given the military language and metaphors of mission that Lü employs in some of her hymns ('Soldiers, soldiers, arise! Put on your full armour/ Soldiers, soldiers, arise! The rifles are already shined ... The Lord will give the various

---

25   Canaan Hymn Selection, no. 664, '中国大有希望'.
26   Canaan Hymn Selection, no. 687, '天父啊我现在向你跪下'.

nations to you as your foundation; the Lord will give the poles to you as your property/ Arise, arise, to battle, we must set out'[27]), the scope for confusion among those not well versed in scripture or in Christian vocabulary as to what is being fought for – the soul of the nation, God's kingdom on earth, or even China's territorial integrity – is not negligible.

If the links between the revival or renaissance of Christian faith in China and the health of the nation may be inferred from several of Lü Xiaomin's hymn texts, the writings of émigré pastor Liu Tongsu make a much more comprehensive case for the new role of a Christian China. The pastor of a Chinese-American church in California, Liu Tongsu is a leading thinker and writer on the house church movement in China. As a US-educated mainland Chinese pastoring an overseas Chinese church, he personifies the transcontinental nature of parts of the Chinese movement. His writings also bring to the fore a question of terminology that is natural in Chinese but often linguistically and conceptually problematic for others. In modern standard Chinese, 'overseas Chinese' (*huaqiao* 华侨) and 'ethnic Chinese' or foreigners of Chinese origin (*huayi* 华裔) are all regarded as 'Chinese' (*huaren* 华人), which is primarily an ethnic and cultural distinction. While the specific term *Zhongguo ren* (中国人 Chinese) refers to PRC nationals, Taiwanese, Chinese Malaysians and British-born Chinese are all embraced in the broader terminological *oikoumenē* of 'Chinese'. Just as He Guanghu's 'mother-tongue theology' incorporates all writings in Chinese, for many Chinese speakers the 'Chinese church' signifies the church of Chinese people, gathered anywhere in the world; ethnicity functions as denomination might in a term such as 'the Anglican Church'.

In an article based on a speech given in Seoul in 2011, 'Portering the Faith: The Role of the American Chinese Church in the Movement to Spread the Gospel in China', Liu Tongsu commends the role of the Chinese American church in spreading the faith to China, and sees in that role a historic importance out of all proportion to its tiny congregation (Liu 2011). In a thesis of which Samuel Huntingdon would be proud, Liu argues that, as the US and China trade places as world leader, the Chinese church in America has been given a pivotal role to play in world history. The reason for China's eclipse of the US, and the prerequisite for it taking on the mantle of world leader, is faith. As even the Communists recognised, it takes something that transcends culture to renew culture, and faith is the strongest contender:

---

27   Canaan Hymn Selection, no. 644, '战士啊起来吧', http://www.liutongsu.net/?p=1162, posted 26 August 2011, accessed 7 May 2017.

This kind of comprehensive cultural renewal based in faith is the pre-requisite for China to return once again to the centre of world history. China's hope does not lie in China; China's hope is in its trust in God. The centre of the world is God; any culture with a central position is only the visible sign of God's sovereign power.

LIU 2011

As China's culture is swept on a high tide of faith, its future position will inexorably be at the centre of the world, while America, the past rampart of faith, has drifted towards the false gods of humanism and is in danger of being cast completely adrift from God by its submergence in materialism and individualism. 'China's Rise' in Liu's analysis is not driven by economic power but ultimately by faith, since God's blessing is manifest in the strength of a nation. Without God, argues Liu, there is no motive force for developing culture, and 'a faithless culture is a dead culture'. Westernisation itself will not bring about a shift in the centre of culture, as is shown by the case of Japan: only a faith centre can become a global cultural centre.

Since the church is the medium through which faith influences culture, it is only in as much as the Chinese church is Sinicised that it can have an impact on Chinese society; Christian faith, holds Liu, can act as an effective agent of cultural renewal in China only by being a living part of Chinese culture. As Liu notes, the twofold separation forced on the Chinese church, from society and from the universal world church, gave the church the opportunity to maintain the purity of its faith, and to become inculturated and break with its inherited Western social and cultural forms, as it was forced to 'create a church out of thin air'. While the culturally conservative Chinese American church has little opportunity to affect US society, suggests Liu, it is poised to play a unique God-given role in world history, as a channel linking the two cultures. Given that the transmission of faith traditions is central to the shift of the centre of world history from the US to China, Chinese people working and researching in the US have played an important role in witnessing to China, just as the Chinese American church has been instrumental in transmitting the 'hardware' of faith and in its financial and technical help.

Even among house church friends and colleagues, there is a spectrum of views, and it is instructive to place the recent writings of house church pastor Wang Yi alongside those of Liu Tongsu. In his earlier writings, Wang, a former law professor, combined a pastoral response to the question of Chinese Christian identity with a scriptural exploration of the themes of patriotism and an ethical consideration of the nature of nationalism and its links to totalitarianism. As Carsten Vala and Huang Jianbo show in their analysis of

Wang's blog postings – he has a substantial online following – these distinguish between nationalism and patriotism, grounding the latter in biblical motifs while accusing the official Three-Self church of being tightly bound to the Communist Party's nationalist agenda (Vala and Huang 2016). But in a striking document posted in August 2015, Wang and co-authors from his church offered a strong refutation of Chinese exceptionalism, and described the Chinese church very much as part of one (global, transcendent) kingdom of Christ, on earth but not of the earth. Entitled 'Reaffirming our Stance on the House Churches: 95 Theses', and signed by two pastors and five elders from his Early Rains church, Wang Yi and his co-leaders set out in some detail their beliefs on a range of church issues, including the 'Sinicisation' of Christianity; relations between church and state; and their opposition to the TSPM (Wang 2015). Their strong stance on the nature of the church in the world counters some of the house church standpoints discussed above, and offers a clear vision for global church relations in its rejection of any Sinicisation of the Chinese church that might 'distort the gospel through culture' or 'sever the church from universal traditions of belief' (no. 38), and in its explicit separation of the spheres of church and state. As the authors explain, the church is a spiritual kingdom in the world, scattered in various countries but pledging its loyalty only to Christ (no. 44). China is already under the sovereign power of Christ, insist the authors: 'In terms of spiritual substance, it is the resurrected Jesus who governs and is in charge of the country's history and the hearts of its people, and not any rulers, political parties, cultures or wealth on earth' (no. 43). While God has given the power of the sword to secular rules, the church holds the keys to heaven: no country is able to limit the church's mission.

While we might contend that the authors' understanding of the Sinicisation of Christianity by other church groups misreads their stance on inculturation (Starr 2016b), the change in perspective is striking – from a human viewpoint bounded by national borders and limited by local governance and regulations, to an eagle's or Godly perspective from above, a spiritual view of the kingdom's relations and networks. The breakdown of earthly boundaries within the (world) church and the rejection of co-religionists who work with the state have clear implications for relations with the outside. It is worth noting, however, that the force of the pushback in this document indicates the strength of the perceived problem: almost every clause, whether berating China for its former culture of idol worship or denying that the church could 'belong' to the People's Republic, is focused on China; the denunciation of a China-centred ideology and promotion of the universal is calibrated in Chinese terms.

At the furthest end of the unregistered Chinese church spectrum, in the zone referred to by the government as *xiejiao*, or evil cults, there are other groups that claim a direct and universal scope. It is all too easy to dismiss these as transient congregations, but even a cursory glance at the website of an organisation such as the Church of Almighty God (formerly known as Eastern Lightning) shows the slick professionalism, financing and numeric strength of some congregations or cults, with multilingual websites, real-time live-chat features, grand-scale operatic videos of the gospel message – and entirely heretical theologies. The Church of Almighty God, whose revelatory scriptures are reproduced in such texts as *The Word Appears in the Flesh* (话在肉体显现), has an extensive theology based on the three ages of the Law, the Age of Grace and the Age of the Kingdom, as well as global aspirations (and aggressive proselytization, with members convicted of the murder of unwilling converts).[28] The Age of the Kingdom was ushered in from 1991, when Almighty God, the last Christ, was incarnated in China as Yang Xiangbin, a woman now resident in the US, the centre of the church's media operations. In this new era, the gospel message will come out of the East to all: as the website proclaims, 'My kingdom takes shape in the entire universe.' When the kingdom spread in mainland China, 'God took back all of the working of the Spirit from the entire universe and focused it on this group of people who accepted God's end-time', the 'predestined' and those who earnestly sought the true way. All other denominations and sects have become a 'wasteland' and have lost the Holy Spirit, who is drawing everyone back to be reconciled in one true church. As Emily Dunn shows in her study of the cult, one of the 'heretical' or heterodox aspects of the group is precisely its cultural iconoclasm and negative depictions of the Chinese people and the Chinese nation, which are out of kilter with national narratives (Dunn 2015: 67–8).

Conclusions

The interplay between the national and the global in Chinese views of itself and its role in the world has impacted on the development of Chinese Christianity and its relations to the world, just as Christianity has contributed to China's global capital and migration flows and to perceptions of nationhood.

---

28   Accessed at https://www.holyspiritspeaks.org/about, with a Chinese web address at https://www.kingdomsalvation.org (the website addresses for this organisation are subject to frequent change). For a new study of this group, see Dunn (2015); on murders, see, for example, 'Inside China's Most Radical Cult', *The Daily Telegraph*, 2 February 2015.

China is, of course, far from unique in expressing its faith in national imagery – or in its church being riven by its relationship to the state – but the Chinese case reminds us that the global, and to some extent the universal, is also the product of a local imaginary. The expansionary-minded nature of certain sections of Chinese Christianity can be couched both in the frame of mission and in political or global hegemonic language. This chapter has argued that particular expressions of Christianity in China have given rise to specific understandings of the issue of the church worldwide, and that these have theological and practical implications for the world church that have yet to be assimilated into debates. The connection between faith, relationship with the state and relations with the outside world has played out very differently in different sectors of the Chinese church, precisely because of the historical and political ramifications of faith-based action on matters such as the relations between earthly and transcendent kingdoms. Theologies matter, and beliefs about church–state relations have had a profound effect on church development within China and in mediating different sectors' relations with the 'world church'.

As the examples in this chapter show, we need to factor political, historical and national narratives into debates on what 'World Christianity' means to its various constituents. Relations among church bodies are as much political as they are theological in a country such as China, and relationships with outside bodies may be entirely governed by state fiats and ideologies – or they may subvert them, as in cases where diffused, lay leaderships exist in larger transnational networks beyond state control (see Lee 2014). World Christianities can be viewed only from within each country's and culture's views of the world and from within particular lexicons. The language of the 'global South', for example, is not part of a Chinese concept of the world; rather, as the discussion of Liu Tongsu's writings show, China's own view of its role and (Christian) destiny in the world supposes a much wider vision.

The relations between narratives of nation in a society and churches' narratives of belonging are naturally complex, and, as some of the Protestant house church examples given here suggest, raising a prophetic voice in one area does not preclude supporting prevalent views in another. The 'wresting back' of the Chinese church from mission groups and mission history was a shared aim for many from varying political and theological persuasions, as well as being a government desideratum. While some Christian groups have been adamantly opposed to the excesses of state authority over religion, and locate their identity – to the point of civil disobedience or even death – in transnational bodies, and their ultimate belonging in transcendent realms, a persistent support for 'China' and solidarity with the Chinese people are also present in sectors of the underground church. This tension, and its effect on understandings of the world church, demands further exploration. A final point to note in this connection is how the global has had an impact in creating the export of national visions, as well as in creating cohesion among Chinese-language speakers across borders. This has been most readily seen in the sprouting of Confucius Institutes around the world, but is present here on a smaller scale in the international funding and marketing of Lü Xiaomin, or the study abroad of Liu Tongsu, and pre-eminently in the use of the internet for publishing and publicity by the house church leaders discussed. The Chinese church is fast becoming a global entity, while its contested adherence to a universal gives pause for thought, at home and abroad.

References

Aikman, D. (2003) *Jesus in Beijing*. Washington DC: Regnery.

Anderlini, J. (2015) '"Western Values" Forbidden in Chinese Universities', *Financial Times*, 30 January 2015.

Ashiwa, Y. and D. L. Wank (eds) (2009) *Making Religion, Making the State*. Stanford CA: Stanford University Press.

Bays, D. (2012) *A New History of Chinese Christianity*. Chichester: Wiley-Blackwell.

Chin Ken-Pa (2011) 'The Paradigm Shift: From Chinese Theology to Sino-Christian Theology – A Case Study on Liu Xiaofeng' in Lai Pin-chiu and J. Lam (eds), *Sino-Christian Theology: A Theological Qua Cultural Movement in Contemporary China*. Frankfurt: Peter Lang.

Criveller, G. (2003) 'Three Documents: A Commentary', editorial, *Tripod* 23 (130).

Dirlik, A. (2015) 'Born in Translation: "China" in the Making of "Zhongguo"', *Boundary 2* (July).

Dunn, E. (2015) *Lightning from the East: Heterodoxy and Christianity in Contemporary China*. Leiden: E. J. Brill.

Goossaert, V. and D. A. Palmer (2011) *The Religious Question in Modern China*. Chicago IL: University of Chicago Press.

Harding, H. (1993) 'The Concept of "Greater China": Themes, Variations and Reservation', *The China Quarterly* 136: 660–86, special issue on 'Greater China'.

Hattaway, P., Brother Yun, P. Xu Yongze and E. Wang (2003) *Back to Jerusalem: Three Chinese House Church Leaders Share Their Vision to Complete the Great Commission*. Downers Grove IL: InterVarsity.

He Guanghu (2014) '從鳳凰涅槃到鳳凰共舞 – 中國宗教學研究的回顧與展望' in He Guanghu and Zhou Xinping, with Ying Fuk Tsang (ed.), 當代中國社會政治處境下的宗教研究 (*Religious Studies in Contemporary China: The Socio-Political Context*).

Occasional Paper Series no. 24. Hong Kong: Centre for the Study of Religion and Chinese Society.

Kuhlmann, D. (2014) 'Negotiating Cultural and Religious Identities in the Encounter with the "Other": Global and Local Perspectives in the Historiography of Late Qing/ Early Republican Christian Missions' in T. Jansen, T. Klein and C. Meyer (eds), *Globalization and the Making of Religious Modernity*. Leiden: E. J. Brill.

Lee, J. Tse-Hei (2001) 'The Overseas Chinese Networks and Early Baptist Missionary Movement across the South China Sea', *The Historian* 63 (4): 752–68.

Lee, J. Tse-Hei (2014) 'The Christian Century of South China, Church, State and Community in Chaozhou (1860–1990)' in T. Jansen, T. Klein and C. Meyer (eds), *Globalization and the Making of Religious Modernity*. Leiden: E. J. Brill.

Li Xiangping (李向平) (2015) '"宗教复兴"还是"信仰重构" – 兼论中华文明特性' ('Religious Revival or Faith Reconstruction – On the Particular Characteristics of Chinese Civilization'). Religion in Global Politics Conference Proceedings. Beijing: Renmin University.

Lian Xi (2010) *Redeemed by Fire: The Rise of Popular Christianity in Modern China*. New Haven CT: Yale University Press.

Liu Tongsu (刘同苏) (2001) 'Keeping Watch for Freedom Under Heaven: On Shouwang Church's Second Outdoor Service', 23 April 2001, http://www.chinaaid.org/2011/04/ chinese-pastor-writes-on-shouwang.html, accessed 7 May 2017.

Liu Tongsu (刘同苏) (2011) '信仰的搬运工 – 美国华人教会在中国福音运动中的角色' ('Portering the Faith: The Role of the American Chinese Church in the Movement to Spread the Gospel in China'), http://www.liutongsu.net/?p=1162, accessed 7 May 2017.

Lü Xiaomin (吕小敏) (2001) *Jia'nan shixuan* 迦南詩選 (*Canaan Hymns*). Volumes 1, 2 and 3. Taipei: Taipei CMI Publishing.

MacInnis, D. (1989) *Religion in China Today: Policy and Practice*. Maryknoll NY: Orbis Books.

Madsen, R. (1998) *China's Catholics*. Berkeley CA: University of California Press.

Madsen, R. and E. Siegler (2011) 'The Globalization of Chinese Religions and Traditions' in D. A. Palmer, G. Shrive and P. D. Wickeri (eds), *Chinese Religious Life*. New York NY: Oxford University Press.

Meyer, C. (2014) 'How the "Science of Religion" (*zongjiaoxue*) as a Discipline Globalized "Religion" in Late Qing and Republican China, 1890–1949 – Global Concepts, Knowledge Transfer and Local Discourses' in T. Jansen, T. Klein and C. Meyer (eds), *Globalization and the Making of Religious Modernity in China*. Leiden: E. J. Brill.

Nedostup, R. (2009) *Superstitious Regimes: Religion and the Politics of Chinese Modernity*. Cambridge MA: Harvard University Asia Center.

Pew Research Centre (2011) 'Table: Christian Population in Numbers by Country', Pew Research Centre website, 19 December, http://www.pewforum.org/2011/12/19/table -christian-population-in-numbers-by-country/, accessed 22 May 2017.

Phillips, T. (2015) 'China Arrests Christians Who Opposed Removals of Crosses', *The Guardian*, 27 August, http://www.theguardian.com/world/2015/aug/27/china-arrests-christians-opposed-cross-removals-zhejiang, accessed 27 August 2015.

Starr, C. (2014) 'Sino-Christian Theology: Treading a Fine Line between Self-determination and Globalization' in T. Jansen, T. Klein and C. Meyer (eds), *Globalization and the Making of Religious Modernity in China*. Leiden: E. J. Brill.

Starr, C. (2016a) *Chinese Theology: Text and Context*. New Haven CT: Yale University Press.

Starr, C. (2016b) 'Wang Yi and the 95 Theses of the Chinese Reformed Church', *Religions* 7 (12): 142.

Ting, K. H. (Ding Guangxun) (1985) 'Retrospect and Prospect', *Chinese Theological Review*, http://www.amityfoundation.org/eng/sites/default/files/publication_pdf/CTR_1_1985.pdf, accessed 7 May 2017.

Vala, C. T. and Huang Jianbo (2016) 'Three High-profile Protestant Microbloggers in Contemporary China: Expanding Public Discourse or Burrowing into Religious Niche on Weibo (China's Twitter)?' in S. Travagnin (ed.), *Religion and the Media in China*. London: Routledge.

Wang Yi et al. (2015) '我们对家庭教会立场的重申 – 95 条' ('Reaffirming our Stance on the House Churches: 95 Theses'), http://weibo.com/p/1001603881634431670754, accessed 7 May 2017.

Xin Yalin (2009) *Inside China's House Church Network: The Word of Life Movement and its Renewing Dynamic*. Lexington KY: Emeth.

Yang Fenggang (1999) Chinese Christians in America: *Conversion, Assimilation, and Adhesive Identities* Philadelphia PA: Pennsylvania State University Press.

Yang Huilin (2014) *China, Christianity and the Question of Culture*. Waco TX: Baylor University Press.

Yu Jie (余杰) and Wang Yi (王怡) (2010) *Yisheng yishi de yangwang* 一生一世的仰望 (*The Expectation for Whole Life*). Taipei: Jiwen.

Zhao Zichen (趙紫宸) (2009) *The Collected English Writings of Tsu Chen Chao*. Volume 5 of *Zhao Zichen wenji* 趙紫宸文集 (*Collected Works of Zhao Zichen*). Beijing: Shangwu.

CHAPTER 9

Anthropological Perspectives on World Christianity

Joel Robbins

Introduction: World Christianity and the Rise of the Anthropology of Christianity

The goal in this chapter is to suggest that anthropology has a lot to contribute to our understanding of world or global Christianity. But before I go on to make my argument in this regard, I should start by pointing out that readers would be well within their rights to imagine that it is going to be difficult for me to make my case. As recently as twenty years ago, anthropologists rarely studied Christianity at all, at least compared with how often they studied almost all other religions, from tiny indigenous traditions to worldwide faiths such as Hinduism, Buddhism and Islam. To mention perhaps the most obvious reason for this tradition of neglect, though not the only one, from the start anthropology defined itself as the study of 'other' cultures or societies – the further away from home and more ostentatiously different from ourselves the better (Robbins 2003). And in maps of the world that split it into people like 'us' anthropologists and then others, Christianity anywhere was always destined to be too much like us. As early as 1938, the very influential anthropologist Isaac Schapera captured the traditional situation of the anthropologist confronting Christianity when he wrote the following about his fieldwork among the Kxatla of South Africa:

> The first essential in a modern fieldwork study is to obtain as full an account as possible of the existing tribal culture. In this due prominence must be given to elements taken over from or introduced by the Europeans ... Christianity, in so far as it has been accepted, must be studied like any other form of cult, in its organization, doctrines, ritual, manifestations in tribal life, attitudes towards it of individual natives, and so on ... This is easy enough to say. In practice it is sometimes difficult to apply, not so much because of technical obstacles as because of the outlook engendered by the training that most anthropologists receive before going into the field. If I may refer to my own experience, I found it difficult, when actually in the field, not to feel disappointed at having to study the religion of the Kxatla by sitting through an ordinary Dutch Reformed

Church service, instead of watching a heathen sacrifice to the ancestral spirits; and I remember vividly how eagerly I tried to find traces of a worship that was in fact no longer performed. And it seems so silly to record the details of a Christian wedding or confirmation ceremony with the same fidelity, let alone enthusiasm, with which one would note down the 'doctoring' of a garden or a new hut.

SCHAPERA 1938: 27

During the sixty-odd years of the twentieth century that followed after Schapera penned these courageously self-revelatory lines, Christianity would spread rapidly in Southern Africa and in many of the other parts of the world filled with the kinds of 'other' societies and cultures that anthropologists were then drawn to studying. But, somewhat shockingly, anthropological attitudes towards studying the world's largest religion would hardly change at all. Even in 1995, one collected lots of scholarly points for witnessing an ancestral sacrifice, and almost none at all for sitting through any kind of Christian ritual.

By the end of the last century, however, things had begun to change in the relationship of anthropology to Christianity. As firm and long-standing as the anthropological habit of indifference towards the Christian faith had been, it has rapidly faded over the last twenty years. Nowadays, many young anthropologists study Christianity, and some more senior ones have taken up the subject with all the energy and ingenuity they used to devote to studying other religions. I do not know anyone who has tried to work up figures on this by looking at publication numbers or thesis titles, but it is certainly folk wisdom in anthropology that the turn to studying Christianity is one of the bigger trends to roll through the contemporary discipline. So steady has the growth been, it is now taken for granted that Christianity is a reasonable topic of anthropological interest. Perhaps Schapera would be relieved, and in any case he would certainly recognise that something had changed in the discipline he called his own.

I do not want to dwell here on the reasons anthropological attitudes towards Christianity have changed so radically over the last fifteen or twenty years.[1] I suspect that some of it has to do with the explosive growth of Pentecostal and Charismatic Christianity around the globe since the 1960s. A reasonable estimate made in 2011 held that there were then 580 million Pentecostal and Charismatic Christians in the world, the majority of them in parts of the global

---

1   I treat this subject more fully in Robbins (2014). See also Jenkins (2012).

South that have long fascinated anthropologists.[2] So impressive has been the global growth of what I will henceforth for reasons of expressive economy simply call Pentecostalism that some Christian scholars now float the idea that it should be treated as a separate fourth stream of the Christian tradition, alongside Catholicism, Orthodoxy and Protestantism (Jacobsen 2011). Inasmuch as this kind of faith insists of making itself relevant to and evident in all areas of life (Pentecostals frequently pray, for example, at the outset of many important social activities), and given its extensive resort to ritual expression (Lindhardt 2011), Pentecostalism proves to be a kind of Christianity anthropologists find hard to ignore in the field. They also find it somewhat easier than more interior forms of the faith to study with their usual fieldwork methods: enthusiastic and demonstrative, Pentecostal religious gatherings are certainly different kinds of social events from the 'ordinary' Dutch Reform Church services that left Schapera feeling a bit let down among the Kxatla. Given these aspects of Pentecostalism, it should perhaps come as no surprise that the first decade of work on Christianity in anthropology was disproportionately devoted to its study. It has only been in recent years that studies of other Christian traditions, such as Catholicism, Orthodoxy, liberal Protestantism and even fundamentalism, have begun to catch up. So it is fair to say that the rise of Pentecostalism as a major global force has had something to do with the rise of Christianity as an anthropological topic.

It is also the case, however, that the 1990s and early 2000s were arguably times of major change in the way in which many Christians around the globe perceived their own faith, and some of these changes may have helped clear the path by which anthropologists found their way to the study of this religion. The change in Christian self-perception I have in mind here is precisely the one that is marked by the title of this volume: over the same two decades that anthropologists in large numbers began to study Christianity, many Christians began to define a key aspect of their religion as its 'worldwide' or 'global' character. Of course, one needs to know only the very rudiments of the history of Christianity to know that it has been spreading geographically from the start, and that it reached many parts of the world a very long time ago. But, and here I am drawing on historical work being carried out by Joel Cabrita,[3] it is really only since the 1990s that this global character of the faith began to seem to many Christians as if it is not just a fact about their religion, and a key feature

---

2 'Christian Movements and Denominations', Pew Forum Religion and Public Life Project, 19 December 2011, http://www.pewforum.org/2011/12/19/global-christianity-movements-and -denominations/, accessed 28 May 2014.

3 Personal communication.

and outcome of its missionary character, but that it is also very much wrapped up in its nature as a faith and of huge importance for its future (see also Noll 2014; Shaw 2012).

One watershed moment in the public recognition of this change was the publication of Jenkins' 2002 book *The Next Christendom: The Coming of Global Christianity* (2002a) and the widely read digest of it that featured in the magazine *The Atlantic* (2002b). Through a mix of compelling narrative history and bold, clearly explained demographic speculation, Jenkins argued not only that Christianity was growing very quickly in the global South, but that its power centres would soon shift in that direction, making it global not only in the varied locations in which the faithful lived, but in the multicentric quality of the struggles soon to ensue over issues of doctrine and practice. One way to express this key point that Jenkins was making is that Christians around the world were beginning to find themselves relevant to one another in new ways, or at least that Northern Christians were coming to find Southern ones relevant in matters of the faith beyond those that occupied missionaries, and that Southerners were becoming conscious of this. The tensions over gender and sexuality that were beginning to roil the Anglican Communion were cases in point for Jenkins, and their rapid intensification served to give his arguments ever wider public play.

As with any massively influential and also somewhat popularising text, Jenkins' book has been widely criticised. And its story is so neatly told that it is hard not to wonder what complexities the author had to leave out in the course of crafting such an elegant account. Robert Wuthnow (2009), for example, has strongly argued that arguments such as Jenkins' that claim that the centre of Christianity is shifting south ignore the continuing financial and cultural power of North American Christianity. But my point is not to judge Jenkins' work on its accuracy. I simply want, in anthropological fashion, to hold up its publication and reception as a key moment in the coming to Christian self-consciousness of a range of ideas that would cohere into the now taken for granted notion (or what Wuthnow (ibid.: 38) called a 'new paradigm') that holds that we can talk about something like world or global Christianity, rather than simply about the fact that there are Christians almost anywhere one might travel.

And looking back, I am intrigued by the fact that anthropology took up the study of Christianity in a big way at the moment when Christian historians including Jenkins and his key historical and theological precursors such as Lamin Sanneh (1989), Andrew Walls (1996) and Dana Robert (2000) began to treat Christianity as a religion that is global or worldwide by nature. One wonders at possible connections here; is it possible that, once Christianity became broadly conceived as global or worldwide rather than Western in its very nature, it finally became 'exotic' or 'other' enough to warrant anthropological attention? I do not have a smoking gun here that would allow me to argue for any direct influence that changes in Christian self-perception had on anthropology, except to say that all the early anthropologists who participated in the development of what would end up being called the anthropology of Christianity were reading Jenkins, Sanneh, Walls and others and had a sense, even if it was inarticulate, that something was afoot in the way in which many Christians in general and certainly Christian academics in particular were understanding themselves. And, of course, the stunning growth of Pentecostal Christianity was a huge part of Jenkins' own argument, which means that he was attending to some of the same phenomena that were independently catching the attention of anthropologists in the field (a fact he notes in footnotes to his second edition in 2007). At the very least, then, the movement of Christians towards a global self-conception of their faith and the movement of anthropologists towards studying Christianity have some similar roots, and it is hard to dispute that anthropologists, missiologists, historians, theologians and all kinds of scholars interested in Christianity worldwide have been swimming in some of the same waters over the last two decades. What I hope to do in the rest of this chapter is consider some things anthropologists have learned that might be of interest to those coming to worldwide, global Christianity from some of these other academic points of view.

By now there exists a number of reviews of the anthropology of Christianity as a field (for example, Jenkins 2012; Lampe 2010; McDougall 2009; Bialecki et al. 2008; Robbins 2012; 2014). These discuss in detail many of the themes that have come to mark work in this area. Rather than cover the kind of extensive territory these works traverse, I here pick out three issues that have been well discussed and that together, I think, provide a distinctively anthropological view on what it might mean to think of Christianity as a worldwide or global religion. These themes are: (1) the role Christianity frequently plays in driving or at least shaping radical cultural change; (2) the sense in which Christians around the globe, even many of those living in some of its furthest-flung, most remote locales, understand themselves to be participating in a worldwide faith; and (3) the extent to which some kinds of Christianity may encourage people to adapt themselves to one of the other most important contemporary global institutions – the market – and to do this by leading people to see and value themselves in the first instance as individuals rather than as members of communities. Taken together, these three themes paint one – though only one – picture of the way in which Christianity shows up as meaningfully global in the places in which anthropologists often encounter it.

This map of the rest of the chapter in place, let me quickly add two caveats about how extensively I will cover the anthropological literature in the three areas I address. The first caveat follows from the fact that my own research has mostly focused on Pentecostalism. For this reason, and also because, as I mentioned earlier, Pentecostals have been over-represented in anthropological work until recently, I am going to focus mostly on Pentecostal cases here, leaving comparisons with other branches of the Christian tradition for another venue. The second caveat is that, in illustrating the points I make with concrete examples, I will give priority to my own fieldwork among the Urapmin of Papua New Guinea. This will make for a more vivid account than if I had proceeded otherwise. But rest assured that on every point I make, there are many other well-developed examples one could turn to, some of which I will refer to as I go along.

Christianity and Cultural Change

With these caveats in mind, let me turn to my first theme: the claim that, as it spreads around the world, Christianity is a powerful force for cultural change. One might think that this would be an obvious point to make when one is studying a religion that stresses conversion to a complex faith that in all of its many manifestations brings with it cosmologies, liturgies and ethical systems of its own. How could a turn to such a religion not be a force for cultural change? But, in fact, this point has not been so obvious to anthropologists. Dedicated to studying cultures and traditions, and defining these as things that are important in part because they endure through time, for much of the history of their discipline anthropologists tended to explain away changes wrought by Christian conversion. In places where Christianity was relatively new, change could be set aside by focusing on how Christianity was something with which people engaged only for pragmatic reasons – as 'rice Christians' – and that they did not allow to tamper with the fundamentals of their own traditional religions. In more sophisticated theoretical terms, anthropologists could say that people actively 'resisted' the Christian message, or adopted it on superficial terms just to protect themselves from further missionary or government intrusion as they clandestinely carried on as before (Robbins 2007). And in places such as Latin America, where Christianity had been around for so long that it was hard to argue that it had had no real effect on the ways in which people thought and lived, anthropologists could resort to models of syncretism that allowed them to spy indigenous traditions beneath the Christian surface, and often to argue that those traditions were what was really providing the structure and main substance of people's religious lives (Ingham 1986).

The new anthropology of Christianity has largely left behind this bias towards stressing cultural continuity in the face of Christian conversion. The claim made by anthropologists of Christianity is not that one never finds situations in which Christianity lies very lightly on the shoulders of its only apparent converts, but that conversion does not always – or even perhaps all that often – work out this way. Pentecostalism in particular, anthropological work reveals, tends to demand major changes and often succeeds in leading converts to bring about radical transformations of their religious lives of an order that these older models of syncretism and resistance could not imagine. It does this in somewhat subtle ways, for it does not reject the reality of the traditional spiritual beings converts once worshipped or found themselves battling against. Instead, it fully accepts the reality and power of these beings, but demands that converts see them all as wholly evil in intent, and that they turn to the Christian God for help in combatting them. In doing so, it insists that converts must also leave behind all of the traditional rituals through which they once approached these figures, relying only on Christian rites to help them navigate life from now on (for a review of these lines of argument, see Robbins 2004b).

The Urapmin people with whom I worked provide a striking example of the kinds of changes often wrought by Pentecostal conversion – and, furthermore, of the other kinds of changes these religious transformations can bring in their wake. So, in relation to this point in particular, I will rely on Urapmin material to make my case.

At this point, I should say a few words to introduce the Urapmin. The Urapmin are a language group of roughly 400 people living in the West Sepik Province of Papua New Guinea, near the geographic centre of the island. The region in which they live was one of the last areas of Papua New Guinea to be colonised. Direct contact with Westerners came only during the Second World War, with colonisation following in the late 1940s. Missionaries from the Australian Baptist Missionary society arrived at the regional government centre of Telefomin soon afterwards, in the early 1950s. But Urapmin is a hard six- or seven-hour mountainous walk from Telefomin, and missionaries rarely made it there. Eventually, in the 1960s, they sent a Telefomin man they had converted to evangelise the Urapmin, but he quickly found himself in trouble with a local young woman and was expelled. From that time forward, the bulk of the initiative to learn about Christianity came from the Urapmin side. Noticing that many of their neighbours, with whom they were part of a complex regional ritual system, had taken up the new religion, some Urapmin adults decided to send their children to Telefomin to stay at the mission station and study Christianity. Many of these young people converted, and a large number of the men became paid evangelists to even more remote populations. They also brought their understanding of Christianity home to Urapmin, and taught many in the community a good deal about the Christian faith. But they made few converts at home: young people traditionally had no religious authority at all in Urapmin, and these young Christians were not in a position on their own to transform the faith of their parents. By the mid-1970s, then, Urapmin was a community in which many people knew about Christianity, but few practised it. Traditional religion remained at the centre of community life.

The religious situation in Urapmin changed radically in 1977. That year, a Charismatic Christian revival that had started in New Zealand and travelled first to the Solomon Islands made its way to Papua New Guinea. Once it reached the island, it was rapidly carried from place to place by local people. Some young Urapmin men who experienced the revival at a local bush Bible college in their region rushed home and began to pray with people that the Holy Spirit would come to their community. Soon, many people began to have experiences of being 'kicked' by the Spirit, as they put it. They shook violently, felt hot and became convinced of their own sinfulness. Some were given gifts of preaching, healing and seeing the sins of others. Within a year, every adult and teenager in the community either had had such Charismatic experiences or had watched as their relatives had them. This convinced people – again, as they put it – that God truly exists. By the end of 1977, everyone in the community was Christian.

As the revival unfolded, some of the younger people who had converted in previous years led the charge to dismantle traditional religion. Cult houses were dismantled and the ancestral bones they harboured were 'thrown out' in the bush. Magical stones and seeds and other materials were burned or thrown down the pit latrines the government had made the Urapmin dig. Equally strikingly, people set aside an elaborate system of taboos put in place by the Urapmin creator spirit Afek and by nature spirits who owned all the natural resources of the Urapmin landscape. All kinds of people began to eat all kinds of food and with all kinds of other people. Hunters began to hunt in formerly taboo parts of the forest and gardeners started to garden on formerly taboo ground. God, the Urapmin now argued, made all the things of the earth and he wanted everyone to use them. To disregard his wishes by observing taboos came to be seen as a sin. Now that they are Christians, the Urapmin say, using terms that have been borrowed from English, it is 'free time' – people do not have to, and indeed should not, follow any taboos.

I hope that I have said enough to give a sense of how radically Christian conversion transformed Urapmin culture.[4] But just to make sure that this point is not missed, I have saved one of the other, most momentous, changes till last. Traditional Urapmin religion contained many taboos restricting various forms of contact between men and women. Men and women, for example, had separate paths on which to walk through Urapmin territory. Men and women also ate separately. And women and children slept in single-family 'women's houses' that made a ring around each village, while men slept in communal men's houses in the centre. Urapmin say that all of these taboos were abandoned by the end of the revival. Certainly, by the time I arrived for my fieldwork at the very end of 1990s, thirteen or fourteen years after the revival had begun, there was no sign of separate paths, men and women ate together, and men and women all slept in the women's houses. One village in which I did not live had kept its men's house, but there were no ancestral relics inside, no one appeared to sleep there, and one of the times I visited I noticed a woman inside. Along with religious ideas and ritual life, gender relations emerged profoundly transformed by Urapmin conversion.

In the early 1990s period of my fieldwork among them, Urapmin were a very recognisably Christian community. People went to church regularly – always on Saturday, Sunday and Wednesday, but often on other days as well. And one could hear people saying Christian prayers almost whenever one chose to listen, except in the very dead of night, and sometimes even then. Urapmin, having become very familiar with dispensational premillennialist doctrines that had been central to the revival, were convinced that Jesus could return at any moment and were preoccupied with leading moral, 'Christian' lives so as to be ready for him whenever he arrived. Christianity saturated every part of their lives. Given this, and given the depth of their Christian thought, of which I will give one example later, it is hard to think of them as rice Christians or syncretists, and – even more relevant to the point I am making here – it is impossible not to see them as people who have lived through a radical period of cultural change.

At this point, I have laid out my first anthropological theme: Christian conversion, at least in the contemporary world, often leads to dramatic cultural changes. On its own, this observation does not really speak to the issue of the worldwide quality of Christianity today, although it does register one of the key effects of this religion as a global force. To bring the global nature of Christianity itself into greater focus, one has to look in detail at some of the new ideas and

---

4   I discuss the Urapmin case in great detail in Robbins (2004a).

practices Christian conversion often introduces, rather than the success it has in installing them and sending older ones away. The other two themes that are prevalent in the literature of the anthropology of Christianity that I have chosen to discuss address precisely this issue.

Conversion to a Consciously Worldwide Faith

Many of the converts anthropologists study see themselves as joining a new religion that both pertains to and connects them with a larger world than the one to which their previous religion did. I remember hearing a man start a prayer at a Sunday service in Urapmin with the exclamation: 'God, people everywhere are praying to you.' Shouted out at a prayer service in one of the world's more remote corners – Urapmin has no electricity and no vehicular roads connecting it to anywhere else – this tiny example speaks volumes about the ability of Christianity to provide people living on the global periphery with a sense that at least in some respects they are part of a worldwide community. And, continuing this theme, once when I asked someone in Urapmin why he thought people preferred Christianity to their traditional religion, he offered that Christianity helped people make sense of things relating to the colonial and postcolonial world in which the Urapmin had been living that traditional religion, with its local spirits exercising power over local spaces, had no way to explain. As he put it, more pithily than I just have, 'Christianity just explains more'. What it helps explain is a global world that now encompasses what Urapmin people have recently come to see as their decidedly local one.

The idea that Christianity lays out a larger world for those who embrace it is not a new one in anthropology. Long before the rise of the contemporary anthropology of Christianity, Robin Horton (1971; 1975a; 1975b) influentially argued that Africans move from their traditional faiths to world religions such as Christianity and Islam when they cease to live only in the 'microcosm' of their local society and begin to have to contend with larger 'macrocosmic' social arrangements such as the state. But what is new in what anthropologists are documenting now is how often converts quite explicitly turn to Christianity as a framework not only for explaining larger arenas of social life, but also for identifying with these larger global worlds over and against the states they see as mistreating their local societies. As the prominent sociologist David Martin (2002: 26) has phrased it, converts in many parts of the world find 'in Pentecostalism a chance to leap over their immediate environment to a wider world'. When Urapmin pray with everyone else in the world on Sunday, they see themselves, to use their terms, as linking up with the 'white' Christian world as opposed to what they take to be the disappointing 'black' nation of Papua New Guinea, a nation that is full of chaos and danger and that has marginalised the Urapmin and rendered them peripheral (Robbins 1998). In other cases, particularly well documented for sub-Saharan Africa, the rejection of the nation is in part a response to traditionalising state efforts to promote the very local religions Pentecostals aim to displace as the foundations of national identity (Meyer 1998; van Dijk 1998). Sometimes, too, conversion to Pentecostalism can be a way of throwing off the religion of a dominating power, as when the Chukchi people of north-eastern Siberia adopt Pentecostalism in order to shed their stigmatised status as pagan without having to 'adhere to values imposed by Russians' (Vaté 2009: 42), or when the Maale people of southern Ethiopia convert to global evangelicalism (fundamentalist in this case) in order to bypass the orthodoxy of the politically dominant northerners (Donham 1999: 95, 101). What links all of these cases is a moral condemnation of the nation-state in which converts are embedded paired with a new identification with a broader, global community that converts now understand to uphold their most important values. Here we see converts putting the worldwide nature of Christianity as they understand it to work in projects of situating themselves in the world in more satisfying terms than they were able to do before adopting their new faith.

Having made this point, I want to open a very brief parentheses concerning something that anthropology is particularly well positioned to bring to the interdisciplinary study of Christianity as a global faith. As a fieldwork-based discipline, anthropology works very close to the ground, staying constantly in touch with the changing ways in which people live. I make this point here because, on the basis of this kind of work, one can notice hints of a recent shift in the pattern I have just identified of Pentecostals in many places using their connection to the worldwide faith to construct larger-than-local identities for themselves. Until a few years ago, this pattern of people identifying as Christians with a global community of believers rather than with their more proximate (but still distant or oppressive or disappointing) states is one that often showed up in anthropological accounts. But recently a new pattern has begun to emerge. This is a pattern in which forms of Pentecostalism that focus on saving the nation have come to the fore. For instance, Kevin O'Neill's (2010) work in Guatemala has produced a full-scale monograph on what he calls 'Christian citizenship'. O'Neill has studied a megachurch headquartered in Guatemala City known as El Shaddai. Members of this church focus on the responsibility they feel to save Guatemala as a whole. Through individual acts of fasting, prayer and self-governance, and through collective rituals of spiritual warfare in which they attack the demonic spirits at the root of Guatemala's sinful patterns of crime, divorce and corruption, they fulfil their obligations to work towards national salvation. Their goal is not to identify with a world beyond their national home, but to make their nation as a whole a redeemed Christian faith community. And, lest we think that this is just a Latin American phenomenon, I should add that reports like this are now being published from other parts of the world as well, such as Melanesia (Eriksen 2009).

It is unclear as yet how one might explain this shift from worldwide to national identification on the part of Pentecostals. Perhaps this is just a trend sweeping through the tightly interlinked networks of contemporary Pentecostalism and it will soon be replaced. Or perhaps there is something deeper going on that relates to changes in how the wider world looks from its peripheries now that the end of the Cold War has removed some of the supports that once steadied people's sense of an organised global world. But whatever the reason for this change, it serves as a reminder in the present context that people's understanding of the global qualities of Christianity are always subject to transformation and that such changes bear watching on the part of those who are interested in understanding its worldwide nature.

Christianity, Individualism and the Global Market

As well as linking people to a wider world by giving them reasons to think of themselves as part of a global Christian community, many anthropologists have found that Pentecostalism also leads to a second kind of cultural change that helps prepare believers for participation in another world-spanning institution, that of the market. This change is one that leads people to see themselves as individuals – as persons, that is, who are disconnected in important respects from those to whom they are closely related as kin, and who are alone responsible for their success or failure in relation to God. Once people have come to see themselves in this way, the argument goes, they are able to live in cities and to work in market-oriented positions that do not require them to put the interests of their families or communities before their own. This move to the market need not be where a growing sense of individualism leads a convert, but, once people come to think of themselves in individualistic terms, the possibility of making this move becomes thinkable in a way that it would likely not have been before.

A conversation I once had in Urapmin is again a good place to start to get a feel for what individualism as a Christian religious concept looks like, for, in fact, the Urapmin have very little contact with the market and thus make sense of their move to valuing the individual mostly in Christian terms. To follow the snippet of conversation I want to share, it helps to know that the Urapmin are one of those kinds of Papua New Guinea societies that helped give us the anthropological notion of the gift, which has recently become well known across many disciplines. Most food Urapmin people eat will have been given to them by someone else, and in turn they will give away much of the food they grow to others. It is best, Urapmin feel, not to eat your own food: that is what they call 'eating for nothing'. Better to give your taro and sweet potatoes to others to eat, and to consume the taro and sweet potatoes others give you; in that way, food not only nourishes the body, but also nourishes the social relations in which Urapmin lives are embedded. Because food should be used to meet both of these goals, even husbands and wives have separate garden areas within a plot, so that the food they provide each other can count as a gift. And as Urapmin people walk down the paths that connect their villages to one another and to their gardens, they are constantly reaching in their string bags to give a little of the crop they have harvested to those they meet, and they are similarly receiving crops from others. They also frequently give to and receive from each other more elaborate gifts of items such as bows and valuable shells. As one anthropologist put it in relation to another Papua New Guinea society, such is the give and take of everyday life in Urapmin (Schieffelin 1990).

With that as background, I can tell my story. One night, I came across Rom in his house reading his copy of the New Testament in the Papua New Guinea lingua franca, Tok Pisin. Rom was, in my experience, one of the most intelligent and articulate people in the Urapmin community. When I happened by his house on the night in question, he was reading and studying Matthew 25, the parable of the ten bridesmaids, five of whom were wise and had enough oil for their lamps but would not share their oil with the five foolish ones who did not, who then missed out on the bridegroom's coming while they were off seeking fresh supplies.

Now, this parable is important for almost all Urapmin for its final line, about keeping watch because one does not know the day nor the hour of Jesus's return. This line plays a key role in the way in which the Urapmin live with their very intense millennial hopefulness, both pushing them to keep the millennial possibility ever in mind and giving them pause when they hear rumours, which they often do, that someone has determined that the second coming is about to arrive. But for some reason I cannot reconstruct, when I bumped into Rom studying this passage by himself, I did not assume that I knew why he thought the parable was important. Instead, I asked him what it meant. He answered that 'this story means that belief is a big thing. Everyone has to have it for themselves.' 'My wife,' he continued, 'cannot break off part of her belief and give it to me; I cannot break off part of mine and give it to her.' 'Each person,' he repeated, 'must have it for themselves.'

What Rom was expressing in this statement was his understanding that there is a profound difference between Christianity as the Urapmin understand it, which requires that each individual work out his or her own salvation, and their traditional moral understanding, which stresses the deep interconnectedness between people and the sense that it is relationships, not individual persons, that either succeed or fail in moral terms. His assertion that belief is a 'big thing' and as such is different from the crops and material items Urapmin regularly exchange with one another is a crystalline statement of Urapmin understandings of what anthropologists have called Christian individualism as well as of the ways in which embracing it represents a change in Urapmin understanding.

As I have noted, Urapmin Christian individualism does not connect them with the market; however, many reports from elsewhere indicate that there are places in the world where Christian individualism does do this. Birgit Meyer (1999a), for example, has shown how many newly urbanised Ewe of Ghana who join the workforce also join Pentecostal churches that promise them 'deliverance' from evil spirits connected with their ancestors and the living family members who are religiously involved with them – evil spirits that hold these new urbanites back from earning God's favour in the form of economic success and a comfortable life in the city. As social scientists, anthropologists have little trouble interpreting such demands for deliverance as efforts people make to disqualify in moral terms demands that relatives make for cash. One would want to insulate oneself from such demands – 'seal' oneself off from baleful ancestral spiritual influence, as some Malawian Pentecostals put it (van Dijk 1998) – so that one might accumulate a little savings and move oneself up in the urban prestige economy. But it is important to note that most converts do not put things this way. For them, their focus on the purification of their own souls is a Christian religious concern, and one that seeks success in this life at least in part as a sign of assurance of salvation.

My last point, about the religious nature of converts' own understanding of their growing sense of individual autonomy in relation to their social surroundings, is an important one. I do not want to be taken as saying that Christianity is little more than a school for learning the nature of market relations or a handmaiden of capitalism in its march around the world (cf. Comaroff and Comaroff 1991; 1997; Brouwer et al. 1996). There are also lots of hints in the anthropological record that, despite its frequent promotion of individualism, in other ways Christianity often provides a critical vantage point on the global market. For example, the asceticism of many forms of the faith, and in particular of many varieties of Pentecostalism, often leads converts to opt out of and criticise consumerism and consumption-oriented versions of individualism (Meyer 1999b). Furthermore, as the sociologist Bernice Martin (1995) has argued, even as such asceticism appears to produce model workers, these workers also turn out to be ones who sometimes leave their positions abruptly when the Holy Spirit prompts them to devote themselves more fully to God.

Having put in place the caution that Christian individualism is not precisely or always the same as its market-oriented cousin, it would not be fair to close this discussion without noting that this does not mean that it cannot sometimes appear in forms that come somewhat close to this. The Universal Church of the Kingdom of God is one of the churches most frequently mentioned whenever people discuss the globalisation of contemporary Christianity. Originally formed in Brazil in the 1970s, it has gone on to become hugely popular worldwide, and particularly in the global South. Indeed, it is often held up as a prime example of successful 'South–South globalisation'. As one of the many 'prosperity gospel' churches around the world, it is built around promises that God wants his faithful to be successful in this world, but that to earn his favour members must give generously to their churches (Coleman 2000). In the Universal Church case, all members must tithe 10 per cent of their income. Given that many are very poor to start with, this is often an immense hardship, at least when viewed from the outside, not only by observers but also by members of the families of converts who have not themselves joined the church and who sometimes distance themselves from those within their ranks who become members over the issue of income that is lost to the family when it is given as tithes.

My interest is not in suggesting that the enormous success of the Universal Church should lead us to see it as some kind of paradigm of the nature of global Christianity. I have brought it up because I have recently read a richly detailed book by the anthropologist Ilana van Wyk (2014) entitled *The Universal Church of the Kingdom of God in South Africa: A Church of Strangers*. For our purposes, the subtitle of the book reveals its core argument. The church van Wyk studies in Durban – which, of course, may not be representative of all Universal Church of the Kingdom of God churches – does little to build community among its members: there are no small groups, development projects or charitable good works. Rooted in a cosmology that holds that the world is full of demons, many of whom deceitfully take the form of people converts might find appealing, and strongly emphasising that a believer's primary goal should be to become through prayer and tithing a 'strong Christian' who can draw on God's power to fight these enemies, members are never sure that even their fellow church-goers are not in reality eager to drag them into sin. For this reason, and because, as noted above, their tithing practices often put them in conflict with their families, many church members keep mostly to themselves, their lives presenting a good deal of the quality of social isolation that social scientists sometimes imagine would be the result of an individualism that has been allowed to develop almost wholly unchecked by other values. I want to stress that when we reach the Universal Church in Durban, we have come a long way from Rom telling me that his wife cannot break off part of her belief and give it to him. Most of the many churches one can read about now in the anthropological record, even if they promote some kind of shift towards individualism, look nothing like this one in Durban.[5] But the case van Wyk describes does raise the question of some of the places to which individualistic notions of salvation can sometimes lead, and should also encourage us to ask what aspects of the Christian understandings of many other churches that also promote some form of individualism keep their members from reaching this point.

Having ended with this somewhat unusual case, I think I should reiterate my main argument about individualism before moving to my conclusion. The point I have hoped to make is that a move towards individualism is one that often leads Christian converts to be able to imagine themselves drawing closer than they have been before to the mainstream of the global market. Not all will go that far – the Urapmin, for example, have fantasies about entering the market but have not been able to do much to realise them. But for many converts to Pentecostalism, the move towards a more globally prevalent sense of the importance of the individual self is another way in which they can feel part of a larger, global world.

Conclusion

Having made my observations about Christianity and its role in cultural change, expanding social identifications and the introduction of individualism, I will be brief in my conclusions. Perhaps I can start by saying that, in and of itself, being 'worldwide' does not make Christianity in any sense unique these days. After all, lots of things, from AIDS to poverty, and from television to Coca-Cola, are by now nothing if not worldwide. In the face of this observation, what I have wanted to suggest in this chapter is that, viewed anthropologically at

---

5   For an entrée into very active debates about the various versions of individualism promoted by different kinds of Christianity, and some sceptical arguments about the suggestion that they do so at all, see Bialecki and Daswani (2015) and Robbins (2015).

least, 'worldwideness' is part of the nature of Christianity in a way that it may
not be part of the nature of Coca-Cola or of the other things on my rhetorically
short list of examples. For many Christians, the sense of global connectedness
Christianity affords is part of what defines the faith. That its doctrine and ritual
life, in many of the forms they take, allow for this sense of connectedness has
to be counted as a major strength of Christianity as a contemporary religious
tradition. At the same time, we need to acknowledge how closely Christianity can sometimes track other major global institutions, such as the market,
that historically have grown up alongside it. In making and illustrating these
and other points, I hope to suggest that anthropological work on Christianity
has a lot of valuable things to say about the ways in which actually existing
Christianity around the globe, both in its practice and in its aspirations, is self-
consciously worldwide. There is much else, of course, that the anthropological
study of Christianity can contribute to the study of World Christianity. Thus,
for example, I could have expanded the list of topics I have discussed here to
include others that have been central to anthropological discussions of Christianity, such as the nature of Christian views of language (Bialecki and Hoenes
del Pinal 2011). Furthermore, all of my examples have paid careful attention to
the cultural aspects of Christianity, and I hope they have indicated that anthropological research is well suited to deepening our sense of how Christianity
shapes the ways people understand and act in the world. Such work can help
us recognise the immense diversity of World Christianities, even as it can also
open up the question of the extent to which, from an anthropological point of
view, there might be aspects of Christianity as a culture that are widely shared
among the many various expressions of the faith (Robbins 2017). But here, given
the focal topic of this volume, I have chosen to focus on the ways in which the
culture of Christianity is constitutively global for many of those around the
world who embrace it. I hope that this kind of anthropological work might
help to deepen in some small way the growing self-consciousness about the
global nature of the Christian faith among those who study it in the academy
as well.

References

Bialecki, J. and G. Daswani (2015) 'What is an Individual: The View from Christianity',
    Hau: Journal of Ethnographic Theory 5 (1): 271–94.
Bialecki, J. and E. Hoenes del Pinal (eds) (2011) 'Beyond Logos: Extensions of the Lan-
    guage Ideology Paradigm in the Study of Global Christianity(ies)', *Anthropological
    Quarterly* 84 (3). Special issue.

Bialecki, J., N. Haynes and J. Robbins (2008) 'The Anthropology of Christianity', *Religion Compass* 2 (6): 1139–58.

Brouwer, S., P. Gifford and S. D. Rose (1996) *Exporting the American Gospel: Global Christian Fundamentalism*. New York NY: Routledge.

Coleman, S. (2000) *The Globalisation of Charismatic Christianity: Spreading the Gospel of Prosperity*. Cambridge: Cambridge University Press.

Comaroff, J. and J. L. Comaroff (1991) *Of Revelation and Revolution. Volume 1: Christianity, Colonialism and Consciousness in South Africa*. Chicago IL: University of Chicago Press.

Comaroff, J. and J. L. Comaroff (1997) *Of Revelation and Revolution. Volume 2: The Dialectics of Modernity on a South African Frontier*. Chicago IL: University of Chicago Press.

Donham, D. L. (1999) *Marxist Modern: An Ethnographic History of the Ethiopian Revolution*. Berkeley CA: University of California Press.

Eriksen, A. (2009) 'Healing the Nation: In Search of Unity through the Holy Spirit in Vanuatu', *Social Analysis* 53 (1): 67–81.

Horton, R. (1971) 'African Conversion', *Africa* 41 (2): 85–108.

Horton, R. (1975a) 'On the Rationality of Conversion, Part I', *Africa* 45 (3): 219–35.

Horton, R. (1975b) 'On the Rationality of Conversion, Part II', *Africa* 45 (4): 373–99.

Ingham, J. M. (1986) *Mary, Michael, and Lucifer: Folk Catholicism in Central Mexico*. Austin TX: University of Texas Press.

Jacobsen, D. (2011) *The World's Christians: Who They Are, Where They Are, and How They Got There*. Oxford: Wiley-Blackwell.

Jenkins, P. (2002a) *The Next Christendom: The Coming of Global Christianity*. Oxford: Oxford University Press.

Jenkins, P. (2002b) 'The Next Christianity', *Atlantic* (October): 53–68.

Jenkins, T. (2012) 'The Anthropology of Christianity: Situation and Critique', *Ethnos* 77 (4): 459–76.

Lampe, F. (2010) 'The Anthropology of Christianity: Context, Contestation, Rupture, and Continuity', *Reviews in Anthropology* 39 (1): 66–88.

Lindhardt, M. (ed.) (2011) *Practicing the Faith: The Ritual Life of Pentecostal-Charismatic Christians*. New York NY: Berghahn Books.

Martin, B. (1995) 'New Mutations of the Protestant Ethic among Latin American Pentecostals', *Religion* 25 (2): 101–17.

Martin, D. (2002) *Pentecostalism: The World Their Parish*. Oxford: Blackwell.

McDougall, D. (2009) 'Rethinking Christianity and Anthropology: A Review Article', *Anthropological Forum* 19 (2): 185–94.

Meyer, B. (1998) '"Make a Complete Break with the Past": Memory and Postcolonial Modernity in Ghanaian Pentecostal Discourse' in R. Werbner (ed.), *Memory and the Postcolony: African Anthropology and the Critique of Power*. London: Zed Books.

Meyer, B. (1999a) *Translating the Devil: Religion and Modernity among the Ewe in Ghana.* Trenton NJ: Africa World Press.

Meyer, B. (1999b) 'Commodities and the Power of Prayer: Pentecostalist Attitudes Towards Consumption in Contemporary Ghana' in B. Meyer and P. Geschiere (eds), *Globalization and Identity: Dialectics of Flow and Closure.* Oxford: Blackwell.

Noll, M. A. (2014) *From Every Tribe and Nation: A Historian's Discovery of the Global Christian Story.* Grand Rapids MI: Baker Academic.

O'Neill, K. L. (2010) *City of God: Christian Citizenship in Postwar Guatemala.* Berkeley CA: University of California Press.

Robbins, J. (1998) 'On Reading "World News": Apocalyptic Narrative, Negative Nationalism, and Transnational Christianity in a Papua New Guinea Society', *Social Analysis* 42 (2): 103–30.

Robbins, J. (2003) 'What is a Christian? Notes Toward and Anthropology of Christianity', *Religion* 33 (3): 191–9.

Robbins, J. (2004a) *Becoming Sinners: Christianity and Moral Torment in a Papua New Guinea Society.* Berkeley CA: University of California Press.

Robbins, J. (2004b) 'The Globalization of Pentecostal and Charismatic Christianity', *Annual Review of Anthropology* 33: 117–43.

Robbins, J. (2007) 'Continuity Thinking and the Problem of Christian Culture: Belief, Time and the Anthropology of Christianity', *Current Anthropology* 48 (1): 5–38.

Robbins, J. (2012) 'Transcendence and the Anthropology of Christianity: Language, Change, and Individualism (Edward Westermarck Memorial Lecture, October 2011)', *Journal of the Finnish Anthropological Society* 37 (2): 5–23.

Robbins, J. (2014) 'The Anthropology of Christianity: Unity, Diversity, New Directions. An Introduction to Supplement 10', *Current Anthropology* 55 (S10): S157–S171.

Robbins, J. (2015) 'Dumont's Hierarchical Dynamism: Christianity and Individualism Revisited', *Hau: Journal of Ethnographic Theory* 5 (1): 173–95.

Robbins, J. (2017) 'Can There Be Conversion Without Cultural Change?', *Mission Studies* 34 (1): 29–52.

Robert, D. L. (2000) 'Shifting Southward: Global Christianity since 1945', *International Bulletin of Mission Research* 24 (2): 50–8.

Sanneh, L. (1989) *Translating the Message: The Missionary Impact on Culture.* Maryknoll NY: Orbis Books.

Schapera, I. (1938) 'Contact between European and Native in South Africa. 2. In Bechuanaland' in B. Malinowski (ed.), *Methods of Study of Culture Contact in Africa.* London: Oxford University Press.

Schieffelin, B. B. (1990) *The Give and Take of Everyday Life: Language Socialization of Kaluli Children.* New York NY: Cambridge University Press.

Shaw, M. (2012) 'Robert Wuthnow and World Christianity: A Response to Boundless Faith', *International Bulletin of Mission Research* 36 (4): 179–84.

van Dijk, R. (1998) 'Pentecostalism, Cultural Memory and the State: Contested Representations of Time in Pentecostal Malawi' in R. Werbner (ed.), *Memory and the Postcolony: African Anthropology and the Critique of Power*. London: Zed Books.

van Wyk, I. (2014) *The Universal Church of the Kingdom of God in South Africa: A Church of Strangers*. Cambridge: Cambridge University Press.

Vaté, V. (2009) 'Redefining Chukchi Practices in Contexts of Conversion to Pentecostalism' in M. Pelkmans (ed.), *Conversion After Socialism: Disruptions, Modernisms and Technologies of Faith in the Former Soviet Union*. New York NY: Berghahn Books.

Walls, A. F. (1996) *The Missionary Movement in Christian History: Studies in the Transmission of Faith*. Maryknoll NY: Orbis Books.

Wuthnow, R. (2009) *Boundless Faith: The Global Outreach of American Churches*. Berkeley CA: University of California Press.

PART 4

Migration and Diaspora

∴

CHAPTER 10

Defender of the Faith: The United States and World Christianity

Andrew Preston

The United States is in something of a unique position in world religious terms. It is a mosaic of various world religions, yet its primary identity is of a Christian nation. This is despite the fact that the separation of church and state is enshrined in the Bill of Rights and the fact that the Constitution is almost completely silent on religious matters aside from prohibiting religious tests for government posts and elected officials. As early as 1796, John Adams, the second president, reassured the Muslim rulers of the Barbary states that 'the Government of the United States of America is not in any sense founded on the Christian Religion'.[1]

However, the reality is rather more complicated. While American society has undoubtedly become more religiously pluralistic over time, it nonetheless has remained in large part a Christian nation up to the present day, culturally as well as spiritually. The United States has received an enormous number of immigrants from all over the world, particularly over the last century and a half, and one might expect this constant inward flow of newcomers to dilute the prevalence and authority Christianity enjoys. One might also expect that the development of one of the most modernised and globalised societies in the world, a development that has continued relentlessly for over a century, would also have inculcated a more secular and less religious society. Yet the privileged standing of Christianity in America is not despite, but because of, the processes of immigration, modernisation and globalisation. The overall result is a society characterised by a unique blend of bewildering multicultural diversity and bold modernity, even post-modernity, but with surprising religious conformity. This Christian cosmopolitanism, for lack of a better term, is something that is also reflected in America's engagement with the wider world, including in the formulation and execution of its foreign policy. In an era of renewed and

---

1 'Treaty of Peace and Friendship', signed 4 November 1796 and ratified 10 June 1797 (in *Treaties and Other International Agreements of the United States of America*, vol. 11. Washington DC: Government Printing Office, 1976, p. 1072).

increasingly intense sectarian conflict, when Christians around the world feel besieged by rival religions or by the advance of secularism in the West, the United States has positioned itself as a defender of the faith.

Immigration and Globalisation

Much of the American story can be told through the prism of religious pluralism, variety and tolerance, with all three growing over time due to the incessant pressures of human migration.

From the Civil War until the outbreak of the First World War in Europe made private, transatlantic shipping perilous and prohibitively expensive, American society was thoroughly transformed by a process now known as the New Immigration. Beginning in the 1870s, several million immigrants, from groups who had never before embarked for America, emigrated to the United States, including Italians, Greeks, Poles, Hungarians, Romanians, Ukrainians, Russians and Scandinavians. Besides their countries or regions of origin, there was much that was new to the United States about these 'new immigrants'. For one thing, they spoke languages that had never had much of a presence in North America; for another, unlike earlier generations of immigrants from northern Germany and the British Isles, they were largely drawn from the rural peasantry and could work only as unskilled labourers. But what was perhaps most radically new, in the American context at least, was the religious faith and practices of these new immigrants: Roman Catholics from Ireland, Italy, Germany and Poland, Orthodox from Greece, Russia and Ukraine, and Lutherans from Norway, Sweden, Denmark and Germany, in addition to the more familiar Protestant influx of Anglicans, Methodists and Presbyterians from England, Scotland, Wales and Northern Ireland. Perhaps most novel was the surge of Jewish immigration from all across Eastern Europe, but especially Russia. Previously, large pockets of Irish Catholics, themselves relative newcomers in the 1830s and 1840s, were the only major anomaly in a nation that was dominated by various strands of Protestantism from the British Isles and northern German states, and Calvinist dissidents from the Netherlands, Switzerland and France. Now, thanks to the new immigrants of the Gilded Age, the United States became a much more religiously diverse society than ever before.

After a hiatus between the First World War and the high point of the Cold War – not coincidentally, a period economic historians have termed 'de-globalisation', when national borders hardened, societies were devastated by conflict, and the flow of capital, people and trade declined (Findlay and O'Rourke

2007: 429–35) – further waves of human migration accentuated the changes in America's religious complexion. Beginning in the 1960s, with President Lyndon B. Johnson's Great Society reforms (especially the Civil Rights Act of 1964 and the Immigration Act of 1965), greater protections for racial and cultural diversity and rising levels of transnational migration saw the advent of another round of new immigration, with people now coming from newer places still. Latin Americans brought with them their own varieties of Catholicism, people from the Middle East introduced Islam, immigrants from South Asia brought Hinduism, East and South-east Asians transplanted Buddhism, and African immigrants imported both Islam and Christianity. On top of all this, another wave of Russian Jews arrived in the 1970s, followed by yet another in the 1990s following the collapse of the Soviet Union.

These successive waves of religious immigrants – for that was what they were, in addition to being economic migrants and political refugees – entrenched faith, spirituality and religious culture more deeply within American society. But they did not create a religious society, for the United States was already a deeply devout nation.

The inward migration of millions upon millions of people from literally every part of the world, a process that has ebbed and (mostly) flowed for 150 years, has transformed the United States from a mostly Anglo-Saxon culture to a thoroughly global amalgam. At the same time, American ideologies of political economy have fuelled global economic trends, from Fordist industrialisation before the 1970s to the neoliberal, deregulated, service-based innovation economy that has prevailed ever since (Maier 2006: 191–284). The United States, then, has been an instigator as well as an incubator of globalisation; not coincidentally, many of the monikers for global interdependence, such as 'McWorld' or 'Coca-Colonization', stem from a blending of American consumerist soft power and the US military's rather more traditional hard power (Wagnleitner 1994; Barber 1995).[2] The United States has been a crucible of globalisation, with American society transforming the world and, in turn, the world transforming America.

Religion has played a large part in these reciprocal processes. Globalisation is perhaps the highest form of modernism, yet the United States continues to be a highly religious society. As such, it has defied the predictions of secularisation theory for over a century. According to secularisation theorists, as the world becomes more modern it will also become more secular – it cannot be other-

---

2 The literature on the intermingling of Americanisation and globalisation is enormous, but see especially Mann (2013).

wise.[3] But if this is accurate, how do we account for the United States, which has simultaneously been one of the most modern societies on earth yet also one of the most consistently religious? One response is to suggest that secularisation itself is a flawed concept because it is a reflection of the biases of its adherents rather than an analysis of the world as it actually is (Casanova 1994; Asad 2003; Clark 2012). Another is to illustrate the ways in which modernity and religion are not incompatible or contradictory but complementary, even synergistic. The career of the sociologist Peter Berger, one of the most distinguished analysts of religious life, is perhaps instructive: after contributing to secularisation theory in the 1960s, Berger was then confronted with the spectacular growth of religion worldwide over the ensuing three decades. Rather than modify the secularisation paradigm to fit the new circumstances, in the 1990s Berger argued that globalisation was in fact aiding the spread of faith (Berger 1967; 1996). Since then, other scholars have explored the ways in which American religion has pioneered the globalisation of religion more broadly (Noll 2009).

The United States thus stands as the exemplar of a different trend in the modern world: a highly modernist society but also a highly religious one, which, because of this powerful confluence, acts as a self-appointed guardian of religion. In this view, the United States is not a defender of *the* faith, or *a* faith, but a defender of faith in general. By incorporating religious refugees across the centuries – from the English Puritans and other non-conformists in the seventeenth and eighteenth centuries, to the Jews of the Russian and Austro-Hungarian empires in the nineteenth century, to the Muslims, Hindus and Buddhists of the global South in the twentieth and twenty-first centuries – the United States is often perceived to be and portrayed as a global haven for religious freedom. It thus has a unique position in the world as a highly pluralistic and tolerant religious society, one in which the broader national politics and culture welcome the believers of any faith simply on the basis that they have a faith.

Americans have reinforced their guardianship of global religious pluralism with similar priorities at home. Domestically, the United States has been a dynamic site of religious experimentation in three important ways. First, in terms of religious innovation, the protections afforded by the First Amendment's separation of church and state (through the 'establishment clause' and the 'free exercise clause') enabled the emergence of an unregulated 'religious

---

3   Variants of secularisation theory are long-standing and can be found in the ideas and writings of Marx, Freud and Nietzsche, among others. For more recent iterations, see Bruce (2002; 2011).

marketplace' in which indigenous faiths could emerge, grow and flourish (Finke and Stark 2005). New, distinctly American Christian denominations were the first to take root in the nineteenth century, against the backdrop of the 'spiritual hothouse' of the Second Great Awakening that unfolded across the nation during the first half of the century; these new Christian denominations included Mormonism, Seventh Day Adventism and, at the turn of the century, Pentecostalism. Existing denominations, particularly Evangelical Baptists and Methodists, witnessed explosive growth in this period as well. Later, thanks to the freedoms provided by the official separation of church and state and the competitive atmosphere fostered by the spiritual marketplace, they were followed by non-Christian innovations such as the Nation of Islam and Conservative Judaism.

Second, immigration fed into, and amplified, the effects caused by the separation of church and state and the spiritual marketplace, leading to the growth of a broad spectrum of religious diversity. Already before 1776, British North America possessed a wide range of Christian denominations, but the Bill of Rights (which included the separation of church and state) and the non-hierarchical political culture of the new republic encouraged the spread of yet more diversity, and, as a result, the 'democratization of American Christianity' (Hatch 1989). By the twentieth century, endless variants of Christianity, many of them creations of the American religious practice and imagination, jockeyed with an impressive array of non-Christian faiths.

Third, unlike in Western Europe, Christianity continued to grow in the United States. With a couple of exceptions, such as the so-called and rather exaggerated 'religious depression' of the 1930s (Handy 1960), religious adherence in the United States saw either growth or continued strength through the nineteenth and twentieth centuries – indeed, this continued even through the 1960s, when other closely related Western societies were witnessing a precipitous decline in faith.[4] Secularisation theorists may not have faced their own crisis of faith had it not been for the strange case of the United States.

---

4 See, for example, Brown (2001), which analyses the secularisation of Great Britain. Aside from fellow settler societies such as Australia and Canada, Britain is probably the closest comparative case study to the United States.

Secularisation, Pluralism and the Judeo-Christian 'Tradition'

The dominant conclusions about religion in American society, then, are that the United States is not a Christian nation; that the nation has been a source of tremendous religious innovation; that it has been hospitable to new domestic faiths as well as to the absorption of different religious faiths and practices from around the world; and that much of this stems from a constitutional order and political culture that prioritise freedom of worship and conscience at the expense of religious conformity and state interference.

But what if these conclusions are only partly true? What if they reflect a more limited religious landscape in the United States? And if the story of American religious pluralism is only partly true, or is complicated by other factors, what in turn does that tell us about the historical trajectory of World Christianities? There are two key objections to the notion that, in practice, the United States is a uniquely diverse religious society. Americans might very well value the principle of religious pluralism, but the reality has been – and continues to be – very different for two reasons: the first is the surprising strength of secularism, a force that is growing apace as time goes on; the second, somewhat paradoxically, is the enduring power of Christianity in the American imagination and Protestantism in American public life.

As we have seen, the limitation of secularisation theory, at least in the American context, is one of the most important pillars for the notion that America is a bastion of religious diversity. Yet secularisation theorists can take some comfort in the United States, for it is indeed a case of partial secularisation, particularly over the last fifty years. Historians have uncovered a long history of American secularism, and the notion that the United States has always been a nation comprised wholly of fervent believers is now no longer accepted (Porterfield 2012).[5] Even during the colonial era, when most colonies had an established church and had been populated to some extent by religious dissenters from Europe, religious faith waned as well as waxed (Butler 1990). Today, one of the fastest-growing religious groups in the United States is the 'nones' – that is, those who do not identify with a religion, claim to doubt the legitimacy of organised religion, or profess no faith at all (Hedstrom 2016). Some regions of the United States, particularly the states of the mid-Atlantic and north-east regions, are more similar in their religious complexion to Canada and Western Europe than they are to more outwardly devout regions of their own country,

---

5 For cogent overviews that also examine the inroads secularisation has made in American society, see Hollinger (2001), Smith (2003) and O'Brien (2010).

such as the south and the plains; New England, for example, has very low rates of church attendance. Even in the north-east, however, outright hostility to religion remains rare, and atheism is not growing all that quickly (Jacobsen 2011: 231).

Moreover, as Tracy Fessenden (2007) and David Sehat (2011) have shown, America's vaunted religious tolerance has also been historically exaggerated. Whether religious freedom is a 'myth', as Sehat provocatively puts it, is an open question, but it is clear from this new work that religious pluralism and tolerance were always a work in progress in the United States. Instead, until well into the twentieth century, Americans lived under a government that was ostensibly neutral in religious matters but in fact prioritised one particular faith, Protestantism, at the expense of Catholics, Jews, Mormons and others. Fessenden's work reveals the deep-seated prejudices that favoured mainstream Protestants in literature and culture; Sehat has done the same for legal norms pertaining not only to religion but also to gender and race. Similarly, the legal historian Philip Hamburger has demonstrated that the First Amendment's separation of church and state remained mostly theoretical until the post-1945 era. Until then, none of the three branches of government, including the courts, interpreted the First Amendment's free exercise and separation clauses as prohibiting government activity in religious affairs, or vice versa, including the bestowing of preferential treatment on specific faiths. Again, in Hamburger's account, Protestants emerge as the historic winners in America's competitive religious politics (Hamburger 2002).

The post-war era ushered in something approximating a genuine separation of church and state. Since the *Everson* case of 1947, in which the Supreme Court for the first time in its history invoked Thomas Jefferson's metaphor of a 'wall of separation', religious culture and practice have been steadily, and rigorously, divorced from the institutions of government at the federal, state and local/municipal levels (Viteritti 2007: 120–2). The Supreme Court itself, as an institution, is an exemplar of the decline of Protestant hegemony that has followed in the wake of the separation of church and state: in 1988, the nine justices of the court were all Protestants, but since the appointment of Elena Kagan in 2010, the bench of the highest judicial body in the country has not included a single Protestant (six are Catholic, three are Jewish).[6] This, of course, is a remarkable transformation, virtually unthinkable even a few decades ago. Yet vestiges of Protestant dominance remain. The US Senate, for instance, still has a chaplain, a Seventh-day Adventist named Barry C. Black. Of the sixty-

---

6 See http://www.supremecourt.gov/about/biographies.aspx, accessed 9 May 2017.

two people who have served in the role, all have been Christians; only one has been a Roman Catholic, and none has been Mormon.[7] Similarly, with one exception – the Roman Catholic John F. Kennedy – all US presidents have been Protestants of some variation.

Even if we account for the waning of Protestant dominance, however, we are still left with a Judeo-Christian elite, a phenomenon that is reflected more broadly throughout American culture and society. This should perhaps be expected given the power Christianity has had in the nation since its inception. 'America' – as a concept, an unfolding project, and a specific place that eventually came to be embodied in the nation-state of the United States – was deeply grounded in Christian exceptionalism from the first moments of European colonisation. That social bond proved to be enduring, providing one of the basic constants of American identity (the other being race, which itself became inextricably bound up with Christianity). Indeed, the Christian basis of national identity and social cohesion transcended the colonial, early national, antebellum and modern eras, and remains to the present day. From the conceit that England's American colonies were a New Jerusalem to Ronald Reagan's adoption in 1980 of the Puritan idea of the United States as a 'city on a hill', Christian notions that Americans were a chosen people and that the United States was a blessed land have shaped the very basis of who Americans think they are, and ought to be.[8]

The place of Christianity – or at its broadest, Judeo-Christianity – has been accentuated rather than diminished by immigration. The successive waves of 'new' immigration, from the Russians, Norwegians and Italians of the Gilded Age to the Mexicans, Nigerians and Koreans of the past thirty years, have certainly changed the racial, ethnic and cultural composition of the United States. But they have done surprisingly little to change the religious character of American society. In the 1865–1914 period, many of these immigrants were Christian. With one major exception, discussed below, the others were mostly Buddhists or Confucians from China and Japan, although their numbers were so small that they did little to alter the religious complexion of the United States outside concentrated pockets in California, Washington and the intermountain west.

---

7   The only Catholic chaplain was Charles Constantine Pise in 1832–33: see http://www.senate .gov/artandhistory/history/common/briefing/Senate_Chaplain.htm, accessed 9 May 2017.

8   The literature on the Christian roots of American exceptionalist identity is large, but see, most recently, Guyatt (2007), McKenna (2007) and Preston (2012). On the complicated intertwining of race and religion, see Noll (2008).

Since the 1965 Immigration Act removed racial quotas on new entrants, the United States has seen a dramatic surge in people arriving from the global South. Again, this has transformed the look of American society: millions of people from Latin America, the Caribbean, sub-Saharan Africa, the Middle East, South Asia, Indochina and East Asia have diluted America's previously overwhelmingly European basis. This is a process that has transformed other Western settler societies, too, such as Canada and Australia, but, as always, the scale of developments has been much greater in the United States. Unlike the first era of new immigration, however, these recent new immigrants may have changed the look of the country but they have done little to alter its soul. The vast majority of Latino immigrants, for instance, are Roman Catholic, although a significant minority are Pentecostal (itself originally an American export). Most of the Koreans who have moved to the United States are either Pentecostal or Presbyterian, while most of the arrivals from Vietnam are Catholic (Jenkins 2007: 116–24). The effects on the American religious landscape have been profound – if anything, true diversity is still an objective, or a dream, or a myth, but it is not yet a reality. As the historian Kevin M. Schultz points out, 'most of America's non-Christian population claims to have no religion at all (almost 20 percent of the population)', while all the other religious minorities – Jews, Muslims, Hindus, Buddhists, and all the rest – *all together* total just 5.3 percent of the population' (Schultz 2016: 273, italics in the original). And even most of these 'nones' are what we might call lapsed Christians who are comfortable in a secularised but culturally Christian (especially Protestant) society.

There is also the effect of a feedback loop that reinforces America's position in the world as a bastion of Christianity: most of the new migrants coming to the United States are Christian, but in turn American Christians propel themselves outwards, to the rest of the world, in sending forth ever greater numbers of Christian missionaries to the global South and propagating faiths that began in America and have a decidedly American flavour despite their transplantation and evolution in other countries and on other continents (Noll 2009). Pentecostalism is perhaps the best example of this phenomenon, but other fast-growing and quintessentially American faiths, such as Mormonism, also fall into this category. That is not to say that the United States generates or propagates World Christianities on its own, or even that it is the most important Christian society, just as it is not the creator of world-historical processes such as globalisation. But just as America is probably the most important influence on globalisation, because it is an open society with the world's largest economy, it is also probably one of the most important influences on the shape of World Christianities – although it is by no means the only one.

Overall, then, the United States remains what it has always been: a remarkably Christian nation that nonetheless celebrates the idea of religious diversity. But there have been historical exceptions to this Christian norm. The most notable and influential exceptional group, from the first era of new immigration, was comprised of Jewish immigrants from Romania, Austria-Hungary, and especially Russia. Their numbers were not small – nearly 3 million – and their impact was profound and widespread. Although their numbers were concentrated in major cities in the east, such as New York, their influence was felt nationally rather than simply regionally or locally. Supported by Catholics, as well as by dissident Protestant sects such as Jehovah's Witnesses, Jews successfully challenged the primacy of Protestantism in American public life. By seeking entry into the mainstream of politics, culture and education, Jews forced Protestants to broaden the boundaries of religious acceptability. The result was the invention of the Judeo-Christian tradition; this began in the 1930s, gained traction with revulsion at the Holocaust and the onset of the Cold War against 'godless' Communism, and culminated in Will Herberg's famous 1955 characterisation of American society as 'Protestant-Catholic-Jew' (Herberg 1955).[9] According to this invented tradition, Judaism had a special place in American society because it was the wellspring of Christianity as well as a custodian of much of what constituted Christian theology and culture. In the eyes of many, America went from being a Christian nation to one that was Judeo-Christian. Jews were thus given a privileged place in American society and culture, often excepted from the constraints aimed at other ethnic or religious minorities.[10] To be sure, antisemitism did not disappear, but it did decrease, dramatically, and has remained on the radical fringes of American life for the past half-century (Dinnerstein 1994).

Jews were thus the exception that proves the rule, a religious minority that was accepted largely on Christian terms and for Christian purposes. By enfolding Jews into a new, Judeo-Christian national culture, they helped served a dual purpose of demonstrating America's commitment to religious pluralism while at the same time reinforcing the dominance of its Christian identity.

---

9   On the invention and flourishing of the Judeo-Christian tradition, see Wall (2008) and Schultz (2011). The literature on the acculturation of American Jews is vast, but for an especially cogent analysis see Hollinger (1996).

10   An example was the 1917 Immigration Act, also known as the Asiatic Barred Zone Act, which specifically exempted Jewish immigrants from many of the tests designed to keep Chinese and Japanese out (Gerstle 2001: 96–7).

The Foreign Policy of a Christian Nation

As the continuation of the office of the Senate chaplain demonstrates, religion, and more specifically Christianity, is not completely absent from the affairs of state. Where it remains, it is largely ceremonial (indeed, as in the case of the Senate chaplain), and it remains under strict conditions of substantive non-interference – but remain it does.

Christianity's pride of place lives on in matters of policy as well, and nowhere more strongly than in foreign policy. Thanks to issues such as abortion, same-sex marriage and transgender rights, religion, especially Christianity, has become a lightning rod in domestic politics. Once a unifying force in American public life, faith is now almost as divisive as race. Conservative Christians feel that they are in a war for the soul of America, and on these cultural issues relating to family, sexuality and gender we see the power of both religious culture and secularisation in full flow, albeit from opposite directions. But in foreign policy, Christianity has a freer hand to play a role.

On the one hand, this is surprising. The separation of church and state applies to the conduct of external affairs; the Pentagon and the National Security Council are not exempt from the First Amendment's religious stipulations. And, traditionally, the State Department's foreign service officers have been among the most secular government officials in the executive branch, both in their own personal belief and in how they approach the statecraft of the nation. And yet the conduct of US foreign policy has been consistently supported by invocations of faith – first Christian and then, from the late 1930s onwards, Judeo-Christian. John Adams may have told the Barbary states that his country was not based on religion, but he was an aberration, not the norm. More common have been ringing declarations of American fidelity to faith as well as to religious freedom. And, in fact, such declarations became more frequent over time, beginning with the presidency of Franklin D. Roosevelt but accelerating rapidly after the end of the Second World War when, paradoxically, the Supreme Court began to heighten and harden the wall of separation between church and state. There have been exceptions – most notably John F. Kennedy and Jimmy Carter, who both explicitly removed religion from the formulation and explanation of US foreign policy – but, overall, religion has been an integral component of the ideological foundations of America's approach to the wider world (Preston 2012; 2016).

Today, the separation of church and state is more firmly established than ever before in American public life. Ironically, that very separation now provides a good deal of the fuel that drives the culture wars and bitter partisan politics between liberals and conservatives over abortion and gay rights. But even more ironically, perhaps, religion still seems to be afforded a privileged place in foreign policy. Sometimes this has come in the form of promoting religious liberty, in tandem with the freedom of conscience. American leaders have held the United States up as a model society in which religion itself is protected from government interference or attack, which in turn creates an environment in which all religions can flourish in peace and tolerance. This is a powerful current in the history of American foreign relations, going back in its modern guise to Roosevelt's 1939 State of the Union address:

> Storms from abroad directly challenge three institutions indispensable to Americans, now as always. The first is religion. It is the source of the other two – democracy and international good faith.
>
> Religion, by teaching man his relationship to God, gives the individual a sense of his own dignity and teaches him to respect himself by respecting his neighbors.
>
> ... In a modern civilization, all three – religion, democracy and international good faith – complement and support each other.
>
> Where freedom of religion has been attacked, the attack has come from sources opposed to democracy. Where democracy has been overthrown, the spirit of free worship has disappeared. And where religion and democracy have vanished, good faith and reason in international affairs have given way to strident ambition and brute force.
>
> An ordering of society which relegates religion, democracy and good faith among nations to the background can find no place within it for the ideals of the Prince of Peace. The United States rejects such an ordering, and retains its ancient faith.[11]

Roosevelt's faith-based version of democratic peace theory – that democracies have the interests of the people at heart and therefore do not instigate wars – has held a powerful grip on the American world view ever since. Most presidents have reiterated it in some form. This includes Obama, who made religious liberty the centrepiece of his most famous foreign policy speech, a direct address to the Muslim world in Cairo, in June 2009, as well as of other major speeches in countries with few protections for the freedom of worship,

---

11   Franklin D. Roosevelt, 'Annual Message to Congress', 4 January 1939, *The American Presidency Project*, http://www.presidency.ucsb.edu/ws/index.php?pid=15684, accessed 9 May 2017.

such as China.[12] 'Freedoms of expression and worship, of access to information and political participation, we believe are universal rights,' Obama said to an audience in Shanghai later that year. And while he admitted that the United States had many faults, 'it is that respect for universal rights that guides America's openness to other countries, our respect for different cultures, our commitment to international law, and our faith in the future'.[13]

That commitment was deepened in 1998, when Congress passed the International Religious Freedom Act (IRFA). The end of the Cold War had been caused, in part, by the emergence of a transnational human rights movement in the late 1970s; religious freedom was a significant aspect of that movement as it unfolded across Eastern Europe and the Soviet Union (Snyder 2011). Around the same time, conservative Christians in the United States, represented by an unprecedented ecumenical alliance between Protestants and Catholics, launched a grassroots political movement to steer the Republican Party in a more rightward direction on moral/cultural issues such as abortion and school prayer, and, in the process, to reshape American politics. This movement, subsequently dubbed the 'Religious Right', coalesced in 1980 with the founding of the non-governmental pressure group Moral Majority. It had greater success and political impact than its founders probably ever dreamed, propelling Republicans to the presidency for three consecutive elections (1980, 1984, 1988) and shifting the centre of gravity of American politics to the right (Williams 2010; Dochuk 2011). Bill Clinton, the Democratic president in the 1990s, tacked to the middle by embracing conservative principles such as balanced budgets, welfare reform and a sterner approach to criminal justice (Berman 2001). Buoyed by their success, Evangelical Protestants pushed Congress to pass IRFA over the objections of the Clinton administration. Once implemented, IRFA required the State Department to monitor other countries' records on observing the religious liberties of their own people. Countries that did not respect freedom of religion were named and shamed in an annual State Department report, which meant that violators were not simply subject to ridicule and censure but also to possible US economic and diplomatic sanctions. Some American allies followed suit, either by establishing their own

---

12   Barack Obama, 'Remarks in Cairo', 4 June 2009, *The American Presidency Project*, http://www.presidency.ucsb.edu/ws/index.php?pid=86221&st=&st1=, accessed 9 May 2017. The best investigation and analysis of the Cairo speech is Birdsall (2015).

13   Barack Obama, 'Remarks at a Town Hall Meeting and a Question-and-Answer Session in Shanghai', 16 November 2009, *The American Presidency Project*, http://www.presidency.ucsb.edu/ws/index.php?pid=86909&st=&st1=, accessed 9 May 2017.

monitoring organisations (Canada) or by simply borrowing from and/or reprinting the State Department's report.

This is all pretty general stuff that relates religion, in the abstract, to politics, political thought and international relations. In several instances, however, Christianity and/or the Judeo-Christian tradition have been given centrality in specific US foreign policy goals, often under the guise of general protections for religious liberty and usually by putting the authority of IRFA into motion. A paradox, for the most part unnoticed, characterises a key ideological component of US foreign policy: while it seeks to defend religious liberty, and pluralism, in general, it ends up protecting the religious liberties of certain groups, usually Christian and Jewish, in particular.

Perhaps the most notable example is the case of Vietnam, a one-party communist state that imposed restrictions on the practice of religion after the Socialist Republic was proclaimed in 1976. The United States and Vietnam had a tense and mostly distant relationship following the end of the Second Indochina War in 1975, but relations improved with Vietnam's *doi moi* reforms in the 1980s and the end of the Cold War in 1989–90. The two countries normalised relations in 1995, and that same year Vietnam joined the Association of Southeast Asian Nations (ASEAN), a market-friendly multilateral institution comprised of stalwart US allies such as Thailand and the Philippines. A decade later, in 2006, the United States did not use its effective veto to block Vietnam's application for membership of the World Trade Organization (Bradley 2009: 174–96). However, this cordial new relationship, and the intertwining of Vietnam's economy with those of other Pacific Rim nations, including America, brought with it new US demands, specifically on Vietnam's treatment of religious minorities. The largest of these minorities is Roman Catholic, but Vietnam has been home to a growing number of Protestants as well. Using its economic and political leverage in a world system that Vietnam had just joined, the United States pushed Hanoi to relax its constraints on Vietnamese Christians. In 2007, the imprisonment of a Vietnamese Catholic priest, Father Thadeus Nguyen Van Ly, provided American officials with a focal point around which to rally. Led by Barbara Boxer, a Democrat from California, and with evidence supplied by the State Department's religious liberty monitors, the Senate pushed for greater religious freedom in Vietnam, albeit with limited success. While American officials championed the rights of Cham Muslims and independent Buddhists, the focus fell upon the status of Vietnam's Christians, most notably its Catholics.[14]

---

14   Press release, 'Senator Boxer Reintroduces Vietnam Human Rights Legislation', 22 May

Turmoil in the Middle East has provoked a similar response from Americans. Conflict in the region is not inherently sectarian, but interreligious strife
is one of the most intractable drivers of interstate tension. With its frequent
military interventions, the United States has merely exacerbated these tensions, for example between Shiite and Sunni Muslims. The resulting wars have
created an overlapping series of major humanitarian disasters, not least the
Syrian refugee crisis, to which some Americans have responded in a revealingly
religious way. *Christianity Today*, the authoritative voice of American evangelicalism and one of the largest-circulation religious periodicals in the world,
warned that the destruction of Syria and Iraq's ancient Christian communities
amounted to a form of ethnic cleansing that it called 'religicide'. The Obama
administration, admonished the magazine's correspondent in Jordan, had to
act specifically in favour of Middle Eastern Christians to prevent their total
destruction (Gavlak 2011).[15] Jeff Jacoby, a prominent columnist for the *Boston
Globe*, compared the suffering of Copts and other Christians of the Middle
East to the destruction the Nazis meted out to German Jews during the 1938
Kristallnacht campaign (Jacoby 2013). Senator Rob Portman, a Republican from
Ohio, introduced a Senate resolution calling on the United States to protect
Christian minorities caught in the midst of sectarian conflict (Fitzgerald 2014).
In 2015, running for the Republican presidential nomination, front runner Don-
ald Trump castigated the federal government for allowing Muslim refugees –
whom he said were cultural undesirables and security risks – entry into the
United States at the expense of Syrian Christians. Chris Smith, a Republican
from New Jersey who chaired the powerful House Subcommittee on Global
Human Rights, agreed: 'Clearly, there's a discriminatory process that excludes
Christians,' he said of both the United Nations and the Obama administration.
'It needs to be changed.'[16] Sensing a vote-winning issue, so did Trump's rival
Ted Cruz, a senator from Texas, who said he would enforce a refugee policy
that would ban Muslims while admitting Christians (Chambers and Schwab
2015).

2009, https://www.boxer.senate.gov/?p=release&id=1007, accessed 12 June 2016; '37 US
Senators Urge Vietnam to Free Imprisoned Priest', *New York Times*, 2 July 2009, http://query
.nytimes.com/gst/fullpage.html?res=9E0DE0DB1639F931A35754C0A96F9C8B63,
accessed 9 May 2017. For the most recent official US assessment of religious freedom in
the Socialist Republic of Vietnam, see USCIRF (2015: 126–31).

15   For a milder version that also pointed to 'religicide' in the Middle East but explicitly
rejected the use of armed intervention as a solution, see Reid (2013).

16   Smith quoted in Hattem (2015). See also Lee (2015).

The fact that virtually all of those drawing attention to the welfare of Arab Christians (either in terms of religious liberty or physical protections) and calling for the prioritising of Christian refugees from the Middle East were from the Republican Party is not a coincidence. Religion was once the main unifier in American political culture. It provided a common ground around which Americans could unite, especially against foreign enemies. Over time, the basis of that religious common ground has been broadened, although it also retains what is essentially a Christian core. Initially, until the late nineteenth century, the common ground was Protestantism, and the external threat was to a large extent Catholicism, from the colonial wars against France and its colonies to the Spanish–American War of 1898. During the First World War, the common ground became a more broadly and loosely defined Christianity, as Catholics 'Americanised' and entered the cultural mainstream. The pressures of the Second World War and the Cold War widened the religious basis of American identity further still, from Christian to Judeo-Christian. Against the pagan, idolatrous forces of National Socialism and the godless agenda of international Communism, it no longer mattered to Americans whether they were Methodist or Episcopalian, Protestant or Catholic, or even Christian or Jew.[17]

The world was being divided between believers and non-believers, and as the world's leading power, as well as a highly religious nation, the United States cast itself as the defender of faith. Yet sometimes that mission for all religions against the forces of godlessness could slip into something altogether more parochial – and quintessentially American. Dwight D. Eisenhower put it succinctly during his successful run for the White House in 1952: 'Our form of government has no sense unless it is founded in a deeply felt religious faith, and I don't care what it is.'[18] Eisenhower has been ridiculed ever since for uttering this banality, at once both arrogant and naïve, but his message actually struck a deep chord in the most sacred traditions of American political thought. Much like Franklin Roosevelt's 1939 State of the Union address, Eisenhower meant that democracy had its basis in the freedoms of conscience and religion; without them, together, there was no stopping the power of the state over the minds and actions of its citizens. And to Eisenhower, that was the essence of America's struggle in the world after 1941, and particularly after 1947.

---

17   For the historical background prior to the Cold War, see Preston (2012: 46–70, 109–21, 161–74, 198–290). Excellent treatments of the interfaith character of the Cold War struggle against Communism include Inboden (2008) and Herzog (2011).

18   'President-Elect Says Soviet Demoted Zhukov Because of Their Friendship', *New York Times*, 23 December 1952, p. 16.

According to Frederic Fox, one of Eisenhower's closest White House advisers and himself an ordained Congregationalist minister, the president was now 'not only the Upholder of the Constitution; he is the Defender of the Faith' (Preston 2012: 444).

Just as the two notions of religious pluralism ('and I don't care what it is') and Christian exceptionalism ('Defender of the Faith') rested uneasily in Eisenhower's White House, they lie at the heart of America's religious identity. Despite John Adams' avowal to the Islamic states of Barbary North Africa more than 200 years ago, despite the separation of church and state found in the First Amendment (and case law), and despite the twin pressures of globalisation and immigration that have remade America and remade it again, the United States remains, to a large extent, a Christian nation.

References

Asad, T. (2003) *Formations of the Secular: Christianity, Islam, Modernity*. Stanford CA: Stanford University Press.

Barber, B. (1995) *Jihad vs. McWorld: How the Planet Is Both Falling Apart and Coming Together and What This Means for Democracy*. New York NY: Times Books.

Berger, P. L. (1967) *The Sacred Canopy: Elements of a Sociological Theory of Religion*. Garden City NY: Doubleday.

Berger, P. L. (ed.) (1996) *The Desecularization of the World: Resurgent Religion and World Politics*. Grand Rapids MI: Eerdmans.

Berman, W. (2001) *From the Center to the Edge: The Politics and Policies of the Clinton Presidency*. Lanham MD: Rowman & Littlefield.

Birdsall, J. B. (2015) 'A Great Leap Faithward: Barack Obama and the Rise of Religious Engagement in American Diplomacy'. PhD thesis, University of Cambridge.

Bradley, M. P. (2009) *Vietnam at War*. Oxford: Oxford University Press.

Brown, C. G. (2001) *The Death of Christian Britain: Understanding Secularisation 1800–2000*. London: Routledge.

Bruce, S. (2002) *God is Dead: Secularization in the West*. Oxford: Blackwell.

Bruce, S. (2011) *Secularization: In Defence of an Unfashionable Theory*. Oxford: Oxford University Press.

Butler, J. (1990) *Awash in a Sea of Faith: Christianizing the American People*. Cambridge, MA: Harvard University Press.

Casanova, J. (1994) *Public Religions in the Modern World*. Chicago: University of Chicago Press.

Chambers, F. and N. Schwab (2015) 'Hillary and Trump at War on Syrian Refugees', *Daily Mail*, 17 November, http://www.dailymail.co.uk/news/article-3322101/Ted-Cruz

-introduce-bill-ban-Muslim-Syrian-refugees-America-saying-plans-bring-tens
-thousands-lunacy.html#ixzz47PiiZojN, accessed 9 May 2017.

Clark, J. C. D. (2012) 'Secularization and Modernization: The Failure of a "Grand Narrat-ive"', *The Historical Journal* 55 (1): 161–94.

Dinnerstein, L. (1994) *Antisemitism in America*. New York NY: Oxford University Press.

Dochuk, D. (2011) *From Bible Belt to Sunbelt: Plain-Folk Religion, Grassroots Politics, and the Rise of Evangelical Conservatism*. New York NY: W. W. Norton.

Fessenden, T. (2007) *Culture and Redemption: Religion, the Secular, and American Liter-ature*. Princeton NJ: Princeton University Press.

Findlay, R. and K. H. O'Rourke (2007) *Power and Plenty: Trade, War, and the World Economy in the Second Millennium*. Princeton NJ: Princeton University Press.

Finke, R. and R. Stark (2005) *The Churching of America, 1776–2005: Winners and Losers in Our Religious Economy*. New Brunswick NJ: Rutgers University Press.

Fitzgerald, S. (2014) 'Sen. Rob Portman: Obama Must Protect Christians in Iraq', *Newsmax*, 30 July, http://www.newsmax.com/Newsfront/Iraq-Christians-Persecution -SenRob-Portman/2014/07/30/id/585796/, accessed 9 May 2017.

Gavlak, D. (2011) '"Religicide" in Iraq', *Christianity Today*, 16 February, http://www .christianitytoday.com/ct/2011/february/religicide.html, accessed 9 May 2017.

Gerstle, G. (2001) *American Crucible: Race and Nation in the Twentieth Century*. Princeton NJ: Princeton University Press.

Guyatt, N. (2007) *Providence and the Invention of the United States, 1607–1876*. Cambridge: Cambridge University Press.

Hamburger, P. (2002) *Separation of Church and State*. Cambridge MA: Harvard University Press.

Handy, R. T. (1960) 'The American Religious Depression, 1925–1935', *Church History* 29 (1): 3–16.

Hatch, N. O. (1989) *The Democratization of American Christianity*. New Haven CT: Yale University Press.

Hattem, J. (2015) 'UN: Critics Wrong on Christian Syrian Refugees', *The Hill*, 20 December, http://thehill.com/policy/national-security/263795-un-critics-wrong-on -christian-syrian-refugees, accessed 9 May 2017.

Hedstrom, M. S. (2016) 'Rise of the Nones' in M. A. Sutton and D. Dochuk (eds), *Faith in the New Millennium: The Future of Religion and American Politics*. New York NY: Oxford University Press.

Herberg, W. (1955) *Protestant, Catholic, Jew: An Essay in American Religious Sociology*. Garden City NY: Doubleday.

Herzog, J. P. (2011) *The Spiritual-Industrial Complex: America's Religious Battle against Communism in the Early Cold War*. New York NY: Oxford University Press.

Hollinger, D. A. (1996) *Science, Jews, and Secular Culture: Studies in Mid-Twentieth-Century American Intellectual History*. Princeton NJ: Princeton University Press.

Hollinger, D. A. (2001) 'The "Secularization" Question and the United States in the Twentieth Century', *Church History* 70 (1): 132–43.

Inboden, W. (2008) *Religion and American Foreign Policy, 1945–1960: The Soul of Containment*. Cambridge: Cambridge University Press.

Jacobsen, D. (2011) *The World's Christians: Who They Are, Where They Are, and How They Got There*. Oxford: Wiley-Blackwell.

Jacoby, J. (2013) 'Yesterday's Atrocities Are Happening Again', *Boston Globe*, 28 August, http://www.bostonglobe.com/opinion/2013/08/28/yesterday-atrocities-are -happening-again-yesterday-atrocities-are-happening-again/ pJyAblR5sBrNBW77ZxHuiL/story.html, accessed 9 May 2017.

Jenkins, P. (2007) *The Next Christendom: The Coming of Global Christianity*. Revised edition. Oxford: Oxford University Press.

Lee, M. (2015) 'Why Are There Only 53 Christians Among America's 2,184 Syrian Refugees?', *Christianity Today*, 20 November, http://www.christianitytoday.com/ct/2015/ november-web-only/why-only-53-christians-2184-syrian-refugees-resettlement .html, accessed 9 May 2017.

Maier, C. S. (2006) *Among Empires: American Ascendancy and its Predecessors*. Cambridge MA: Harvard University Press.

Mann, M. (2013) *The Sources of Social Power. Volume 4: Globalizations, 1945–2011*. Cambridge: Cambridge University Press.

McKenna, G. (2007) *The Puritan Origins of American Patriotism*. New Haven CT: Yale University Press.

Noll, M. A. (2008) *God and Race in American Politics: A Short History*. Princeton NJ: Princeton University Press.

Noll, M. A. (2009) *The New Shape of World Christianity: How American Experience Reflects Global Faith*. Downers Grove IL: IVP Academic.

O'Brien, M. (2010) 'The American Experience of Secularisation' in I. Katznelson and G. Stedman Jones (eds), *Religion and the Political Imagination*. Cambridge: Cambridge University Press.

Porterfield, A. (2012) *Conceived in Doubt: Religion and Politics in the New American Nation*. Chicago IL: University of Chicago Press.

Preston, A. (2012) *Sword of the Spirit, Shield of Faith: Religion in American War and Diplomacy*. New York NY: Alfred A. Knopf.

Preston, A. (2016) 'America's World Mission in the Age of Obama' in M. A. Sutton and D. Dochuk (eds), *Faith in the New Millennium: The Future of Religion and American Politics*. New York NY: Oxford University Press.

Reid Jr., C. J. (2013) 'War Begets War, Violence Begets Violence', *Huffington Post*, 4 September, http://www.huffingtonpost.com/charles-j-reid-jr/war-begets-war-violence -b_b_3860641.html, accessed 9 May 2017.

Schultz, K. M. (2011) *Tri-Faith America: How Catholics and Jews Held Postwar America to its Protestant Promise*. New York NY: Oxford University Press.

Schultz, K. M. (2016) 'The Blessings of American Religious Pluralism and Those Who Rail Against It' in M. A. Sutton and D. Dochuk (eds), *Faith in the New Millennium: The Future of Religion and American Politics*. New York NY: Oxford University Press.

Sehat, D. (2011) *The Myth of American Religious Freedom*. New York NY: Oxford University Press.

Smith, C. (ed.) (2003) *The Secular Revolution: Power, Interests, and Conflict in the Secularization of American Public Life*. Berkeley CA: University of California Press.

Snyder, S. B. (2011) *Human Rights Activism and the End of the Cold War: A Transnational History of the Helsinki Network*. Cambridge: Cambridge University Press.

USCIRF (2015) *2015 Annual Report*. Washington DC: United States Commission on International Religious Freedom (USCIRF).

Viteritti, J. P. (2007) *The Last Freedom: Religion from the Public School to the Public Square*. Princeton NJ: Princeton University Press.

Wagnleitner, R. (1994) *Coca-Colonization and the Cold War: The Cultural Mission of the United States in Austria After the Second World War*. Chapel Hill NC: University of North Carolina Press.

Wall, W. L. (2008) *Inventing the 'American Way': The Politics of Consensus from the New Deal to the Civil Rights Movement*. New York NY: Oxford University Press.

Williams, D. K. (2010) *God's Own Party: The Making of the Christian Right*. New York NY: Oxford University Press.

CHAPTER 11

The Death Throes of Indigenous Christians in the Middle East: Assyrians Living under the Islamic State

Naures Atto

Christianity emerged in the Middle East, became a majority religion, and then expanded into various geographical directions. Although the faith suffered a decline under Arab Muslim rule from the eleventh century, the region nonetheless remained an important spiritual centre for Christianity until about the thirteenth century. Today, however, local Christians express fear about the end of their existence in the region, their ancestral home. This fear is also shared by scholars and experts, who ask whether Christianity has a future in the Middle East (Jenkins 2014; Tamcke 2016). In this way, the narrative of the steady decline of Christianity in the Middle East serves as a powerful counterweight to the more frequently told triumphalist story of the explosive worldwide growth of Christianity in recent decades (Jenkins 2011).

In the collective memory of Assyrians,[1] their traumatic past – transmitted through generations – continues to play a central role in their life (Atto 2017). One could say that each generation has experienced a form of continued dispossession, and these experiences have accumulated in the inherited memory of individuals. For example, together with Armenians and Greeks, Assyrians worldwide began 2014 with preparations for the commemoration of the centenary of the 1915 genocide of Christians in Ottoman Turkey. Yet in 2014 they were confronted with yet another genocide – another systematic and intentional attempt to destroy their people, but one occurring in the present. Today, Christian communities in the Middle East are targeted by the Islamic State (IS) and other radical militant Islamist groups. Areas occupied by IS in Syria and Iraq have now been entirely cleansed of Christians, while those Christians living in Lebanon and Turkey along the border with Syria and Iraq follow unfolding developments with great fear. Hundreds of thousands of people have been displaced from what they consider to be their homeland.[2] Until recently,

---

1 Assyrians is used here as a cross-denominational name for the various Oriental churches in the Syriac tradition; it can be used synonymously with Syriacs and Arameans.

2 Assyrians do not define their homeland in terms of the modern national borders of the

the 1915 genocide may have been experienced as an abstract historical event by the younger generations of Assyrians who were born in the Western diaspora. However, witnessing what is happening to their people now, Assyrians invoke deep-rooted inherited memories of the 1915 genocide. The current genocide by IS has served to increase their awareness of both a persecuted past and an unknown future, both in the Middle East and in the diaspora.

This chapter examines the predicament of Christians in the Middle East, focusing specifically on the Assyrian community, which has been forcibly displaced in extensive patterns of migration and asylum seeking. It discusses how members of the world's first Christian communities feel that their existence is threatened in their historical homeland and how they deal with the dilemma of choosing whether to leave or to stay in the region in an attempt to save not only their individual lives but also their existence as a people with historical roots in the Middle East. After a short account of the position of Christians in the modern history of Turkey, Syria and Iraq, the chapter discusses the consequences of the rise of IS for local Christians in Syria and Iraq. The last part of the chapter addresses some popular and prevalent debates surrounding Christians' strategies for survival. This chapter is based on an analysis of newspaper articles and television reports and on individual interviews conducted by myself, either by telephone or during fieldwork conducted up to February 2017. I was born into the group under study and raised in a European diaspora context as the child of refugees, and so I am undoubtedly writing from an engaged insider's perspective. This closeness has required a reflexive approach regarding both my own position and the media sources studied, especially those generated by protagonists battling for survival.

Post-1915: Persecution Continues

As traumatised survivors of a genocide who had lost more than half the population, in the period after the First World War, Assyrians' most urgent need was sheer physical survival. Their property and their cultural heritage had been destroyed or re-appropriated and they consequently became increasingly less visible in society (Gaunt et al. 2017). Characteristic of the attitude of survivors in the following decades has been their attempt to remain anonymous and live

---

Middle East, which were decided after the collapse of the Ottoman Empire, but rather in terms of the historical roots of their people in the whole Syro-Mesopotamian region and beyond, while simultaneously stressing northern Mesopotamia to be the centre of their homeland today (Atto forthcoming).

a more isolated life; these are classic survival mechanisms of a minority living with a prevalent mistrust of the majority society. Their religious leaders have often tried to convince community members to obey the ruling government or regime, which has often meant succumbing to the assimilation policies of the Turkification, Arabisation or, more recently, Kurdification of their collective identity. These threats to their survival in Muslim majority societies have often made Assyrians living in these countries more conscious of their Christian identity and determined to self-consciously maintain it. In practice, this has often meant explicitly supporting dictatorial regimes in return for being tolerated as Christians. This can be seen as a continuation of their position as *millet* (a religious community) in the Ottoman Empire and under earlier Arab Muslim rulers, when Christians had to pay the *jizya* tax and live according to certain regulations in exchange for 'protection' (or toleration), which meant that they lived as second- or third-class loyal citizens.

From the late nineteenth century onwards, Assyrian families also emigrated to North America in search of safety and survival. It is common for members of successive generations to have been born in different countries: for example, this is the case for the family of Samer Kefargis, an Assyrian from the village of Tel Goran on the Khabur River in Syria, who escaped IS (Henk and Susebach 2016). His grandfather was born in the Ottoman Empire, his father in today's Iraq, he himself in Syria – and now he has fled to Australia, where the next generation will be born. Samer says: 'You can't get farther away than this. With the next expulsion we will have to go to the moon.' Assyrians often lament the number of times they have had to flee and start life afresh elsewhere.

Until the 1960s, the migration of Assyrians from the Middle East was mostly directed towards North and South America. This changed in the 1960s when the first Assyrians made use of the *Gastarbeiter* system[3] to settle in Germany, and in 1967 the first group of Assyrians from Lebanon was invited to settle in Sweden as stateless refugees (Atto 2011). Subsequently, more than 300,000 Assyrians settled in Europe, arriving from Turkey, Syria, Lebanon, Iraq and Iran. Hundreds of thousands more went to Australia and America. They chose to emigrate to Western countries that they considered 'Christian' and where they expected to be welcomed with open arms as co-religionists, based on their assumption that religion in the West had the same role in society as in the Middle East. However, after their resettlement they came to understand that

---

3   This was a 1961 bilateral agreement between Germany and Turkey that made it possible for individuals with Turkish citizenship to work temporarily in Germany with the expectation that they would return home if they became unemployed.

religion in the West played a profoundly different role, and that policymakers in particular did not favour them more than any other immigrant group just because they were Christians. Also, in Europe their oppression in the Middle East was not recognised in juridical terms; this was reflected in the fact that only a very few received political refugee status and most were allowed to stay for 'humanitarian reasons' (Atto 2011). All this has resulted in a situation in which the majority of Assyrians have established themselves in the West, while only a tiny minority remain in the Middle East.

Christians as Scapegoats in Society

As one of the most vulnerable groups in society, any situation of crisis in the Middle East has had dire consequences for the local Christians. To mention only a few recent examples, the situation of Christians deteriorated drastically after the Gulf and Iraq wars (1991 and 2003), the war in Syria (since 2011), and especially the rise of IS. Even before the expansion of IS, the wars in Iraq and Syria had driven out many Christians from their homes, through either direct or indirect threats and fear. After the American invasion of Iraq in 2003, local Christians began to be targeted, being blamed in particular for aiding the Americans. On the Sunday of 1 August 2004, six churches were simultaneously bombed in Baghdad and Mosul, along with nearly thirty other churches throughout the country. In Iraq alone, between June 2004 and August 2013, 118 churches were bombed or attacked (Knights of Columbus 2016: 194–9). While the Christian population in Iraq was estimated at 1.4 million in 2003, in 2015 this figure had dropped to 275,000 (ibid.: 223). In Syria, the number of Christians decreased dramatically from 1.5 million in 2011 to 500,000 in 2016.

The following sections focus on three geographical areas where Assyrians fell victim to IS and/or to majority groups involved in the ongoing wars in the Middle East.

Mosul and Nineveh Plain

In June 2014, the local Christians in the Nineveh Plain and Mosul, as well as newly settled refugees, were overwhelmed by the destructive occupation of the city of Mosul. The Iraqi army abandoned its positions as soon as IS overran the city, and, on 29 June 2014, Abu Bakr al-Baghdadi declared the existence of a caliphate, an Islamic state, with himself as the reigning caliph. The emergence and development of IS are often explained in relation to the US invasion of Iraq in 2003 and the marginalisation of Sunnis from power, which in turn led to the radicalisation of this group as well as to the development of a policy vacuum in which IS seized the chance to flourish (Haykel 2015: USCIRF 2015). While the initial aims of IS were to topple the regimes in Iraq and Syria, its ultimate goals became world conquest and the establishment of Islamic rule throughout the globe (Haykel 2015).

Ordinary people were not ready for the rapid military successes of IS; nor were they prepared to take the speedy action needed to save their lives and belongings. The manner in which people fell victim to jihadi warfare depended mostly on their religious affiliation and their interpretation of Islam. In the newly conquered areas, IS forced all people to live under the rule of a Salafist interpretation of Islamic law dating to the seventh century. The jihadists painted the Arabic letter 'N' for *Nasrani* (Christian) in red paint on Christians' homes and other property and announced on 14 July 2014, in mosques and on the radio in Mosul, that if Christians wanted to continue their life in the caliphate they would have to convert to Islam, pay the special *jizya* tax (as instructed in the Qur'an: Chapter 9, 'al-Tawba', verse 29) and consider themselves subdued.[4] Otherwise, they should leave the area within five days – by 19 July at noon – or else be killed by the sword.[5]

Following this declaration, Christians fled en masse with nothing more than their clothes to the Assyrian villages of the Nineveh Plain (north-east of Mosul), later spreading further into the Kurdish-governed area of northern Iraq, finding shelter in churches, community centres and unoccupied buildings, or living outside until tents could be provided. They lost everything in a matter of days, or, in some cases, hours. Patriarch Louis Sako of the Chaldean Church reminded the world in an interview: 'For the first time in the history of Iraq, Mosul is now empty of Christians'.[6] The 30,000 Assyrians still living in Mosul after the American invasion of 2003 were expelled; this was the first time in recorded Christian history that no masses were held in the city.

After Mosul, IS also captured Qaraqosh, the largest Christian city in Iraq, on 6 August 2014, followed by other towns and villages on the Nineveh Plain. The Kurdish *Peshmerga*, who were in charge of defending Qaraqosh and the Nineveh Plain, had retreated, as the Iraqi army had done earlier in Mosul. Expelled Christians from Mosul were followed by about 200,000 more Chris-

---

4   In reality, IS was not interested in the *jizya* but aimed to eliminate non-Muslims (see Knights of Columbus 2016: 12–13; also Nicholson 2016: 17–21).

5   'ISIS Statement Ordering Christians to Convert or Die', Assyrian International News Agency (AINA), 20 July 2014, http://www.aina.org/news/20140720051600.htm, accessed 8 March 2016.

6   'Convert, Pay or Die: Iraqi Christians Flee Mosul after Islamic State Ultimatum', Russia Today (RT), 19 July 2014, https://www.rt.com/news/174104-iraqi-christians-isis-ultimatum/, accessed 8 March 2016.

tians from Qaraqosh and the villages of the Nineveh Plain east and north of Mosul in early August. They were unable to defend themselves as they were not allowed to establish their own militias; on 14 July 2014, the inhabitants of Qaraqosh (Baghdeda), Karamles and Bertella (all home to Christians) had been requested by the security committee in al-Hamdaniyya (Qaraqosh/Baghdeda) to surrender their weapons.[7] If they had failed to co-operate, they would have been 'subjected to the harshest disciplinary actions'. Their disarmament happened only weeks before IS attacked them.

Assyrians worldwide received this news with great sadness and consternation. On social media, the Arabic letter 'N' became the profile of many Facebook users and was also used as a hashtag on Twitter to express solidarity with the expelled Christians. In further acts of solidarity with their people in the Middle East, Assyrians organised demonstrations and flash mobs in order to call the international community's attention to the acts of IS. And to meet the refugees' immediate needs after fleeing, existing[8] and newly established[9] Assyrian foundations in the diaspora initiated humanitarian actions such as sending clothes, food and medical aid to the displaced refugees. But solidarity and material help did not change the bitter reality of the victims. Displaced individuals interviewed six weeks after they were expelled from their homes expressed anger and disbelief about what had befallen them as the indigenous population of Mosul. An expelled woman said:

> Yes, they expelled us from our original land, from our original land! They told us: 'Go away! This is not your land. Go to your Christian people and to your pastors. Let them feed you, shelter you and give you homes.' He said to me and my sister: 'Bring your money and give it to us. If not, each one of you will be shot in the head' ... Why this injustice? What have we done to you? What have all these Christians done? ... This is just like the Lord Jesus said: 'I send you out as sheep in the midst of wolves.'[10]

---

7   'ISIS Orders All Former Church Guards to Surrender their Weapons', AINA, 14 August 2014, http://www.aina.org/news/20140814133038.htm, accessed 6 March 2016.

8   For example, Christian Aid Program Northern Iraq (CAPNI, http://www.capni-iraq.org/index.php/en/), Hatune Foundation (http://hatunefoundation.com/international/), Assyrier Utan Gränser (http://assyrierutangranser.se) and Assyrian Aid Society of American (http://www.assyrianaid.org; all accessed 18 March 2016).

9   Among them, A Demand For Action (http://www.ademandforaction.com), We Are Christians (http://wearechristians.de/we-are-n/) and Save our Souls (https://www.facebook.com/1915.de/info/?tab=page_info; all accessed 18 March 2016).

10   Interviews with a displaced family from Mosul on Ishtar TV, 23 April 2014, https://www.youtube.com/watch?v=QZl5wVbFjHM, accessed 10 January 2016.

This reference to Jesus's words is very common among Christians in the Middle East when discussing their socio-political situation. This expresses their vulnerability within the socio-political context of the Middle East and simultaneously emphasises their faith as followers of Jesus.

Villages on the Khabur River

IS also targeted thirty-five Assyrian villages along the Khabur River in Syria that had been built by Assyrians who originated from the Hakkari mountains in south-east Turkey, survivors of the 1915 genocide. First they had fled to Iraq, but in August 1933, a year after the British handed over rule to the Iraqis, 600 Assyrians were massacred and about sixty Assyrian villages north of Mosul were pillaged by the Iraqi army in what has become known as the Simele massacre (Joseph 2000: 196–7).[11] This massacre caused many Assyrians to leave Iraq and establish settlements for the victims along the Khabur River in French mandated Syria. Eight decades after their arrival, IS overran their villages in February 2015. IS forces killed nine Assyrians who were defending their villages and took 253 people hostage. Three of the abducted men were killed; their deaths were recorded on a video that was distributed to the media on 23 September 2015.[12] In the same video, the jihadists requested ransom money for the release of the remaining hostages. Since then, most of the Khabur hostages have been released in exchange for millions of dollars collected by the Assyrian community worldwide.

In a long article, Henk and Susebach (2016), journalists of the German magazine *Der Zeit*, followed the routes and the stories of the people who managed to flee IS from the village of Tel Goran on the Khabur River, illustrating what the IS jihadist war has meant for a community in one small village, for Christianity in the region, and for their future as a people. The residents of Tel Goran can now be found in the four corners of the globe. This dispersion is representative of these people's situation and will therefore have long-term effects on their future.

---

11   Other Assyrian sources mention 3,000 victims of the Simele massacre. The lawyer Raphael Lemkin coined the term 'genocide' and initiated the Genocide Convention after he became aware of the Christian genocide in 1915 and the Simele massacre in 1933.

12   'ISIS Execute Three Assyrians in Syria', AINA, 8 October 2015, http://www.aina.org/news/20151008022445.htm, accessed 14 March 2016.

Kamishli

Another location where Christians have been specifically targeted is the city of Kamishli in the al-Hasakah province of northern Syria. The people here had not felt the IS threat as much as in other areas of the war-torn country, largely because, alongside the Syrian army, the Kurdish YPG (People's Protection Units) have been defending the area in great numbers with the aim of forming a Kurdish autonomous region.

After the First World War, Assyrians in Turkey who had survived the 1915 genocide crossed the border into Syria to live under the mandate of the French, as a Christian power. Kamishli was then a desert-like area. Assyrians consider themselves to be the founders of Kamishli and to have shaped its twentieth-century history. Although many had already emigrated before the war started in 2011, of the approximately 35,000 remaining Assyrians in Kamishli before the war, only 7,000 were still living there at the beginning of 2016, of whom about 80 per cent were over the age of fifty. For the remaining Christians in this city, fear for their lives increased on the evening of 30 December 2015 when three bombs exploded at the same time in the centre of their neighbourhood, Al Wusta, where 90 per cent of the inhabitants are Christians of different denominations. The explosions caused sixteen deaths and left more than thirty badly injured. The media reported IS responsibility, but the local Christians themselves doubted this and several speculations about other motives and possible scenarios began to circulate. Two more bombs exploded in the same neighbourhood on 12 January 2016 and killed another four Christians. On 7 March 2016, another bomb exploded outside the Mor Gabriel school, a few minutes before 300 Christian pupils were about to leave for home.[13] Although the blast caused injuries to only five people, fear within the community increased. Souleman Youssef, who was interviewed by Assyria TV, said that these events should be understood in the context of the earlier explosions – as a message to his people 'that you should leave this place'. He also asked why their (Christian) neighbourhood and not the other neighbourhoods of Kamishli were under attack, and expressed his alarm that not one ambulance arrived after any of the explosions in the Al Wusta area. The crimes committed by IS against religious minorities in Iraq and Syria have been recognised as an act of genocide by different international institutions and governments, among them the US Government,[14] US House of Representatives

13   Interview with an inhabitant of Kamishli: 'Souleman Youssef about Latest Explosion in Qamishli', Assyria TV, 7 March 2016, http://www.assyriatv.org/, accessed 14 March 2016.

14   'John Kerry: ISIS Responsible for Genocide', CNN Politics, 17 March 2016, http://edition.cnn.com/2016/03/17/politics/us-iraq-syria-genocide/index.html, accessed 17 March 2016.

(Boorstein 2016) and the European Parliament.[15] So far, no specific action has been taken regarding any of the victim groups.[16]

The Future

Assyrians greeted the rise of IS with bitter surprise. Considering themselves a 'stateless people', Assyrians in the homeland and in the diaspora have provided immediate help to the displaced, a population that is exhausted, terrified and concerned about its future existence. The forcibly displaced Assyrians on the Nineveh Plain 'fear that they will never return to their ancestral lands, and that the Christian presence in the region might disappear' (Windsor 2015a). In Tur Abdin in south-eastern Turkey, the local Christians saw the latest developments as part of a seamless history of persecution since 1915, fearing that oppression by IS would become the last *Sayfo* (literally 'Sword') genocide – the one that brings to an end 2,000 years of Christianity in the region.[17] In a 2013 documentary, Chaldean Patriarch Louis Sako answered the reporter's question 'Do you see any future in Iraq' with: 'I am very afraid about the future; it is not clear.' Below, I discuss several options open to Assyrians regarding their struggle for continued existence in the Middle East.

Stay and Resist

A small number of people, whom I shall dub the idealists, plan to stay and resist IS's efforts to erase them. This stance is also shared by their religious leaders, who invoke potent discourses of the ancient indigeneity of Christianity in the Middle East. They back this up by appealing to the international community, and especially to Christians worldwide, to aid them with both humanitarian and political support in order to achieve their aim. For example, Assyrian organisations have lobbied their governments in the West to recognise IS acts as

---

15 'European Parliament Resolution of 4 February 2016 on the Systematic Mass Murder of Religious Minorities by the So-called "ISIS/Daesh" (2016/2529(RSP))', 4 February 2016, http://www.europarl.europa.eu/sides/getDoc.do?type=TA&reference=P8-TA-2016-0051& language=EN, accessed 6 February 2016.

16 Ewelina Ochab, author of *Never Again* (2016), has documented the ongoing genocide of Christians and other religious minorities in Syria and Iraq and highlights the international community's failure to end the carnage. The book provides a blueprint for adapting international laws on genocide to make them an adequate response to terrorist groups such as ISIS.

17 Communication with people in Tur Abdin, 2015.

'genocide' and to empower their people politically to sustain themselves in their homeland.[18] They prefer to risk being attacked while defending their homeland than leave without having tried to defend it. Emarceen Youssef, a young victim of the Kamishli bomb blast of 30 December 2015, said in an interview four days after he lost one of his legs that 'the message of the perpetrators … is very clear: they want us to leave so they can take over our land and property. But what has happened has strengthened us and not weakened us.'[19] Emarceen's father, Souleman Youssef, expressed his opinion in the same interview:

> [O]ur people in Kamishli were those who built and developed Kamishli after a genocide [1915 in Ottoman Turkey] … We as a people should be proud that these survivors did not stay in Turkey to only mourn their deaths but they came and built up Kamishli together with the Armenian survivors … and we should do the same [now]; we should stay and continue developing it. And keep hope for the future … and not only cry.

Mr Youssef was well aware that his message was being heard by community members worldwide, from whom he received many telephone calls after the bomb blasts, and explained that 'their reaction showed that they are with us here in the homeland'. Referring to the strength of earlier ancestral genocide survivors and the possibility of yet again establishing a new life in a desert-like place, he was consciously communicating an inspiring message of hope. Such messages are also posted on Facebook by displaced Assyrians from their places of refuge, sometimes only a few kilometres away from IS; they make music and joyously celebrate their secular and Christian holidays and develop educational projects for displaced children and students.[20]

---

18   One such initiative is the letter sent on behalf of several organisations to United States Secretary of State John Kerry in support of the Department of State's investigation into whether IS's treatment of Assyrian Christians in Syria and Iraq can be considered 'genocide' (Nicholson 2016).

19   'Interview with Emarceen Youssef and his Father Souleman Youssef', Assyria TV, 3 January 2016, http://www.assyriatv.org/page/3/, accessed 4 January 2016.

20   See, for example, a picture posted by Shlama Foundation (https://www.facebook.com/shlamafoundation/posts/867327006711726:0, accessed 19 March 2016) and the video of Assyrians singing a secular song about Alqosh during Palm Sunday celebrations in Alqosh in 2016, which was shared more than 800 times within two days (https://www.facebook.com/page.khoranat.alqosh/videos/1721931478028634/?pnref=story, accessed 21 March 2016). See Etuti.org for educational projects by the Etuti Institute (http://www.etuti.org/education/, accessed 30 January 2017).

Christian leaders have also strongly supported their members in attempts to stay in the region by visiting them at times of urgent crisis, by addressing their problems in the media, and by offering financial help. Patriarch Ephrem II declared in his Christmas message that 'despite the deaths and the killings which are taking place everywhere we should keep our faith and hope in the ancestral homeland'.[21] A week later, in his statement after the December Kamishli bomb blasts, he specifically addressed his church members in the city:

> You refused humiliation and submission [conversion to Islam] and you did not accept a substitute for your land [emigration]. We believe that these terrorist attacks will not separate you from your land; these explosions, however violent and bloody they may be, will not uproot you from your country.[22]

Before IS attacked in 2013, Patriarch Louis Sako of the Chaldean Church answered a reporter's question about why people stayed: 'I think we should be courageous to persist, to persevere ... to give up our life, to be martyred. We are ready.'[23] Interviewed three years later, he remained steadfast, avowing that 'nothing can ever expel Christianity from the Middle East, despite all the difficulties, as long as there are Christians determined to stay in the land of their birth, proud of their identity and their mission in this part of the world'.[24]

While enduring the challenges of survival in the Middle East, many Christians in the region, including their religious leaders, express their disappointment with Western governments that have not supported them politically in their attempts to stay in their homeland. A frequent criticism made by Assyrians is that political debates about the Middle East typically ignore Christians. They view mainstream Western politicians as being 'politically correct' by avoiding the use of religious categories, as is considered befitting to a modern

---

21   'Christmas Message: H. H. Patriarch Ephrem II', Assyria TV, 23 December 2015, http://www.assyriatv.org/page/3/, accessed 6 January 2016.

22   'Statement Issued by Syriac Orthodox Patriarchate of Antioch and All the East', Damascus, 31 December 2015, http://syriacpatriarchate.org/wp-content/uploads/2015/12/Qamishly.jpg, accessed 22 February 2016.

23   'Iraqi Christians in Peril: Faith Matters', 5 February 2013, https://www.youtube.com/watch?v=YdWMIZU4gsA, accessed 3 May 2017.

24   'Chaldean Patriarch: No "Christian Militia" to Free Land Occupied by Jihadists', Official Vatican Network, 2016, http://www.news.va/en/news/asiairaq-chaldean-patriarch-no-christian-militia-t, accessed 15 March 2016.

secular state. Moreover, Assyrians observe that, when Western politicians do intervene in the Middle East for the sake of their own geo-political interests, they avoid speaking about persecuted Christians, even if they are indeed persecuted because of their religion.[25] The expelled Archbishop of Mosul lamented in an interview:

> The people are just being thrown out, as if they do not belong anywhere. There is no more humanity in this world ... And all those [countries] who say they have human rights, they are all liars! ... They were all watching what was happening to this people for the last three months and no one came to help ... we are screaming that the people are lying in the streets, help us before winter and rain arrive.[26]

Christians in the Middle East believe that the unpopularity of the West in the region has a negative impact on them as local Christians because they are perceived by Muslims to be co-religionists with Christians in the West. In such a context, local Christians become easy targets of angered local Muslim groups. This is one of the reasons why Patriarch Louis Sako of the Chaldean Church reacted negatively to US President Donald Trump's policy to ban nationals of seven Muslim-majority countries from entering the United States for at least ninety days.[27] He also criticised the leeway given to the Department of Homeland Security to prioritise refugee claims 'on the basis of religious persecution' as long as the person applying for refugee status is an adherent of 'a minority religion in the individual's country of nationality' (Sanchez and Park 2017).[28] With this stand, the Patriarch sides with the local populations of the Middle East, irrespective of their religious affiliation, in order not to attract negative attention from his Muslim neighbours. Yet not all agree with

---

25   'Iraq Prelate Backs Preference for Minority Refugees Fleeing Genocide', Crux, 2 February 2017, https://cruxnow.com/interviews/2017/02/02/iraq-prelate-backs-preference-minority-refugees-fleeing-genocide/, accessed 7 February 2017.

26   'Bishop of Mosul Is Weeping', Suroyo TV, 3 November 2014, https://www.youtube.com/watch?v=ljAo8GZ615g, accessed 15 December 2015.

27   'Full Text of Trump's Executive Order on 7-Nation Ban, Refugee Suspension', CNN Politics, 28 January 2017, http://edition.cnn.com/2017/01/28/politics/text-of-trump-executive-order-nation-ban-refugees/index.html?sr=fbCNN012917text-of-trump-executive-order-nation-ban-refugees1220AMVODtopLink&linkId=33891087, accessed 2 February 2017.

28   See also 'Irak: US-Flüchtlingspolitik ist "Falle für die Christen"', Radio Vatican, 30 January 2017, http://de.radiovaticana.va/news/2017/01/30/irak_us-flüchtlingspolitik_ist_„falle_für_die_christen"/1289254, accessed 31 January 2017.

the Patriarch: different opinions have been voiced by the Chaldean Archbishop Bashar Matti Warda in Erbil[29] and Samuel Tadros (2017), who both argue in favour of Christian minorities being given special priority as migrants.

Unity in Defence

On several occasions, Christian leaders have expressed the view that they need to unite as Christians in order to increase their chances of survival in the Middle East. In August 2014, Patriarch Louis Sako of the Chaldean Church (visiting the region during the historical meeting of the Five Patriarchs) addressed displaced community members in northern Iraq:

> Today, what is required for us is that wherever we are we must have one voice, one stand, one feeling. In the end we are one church. As much as we are one church we will be a stronger church and we will have a future.
>
> BETBASOO 2014

The Patriarchs also met with President Obama in the United States, with the aim of raising awareness of the dangers Christian communities are facing in the Middle East (Harmon 2014). A symbolic show of unity took place after the Kamishli bomb blasts in December 2015: the seven Christian denominations in Kamishli organised one service for all the victims and buried them in a single grave.

Emigration

The mass emigration of Assyrians is discussed less openly than their persecution on their media platforms. Often, emigration is debated in relation to other alternatives, but always with an undertone of fear of the impending worst-case scenario. While Patriarch Ephrem II of the Syriac Orthodox Church has shown great support for attempts to remain in the homeland, in his latest Patriarchal Encyclical he discussed leaving as a realistic and viable alternative to staying:

> Though we urge all to hold firm to the land of our forefathers, under such persecution, we have the duty to help them [refugees] ... emigration is an action expressing the refusal of submission and giving up to the

---

29   'Iraq Prelate Backs Preference for Minority Refugees Fleeing Genocide', Crux, 2 February 2017, https://cruxnow.com/interviews/2017/02/02/iraq-prelate-backs-preference -minority-refugees-fleeing-genocide/, accessed 7 February 2017.

conditions imposed on us. It reflects the desire to lead a dignified life, preserve the basic elements of life and keep one's rights and freedoms.[30]

Here, the Patriarch explains emigration as a necessary solution in the face of threatened subjugation to IS and the associated hardships. This change of discourse occurred only a few months after his December 2015 statement in which he expressed great hope that, despite the violence, his community members would be able to resist and stay in their homeland. The Patriarch's Archbishop, Dawud Sharaf, said in relation to subjugation after being expelled from Mosul in August 2014:

> So here we are, dying before the eyes of the world. We will never agree to live as *dhimmis* ... A *dhimmi* is a slave. We are not, and will never agree to be *dhimmis*. Anyone who agrees to be a *dhimmi* is better off dead ... God created us free, and free we shall die.

If emigration is the only alternative to the *dhimmi* status (living in a subordinated position in relation to Muslims), the immediate consequence of this will be that Assyrians are uprooted from the Middle East. Certainly, not all Christian religious leaders in the Middle East are happy with the initiatives of some Western institutions to support the immigration of Christians from the region. In an interview with Agence France-Presse, Archbishop Antoine Audo of the Chaldean Church in Aleppo stated that: 'No one cares about whether we stay or leave ... The priority for the West is economic power ... It does not see the historic importance of our presence.'[31] He mourned the decline in the number of Christians in his city from 150,000 before the war to 50,000 at the beginning of 2016 and stated that Europe should have kept its borders closed.[32]

However, despite these protests from their local religious leaders, the great majority of Assyrians do in fact want to leave because they have lost hope in a future for Christians in the Middle East. Reporting from northern Iraq, Miles

---

30   'Patriarchal Encyclical of the Great Lent 2016', 11 March 2016, http://www.soc-wus.org/page
      .php?id=481, accessed 11 March 2016.
31   'Aleppo Bishop Speaks Out Against Christian Kidnappings', *Naharnet*, 26 February 2016,
      http://m.naharnet.com/stories/en/70711-aleppo-bishop-speaks-out-against-christian
      -kidnappings, accessed 22 May 2017. For more about the wish of religious leaders to keep
      a Christian presence in Syria, see Windsor (2015b).
32   'Bishop Blames Europe for Near Extinction of Christianity in Syria', Daily Caller News
      Foundation, 24 February 2016, http://dailycaller.com/2016/02/24/bishop-blames-europe
      -for-near-extinction-of-christianity-in-syria/, accessed 26 February 2016.

Windsor (2015a) observes that it is young adults in particular who want to leave for the West. This is also the case in Syria.[33] And only the very poor, those who lack transnational connections, the elderly and the idealists choose or are obliged to stay. The first visits to areas liberated from IS since October 2016 have only increased Christians' general lack of hope in a future in the Middle East, despite the fact that, in the first videos recorded when visiting their towns after the expulsion of IS, those who witnessed the extent of the destruction expressed strong feelings of optimism; these early visitors were often priests, local Christian militiamen and community members. Together, they make a provisional cross (from any material available to them in their surroundings) to be placed at the top of the local, ruined church; they ululate, cry, ring the church bells, and say a prayer to bless the church after it has been desecrated and destroyed by IS during a period of occupation of more than two years. Although these rituals are expressions of their hope of returning to their homes after liberation, in reality, for most displaced Christians, they can also be understood as the rituals of a last farewell before leaving for good, because they experience a deep sense of being helpless in a situation of total devastation. Not only have all their churches been destroyed, but also the homes of Christian residents have been looted and either are occupied by local Muslim neighbours or have been burned down (Ochab 2017; Jeffrey 2017; Chick 2017). Security has become an even greater issue than the material damage; the victims and their community leaders have appealed for an international protection force to ensure their safety, to give them hope that it would be possible to rebuild. The displaced residents expressed strong distrust in any effective security measures to be taken by local governments in order to protect them from similar atrocities in the future (Farley 2017; Ochab 2017; Shamon 2017).[34] A young woman described her traumatic experience after witnessing how her birthplace had been turned into a ghost town: 'They destroyed our dreams and our memories' (Chick 2017). Another woman, who also decided not to stay despite the urging of her religious leaders, asked the question: 'What if something even worse than ISIS comes?'[35] In line with these existential fears, in the report *Ensuring Equality*, several smaller non-governmental organisations (NGOs) wrote of their concern about the exclusion of Christians and other religious minorities from the national settlement plan being put together by Iraq and other regional powers and presented

---

33   Communication with Assyrians in Syria, March 2016.

34   See also 'What if Something Even Worse than ISIS Comes?', World Watch Monitor, 3 February 2017, https://www.worldwatchmonitor.org/coe/4808095/4896473/4901301, accessed 5 February 2017.

35   Ibid.

to the UN (World Watch Monitor 2017). The report warns that this plan and its proposed goals will make it even more likely that the internally displaced people will not return to their former homes after IS is defeated.

This state of continuous emigration has increased a fear among Assyrians of becoming entirely uprooted from what they perceive to be their ancestral homeland. What matters to them is their survival as a people, which they believe is impossible without maintaining connections to the homeland. Assyrians embed their Christianity within a specific tradition, history and region. Fears for the end of their existence in what they consider to be their historical homeland therefore goes together with anxiety over their survival as churches and a people in the diaspora. Becoming disconnected from this heritage will have consequences for their Christianity and their ethnic identity. Metaphorically, the homeland is viewed by Assyrians as a type of soil within which culture develops and flourishes. The homeland is where Assyrians' pre-Christian and Christian heritage is embedded in tangible and intangible culture. And the ancestral homeland has the function of connecting and reconnecting the members of its imagined community in the diaspora. From this essentialist perspective on the role of the ancestral homeland as the necessary soil of their culture, Assyrian Christians believe that losing their connections to the Middle East will mean that their culture will wither. They consider that Assyrians' assimilation in the West is occurring too rapidly for their distinctive identities to survive. Having witnessed the assimilation experienced by earlier generations (especially in North and South America), activists and church leaders fear that life in the diaspora, and concomitant experiences of freedom of expression, will not necessarily result in a distinct communal identity, a strong church, or the survival of Assyrians as a people.[36] The threat of assimilation was also addressed by Patriarch Ephrem II in his 2016 Lent Encyclical:

> We, therefore, impress upon our faithful who are resettling in the west to hold on to certain aspects of our culture that we do not want to change our identity which we have to preserve and our Oriental Christian heritage which may be compromised in the West. We also need to work on reconciling many aspects of our culture with that of the western society without being affected by western atheism and secularism which may clash with our Christian values. Most importantly, we need to find ways

---

36   See, for instance, Polycarpus Augin Aydin's paper 'The Syriac-Orthodox Church in the Diaspora: Challenges and Opportunities', presented at the University of Cambridge, 5 March 2014.

to create harmony between the cultures of the East and the West so that emigration does not become a reason for the extinction of our culture.[37]

The Patriarch, like other community members, discusses identity as a rational process that can be steered and managed. Of course, in reality, changes take place imperceptibly without explicit reflection on the part of those newly arrived in the West. In the process of acculturation, Assyrians naturally begin to include new practices in their collective identities, while excluding others. The last five decades have clearly shown that Assyrians in the diaspora have flourished within a relatively short period of time, but they have also witnessed changes that have greatly unsettled the identity of the community, such as the second and third generations losing their mother tongue, Aramaic, and declining church attendances.

A dominant discourse among Assyrians is therefore that if emigration is a necessary evil, one should take every measure possible to ensure cultural and religious survival in the diaspora.[38] Activists and educators aim to develop new initiatives in order to help Assyrians sustain the central elements of their traditions, such as their classical Syriac and modern Aramaic languages.[39] The use of internet platforms and telecommunications has been instrumental in maintaining and developing new networks among Assyrians, networks that – tellingly – were largely absent before their dispersal. After emigration, very local, isolated and agrarian-based ethno-religious identities in the Middle East have largely broken down, while new transnational networks, predicated on new social media, have been developed. Today, these new technologies are central and driving forces in the dynamics between community members. Modern technology has been used so that people can remain in touch with each other on a social level as well as more actively as a medium used by activists to express their views and to influence and mobilise people for their

---

37   'Patriarchal Encyclical of the Great Lent 2016', 11 March 2016, http://www.soc-wus.org/page .php?id=481, accessed 11 March 2016.

38   When explaining the migration experiences of the 'formerly missionized' communities of the postcolonial world, Afe Adogame and Shobana Shankar (2013: 1–2) use the concept of 'reverse mission' and discuss various dynamics of 'religious expansion' in a global world. The case of Assyrians differs from this conceptualisation as the main reasons for their mass emigration to the West is their survival both physically and culturally, rather than having a missionary zeal in the sense of 'reawakening' Western societies.

39   An example of such an initiative is the Aramaic Online Project, which teaches modern Surayt Aramaic to adult learners. The American-based organisation Rinyo is developing online games and songs for children to learn Surayt.

political aims. The internet has also allowed space for cultural development: Assyrian artists can present their work and educators make use of new technology to teach modern Aramaic dialects and Syriac, which were often not allowed to be taught in educational institutions in the homeland. At more local levels in the diaspora, too, the establishment of churches and secular institutions wherever Assyrians have settled has been the most important means of retaining strong connections among community members.

Newly arrived refugees who settle among their community members in the diaspora are soon confronted with these complex dynamics in their host countries. They arrive in anticipation of connecting with Assyrians who share similar norms and values, but in reality they often find that the first newcomers from a few decades ago have entirely adapted themselves to their new societies, creating a gap between the lifestyles of the established Assyrian diaspora and the newly arrived refugees. This dynamic has been experienced by Samer Kefarkis, who settled in Australia a few months before IS attacked his village in the Khabur area of Syria in July 2014 (Henk and Susebach 2016). He now believes that his culture will not survive in Australia, especially when he observes the norms, values and lifestyle of his teenage niece. He is still grappling with the shocking aftermath of the loss of his cultural identity, his house and his entire village. Samer has not been in Australia long enough to grasp how others in the Assyrian diaspora can help him retain his cultural heritage.

Conclusion

This chapter has discussed how the latest wars in Syria and Iraq, and especially the rise of IS, have led to tensions between Christians and Muslims in these countries, resulting in the forced displacement and worldwide dispersal of the former. With the absence of international protection and material help, Assyrians are no longer hopeful of regaining a place for themselves in their historical homeland and instead aim at settling in Western countries. Initiatives among Assyrians both in the Middle East and in the diaspora have also been unsuccessful in ending their plight. What is now greatly feared by Assyrians is their impending extinction as a people in the Middle East as well as the loss of their ancestral homeland to the majority groups in the region. Some Christians in the Middle East see themselves as local victims of international, or Western, political involvement in the Middle East, while at the same time they are ignored by these powers and left to their own fate. Not finding any viable solutions, they have come to perceive themselves as latter-day Christian martyrs.

On the one hand, Assyrians' settlement in mainly Western countries has given them the chance to establish themselves in what they perceive as democratic and Christian societies in which they are able to express their religious and ethnic identity freely, and where they have flourished. On the other hand, based on experiences in the last few decades, Assyrians have also been confronted with a situation in which they view assimilation into their Western host societies as a great threat to their cultural existence, especially in relation to their fast-disappearing foothold in the Middle East. Nevertheless, an essentialised ideal of their homeland, powerful cultural traditions and the courage of those who remain are important means for challenging these existential difficulties and for keeping alive their hope for an existence in their homeland.

References

Adogame, A. and S. Shankar (2013) *Religion on the Move! New Dynamics of Religious Expansion in a Globalizing World*. Leiden: E. J. Brill.

Atto, N. (2011) *Hostages in the Homeland, Orphans in the Diaspora. Identity Discourses among the Assyrian/Syriac Elites in the European Diaspora*. Leiden: Leiden University Press.

Atto, N. (2017) 'What Could Not Be Written: A Study of the Oral Transmission of Sayfo Genocide Memory Among Assyrians', *Genocide Studies International* 10 (2): 183–209.

Atto, N. (forthcoming) 'Diaspora Assyrians and the Perception of Homeland'.

BetBasoo, P. (2014) 'The Historic Visit of Five Patriarchs to North Iraq', AINA, 26 August, http://www.aina.org/releases/20140826162613.htm, accessed 3 May 2017.

Boorstein, M. (2016) 'The U.S. House Just Voted Unanimously that the Islamic State Commits "Genocide." Now what?', *The Washington Post*, 15 March, https://www.washingtonpost.com/news/acts-of-faith/wp/2016/03/15/the-u-s-house-just-voted-unanimously-that-the-islamic-state-commits-genocide-now-what/, accessed 15 March 2016.

Chick, K. (2017) 'Iraqi Christians: Will They Go Home?', *Christian Science Monitor*, 14 January, http://www.csmonitor.com/World/Middle-East/2017/0114/Iraqi-Christians-Will-they-go-home?cmpid=gigya-tw, accessed 4 February 2017.

Farley, H. (2017) '"Jihadists Used Our Church as a Shooting Range": Iraqi Christians Return Home to Devastation', *Christianity Today*, 24 January, http://www.christiantoday.com/article/jihadists.used.our.church.as.a.shooting.range.iraqi.christians.return.home.to.devastation/104143.htm, accessed 1 February 2017.

Gaunt, D., N. Atto and S. O. Barthoma (2017) *Let Them Not Return: Sayfo – The Genocide against the Assyrian, Syriac, and Chaldean Christians in the Ottoman Empire*. Oxford and New York NY: Berghahn Books.

Harmon, C. (2014) 'Eastern Christians Meet with Obama, Call for Solidarity in the Face of Persecution', *Catholic World Report*, 12 September, http://www .catholicworldreport.com/Blog/3365/eastern_christians_meet_with_obama_call _for_solidarity_in_the_face_of_persecution.aspx, accessed 20 March 2016.

Haykel, B. (2015) 'Isis: A Primer', *Princeton Alumni Weekly*, 3 June, https://paw.princeton .edu/issues/2015/06/03/pages/0027/index.xml, accessed 22 February 2016.

Henk, M. and H. Susebach (2016) 'The Exodus', *Die Zeit*, 16 February. Translated by Josh Ward, http://www.zeit.de/politik/ausland/2016-02/syria-is-war-tel-goran -christians, accessed 17 February 2016.

Jeffrey, P. (2017) 'Iraqi Christian Leader Visiting Mosul Sees Little Future for Christians', *National Catholic Reporter*, 31 January, https://www.ncronline.org/news/world/iraqi -christian-leader-visiting-mosul-sees-little-future-christians, accessed 1 January 2017.

Jenkins, P. (2011) *The Next Christendom: The Coming of Global Christianity*. Oxford: Oxford University Press.

Jenkins, P. (2014) 'Is This the End for Mideast Christianity?', *Christianity Today*, 4 November, http://www.christianitytoday.com/ct/2014/november/on-edge-of-extinction .html, accessed 26 March 2016.

Joseph, J. (2000) *The Modern Assyrians of the Middle East*. Leiden: E. J. Brill.

Knights of Columbus (2016) *Genocide against Christians in the Middle East. A Report Submitted to Secretary of State John Kerry by the Knights of Columbus and in Defense of Christians*. New Haven CT: Knights of Columbus, http://www .stopthechristiangenocide.org/scg/en/resources/Genocide-report.pdf, accessed 20 March 2016.

Nicholson, R. (2016) 'An Open Letter to John Kerry: Genocide against Assyrian and Other Iraqi and Syrian Christians in ISIS-controlled Territory', Philos Project, 8 March, https://philosproject.org/an-open-letter-to-john-kerry-genocide-against -assyrian-christians-in-isis-controlled-territory/, accessed 24 March 2016.

Ochab, E. (2016) *Never Again: Legal Responses to a Broken Promise in the Middle East*. Vienna: Kairos.

Ochab, E. (2017) 'What Shook Me the Most in the Liberated Ninevah Plains', *Forbes*, 30 January, http://www.forbes.com/sites/realspin/2017/01/30/what-shook-me -the-most-in-the-liberated-ninevah-plains/#7169df915f3a, accessed 7 January 2017.

Sanchez, R. and M. Park (2017) 'What to Know about Trump's Visa and Refugee Restrictions', *CNN Politics*, 30 January, http://edition.cnn.com/2017/01/28/politics/trump -immigration-refugees-visa-policy/index.html, accessed 2 February 2017.

Shamon, R. (2017) 'The Fate of Iraq's Indigenous Communities', *Fair Observer*, 25 January, http://www.fairobserver.com/region/middle_east_north_africa/iraq-news -yazidi-assyrian-middle-east-news-43540/, accessed 4 February 2017.

Tadros, S. (2017) 'Should Middle East Religious-Minority Refugees Be Prioritized?', Hudson Institute, 30 January, https://hudson.org/research/13289-should-middle-east-religious-minority-refugees-be-prioritized, accessed 7 February 2017.

Tamcke, M. (2016) 'Christen in Syrien: Das Ende einer zweitausendjährigen Geschichte?' BR 2 podcast, 16 March, http://www.br-online.de/podcast/mp3-download/bayern2/mp3-download-podcast-radiowissen.shtml, accessed 20 March 2016.

USCIRF (2015) *Annual Report*. Washington DC: US Commission on International Religious Freedom (USCIRF), http://www.uscirf.gov/sites/default/files/USCIRF%20Annual%20Report%202015%0%282%29.pdf, accessed 23 March 2016.

Windsor, M. (2015a) 'Iraq's Christians Seek Another Country', *The Wall Street Journal*, 12 May, http://www.wsj.com/articles/iraqs-christians-seek-another-country-1431455921, accessed 24 March 2016.

Windsor, M. (2015b) 'Syria's Christian Refugees: Four Wrong Assumptions', *The New York Times*, 19 December, http://kristof.blogs.nytimes.com/2015/12/19/syrias-christian-refugees-four-wrong-assumptions/?_r=1, accessed 24 March 2016.

World Watch Monitor (2017) *Ensuring Equality: A Multi-NGO Report on the Christians and Other Religious Minority IDPs and Refugees in the Middle East*, https://www.worldwatchmonitor.org/research/4882720, accessed 5 February 2017.

CHAPTER 12

Symbolising Charismatic Influence: Contemporary African Pentecostalism and Its Global Aspirations

J. Kwabena Asamoah-Gyadu

This chapter is an examination of the global nature of the sequence of Pentecostal and Charismatic churches that began to emerge in Africa from the 1970s onwards. It shows how the movement's transnational aspirations are central to its immense appeal as a key player in World Christianity. In particular, it analyses widely utilised symbols essential in the construction of a modern international African born-again identity. The combined general expression 'Pentecostal/Charismatic' is used here to refer to Christian churches and movements that value, affirm and consciously promote the experience of the Holy Spirit as part of normal Christian life and worship. There are different types of Pentecostal movements but generally those that come under that designation, as I point out below, are historically older and doctrinally more clearly defined than their Charismatic progenies. What is common to Pentecostal/Charismatic movements – whether they exist as churches, renewal movements within non-Pentecostal churches or as para-church organisations – is an emphasis on the experience of the Holy Spirit and the deployment of spiritual gifts in the life of the religious community. Since its emergence in the early years of the twentieth century, Pentecostalism has gradually developed into a global religious phenomenon. This chapter considers how, in its contemporary forms, the movement has adopted certain symbols meant to depict its worldwide aspirations and influence. These symbols play a significant role in contemporary Pentecostal/Charismatic Christianity as they are related to the central theme of the experience of the Holy Spirit as a source of influence and empowerment for life and ministry at both local and international levels.

Religious symbols are important for all religious traditions. In the history of the Christian church, for example, the cross has become the symbol that defines faith in God who became incarnate in Christ. In addition to the cross, denominational and independent church traditions adopt different symbols that are intended to depict either their religious culture or their doctrinal emphasis. In postcolonial, post-missionary African Christianity, for example, a number of traditional religious symbols have been incorporated into the liturgical lives of mission-founded denominations in order to affirm their inde-

© KONINKLIJKE BRILL NV, LEIDEN, 2017 | DOI: 10.1163/9789004355026_014

pendence and to give meaning to their efforts at contextualisation. The traditional or historical symbol of the Pentecostal/Charismatic movement has been the dove. This was selected due to the fact that it was in the form of a dove that the Holy Spirit is supposed to have descended on Jesus Christ after his baptism, as recorded in the synoptic traditions. Religious symbols often possess some sacramental value for believers as mediators of supernatural power. However, the importance of those discussed in this chapter lies not in their sacramental value but in their worth for the self-definition of contemporary Pentecostals, especially in their unique and developing theologies of prosperity and dominion. Those considered are, firstly, the eagle, representing Charismatic power in its various manifestations; secondly, the globe, signifying contemporary Pentecostal internationalism and global aspirations; and thirdly, the microphone, which depicts the power of the word and the need to broadcast it, and which creates an association with the tools of modernity.

My intention is to use these symbols as a way of pointing to the transnational significance of contemporary African Charismatic Pentecostalism. The examples come mainly from Ghana and Nigeria but are useful for understanding this movement as one with a global reach and importance. The chapter interrogates the ways in which contemporary Pentecostal movements in Anglophone Africa use symbols and idioms of the Holy Spirit to represent their transnational importance in World Christianity. Those familiar with images advertising the Charismatic credentials of contemporary Pentecostal pastors will note that among the most common are those with the 'man or woman of God' holding a microphone to his or her lips. Even the microphone symbolises a transnational agenda because the messages of these pastors are not only considered powerful in their effects, but recordings of them circulate internationally as people listen to their sermons and prophetic declarations as sources of empowerment through the vicissitudes of life. In looking at these new symbols, this chapter recognises that the dove, which is the traditional symbol of Pentecostalism, has not fallen out of use completely but there has been a noticeable transition from this conventional symbol to the eagle. The eagle best captures the sort of religio-theological culture of success, growth, vigour and prosperity that is associated with contemporary Charismatic Pentecostalism.

African Pentecostalism in the Context of African Christianity

In a book using the phrase *To the Ends of the Earth* as its title, Allan Anderson (2013: 3) writes that it is no coincidence that the southward shift in Christianity's centre of gravity during the twentieth century has occurred in tandem with the phenomenal explosion of Pentecostalism. Pentecostalism defines its call-ing in terms of a movement brought into being by God to influence the world. The anchor text that defines its mission orientation is Acts 1: 8 – 'But you will receive power when the Holy Spirit has come upon you; and you will be my witnesses in Jerusalem, in all Judea and Samaria, and to the ends of the earth' (*New Revised Standard Version*). Its orientation as a movement of empower-ment for ordinary lay people enables Pentecostalism in its various streams to spread quickly. Pentecostalism, to draw on Harvey Cox's interpretation in *Fire from Heaven* (1995), is 'reshaping religion' and 'spirituality' in the twenty-first century. In the midst of the phenomenal growth in the Christian presence in Africa, the influence of Pentecostal spirituality on non-Pentecostal churches is significant. Ruth Marshall's (2009) reference to the rise of the movement in Nigeria in terms of a 'revolution' says much about its socio-religious and polit-ical impact.

In Africa, Pentecostal Christianity developed in response to several factors, including what was seen as the neglect of the ministry of the Holy Spirit in historical mission Christianity. Its appeal lay in its ontological similarities with traditional religious world views concerning misfortune and its causes (Bediako 1995: 69). Like shrine priests and diviners, Pentecostal leaders attrib-uted a spiritual explanation to illness and to personal and communal disaster, but they considered the whole African pantheon demonic. True remedy came from possession by the Holy Spirit. Pentecostalism first encountered Africa via classical Pentecostal missions such as the Apostolic Faith Mission, the Assem-blies of God and the Apostolic Faith Church, which arrived on the continent in the 1910s. Within a decade it had given birth to Christian independence across Southern and West Africa, where it rapidly developed its own traject-ory, characterised by African leadership, exorcism, divine healing and white robes. Its leaders or 'prophets', often former evangelists in the historical and Pentecostal churches, drew on a variety of Christian traditions, including mis-sionary revivalism, to evolve their own distinctive traditions, legitimated by access to vernacular scriptures (Maxwell 2006b; Cabrita 2014). Following the African Independent Churches (AICs) and classical Pentecostals, the contem-porary Charismatic Pentecostals who emerged in the late 1970s constituted a third type of Pentecostalism in Africa and are also the newest and most glam-orous in terms of visibility and impact. Christian innovation in Africa did not just shift the centre of global Christianity but also 'radically altered its denom-inational and theological appearance' (Maxwell 2006b: 403).

To that end, the contemporary Charismatic Pentecostals who concern us in this chapter are a historically younger and theologically versatile variant of Pentecostalism. In qualitative terms, the contemporary West African Pentecostals discussed here focus on material success and prosperity as indicative of divine favour. Eschatological issues such as the Second Coming of Christ and the judgement at the end of the age hardly feature in contemporary Pentecostal religious discourses in the West African regions surveyed in this chapter. In contrast to the 'otherworldly' focus of the classical Pentecostals, the contemporary ones uphold a world-affirming view of dominion. The message is grounded in a transcendental view of daily life that offers the hope of overcoming difficulties in one's endeavours and encourages those on their way up that material prosperity is of God. Consequently, a number of new Pentecostals have become actively involved in African public life, including in its economic and political institutions. A number of West African Pentecostals own financial institutions, private educational facilities, and investments in the transport sectors of their countries. This is a movement that is of great global or transnational significance, and I look at some of the ways in which it has sought to underscore its own importance as a world movement through the use of certain symbols.

Contemporary Pentecostals occupy much of the space held by Independent Christianity in the colonial and early postcolonial eras. To place their popularity in some perspective, there is evidence that a number of AICs are going through metamorphoses and emerging as contemporary Charismatic churches in order to remain relevant within a changing and modernising Christian landscape. Moreover, Pentecostal modes of worship now count as the norm in the average African Christian church. One of these churches is the Redeemed Christian Church of God (RCCG), founded in 1952 by a Nigerian prophet, Josiah O. Akindayomi. The RCCG, having shed its AIC image as a vernacular local church for lower-class Nigerians, with its pastors lacking formal education, has now become a contemporary Charismatic Pentecostal church under the leadership of Enoch Adeboye. The evolution of the RCCG towards a prosperity mindset under the leadership of Adeboye, according Asozeh Ukah, 'amounted to an effective rebranding and repackaging of the church as a modern and global corporate organization' (2008: 80).

The sheer amount of research and scholarship that contemporary African Pentecostalism has attracted, especially from Ghana and Nigeria, is indicative of its importance within the changing religious landscape of Christianity on the continent (Gifford 1998; Asamoah-Gyadu 2005; Marshall 2009; Ukah 2008). Ghana and Nigeria have a combined population of over 150 million people, and in Africa they remain the incubators of Christian religious innovation. Historically, Christian leaders from Ghana and Nigeria have directly influenced developments across sub-Saharan Africa, as far as the spread of new religious movements is concerned.

The Faith/Prosperity Gospel

The late Archbishop Benson Idahosa of Nigeria is widely acknowledged as the pioneering founder of contemporary prosperity-oriented movements in West Africa. The most popular contemporary Pentecostal churches associated with Ghana and Nigeria include the Action Chapel International (ACI), led by Archbishop Nicholas Duncan-Williams; International Central Gospel Church (ICGC), led by Pastor Mensa Otabil; Dag Heward-Mills' Lighthouse Chapel International; and Sam Korankye-Ankrah's Royalhouse Chapel International. The popular churches in Nigeria are: David O. Oyedepo's Living Faith Church Worldwide; T. B. Joshua's Synagogue Church of All Nations; and Pastor Enoch Adeboye's RCCG. Their prosperity gospel and dominion mindset are now common themes in African Christianity as a whole, although they are not preached with the same levels of passion and emphasis everywhere. The principle of 'sowing' tithes and offerings and 'reaping' material blessings, for example, although criticised for its formulaic approach to Christianity, has also been incorporated as a fundraising method in many non-Pentecostal churches. They are 'contemporary' because these are popular as Christian movements that are at home with modernity; they are Charismatic because they emphasise the gifts and graces of the Holy Spirit in Christian life and worship, with speaking in tongues, healing, prophecy, visions and revelations; and they are Pentecostal because they share the religious culture of historically older and theologically more formal and articulate classical Pentecostal traditions, such as the Assemblies of God, that evangelised sub-Saharan Africa from the West.

These contemporary Charismatic Pentecostal churches in sub-Saharan Africa are about half a century old. They have been influenced greatly by North American televangelism and prosperity preaching. Their main characteristics are fairly standard across the board: youthful, educated and mega-size congregations; charismatic and well-educated (not necessarily in theology) leadership; extensive and innovative use of modern media technologies and religious advertising; internationalism; religiously exuberant and expressive worship; and the preaching of prosperity in a materialistic sense. Maxwell provides the following apt summary of the nature of contemporary Charismatic Pentecostals – or Born-again Pentecostals, as some would like to call them:

> Its numbers have mushroomed in a context of state contraction, neo-liberal economics, poverty and growing political turmoil ... It has embraced media technologies, particularly the electronic media and religious broadcasting, with great zeal ... It has adopted the faith gospel, drawing from the teachings of Oral Roberts, T. L. Osborn, Kenneth Hagin

and Kenneth Copeland to argue that material success is a sign of faith and
of God's blessing. Its leaders are particularly susceptible to the tools and
some of the values of modernity, especially the values of liberal capitalism. And it casts itself as inter-denominational and global in character.

MAXWELL 2006b: 418

Maxwell's reference to contemporary Charismatic Pentecostalism's embrace of
modern media technologies and neoliberal capitalism and its self-perception
as a global Christian endeavour is important for understanding the religious
symbols that the movement has adopted. Perhaps the single most important
theological development associated with these newer Pentecostals is the faith
gospel of prosperity: this is the belief and message that Christians have the right
to expect God to bless them in order that they do well, both spiritually and
materially, in this life.

Most sectors of African Christianity have continued to expand in the postcolonial era and remain vital, often animated by their own traditions of revival
(Maxwell 2006a). Nevertheless, Pentecostal leaders have done their utmost to
disparage their denominational rivals by stressing the centrality of the Holy
Spirit in their movements and suggesting its absence in all others. In the formative years of the movement, Pentecostal preachers demonstrated a disdain for
theological education by referring to seminaries as cemeteries from where only
dead bones emerged. Young people in particular were challenged to 'come out'
of those churches on account of their supposed dry denominationalism, moral
permissiveness and staid and ordered liturgies, which did not engender supernatural encounters with the Holy Spirit. The theologically articulate but spiritually empty clergy were castigated as supervising and presiding over churches
that were going nowhere. Symbolically, they were referred to as chickens. In
contrast, the new Pentecostals present God's Spirit as the giver of life, and
the Spirit is seen as having embarked on a mission of renewal with the new
churches. 'Come out of the chickens and soar like eagles' was the common
mantra. As Archbishop Nicholas Duncan-Williams, founder of ACI in Ghana,
told me in an interview in 1991: 'God is on the move, but the older churches
have not even sensed it.' The image of the Spirit of God as an eagle who hovers
overhead to make order out of chaos is in part responsible for endearing that
symbol to contemporary Pentecostals.

The themes of success and prosperity associated with contemporary Pentecostalism are communicated in a variety of ways, including through the use of
catchphrases, symbols and images, either as part of church logos or in advertisements for church events. The rhetoric of success also features a certain level
of internationalism that includes establishing branches abroad, the worldwide

peregrinations of the leadership, the invitation of internationally known Charismatic preachers to minister in Africa, media ministries on digital satellite television and the internet, and the publication of books for distribution on the world market. I make the point that, beyond the symbolism of power and transnational influence, the symbols underlying the self-definition of contemporary Pentecostals as transnational movements also underscore their dominion theology. It is true that many of the historical mission churches also have a conception of themselves as global institutions that have responded to Christ's imperative to make disciples of all nations. Their international gatherings – for instance at the Vatican or Lambeth Palace – and the continuous traffic of clergy and laity across continents for fellowship and study are testament to their cosmopolitan nature. Like contemporary Charismatic Pentecostals, they, too, have adopted electronic media to proselytise and encourage the faithful – and with some success, as Pope Francis's 8.9 million Twitter followers attest. However, I argue that Pentecostals identify so strongly with the use of electronic media, a transnational outlook and the prosperity gospel that these have become their defining features, a means of asserting a modern outward-looking, socially mobile identity for their aspiring urban middle-class membership.

Internationalism

Those who have left Africa to establish churches abroad are also helping to keep Christianity as a non-Western religion. Simultaneously, these persons are also keeping the hope of its message alive in what they perceive to be otherwise largely secular areas, for example in Europe. It is not surprising that the African immigrant churches in European countries such as Germany, on observing declining church attendance in these countries, insist on being called 'New Mission churches' and not migrant churches. This name, they claim, avoids an emphasis on their 'foreignness' and instead stresses the reason why they claim to be in Europe: that is, to fulfil a missionary calling from the South to the North (Währisch-Oblau 2009: 35).

   In the light of these developments, especially with the rise of immigrant church communities outside Africa, it may be deceptive to look at these individualised ministries and consider them to be Ghanaian or Nigerian depending on their geographical locations. They may look Ghanaian or Nigerian in terms of ethnic composition, leadership and headquarters location, but each of these contemporary Pentecostal churches has branches across the continent and beyond. They benefit immensely from the high numbers of Africans who migrate from Africa to the West. Immigrants view Pentecostal/Charismatic Christianity as providing a sort of spiritual safety net for survival in spiritually and physically precarious diasporic communities. Most African immigrant churches in Europe and North America, for example, belong to this category of new Christian movements. The establishment of international branches is a major aspiration for many church leaders, as it underlies their claims to being international organisations and affords the leaders the opportunity to travel, something that is important for their curriculum vitae as high-profile Charismatic figures. Additionally, two of the most popular and populous contemporary Charismatic Pentecostal churches in Europe were also founded and are led by Nigerians. These are the London-based Kingsway International Christian Centre (KICC), led by Pastor Matthew Ashimolowo, and the Church of the Embassy of the Blessed Kingdom of God for all Nations, based in Kiev, Ukraine. KICC attracts upwards of 10,000 worshippers every Sunday to its multiple services, while the God Embassy, at the height of its popularity in the mid-2000s, brought together a similar number in its Kiev stadium-like meeting place.

It is evident from the lists provided above that in the expressions and transmissions of the new faith as transnational religious communities, the words 'international', 'worldwide' and 'global' have become important prefixes, suffixes or additions to the names of these churches. Paul Gifford's study of contemporary Pentecostalism in Ghana captures the sort of 'internationalism' associated with Africa's contemporary Pentecostal churches:

> [Ghana's] charismatic churches perpetually host visitors, especially North American and Nigerian, and its church leaders ... are forever going abroad ... Some of the broadcast media and international literature are from overseas. While this research was in progress, the Korean David Yonngi Cho visited Ghana for a crusade and pastors' conference, and the Nigerian David Oyedepo brought his 'Maximum Impact Summit' to Accra in mid-2002, events of great importance for Ghana's charismatic Christianity.
> GIFFORD 2004: X

Popular Christianity, Gifford suggests, is a creative response on the part of ordinary people to the destabilising effects of modernisation. On the interface between contemporary Charismatic Christianity and public life in Africa, Gifford surmises that religion can legitimise new aspirations. Every religion, he notes, involves struggles to conquer, monopolise or transform the symbolic structures that order reality (Gifford 1998: 26).

The expressions 'aspirations', 'conquer' and 'transform' in Gifford's observation above are significant in terms of the mentality of 'dominion' that informs much contemporary Pentecostal theology. The ability to extend one's ministry beyond local borders is something that most pastors aspire to do, and to go international fulfils the ambition that God has called Christian churches and their leaders to exercise territorial dominance and control in world Christian mission. As a form of popular Christianity, the desire for a global impact proceeds in parallel with the belief that the Spirit of God is a Spirit of dominion. This seems to be an important way in which the Charismatic movement seeks to express its theological self-understanding. The Spirit that hovers over the face of the waters is also the Spirit that is universal. Considered from a Pentecostal perspective, it is through the working of the Spirit of God that Christianity becomes a universal faith, giving rise to World Christianity, with each manifestation a facet of a single diamond.

This internationalism, expressed by the dominion mindset, is thus evident in these churches' self-understanding as possessing a worldwide 'apostolic' calling and ministry. The worldwide travels of their leaders, the international array of Charismatic preachers at events, their foreign branches, and the choice of religious symbolism are all meant to underscore this international mindset. The fact that the revival meetings and evangelistic campaigns of new Pentecostal churches carry such secular designations as 'summits', 'conferences' and 'conventions' reveals much, not just about their contemporary and entrepreneurial nature, but also about their self-perception as international, even corporate, religious organisations.

Dominion: An Emerging Theme

Pentecostals usually interpret scripture based on their own experiences, meaning that their theology is usually not systematic. However, there are clearly themes that have emerged from their practices and discourses. Dominion is one such emerging theme in contemporary Pentecostalism in West Africa. In addition to their emphasis on being born-again in Jesus Christ, baptism with the Holy Spirit, speaking in tongues, healing from sickness and disease, and the second coming of Christ, which are all associated with classical Pentecostalism, contemporary West African Pentecostals focus on pursuits linked to prosperity and attaining 'dominion'. They strongly uphold belief in a so-called prosperity theology, which places great emphasis on material success as a prime indicator of God's favour for faithful Christianity. In turn, this prosperity mindset and agenda crystallise around a dominion theology in which it is believed that, with the power of the Holy Spirit, the believer can dominate and influence life and society through the application of certain biblical principles of success. The key biblical text that supports dominion theology is found in Genesis 1: 28, which contemporary Pentecostals like to read in the King James version of the Bible:

> And God blessed them, and God said unto them, Be fruitful, and multiply, and replenish the earth, and subdue it: and have dominion over the fish of the sea, and over the fowl of the air, and over every living thing that moveth upon the earth.

In Ghana, one of the more theologically sophisticated Pentecostals, Pastor Mensa Otabil, founder and leader of ICGC, has developed an entire Charismatic theology around this text, which he has published in his volume *Four Laws of Productivity* (1991). The four laws, as inferred from this verse in Genesis, are listed as: fruitfulness, multiplication, subjugation and dominion. Pastor Otabil has also published another book, *Dominion Mandate*, in which he observes that:

> The word dominion ... carries the idea of contending with something that is wild and untamed in order to bring it under control. The intention of dominion therefore is to empower man with the authority and ability to contend with the wildness of the earth as it was handed over to him, and make it serve useful purposes. God gave us both the authority and ability. He planted in man a hunger for this kind of dominion ... Do not take yourself for granted. Don't ever diminish your value because you have been created with awesome power, with the capacity to be 'fruitful, multiply, replenish and subdue the earth and, to have dominion'.
>
> OTABIL 2013: 8, 14

David O. Oyedepo, founder and leader of the Nigeria-based Living Faith Church Worldwide, has also published several works on prosperity theology, one of them titled *Walking in Dominion* (2006). He runs his own publishing house in Ota, Nigeria, which is simply named Dominion Publishing House. The fact that a private university college founded in Ghana by Archbishop Nicholas Duncan-Williams is named Dominion, as well as that the Ghana branch of London-based KICC is named Dominion Centre, provides useful examples of the importance of the expression 'dominion' as a theological term underpinning the choice of religious symbolism in contemporary Charismatic Pentecostalism in Africa and its diasporic communities. The word 'dominion' thus appears in the titles of books and sermons and also occurs in the names of churches and as the theme of conferences, summits and evangelistic campaigns.

Religious Symbolism and Pentecostalism

Contemporary Charismatic Pentecostalism in Africa and elsewhere is a movement that advocates what David Maxwell describes as 'redemptive uplift', a process of rupture with one's past that leads to the embrace of Jesus as Lord, and which subsequently leads to a constructive lifestyle of change and prosperity (Maxwell 1998: 354). The eagle features prominently in Pentecostal/Charismatic symbolism and illustrations in breakthrough or success and prosperity sermons. It appears as a theme in revival meetings and conferences, or even as the religious emblem of particular Charismatic churches. The image of an eagle can be used to illustrate a particular type of self-belief: an aspirational belief in a rise above mediocrity, enhanced performance in various endeavours, achievement and a general need to be ambitious. It is a symbol that captures the motivational religious philosophy of contemporary Pentecostalism to attain and maintain empowerment or dominion in all areas of life. One Charismatic church, located in the heart of Accra, the capital of Ghana, is even named Eagle Charismatic Centre. The theological rationale behind the penchant for using the eagle in Charismatic West African Christianity relates to the pursuit of power: as the king of the birds, the eagle represents the power of flight, ambition, longevity, vision, height, strength and renewal, as I explain below. Paul Gifford says of the movement's focus on success that discussing African Pentecostalism without discussing its emphasis on success is like discussing a computer without its software (Gifford 2007: 20).

Throughout the history of world Pentecostalism, the dove has been its preferred religious symbol. As an image, it comes from something that happened very early in the ministry of Jesus, when the Holy Spirit, the third person of the Godhead, descended on Jesus at his baptism in the form of a dove. In the gospel according to St Matthew, the key moment is captured as follows:

> As soon as Jesus was baptized, he went up out of the water. At that moment heaven was opened and he saw the Spirit of God descending like a dove and lighting on him. And a voice from heaven said, 'This is my Son, whom I love; with him I am well pleased.'
>
> Matthew 3: 16–17, *New International Version*

As Pentecostalism is a movement of the Holy Spirit, it is thus understandable that the dove remains the standard symbol, just as the crucifix is associated with Catholicism and the cross with mainline Protestantism. The new religious symbols discussed here in relation to contemporary Charismatic Pentecostals are not necessarily objects of cultic veneration; Pentecostals would call any such veneration idolatry, and a number of disagreements between Catholic Charismatics and their denomination have stemmed from the Catholic uses of religious statues and icons. Religious symbolism, when applied to Pentecostals, must therefore be understood in a limited sense. The human being is a *homo symbolicus*, Mircea Eliade argued in the 1950s (Eliade 1959: 95). He pointed out that every religious act and every cult object aims at a meta-empirical reality and usually refers to or points towards supernatural values or beings (ibid.: 95).

Pentecostal/Charismatic Christianity is generally wary of any item that acquires a mediatory role in religion. This stems from the movement's emphasis on the experience of the Holy Spirit as democratising access to the sacred. When filled with the power of the Spirit, anyone can preach, prophesy and speak in tongues, or even exercise a ministry of healing miracles and signs and wonders. Ministry, as understood within Pentecostal contexts, is not the preserve of a few ordained people. The Charismatic leader may carry the anointing in special measure, but in Pentecostalism the Protestant principle of the 'priesthood of all believers' is taken to mean that adherents have a Spirit-enabling ability to function as instruments of God irrespective of their position. The symbols discussed here therefore aim to have a metaphysical reality, not as the focus of worship but rather in the sense that they articulate for users a certain divine self-understanding of their existence and their mission in this world. The statement that best explains this understanding of religious symbols comes from a point made by Eliade, suggesting that such symbols are imbued with existential value. In his words, 'a symbol always aims at a *reality in which human existence is engaged*' – a symbol expresses the 'spiritual as lived' (Eliade 1959: 102). The religious symbol performs a number of functions in its direct engagement with human existence: 'The religious symbol not only unveils a structure of reality or a dimension of existence; by the same stroke it brings a *meaning* into human existence' (ibid.: 102).

On the Wings of the Eagle

As a symbolic representation of the Charismatic Pentecostal theology of power in Africa, the eagle featured as the background image of ACI's Impact 2015 summit, led by Archbishop Nicholas Duncan-Williams. Throughout the year, the contemporary Charismatic Pentecostal churches that are present throughout sub-Saharan Africa hold conventions, revival meetings, evangelistic crusades, Holy Ghost action campaigns, business summits for millionaires, marriage workshops, and a host of other programmes in a constantly evolving menu of religious activities. The billboards, posters, flyers and radio and television advertisements that bring these activities to the attention of the public are common throughout urban sub-Saharan Africa. In November 2015, ACI organised its annual flagship programme, Impact 2015, with the theme 'Mount Up with Wings Like Eagles' (Isaiah 40: 31). The eagle is a much-loved symbol in contemporary Charismatic Pentecostalism because it reflects the theological aspirations of a movement that talks a great deal about dominion and prosperity. The ACI poster and newspaper advertisements had a huge flying eagle as a background image.

The Impact 2015 programme took place in ACI's vast Prayer Cathedral on Accra's Spintex Road. There are a number of things about Impact 2015 that are relevant for the purposes of this chapter: first, its theme, which centred on the eagle; second, the array of international – mainly North American – speakers who featured alongside Archbishop Duncan-Williams; and third, the extent of advertising, which says much about the sorts of aspirations of the churches we are dealing with here. ACI, formerly the Christian Action Faith Ministry International, is one of the most prominent contemporary Charismatic Pentecostal churches in the country. It was founded in 1998 and operated around the Accra airport residential area for a number of years before relocating to the Prayer Cathedral on Spintex Road. Over the years, Archbishop Duncan-Williams, who is the protégé of the late Nigerian prosperity-preaching Charismatic leader Archbishop Benson Idahosa, has cultivated a network of friends, including Bishop T. D. Jakes of the Potter's House Ministry in Texas USA and the American Charismatic prophetess Juanita Bynum. Although there are many contemporary Pentecostal churches that remain small, on the whole, most of them aspire to build transnational religious empires led by religious entrepreneurs and superstars for whom success and prosperity constitute goals of religious faith. The influence of Archbishop Duncan-Williams, like many of his compatriots, goes far beyond the local religious constituency through the use of media, his worldwide tours and his self-designation as an 'Apostle to the Nations'.

Earlier, in July 2013, Ghana's ICGC, led by Pastor Mensa Otabil, ran a series of television and internet advertisements for its annual Destiny Summit. ICGC was founded in 1984 and, like Duncan-Williams' ACI, has grown into a megachurch, with its leader, Pastor Otabil, emerging as one of the most popular Charismatic pastors in Ghana today. Like Duncan-Williams, Otabil also has an extensive international ministry. He has distinguished himself as a pastor with a message of African empowerment and liberation, further contextualising why the eagle is important to his theology. The ICGC advertisement put out by Mensa Otabil began with a flying eagle. The preference for the eagle over

the traditional pneumatic symbol of the dove, which represents peace, is due
to the fact that it stands for everything that relates to power as a global concept:
charisma, potential, possibility, achievement, territorial dominance, control
and renewal (Asamoah-Gyadu 2013: 3). The eagle in the ICGC advertisement
takes off into the skies, its flight accompanied by the spoken words: 'Rise up:
move your life, ministry and business to new heights.'

Waldo César rightly describes the spoken word as the 'motor' that drives
Pentecostal spirituality, and 'oral performance' as 'the most important aspect
of the religious service' (César 2001: 28). The reference to the power of the
spoken word here is significant. In this sort of Christianity, the word as spoken
by those anointed by God has agency in blessing, healing and exorcism. The
advertisement, just like the one from Duncan-Williams' ACI, also featured an
international array of Charismatic speakers and crowds of worshippers. Pastor
Mensa Otabil, to illustrate the importance of the spoken word, wields a microphone. His voice accompanies the flight of the eagle as he invites the public to
a destiny-changing experience at the 2013 Destiny Summit. Mike Murdock, the
African-American prosperity preacher who was one of the guest speakers at
this event, also uses the spoken word in the advertisement. He is depicted saying: 'God reacts to my words not my thoughts.' All this underscores the point
that the images and symbols – a flying eagle, microphone-wielding preachers, the spoken word, internationally known Charismatic televangelists, and
crowds signifying influence – were carefully chosen and packaged to reflect a
certain contemporary Charismatic self-perception as a movement with international significance and therefore important in World Christianity. For these
people, World Christianity is the reality that God, through his powerful Spirit,
is spreading his influence through them into the world.

The Eagle and Dominion Theology

To further illustrate this point, the symbolism of the eagle, reinvented in Pentecostalism to represent the Holy Spirit as the empowering presence of God, is
again relevant. At the beginning of the contemporary Pentecostal movement
in West Africa in the late 1970s, I noted that the eagle featured frequently in the
daily discourses of this new stream of Christianity. The eagle is used as an illustration in many sermons; it is the subject of songs of inspiration; it is the name
of young people's groups; some churches have the word 'eagle' in their name;
and many Charismatic conferences are designated 'eagle summit', 'eagle conventions' or something similar. If the dove is representative of the calmer and
gentler moves of the Holy Spirit, the eagle represents his more aggressive and

conquering side. The eagle can take dominion because it has the advantage of height, strength, endurance, longevity, vision and power over other birds. The critical text for many Pentecostals is Isaiah 40: 27–31:

> Do you not know? Have you not heard? The Lord is the everlasting God, the Creator of the ends of the earth. He will not grow tired or weary and his understanding no one can fathom. He gives strength to the weary and increases the power of the weak. Even youths grow tired and weary, and young men stumble and fall; but those who hope in the Lord will renew their strength. They will soar on wings like eagles; they will run and not grow weary, they will walk and not be faint.

Contemporary pneumatic groups apply this text in a variety of ways, including prayer. In one of his publications, *Power in Prayer* (2001), Bishop Charles Agyinasare of the Perez Chapel International applies the metaphor of the eagle by noting that the eagle is the king of the birds; it is a powerful bird that is able to detect prey many miles away because of its 'powerful microscopic eyes'. The eagle also symbolises the power of renewal. It can live for a generation and when the eagle's feathers start to become weak, it goes among the rocks and uses its sharp beak to remove all its feathers from its skin. After that, it hits the rocks with its beak and talons until they fall off and reveal the soft tissue underneath. As a result, the eagle is unable to eat for a number of days. It is also unable to fly, so it spends the time resting on the rocks. After it has gone through this period of fasting (and waiting), fresh feathers appear and its beak and talons grow back. Through this process, the eagle is renewed to a youthful state and is able to fly even more strongly than before. It does not get weary and is able to hunt its prey more effectively. The new beak is stronger, as are the feathers and talons, so it flies better and gets a better grip on its prey (ibid.: 11–12).

Bishop Agyinasare compares the eagle's period of 'waiting' to periods of fasting and prayer. In his words, 'those who forsake themselves, make sacrifices and pay a dear price to wait on the Lord ... will renew their strength, they will mount up with wings like the eagle' (ibid.: 12). He continues:

> The more one waits upon the Lord, the more he breathes over you and the more his presence overshadows you and you renew your strength ... As you wait on the Lord, God will infuse, inject and vaccinate you with his power and you will be energised to rise to fulfil your God-given destiny.
>
> AGYINASARE 2001: 13

If the dove represented the quiet holiness of classical Pentecostalism, re-treating from the world, the eagle has come to represent the confident, world-embracing prosperity religion that characterises so much of Pentecostalism's contemporary form in African towns and cities.

The Globe in Dominion Theology

The symbol of the eagle is usually combined with the symbol of the globe. The globe is perhaps the most self-evident and vivid depiction of the expansion-ist mission agenda of contemporary Pentecostalism. I have noted that Pente-costalism is a movement that was tasked to reach the world from the out-set. Jesus told the disciples that, when the Holy Spirit came upon them, they were going to be witnesses to him in Jerusalem, Judaea, Samaria and the ends of the world. Although the globe as a symbol does not appear in scripture, it is nonetheless an apt representation of the expression 'to the ends of the earth'.

We have noted that a large number of contemporary Pentecostals therefore underscore their global significance by frequently using 'international', 'global', 'worldwide' and 'transcontinental' in the names of their churches. In Ghana and Nigeria there is *International* Central Gospel Church, *Global* Revival Minis-tries, Perez Chapel *International* and Living Faith Church *Worldwide*. Prophetic declarations that people will have access to international opportunities have become part of contemporary Pentecostal discourse. The influence sought con-sists of both individuals breaking through in life by means of international travel opportunities, and ministries being able to establish branches abroad. Indeed, some West African Pentecostal churches provide prayer camps led by prophets anointed with special powers to break down the bureaucratic strong-holds involved in the delivery of passports and visas necessary for international travel (van Dijk 1997: 2).

A useful example of this process can be seen in the work of the Nigerian Charismatic pastor Sunday Adelaja, in Kiev, Ukraine. His church, established in 1994, has a long name: the Church of the Embassy of the Blessed Kingdom of God for all Nations. Each of these terms was chosen to reflect a certain transnational understanding of Christian mission:

> The Church is the representative of God on the earth – His 'Embassy'. Therefore, we – children of God – are the citizens of His Divine Kingdom and not citizens of this world! The Blessed Kingdom of God [is] a place of destruction of curses. At the head of every kingdom is a king. Our King

is Jesus Christ! He is the Lord of all nations ... Jesus Christ is the Savior for everyone, irrespective of his age, color or skin, nationality and social status.[1]

An appropriate media image has been developed to reflect the philosophy of the name. The logo of God Embassy is a globe with Africa in the centre. The globe, symbolising the world as a mission field, is capped by a golden crown with a cross. Just below the crown is a light emanating from Ukraine, which remains otherwise unmarked. The light from Ukraine shines throughout Europe and the Middle East. Africa figures prominently, but the light and energy of the church emanate from Ukraine and reach around the world (Wanner 2007: 214). In the meeting halls of God Embassy the national colours of the different nations in which the church has a presence are displayed to further demonstrate its global or transnational significance.

The Power of the Word in Dominion Theology

The expression that most captures the core significance of the pneumatology of the eagle and the globe in Pentecostalism is the word 'dominion', which represents power and control. Pentecostalism understands itself as a movement that is called into being by God to dominate the world. It is thus instructive that the slogan of KICC is 'Raising Champions and Taking Territories'. Contemporary Pentecostalism in Africa therefore creates a religious menu that focuses on empowerment and emancipation. The upwardly mobile youth that the movement attracts, as well as professionals, the unemployed and the poor, are all inspired through motivational messages to do something practical to achieve upward mobility by taking dominion. In this new type of pneumatic Christianity, there has been a complete shift from preaching that focuses on morality, the attributes of God, accepting your destiny in life and preparing for heaven, to a message that tells you to build houses, buy cars, travel abroad, expand your business, pursue wealth and improve your lot in this life. In Africa as elsewhere, several of the movement's leaders have established universities to help people achieve these lofty aims, and there is also much preaching on black liberation and empowerment. Here we see why the eagle is important in contemporary Pentecostal discourse, imagery and symbolism – it is empowered by its

---

1   Church of the Embassy of the Blessed Kingdom of God for all Nations, *Eighth Anniversary Brochure*, 2002, Kiev, p. 5.

powerful wings to soar to great heights. This association translates into the provision of opportunities for higher education and seminars on self-improvement and empowerment that have come to be associated with the new Christianity; these constitute the wings on which people are expected to soar to those heights. It is noteworthy that while recently established Pentecostal universities actively spurn theology and the social sciences as appropriate subjects, they promote business and media studies as worthwhile areas of study (Maxwell 2013: 102).

In Charismatic media culture and advertising, the images – a flying eagle, microphone-wielding preachers, the spoken word, internationally known Charismatic televangelists, and crowds signifying influence – are carefully chosen and packaged to reflect a certain contemporary Charismatic cultural paradigm. Historically, it was through the word – in magazines and church newsletters, and later on radio and via televangelism – that Pentecostalism became a global religion. Allan Anderson gives a vivid description of how the global aspirations of Pentecostalism have played out for over a century: 'The experience of the Spirit and belief in world evangelization are hallmarks of Pentecostalism, and Pentecostals believe they are called to be witnesses for Jesus Christ to the farthest reaches of the globe in obedience to Christ's commission' (Anderson 2013: 1). In a very instructive article, Waldo César describes Pentecostalism as a complex movement that combines biblical symbolism with modern forms of communication and global expansion (César 2001: 22). The symbolic, he notes, 'functions as a language which blends what is immanent in the world with the transcendental; the experience of the sacred reveals itself in concrete situations in everyday life' (ibid.: 27). Thus, alongside space and time, César rightly identifies the spoken word as a vital component of Pentecostal spirituality. The spoken word, he notes, 'is the motor which drives this new spirituality, and oral performance is the most important aspect of the religious service' (ibid.: 28).

This power, which is believed to be inherent in the spoken word, is what is symbolised by the use of the microphone in Pentecostal media images and advertisements. In publicising upcoming events, Pentecostal churches make use of posters and handbills as well as images on television, and always the favoured image of the speaker is with a microphone in hand. The microphone signifies many things, including the power of the word in preaching, ministration through singing, and the ability to declare the word of God in tongues, prophecy, word of knowledge, or narrative visions and revelations. It signifies the authority of the believer to cast out demons in the name of Jesus and pronounce blessings and prosperity on those with needs. The spoken word also has a performance effect in Nigerian Pentecostalism. Ruth Marshall observes:

In this context, the language of faith is truly performative and accords to testimony and prayer a force that is genuinely foundational: to invoke God, to praise Him, to pray to Him, and to testify to his works constitutes both the act of faith – what Paul called *performativum fidei* – but also, very literally, an *action* on the world. Through prayer and witness, converts do things with words.

MARSHALL 2009: 4

The performance effect of the spoken word in African pneumatic movements is evidence of the resonances between primal ideas and Christian innovation. In the traditional context, words translate into action, and therefore the power of blessings and curses is very important, especially when they come from figures of authority. Through the word, the forgiveness of sins can be pronounced and evil can be cursed out of the lives of the troubled. The fact that the church of Jamaican American preacher Randy Morrison, in Minnesota, is called Speak the Word Church reflects the importance of the spoken word in contemporary Pentecostalism. The emphasis on the power of the spoken word, more than anything else, is illustrative of a movement that shares a Charismatic culture that has a global presence. The spoken word travels, as a result of which the voices of Charismatic pastors are accessible through recordings and also through their television and internet ministries. Where necessary, these voices are recorded as texts that circulate globally. Pentecostal services, as César explains, also unfold through various sounds transmitted through powerful speakers; oral performances include 'prayers, alleluias, songs, appeals, testimonies, more alleluias, offerings, confessions, casting out of demons, even more alleluias, biblical readings, sales of booklets and pamphlets, distribution of symbolic objects, miracles, and above all, speaking in "strange tongues"' (César 2001: 28). The spoken word is supposed to have the power of transformation and is literally 'received' through imaginary appropriations, whether they come through electronic recording devices or live television, radio or internet services. In this connection, Eastwood Anaba, a leading contemporary Pentecostal leader from Ghana, writes: 'Impossibility should be ruled out of your vocabulary … We have the mandate to change our environment by speaking the word of faith … We have the mandate to set the oppressed free and our boldness in the exercise of our authority is crucial to the blessing of humanity' (Anaba 2004: 38).

Conclusion

At the beginning of the twenty-first century, Kwame Bediako noted that much of the study of Africa seemed to miss the significance of the dramatic growth in Christian adherence across the continent. What was most striking, he noted, 'is the enhanced place of Africa in the modern transformation of Christianity in the world, as indeed, in the renewed significance of religion as a social force in human affairs' (Bediako 2000). The growth of Christianity among Africans has occurred at a time when the faith is in decline in the West in terms of numbers and public expression. It is Bediako's contention that the sheer surprise at the fact that Africa emerged as a major heartland of Christianity at the close of the twentieth century makes it important that we should seek to understand what this might mean for Africa and for the world (ibid.: 304). It was Bediako's mentor Andrew F. Walls who argued that we have to regard African Christianity as potentially the representative Christianity of the twenty-first century. Ghana, Nigeria and other countries in the sub-region of West Africa have established some of the most dynamic and influential contemporary Charismatic Pentecostal churches of our time. Not only have the churches grown into transnational organisations with branches and networks in North America and Europe, but also their Charismatic leaders are taking their place alongside their counterparts from the Northern continents in shaping the theology and practice of Christianity worldwide.

Dutch anthropologist of religion André Droogers argues for the important relationship between individual and society in Pentecostalism, suggesting that the movement's evangelistic campaigns ultimately address the whole of humanity (1994: 34). The symbolic representations of dominion theology discussed in this chapter – the use of the eagle, the globe and the microphone – affirm Droogers' argument in their depiction of the movement's transnational aspirations. Gerrie ter Haar notes that the development of African churches in diasporic communities outside the continent marks a significant departure that should lead to a renewed appreciation of Africa's role in the modern world. To call them 'African' churches, Gerrie ter Haar observes, implies a limitation on their task in Europe. They look at themselves as 'international' churches, expressing their aspiration to be part of the international world in which they believe they have a missionary task (ter Haar 1998: 29). The symbols of the eagle, the globe and the microphone have been adopted as signifying these global aspirations. An understanding of their significance within the context of the work of the Holy Spirit helps us to appreciate and interpret contemporary African Pentecostal/Charismatic Christianity in its own terms as a local movement with global aspirations.

References

Agyinasare, C. (2001) *Power in Prayer: Taking Your Blessings by Force*. Hoornaar, Netherlands: His Printing.

Anaba, E. (2004) *The Workability of Faith*. Bolgatanga, Ghana: Desert Leaf Publications.

Anderson, A. (2013) *To the Ends of the Earth: Pentecostalism and the Transformation of World Christianity*. Oxford: Oxford University Press.

Asamoah-Gyadu, K. (2005) *African Charismatics: Current Developments within Independent Indigenous Pentecostalism in Ghana*. Leiden: E. J. Brill.

Asamoah-Gyadu, K. (2013) *Sighs and Signs of the Spirit: Ghanaian Perspectives on Pentecostalism and Renewal in Africa*. Oxford: Regnum International.

Bediako, K. (1995) *Christianity in Africa: The Renewal of a Non-Western Religion*. Edinburgh: Edinburgh University Press.

Bediako, K. (2000) 'Africa and Christianity on the Threshold of the Third Millennium: The Religious Dimension', *African Affairs* 99 (395): 303–23.

Cabrita, J. (2014) *Text and Authority in the South African Nazaretha Church*. Cambridge: Cambridge University Press.

César, W. (2001) 'From Babel to Pentecost: A Social-Historical-Theological Study of the Growth of Pentecostalism' in A. Corten and R. Marshall-Fratani (eds), *Between Babel and Pentecost: Transnational Pentecostalism in Africa and Latin America*. Bloomington IN: Indiana University Press.

Cox, H. (1995) *Fire from Heaven: The Rise of Pentecostal Spirituality and the Reshaping of Religion in the Twenty-first Century*. Reading MA: Addison-Wesley.

Droogers, A. (1994) 'The Normalization of Religious Experience: Healing, Prophecy, Dreams, and Visions' in K. Poewe (ed.), *Charismatic Christianity as a Global Culture*. Columbia SC: University of South Carolina Press.

Eliade, M. (1959) 'Methodological Remarks on the Study of Religious Symbolism' in M. Eliade and M. Kitagawa (eds), *The History of Religions: Essays in Methodology*. Chicago IL and London: University of Chicago Press.

Gifford, P. (1998) *African Christianity: Its Public Role*. Bloomington IN: Indiana University Press.

Gifford, P. (2004) *Ghana's New Christianity: Pentecostalism in a Globalizing African Economy*. London: Hurst and Co.

Gifford, P. (2007) 'The Prosperity Gospel in Africa: Expecting Miracles', *Christian Century*, 10 July.

Marshall, R. (2009) *Political Spiritualities: The Pentecostal Revolution in Nigeria*. Chicago IL: University of Chicago Press.

Maxwell, D. (1998) '"Delivered from the Spirit of Poverty?": Pentecostalism, Prosperity and Modernity in Zimbabwe', *Journal of Religion in Africa* 28 (3): 350–73.

Maxwell, D. (2006a) *African Gifts of the Spirit: Pentecostalism and the Rise of a Zimbabwean Transnational Religious Movement*. Oxford: James Currey.

Maxwell, D. (2006b) 'Post-colonial Christianity in Africa' in H. McLeod (ed.), *The Cambridge History of Christianity. Volume 9: World Christianities*. Cambridge: Cambridge University Press.

Maxwell, D. (2013) 'Social Mobility and Politics in African Pentecostal Modernity' in R. Hefner (ed.), *Global Pentecostalism in the 21st Century*. Bloomington IN: Indiana University Press.

Otabil, M. (1991) *Four Laws of Productivity: God's Foundation for Living*. Tulsa OK: Vincom.

Otabil, M. (2013) *Dominion Mandate: Finding and Fulfilling Your Purpose in Life*. Accra: Kairos Books.

Oyedepo, D. O. (2006) *Walking in Dominion*. Ota, Nigeria: Dominion Publishing House.

ter Haar, G. (1998) *Halfway to Paradise: African Christians in Europe*. Cardiff: Cardiff Academic Press.

Ukah, A. (2008) *A New Paradigm of Pentecostal Power: A Study of the Redeemed Christian Church of God*. Trenton NJ: Africa World Press.

van Dijk, R. (1997) 'From Camp to Encompassment: Discourses of Transsubjectivity in the Ghanaian Pentecostal Diaspora', *Journal of Religion in Africa* 27 (2): 135–59.

Währisch-Oblau, C. (2009) *The Missionary Self-perception of Pentecostal-Charismatic Church Leaders from the Global South in Europe*. Leiden: E. J. Brill.

Wanner, C. (2007) *Communities of the Converted: Ukrainians and Global Evangelism*. Ithaca NY and London: Cornell University Press.

Relocating Unity and Theology in the Study of World Christianity

Emma Wild-Wood

Introduction

This volume has argued that existing studies of World Christianity have a tendency to be dominated by a focus on multiplicity, pluralism and the diverse stories of local Christianities around the globe. In the introduction, and in various ways throughout the following twelve chapters, the volume has proposed a new approach, one characterised by renewed attention – not solely to diversity, but instead to the common threads and transnational connections that knit together Christians across the world. This afterword offers some concluding reflections on the shift from multiplicity to unity that has been argued for throughout the course of the preceding pages. In its focus on 'unity' and its examination of social science and theological approaches, it provides a particular way of following Joel Cabrita's and David Maxwell's call to trace 'global, comparative connections' by studying the 'complex interplay of the local and the universal in religious belief and practice'.

The first section of the afterword examines how previous chapters demonstrate transregional connections and collaborations among Christians. In summarising themes of unity in the social scientific and historical writings in this volume, this section both prepares the ground and offers a methodological contrast to the subsequent discussion that will focus on the issue of 'unity' through a theological lens. The central part of the afterword seeks to illuminate, with reference to the theological chapters of this volume, the specifically theological ramifications of the proposed unitary approach in the study of World Christianity. Bearing the new focus on 'unity' in mind, the afterword also offers some preliminary thoughts regarding new collaborative research agendas in the study of World Christianity. The intention here is not to discuss ecclesiologies or Trinitarian doctrines, in which theological discussions of unity often lie, but rather to use notions of unity – embedded in social practice and emerging in contemporary theology – as a way of accessing a number of related issues for the interdisciplinary study of World Christianity.

© KONINKLIJKE BRILL NV, LEIDEN, 2017 | DOI: 10.1163/9789004355026_015

Through a discussion of unity, the afterword thus argues for a study of World Christianity that continues to include theological methods in its purview, an approach that is evident in leading journals such as *Exchange* and *Mission Studies*. However, attention to theology is not uncontentious. Cabrita and Maxwell note in the introduction that, in the formation of the field of World Christianity, theology has often played a partisan role. In an era that found the universalising impetus of the modern missionary movement ethically questionable, those theologians and missiologists who re-examined Christian belief in the light of Christianity's worldwide spread tended to highlight the immanent, the cultural and the political. They developed theologies with a local or regional focus, often known collectively as 'contextual' or 'inculturated' theologies. To put it another way, they placed great attention on theologies of incarnation, and insufficient focus on what beliefs of transcendence or unity might mean for Christian communities. However, worldwide theology in the twenty-first century, as the chapters by Peter Phan (Chapter 4) and Dorottya Nagy (Chapter 5) show, has begun to critique this prior focus on difference and attempt to rehabilitate the universal through notions of unity, exchange and interdependence. However, before I turn to discussions of unity in theologies in World Christianity studies, I survey how the social scientific approaches represented in this volume describe networks and linkages that connect Christian adherents, movements and organisations worldwide. By focusing on the mechanisms through which a sense of belonging and consciousness of unity is created, this afterword thus places the theologies that are discussed in the second section – both local and universal – in their own historical context.

Connections, Belonging and Consciousness of Unity

Christian notions of unity are embedded in practices that create connections between Christians. These connectors are vehicles for unity and, as we shall see, at the same time sometimes pose obstacles to that unity. David Maxwell's chapter (Chapter 1) calls for a study of connectivity and consciousness in Christianity that is attentive to processes of homogenisation and localisation. Joel Robbins proposes in his chapter that it is timely to examine certain familiar traits in Christian movements – larger-than-local belongings, individualism and radical social change – that have been given theologically informed explanations through the beliefs and practices of Christians. Although the global spread of Pentecostalism has recently focused scholarly attention on religious transnationalism, as contributors to this volume show, other forms of Christianity also have mechanisms for connecting believers via beliefs, symbols, rituals, organisations and global networks.

Connections between multiple sites and groups occur through church structures, through mission or publishing associations, through informal networks,
and through alliances with significant individuals. New communication technologies of literacy, print and electronic media (Atto, Chapter 11) have provided
a means of connection, and so have nineteenth-century Bible colporteurs
(Feitoza, Chapter 2) and foreign policy (Preston, Chapter 10). It is through these
means and mechanisms that theological ideas and practices travel. Indeed,
connectivity is entangled with issues of mobility: not all Christians move, but
the vehicles that facilitate the movement of ideas, practices and materials also
aid the movement of people. A web of connections and overlapping membership of organisations provide some Christians with opportunities for travel,
collaboration and the sharing of ideas, creating particular sorts of transnational
communities. Others are acquainted with a movement or network through the
dissemination of its ideas and objects in their locality. Transregional networks
are maintained through global, continental or regional networks and by conferences at which much formal theology is produced as papers or reports rather
than as books or articles. The World Council of Churches (WCC), the conferences and encyclicals of the Roman Catholic Church (Chapter 4), the global
Evangelical Lausanne Movement (Kirkpatrick, Chapter 3) and the British and
Foreign Bible Society (Chapter 2) have all played a role in shaping the theology of Christians spread across large spatial distances and straddling cultural
and linguistic divides. Few Christians, or the churches and institutions to which
they belong, see themselves in isolation from theological endeavours in other
parts of the globe. As the chapters in this volume show, they co-operate in
transcontinental collaboration, enabling the cross-fertilisation of theological
ideas.

Confessional connections exist alongside rupture, or the severing of links,
frequently over doctrinal differences. New aggregations and solidarities create
new divisions. Maxwell notes the development of 'the sharper, more formal
identity' of the Anglican Communion at the end of the nineteenth century,
but by the beginning of the twenty-first century its common identity appears
much less certain. Stark disagreements about sexual ethics and biblical interpretation demonstrate both deep fissures within the Anglican Communion
and an underlying tenacity in attempting to find common accord. The Communion has deployed reconciliation strategies from South African theologians
in its internal debates, while the Fellowship of Confessing Anglicans and the
Global Anglican Future Conferences (GAFCON) draw participants from both
the Northern and Southern hemispheres who robustly critique the direction of
the Anglican Communion. Alliances have been made across the autonomous
provinces that form the Communion. Similar types of transregional debates

are explored in David Kirkpatrick's chapter on tensions within the worldwide Evangelical community. His historical study presents debates within global Evangelical networks as being profoundly influenced by Latin American theologians, who, at the same time as some of their Catholic counterparts, mounted a challenge to dominant traditions. They challenged the orthodoxies of mid-twentieth-century evangelicalism while remaining deeply committed to ideas of biblical authority. Evangelical unity through the authority of the Bible had been assumed in theory, but, in practice, as Kirkpatrick shows, that unity was deeply fractured in arguments between North and South Americans over the power dynamics that underpinned many debates surrounding the issue of biblical inerrancy. Connections remained between individuals and associations but they were fraught and conflictual. The role of the Bible, of its translation and interpretation, and of its status as a signifier of divine authority is both a homogenising influence and a source of dissent and dissipation. In calling for more recognition of a Christianity that is worldwide in scope, this volume is far from arguing that seamless agreement and harmony characterise this worldwide communion.

Unity has been an enduring concern among many Christians worldwide despite their frequent conflicts – as between Protestants and Catholics in European history. Ecumenical relations – attempts towards institutional unity or common fellowship – were revived and re-examined from the nineteenth century onwards, efforts that sometimes referenced the ecumenical councils of the patristic era. As the introduction shows, ecumenism had become increasingly important to many Christians as an expression of universality by the mid-twentieth century, even as Christian pluralism increased in a dizzying fashion, especially given the emergence of Pentecostal denominations and ministries worldwide. Of course, one of the most prominent of these global ecumenical organisations is the aforementioned World Council of Churches, which seeks to create platforms that connect Christian churches throughout the world. Thus, the WCC has supported independent networks such as the Ecumenical Association of Third World Theologians (EATWOT) and the Circle of Concerned African Women Theologians. These organisations critique Western theologies for claiming a universalism that they consider unrepresentative, and they disseminate their theology through continental or international conferences. While focusing on the creation of localised theologies, theologians associated with these organisations deliberately drew upon the resources represented in their global links and exchanged theological ideas with interlocuters across the world.

Liberal-minded organisations such as the WCC view such attention to diversity as enriching Christian unity rather than diluting it. Phan, in this volume, notes with approbation the WCC's search for 'convergence' among the diversity of its membership. He contrasts this approach favourably with more centralised Catholic notions of unity maintained through doctrinal uniformity and structural conformity that tend to exclude many of the diverse expressions of Christianity worldwide, including some of those within Catholicism itself. Phan's discussion shows that the particular structures that facilitate transregional connections have embedded within them particular kinds of Christian consciousness. Their very operations – the nature, extent and scale of them – indicate their understanding of Christian unity, and what shape ecumenism ideally should take.

These efforts in the direction of centralisation – even when marked by an awareness of diversity, as in the case of the WCC – are not just found among the higher echelons of church leadership; many ordinary Christians share similar aspirations for unity. The consciousness of belonging to a world religion is attractive to Christians around the globe. Some attempt to straddle geographical, cultural or ecclesial divides because their belief in the unity of Christianity compels them to do so. Included among them are the Roman Catholics, mentioned by Maxwell, who are troubled by a retreat from Ultramontane commitments that appear to distance adherents from the centralised Roman Catholic Church, and Protestant movements such as the East African Revival whose members actively seek to banish ethnic distinctions, to develop international connections, and to reject attempts to render Christianity 'authentically' African. This quest for global identities also goes some way to explain the motivation of Pentecostal churches including the Redeemed Christian Church of God and the Universal Church of the Kingdom of God, which, within forty years, have moved confidently from Nigeria or Brazil and planted churches throughout the world. Kwabena Asamoah-Gyadu's chapter in this volume (Chapter 12) offers examples of these self-consciously 'globalising' Pentecostals. This volume illustrates the aspiration for unity on the part of Christians worldwide, and the institutional and informal structures, networks, practices and disciplines through which unity is pursued.

Theological ideas and imagery work alongside a range of more embodied, affective religious practices and disciplines in shaping the nature of Christianity worldwide. Some Christians use the Bible to guide them in daily life, viewing this as a text that provides a common script for holy living to Christians the world over. Others emphasise church teaching or are inspired by song and symbol, they follow Jesus and they anticipate direction from the Holy Spirit. In doing so, they develop local hermeneutical innovations and draw upon the tradition of their denomination or movement. Christians are affected by what they believe and practise, and they dedicate considerable resources to teaching and learning in settings that range from small prayer groups to university courses. The results, as our contributors variously demonstrate, are often sophisticated, multilayered beliefs and practices embedded in the social life of any given Christian community, and, most crucially, also shared with other Christian groups across the globe.

Pedro Feitoza's chapter on Bible colporteurs discusses the transatlantic dimensions of Evangelical approaches to the Bible, which produced modes of reading and interpretation that were disseminated by relatively humble Protestant Bible sellers. He depicts the role of British charities in the development of a transatlantic hermeneutic through the immediate and personal readings of scripture that were particularly associated with Evangelical and (later) Pentecostal religious observance. These colporteurs fervently believed in the agency of the Bible, translated into vernacular languages, to create followers of Christ across the globe. Furthermore, the Bible was understood to be a text that directly connected its readers to the life of Jesus and the apostles, creating hermeneutical connections not only across vast stretches of space, but also through time. Indeed, one of the merits of Feitoza's contribution is that he provides a much-needed chronological depth to our collection, highlighting the historical origins of the contemporary Latin American evangelicalism discussed in Kirkpatrick's chapter. In Brazil, this Protestant approach came into conflict with Catholic ideas of Holy Scripture; the latter assumed the necessity of priestly interpretation of the texts, while the former emphasised the primacy of individual, lay readings of the Bible. Thus, the two groups developed competing forms of Christian consciousness through methods of homogenisation within their organisations, and these methods were influenced by differing traditions surrounding authority and interpretation. While Protestants stimulated a broader sense of universal faith among their adherents, they did little to improve ecumenical relations within the country. By its very nature, a strong sense of belonging – and, in this case, one defined by clear doctrinal boundaries – often creates new categories of exclusion.

Devotees' own perceptions of the differing 'scales' of their belonging to a larger Christian fraternity are a concern of several contributors to this volume. Chloë Starr (Chapter 8) presents the *oeuvre* of a well-known contemporary Chinese singer/songwriter to demonstrate that, at a popular level, Chinese Christian identity and belief have a strongly nationalistic component. Starr argues that popular theologies, by claiming the Chinese nation for God, may promote national notions of belonging just as readily as they foster local, regional or global identities. In this way, a Christian-inflected nationalism has the potential to defuse aspirations towards universal belonging. Global connectivity, she suggests, is not a priority for all, even among a community that is strongly influenced by its diasporic members. The way in which any part of the Chinese church considers itself to be universal is contested within its membership. In a related fashion, Kwabena Asamoah-Gyadu examines the way in which biblical imagery is deployed in Pentecostal theology to create meanings and associations that operate at a national level and that also claim a powerful presence on the world stage. The shift from eagle to dove is symptomatic of much confident, contemporary Pentecostalism and its radical departure from its roots in holiness evangelicalism. The emphasis on individual conversion away from the 'world' has been replaced by an exuberant appropriation of the nation and the world for God. Charlotte Walker-Said (Chapter 7) tracks the way in which Christian consciousness is formed at macro and micro levels of society through various associations, leagues and unions in Cameroon as she explores the influences of Catholic and Protestant internationalism and their impact on broader societal issues such as marriage, the family and education. In her assessment of the way in which local theologians and pastors utilised Catholic social teaching as a critique of discrimination and abuse in their own societies, Walker-Said brings together the cultural and the political resonances of Christian thought, a theme that is evident in other chapters. Naures Atto (Chapter 11) explores the political ramifications of minority Christian identity in the Middle East, and the distinct beliefs, practices and political limitations that have created them. She identifies familiar Bible verses that Syrian Christians deploy to articulate their ethnic-Christian consciousness in a region where their existence is threatened. She studies their expectation of a Christian solidarity that transcends political borders and linguistic and cultural divides and their resulting mobilisation of global Christian support for their precarious existence through electronic media and diasporic communities. Andrew Preston's chapter (Chapter 10) is concerned with national perceptions. In demonstrating that US foreign policy has been influenced by moral ideas generated over several generations in a Judeo-Christian milieu, it shows the way in which universalising sensibilities have influenced America's sense of nationhood and the perceptions of America on the global stage. Both Atto and Preston examine how far religious identity is imbricated in cultural and political identification, and thus their chapters suggest that Christian aspirations for unity are embedded within larger social or political relationships and may be able to influence communities and governments.

The complexities of thought and action within the Christian groups studied in this volume require a sophisticated appreciation of the way in which theologies are (and are not) deployed within and between Christian communities, especially in the service of articulating notions of unity and connectedness. The contributors to this volume engage with theological, denominational and hermeneutical influences, unlocking the complex discursive traditions of Christianity and showing that theological traditions are a form of connectivity through time. The affective ideas and practices of tradition, even when rein-vented or deliberately contested, can unite Christians in the present age and across the globe with those of a previous age. It matters, for example, that the British and Foreign Bible Society and the Religious Tract Society had a distinct approach to the Bible emerging from within a Protestant framework. It matters that Francophone Africans adapted particular aspects of Catholic social teach-ing in contested ways in Cameroon, and, in so doing, committed to ideologies that connected them beyond their immediate locales. Starr's rationale for an inculturated, 'Sinicised' theology and church structure in the People's Republic of China and Chandra Mallampalli's discussion of competing Sanskritised and Dalit theologies (Chapter 6) show that political and social differences generate significant theological distinctions that in turn have an impact on the limits and boundaries of discussions surrounding Christian unity. The work of theolo-gians has been used to understand sources of particular Christian ideas, which tradition they belong to, and how adaptive they may be in relation to that tra-dition. Likewise, the theologians in World Christianity studies who re-examine Christian belief, to whom we turn now, consider the lived experience of Chris-tians and wider society to be foundational for their theology and have deployed social science and historical methods in their work.

I now focus on the more formal theological endeavours in the direction of ecumenism and unity in the study of World Christianity, having noted how the contributors to this volume have given attention to Christian aspir-ations towards unity embedded in society and culture. The following section rehearses why contextual theologies have focused on regional concerns and examines a turn to new approaches in theology that seek to replace a straight-forward celebration of diversity with a more nuanced awareness of the com-plex co-existence of unity within diversity. This approach is exemplified in the chapters by Nagy and Phan in this volume, but it is also more broadly dis-cernible in a wider set of contemporary theological writings – from Protest-ant, Catholic and, increasingly, Pentecostal traditions – referenced below. If, as Cabrita and Maxwell note, there has been less Catholic than Protestant engage-ment in avowedly 'World Christianity' studies in the West, there has been no similar lack of theological innovation from Catholic theologians worldwide, who influenced and responded to the dynamics of Vatican II discussed in the introduction.

Problems of Unity in New Interpretations of Theological Tradition

Theologians in World Christianities – that is, those theologians worldwide who consider that the global spread of Christianity requires new theological responses – are showing an increasing interest in the connectivity and consciousness practised by Christians worldwide, an impetus that they call 'unity'. Yet, precisely because these theologians recognise the diversity of Christian expression, the achievement of some form of Christian unity remains both an aspiration and a problem. As the chapters by Phan and Nagy demonstrate, in order to achieve a unity of practice in plural situations, these thinkers seek new dialogical methods while at the same time remaining nervous of those theologies that appear to homogenise Christian belief and practice by imposing normative – usually Western – standards upon them.

Many theologians worldwide who are cited below offer robust criticism of efforts to present any one theological tradition as 'normative'. It is in puzzling over the conundrum of unity in plurality – where unity lies and what distinguishes Christian unity – that theologians most closely associated with studies of World Christianity have developed comparative methods, through 'intercultural' and 'interreligious' theologies. Before examining these theologies, however, I will explore the problems theologians have faced over unity and the continued attention to context that informs new interpretations of theological traditions.

Through a critique of classical theology, theologians seeking new responses to the worldwide spread of Christianity developed a regional approach to studies that rendered 'Christianities' local and that overlooked the importance of wider connections and communities. Theologians in Africa, Asia and Latin America have argued that many seminal figures within the European and North American theological canon fail to recognise the overweening influence of European culture on the shaping of that Christian tradition they hold up as normative (Parratt 2004: 7–8). Some of the most cited modern theological approaches offer little assistance in this regard. For example, the influential Radical Orthodoxy school proposes a return to a pre-modern, pre-Enlightenment Christianity uncontaminated by modern distinctions between sacred and secular, private and public, reason and spirit (Millbank 1990). While some theologians may find aspects of this argument compelling, Radical Orthodoxy's avowed commitment to a religious ideal exemplified in the Christendom of medieval Western Europe render the overall import of this theology deeply problematic to theologians situated outside the West.

These theologians have critiqued the dominant role of traditional theological forms and their Western philosophical expectations, arguing that these are ways of illegitimately claiming universal significance for their own theological responses to particular problems. In so doing, they argue, Western theology overlooks local or geo-political inequalities. Contextual African theologies, for example, developed as part of a broader pan-Africanist intellectual movement during colonialism in which claims to authentic, indigenous identities were also significant in constructing nationalist concepts. Traditional wisdom for Christian theology was sourced from local proverbs or conceptions of ancestors (Mulago 1965; Mbiti 1970; Nyamiti 1984). Theologians of liberation in Latin America (Boff and Boff 1987), South Africa (Mosala 1989) and India (Nirmal 1990) have argued that the poverty and marginalisation that result from unequal access to power and wealth are of paramount concern. Feminist theologies and debates over human sexuality also demonstrate contextual division within geographical regions. For example, members of the Circle of Concerned African Women Theologians such as Mercy Odoyoye (1995) and Musa Dube (2003) appraise regional theologies of inculturation written by men and seek to intervene in national and church programmes for the improved health and education of girls and women. Dube argues that women's ability to avoid contracting HIV/AIDS is reduced through the promiscuity of men, and through Christian and traditional expectations of marriage that effectively silence women. Women theologians of the Circle draw on internationalised rights-based language and critiques of patriarchy in order to introduce transregional ideas about gender, which are then applied to a regional context (Phiri and Nadar 2010: 91–2). Male theologians, they say, perpetuate a connection between Christianity and African tradition that favours patriarchal systems, ignoring the need for gendered theology. Furthermore, contextual theologians consider that many unitary Christian traditions not only ignore significant differences among Christian peoples, they also fail to offer a way forward in division. In this volume, Kirkpatrick's close examination of the disappointed expectations of unity within global evangelicalism illuminates the limited ability to respond to division when movements with common causes develop significant differences. For these reasons, many theologians worldwide continue to focus their attention on the regional and incarnational, expecting only to see a greater plurality of theological expression.

These factors also mean that theologians of World Christianity who have turned their attention to transnational connections beyond merely local interests, such as Nagy and Phan in this volume, face a profound dilemma. The contextual theological approaches most closely associated with a World Christianity/ies approach (as Nagy and Phan term it respectively) are too fragmented to be able to assist (focusing primarily on difference, pluralism and local context), while the polemical Radical Orthodoxy approaches that have provoked much productive thought in contemporary Western theological circles have yet to produce a defence of Christian tradition that encompasses diverse belief and practice across the globe. The first polarises by being overly attached to discrete concepts of cultural boundedness, and thus fragments and localises Christian theology. The second homogenises, proposing a return to a uniformity of tradition and structure to avoid conflict. In fact, this dichotomy overstates the problem. Even when focusing on a particular context, theologies within the World Christianity camp betray an ideological pull to a wider whole. Theologians may foreground the local, particular and specific in contesting the nature of the universal in theological thought, but their commitment to engagement across the globe is implicit in their writings. Particular experiences – whether cultural, political or ecclesial in focus or local, regional or international in scale – are brought into conversation with scripture and common Christian traditions (Parratt 2004: 15). It is rather that these theologies contest what it is that can be considered universal in theological traditions, and how far any local form is able to articulate unity as well as propose new dynamic interactions between the local and the universal.

Given this programmatic attention to difference – part of a wider project of contesting a Eurocentric Christianity that positions itself as normative – theologians of World Christianity are seeking and crafting new languages with which to describe unity without erasing the importance of difference (Tan and Tran 2016: Part II). For some time, theologians have proposed that comparative approaches are necessary in order to generate more nuanced theology and to facilitate the connectivity that Christians seek. EATWOT is understood as an early manifestation of an exchange of ideas called 'intercultural theology'. From 1974, the Catholic Federation of Asian Bishops' Conferences developed a dialogical approach with and among the cultures, religions and poor of Asia, bringing together in conversation streams of contextual theology and action that have often been regarded as distinctly inculturated, interreligious or political. From the 1970s onwards, Western theologians convinced by the insights of theologians from Africa, Asia and Latin America developed an 'intercultural' theology, which brought contextual theologies from different places into creative tension with one another. Walter Hollenweger, also known as an early historian of the Pentecostal movement, was among the first proponents of this comparative method, which, he believed, was required to create an enriched and shared Christian theology (Hollenweger 2003: 90). The arrival of the twenty-first century brought renewed calls to identify similarities among difference or to find 'constants in context' (Bevans and Schroeder 2004) and to engage in 'global theological conversation' (Kim 2004a) beyond particularistic impulses. These projects have arisen from a recognition among those persuaded by contextual theological methods that the regionalisation, inculturation or politicisation of theology requires methods of dialogue and an acknowledgement of interdependence so that they may fruitfully interact with one another, and begin to influence systematic theology in the West (McDougall 2014: 162).

Foundational to this theology is the idea that Christian unity is accompanied not only by its shadow, disunity, but also by its vital partner, diversity. Phan, a Catholic theologian, addresses the subject most directly in this volume. He welcomes the diversity of theological thought as a necessary product of an attention to the variety of cultures, an appreciation of popular theological expression, and an engagement with philosophical and religious traditions outside the Western world. He asserts that Christian faith can be accessed only through the many societies, languages and thought patterns in which it appears and that all theology emerges from particular situations. Context, he argues, should be intentionally included when constructing theology. Yet he also claims an important role for Christian unity – the fellowship or communion among Christians and between Christians and God, three-in-one – in an age of Christian pluralism. He notes new interpretations of theological sources that challenge previously normative readings of scripture and tradition that held up Western practice as a template. Phan insists that these interpretations of theological method are no more than new responses to familiar tasks. Catholic theologians, for example, are at pains to show that their interpretation is an outworking of Catholic teaching, developing from the encyclicals of the church, even when this has been contested by organs with the Roman Catholic Church (see, for example, Gutierrez 1975).

The productive tension between unity and diversity is also a major concern in the chapter by Nagy, a Lutheran missiologist. Theology in an age of diversity and connectivity, she suggests, must consider the meaning, manifestation and articulation of unity within and beyond the Christian church. Phan and Nagy refer to Christian notions of what binds together and creates belonging and what prevents such commonality. Recourse to regional systems of thought is brought to bear on the search for unifying approaches for theology in World Christianity by theologians who criticise the perceived homogenisation of classic theology. They are often troubled by 'Western' analyses that presuppose conflict and dissent and that encourage conflictual styles of argument. In order to change the register of engagement, some theologians deploy traditional methods that promote 'harmony' (Chow 2013) for East Asian theologians, 'non-duality' (Aleaz 2000) for South Asian theologians, and 'ubuntu', or communal humanity, for Africans (popularised by Desmond Tutu (1999)). In this critique of modern rationalism, perhaps there is evidence for an instinct that runs parallel to that of Radical Orthodoxy's resourcing from the Western pre-Enlightenment past (Katongole 2017: 35). The holistic means of interaction and aspirations for consensus in some cultures of the global South appear to be close to European pre-modern views.

Evidence of this shift in method can be discerned in corresponding changes in the subject matter of many new theological approaches. Theologians are pioneering new approaches that focus on God the creator or the dynamic, mobile Holy Spirit (see, for example, Yong 2003). There is a related attention to subjects such as reconciliation, globalisation and migration (see, for example, Kwoi 2012; Cruz 2010). Environmental concerns have attracted considerable recent interest. For example, EATWOT has called for a 'planetary' theology, one in which the unitary project includes all living things on earth (International Theological Commission 2012). Global inequality, ecology and universal communion are discussed in Pope Francis's most recent encyclical, *Laudato Si'* (2015). These subjects are no longer territorial in focus, but are presented as having a worldwide impact, affecting most societies, requiring large-scale political and theological interventions, and demanding the attention of all Christians. In responding to them, theologians are increasingly turning to postcolonial theories of hybridity and multiple belonging (Küster 2016: 209–11). While none of the contributors to this volume explicitly address environmental issues, an awareness of global population shifts, migration and the overarching importance of shared physical environments undoubtedly underlies many of the case studies contained here. In his chapter, Phan demonstrates the ways in which a global view on particular issues alters the theological enterprise because it demonstrates an appreciation of cultural, religious and political diversity in the world and a commitment to Christian reflection in these contexts.

One long-standing challenge for theologians has been to conceive of unity when the relevant interlocutors do not share a common commitment to the Christian faith. The encounter between Christianity and other religious faiths is one that is addressed only fleetingly in this volume, yet it is likely that this topic will become ever more relevant to theologians of World Christianities. Interreligious contact can frequently breed conflict: Maxwell writes of breaks and barriers, and, in the chapters by Mallampalli and Atto, the tensions engendered by religious difference are apparent in situations of great political and cultural turmoil. In contrast, Phan mentions in his chapter the attempts to unite across religious differences in the interreligious dialogue that has a long and important history among Asian theologians and which is providing new methods of engagement in other parts of the globe. A growing number of Western theologians, aware of the increased cultural and religious pluralism in Europe, North America, Australia and New Zealand, turn to Christian theologians such as Stanley Samartha (1974) or Edmund Kee-Fook Chia (2016) who draw on imaginative, intellectual and ethical resources found in other faith traditions and engage in dialogue with experts from other religions. For example, the European Society for Intercultural Theology and Interreligious Studies (ESITIS), established in 2005, assumes an interface of secular and confessional stances for the critical investigation of Christianity in other societies and of other religious traditions. Interfaith practices emerge from a consciousness of worldwide common endeavours beyond local differences, crossing boundaries of culture, confession and faith, and they operate as a form of transregional conversation. Often there is an applied element to the dialogue, whether that be development, peace and reconciliation, interethnic policy, or ecclesiastical support. Most significant, as noted in Nagy's chapter, is a new understanding of the theological task as interpretive rather than legislative. Increasingly, intercultural and interreligious theologies investigate the nature of Christianity, examining what different groups consider normative, testing the perceptual boundaries of distinct religious traditions, and discovering ways of engaging across those boundaries.

Contemporary theologians are engaged in the task of accounting for the diversity of worldwide Christian expression as well as articulating deeply felt sentiments of unity – often across considerable borders. This section has described some of the ways in which theologians worldwide have shifted their primary focus from the local to the universal (while still attempting to avoid the old trap of normative, homogenising theology), developing comparative or intercultural theologies and engaging in global conversations in order to seek unity in diversity. While the importance of Christian unity as rooted in Jesus Christ and the church is a deeply held tenet, the Christian traditions within which this central doctrine is affective are contested and debated. The recognition that familiar beliefs and practices are adapted and change in unfamiliar circumstances has given rise to a plethora of new theologies that problematise assumptions that unity is achieved through a single Christian theological tradition. The final section of this afterword looks forward. It suggests that scholars might attend to issues of unity in the very *methods* by which they conduct collaborative research across the globe. It offers a sketch of a reflexive model deployed in theology that may aid successful academic collaborations across disciplinary, geographical, linguistic and cultural divides – giving new methodological meaning to the religious and theological pursuit of Christian unity.

Interdisciplinary Engagements with Scholars Worldwide

As the chapters in this volume have demonstrated, the 'West' can no longer examine the 'rest' as its subject and call it 'the world'. Neither can the 'West' alone examine 'the world'. The number of Western-based contributors to this volume only serves to illustrate the political and social asymmetries between different areas of the world, even while Nagy's chapter draws our attention to the contingent, variable nature of seemingly fixed categories such as 'Western' and 'Eastern' Europe. Sustained and thoughtful interaction between academic elites across different geographical regions can modify the objectification and suppositions of alterity that can still insert themselves into academic work about subjects who cannot easily respond. In order to achieve this interaction, scholars across the globe urgently need to consider how best to collaborate with colleagues worldwide while deploying diverse methods and holding different assumptions of scholarship – all this at a time when the norms of the academy are rapidly shifting as they are adapted across the globe. Scholars of World Christianity require an expansive, inclusive and relational approach – one that offers collaborative ways of exchange in a diverse area – so that the *study* of World Christianity may also be worldwide.

An expansive approach includes developing the potential for theological material and method to enrich historical and social scientific approaches and vice versa. The academic community is far from united in its pursuit of knowledge and understanding. In particular, significant fractures exist within the ranks of those who study religion. There has, for example, been a long-standing debate about the nature and objectives of religious studies and its relationship to theology, which has largely been formed by the Western academy. Some scholars still adhere to a clear distinction between studying *about* and being educated *in* a religious tradition. They express concern about the intrusion of theology into their fields; for them, it confuses the subject of study with the method of study and addresses the metaphysical, moral and existential in a manner that is unconventional in post-Enlightenment disciplines long assumed to be secular and expunged of doctrinal influence (Weibe 2005). However, there is a growing recognition that social science claims are no more unmotivated than any others, and that social science categories have marginalised Christian categories while being a product of them. This acknowledgement has drawn greater attention from anthropologists to the unitary belief systems of Christians. It has also provoked a call to adopt something from the people they study, describe the people they study on their own terms, and be willing to recover certain indigenous categories (theological and otherwise) and to identify their beneficial ways of being (Robbins 2006). Theologians in

World Christianity have also used social scientific studies in order to ascertain from empirical research into speech, symbol and community practice the unitary consciousness of Christians as members of the church (Mugesa 2004: 5–8).

An inclusive approach is one in which scholars study 'with' and 'in' World Christianity, learning from those who are shaping their disciplines in ways different from those that exist in the Western academy. Some scholars are part of the communities they study and contribute to studies in World Christianity a form of scholarship that is emotionally engaged, when the Western academy has traditionally expected a critical distance. In this volume, for example, the immediate and personal quality of Atto's chapter arises from her close association with and activism for Christians in the Middle East. While a professional anthropologist, Atto is also a participant in the community she is describing. She writes of her reflexive process as a 'engaged insider' who knows those subjects whose survival is at stake. In her chapter, Nagy calls for a new comparative approach to the Christian other, in which scholars discover how to evaluate and engage with Christian theologies that transgress the rules of contemporary Western academic practice. Many of the theologians mentioned in this afterword are activist in broad intent, often programmatic, and committed to the outcomes they elucidate in their writing. They have constructed their theologies in response to immediate problems facing their own churches and societies. They are critical of forms of thought that they consider to be insufficiently relevant or to lack societal impact. Their theologies challenge the distinction between private and public expression. For example, they often retain their rough edges and may include stories, autobiographical notes, proverbs and songs alongside expressions of deep dissatisfaction with the status quo.

For this expansive and inclusive approach to be successful, it requires a relational component. This does not merely seek to comprehend the other on their own terms, through a process of personal and disciplinary reflexivity; it is an approach that engages in dialogue and an exchange of assumptions and beliefs together with the other. It is particularly important where there are significant doubts about the premises and rationale of the other. This relational reflexivity is focused not on the other but on the encounter between two or more parties.

One particular engaged and relational approach to the study of religion, developed from the comparative theological work mentioned above, operates on a number of levels and is helpfully elucidated by Oddbjørn Leivik (2014). This approach attempts to hone interdisciplinary enquiry and reflexivity in order that scholars from different disciplines – theology, religious studies, social sciences, law and history – are able to learn from each other. It aims to achieve mutual understanding and consensus through dialogue between researchers of different religious traditions and none. It does this by deliberately exploring confrontational elements between the represented parties. Participants are expected to own their own religious influences and those of others, while drawing on outsider perspectives of the research in hand to gain critical distance. The negotiation of emic and etic forms of research and the ways in which they intrude upon one another can be applied differently by different scholars working on particular projects. For example, the issues of 'inducement' and 'conversion' in the Indian context that Mallampalli addresses in his chapter demonstrate fraught and complex relationships developed over time and which play out in contemporary society. Careful historical construction, like that supplied by Mallampalli, is able to provide a useful resource for those theologians from Dalit and Vedic traditions who wish to establish a constructive dialogue on a divisive issue (Kim 2004b: 58). In expecting a high level of intersubjectivity about researchers' own disciplinary and faith positions, the questioning of attitudes, values, assumptions, thoughts and actions is not an interior activity carried out alongside and somehow supplementary to research, but rather a corporate activity embedded in the research itself.

This approach of relational reflexivity – with its expectation of self-examination, its resistance to assumptions of neutrality or secularity that stands at odds with its subjects or interlocutors, and its high level of religious literacy and sensitivity – may be deployed within studies in World Christianity. Its value is twofold. First, the epistemic reflexivity on religious belief and practice as they influence all areas of life places the religious self-understanding of scholars within the orbit of the enquiry itself, rather than beyond its reach. This approach asks how the religious or non-religious beliefs or assumptions of researcher and research subject exert a mutual influence upon each other. It denies academic neutrality or the unacknowledged inclusion of belief, preferring the open discussion of subjectivities. Theory, practice and observation are bound together in mutual engagement and critique. Second, the reflexive process is carried out relationally. Participants gaze upon each other with equal intensity, the boundaries between researchers and subjects are dismantled, and interlocutors meet as equals in the study of World Christianity. Without such self-critical reflexivity, World Christianity studies may perpetuate what they most seek to avoid: the exoticising gaze of Western-trained, Enlightenment-influenced scholars on the practices of others outside Western Europe and North America. With such an expansive, inclusive and relational approach, the *study* of World Christianity can also be worldwide.

References

Aleaz, K. P. (2000) *A Convergence of Advaita Vedanta and Eastern Christian Thought*. Delhi: ISPCK.

Bevans, S. and R. Schroeder (2004) *Constants in Context: A Theology of Mission for Today*. Maryknoll NY: Orbis Books.

Boff, L. and C. Boff (1987) *Introducing Liberation Theology*. Translated from the Portuguese by P. Burns. London: Burns & Oates.

Chia, E. K.-F. (ed.) (2016) *Interfaith Dialogue: Global Perspectives*. New York NY: Palgrave Macmillan.

Chow, A. (2013) *Theosis, Sino-Christian Theology and the Second Chinese Enlightenment*. New York NY: Palgrave Macmillan.

Cruz, G. T. (2010) *An Intercultural Theology of Migration: Pilgrims in the Wilderness*. Leiden: E. J. Brill.

Dube, M. (2003) 'A Vision for Mission in the 21st Century: Ways Ahead for Ecumenical Theological Education: HIV/AIDS and Other Challenges in the New Millennium'. Keynote address at St Paul's United Theological College, Limuru, 3 June, http://thecirclecawt.com/focus_areas3d57.html?mode=content&id=17293&refto=2629, accessed 17 February 2017.

Gutierrez, G. (1975) *A Theology of Liberation: History, Politics and Salvation*. Translated from the Spanish and edited by Sister Caridad Inda and J. Eagleson. London: SCM Press.

Hollenweger, W. (2003) 'Intercultural Theology: Some Remarks on the Term' in M. Frederiks, M. Dijkstra and A. Houtepen (eds), *Towards an Intercultural Theology: Essays in Honour of Jan A. B. Jongeneel*. Zoetermeer: Uitgeverij Meinema.

International Theological Commission (2012) 'Towards a Work Agenda for Planetary Theology', *Voices* 3–4: 15–24, http://eatwot.net/VOICES/VOICES-2012-3&4.pdf, accessed 16 February 2017.

Katongole, E. (2017) *Born from Lament: The Theology and Politics of Hope in Africa*. Grand Rapids MI: Eerdmans.

Kim, K. (2004a) 'Missiology as Global Conversation of (Contextual) Theologies', *Mission Studies* 21 (1): 39–53.

Kim, K. (2004b) 'India' in J. Parratt (ed.), *An Introduction to Third World Theologies*. Cambridge: Cambridge University Press.

Küster, V. (2016) 'From Contextualization to Glocalization: Intercultural Theology and Postcolonial Critique', *Exchange* 45 (3): 203–26.

Kwoi, P.-L. (2012) *Globalisation, Gender and Peacebuilding: The Future of Interfaith Dialogue*. New York NY: Mahwah.

Leivik, O. (2014) 'Interreligious Studies: A Relational Approach to the Study of Religion', *Journal of Interreligious Studies* 13: 15–19.

Mbiti, J. (1970) *Concepts of God in Africa*. London: SPCK.

McDougall, J. A. (2014) 'Contemporary Landscapes and New Horizons: The Changing Maps of World Christianity', *Theology Today* 71 (2): 159–63.

Millbank, J. (1990) *Theology and Social Theory: Beyond Secular Reason*. Oxford: Blackwell.

Mosala, I. J. (1989) *Biblical Hermeneutics and Black Theology in South Africa*. Grand Rapids MI: Eerdmans.

Mugesa, L. (2004) *Anatomy of Inculturation: Transforming the Church in Africa*. Maryknoll NY: Orbis Books.

Mulago, V. (1965) *Une Visage africaine de Christianisme: L'union vitale Bantu face à l'unité ecclésiale*. Paris: Présence Africaine.

Nirmal, A. P. (ed.) (1990) *A Reader in Dalit Theology*. Chennai: Gurukul Lutheran Theological Seminary.

Nyamiti, C. (1984) *Christ as Our Ancestor: Christology from an African Perspective*. Gweru, Zimbabwe: Mambo.

Odoyoye, M. A. (1995) *Daughters of Anowa: African Women and Patriarchy*. Maryknoll NY: Orbis Books.

Parratt, J. (2004) *An Introduction to Third World Theologies*. Cambridge: Cambridge University Press.

Phiri, I. A. and S. Nadar (2010) 'African Women's Theologies' in D. B. Stinton (ed.), *African Theology on the Way: Current Conversations*. London: SPCK.

Robbins, J. (2006) 'Anthropology and Theology: An Awkward Relationship?', *Anthropological Quarterly* 79 (2): 285–94.

Samartha, S. (1974) *The Hindu Response to the Unbound Christ*. Madras: The Christian Literature Society.

Tan, J. Y. and A. Q. Tran (2016) *World Christianity: Perspectives and Insights*. Maryknoll NY: Orbis Books.

Tutu, D. (1999) *No Future without Forgiveness*. London: Rider.

Weibe, D. (2005) 'Religious Studies' in J. R. Hinnells (ed.), *The Routledge Companion to the Study of Religion*. Abingdon: Routledge.

Yong, A. (2003) *Beyond the Impasse: Toward a Pneumatological Theology of Religions*. Grand Rapids MI: Paternoster Press.

Index

Printed in the United States
By Bookmasters